OPEN GAZA

Open Gaza is dedicated to the memory of Michael Sorkin,
who fought tirelessly for the social and spatial justice of Palestinians
and whose vision enabled this book to come into being.

First published in 2021 by
The American University in Cairo Press
113 Sharia Kasr el Aini, Cairo, Egypt
One Rockefeller Plaza, 10th Floor, New
York, NY 10020
www.aucpress.com

ISBN 978 1 649 030719

Library of Congress Cataloging-in-
Publication Data

Names: Sorkin, Michael, 1948–2020,
    editor. | Sharp, Deen, editor.
Title: Open Gaza : architectures of
    hope / edited by Michael Sorkin
    and Deen Sharp.
Description: First edition. | New York :
    Terreform : The American
    University in Cairo Press, 2021 |
    Includes bibliographical references.
Identifiers: LCCN 2020028150 (print) |
    LCCN 2020028151 (ebook) |
    ISBN 9781649030719 (board) |
    ISBN 9781649030733 (pdf).
Subjects: LCSH: Architecture—Gaza
    Strip. | City planning—Gaza Strip. |
    Gaza Strip—Environmental
conditions.
Classification: LCC NA1478.G39 O64
    2021 (print) | LCC NA1478.G39
    (ebook) | DDC 720.95694/3—dc23

1 2 3 4 5   25 24 23 22 21

Printed in China

Deen Sharp
Michael Sorkin
Editors in Chief

Nic Cavell
Maria Cecilia Fagel
Vyjayanthi V. Rao
Senior Editors

Sarah Abdallah
Corinne Butta
Research Assistants

Isaac Gertman and
Jenny Rosenberg,
The Independent Group
Book Design

Marieke Krijnen
Copy Editor

Stephen Hoban
Proofreader

Terreform is a non-profit, urban
research studio and advocacy group.
Founded in 2005 by Michael Sorkin,
its mission is to investigate the forms,
policies, technologies, and practices
that will yield equitable, sustainable,
and beautiful cities for our urbanizing
planet.

Terreform and all the contributors to
Open Gaza: Architectures of Hope
are deeply grateful for the generous
support to this book by:

Omar Al-Qattan

Jay Schnitzer and Sara Roy

Fonna Forman and Teddy Cruz at the
Center on Global Justice, University
of California, San Diego

Malkit Shoshan at the Foundation for
Achieving Seamless Territory (FAST)

Open Gaza: Architectures of Hope is
part of the Middle East Urban Studies
series edited by Deen Sharp and
Noura Wahby. Published by the
American University in Cairo Press,
the series explores new research
from a progressive and critical lens on
the wide-ranging implications of
urban transformation in the Middle
East. It engages with the intensifying
processes of urbanization across the
region, from large-scale infrastructure
projects to the construction and
destruction of new cities and urban
regions.

OPEN GAZA

Edited by Michael Sorkin and Deen Sharp

TERREFORM

The American University in Cairo Press

Cairo   New York

CONTENTS

PREFACE

Sara Roy

The Gaza Strip is a part of the world whose small size belies its profound significance. Gaza has always been the heart of Palestinian nationalism and the core of popular defiance, adamant and unrelenting in its resistance to Israeli occupation and in its rejection of any attempt to displace it, insisting on its presence in the world. Because of this, Gaza, fundamentally, has defined Palestine's relationship with Israel.[1] In this vein, Edward Said writes:

> To the Israelis, whose incomparable military and political power dominates us, we are at the periphery, **the image that will not go away.** Every assertion of our nonexistence, every attempt to spirit us away, every new effort to prove that we were never really there, simply raises the question of why so much denial of, and such energy expended on, what was not there? Could it be that even as alien outsiders we dog their military might with our obdurate moral claim, our insistence . . . that 'we would prefer not to,' not to leave, not to abandon Palestine forever?[2]

This refusal to leave is most powerfully expressed in Gaza. From the beginning of the occupation over fifty years ago, Israel has never really known what to do with Gaza. Gaza is dogged and relentless, the "image that will not go away." Despite the many attempts to subdue and disable it, Gaza's place in Palestine is assured, for there can be no meaningful resolution to the Israeli–Palestinian conflict without it.

Israel's principal strategy from the outset—in terms that were clearly articulated to me by Israeli officials over thirty years ago— was to prevent the emergence of a Palestinian state, to ensure that no viable political or economic entity would ever be established on land Israel claimed as its own. A key feature of Israel's strategy was the division and separation of Palestinians living under occupation, which meant separating and isolating Gaza—the source of nationalist resistance—from the West Bank and Jerusalem, which Israel sought to annex. Gaza's transformation into something distinct and apart, removed from any meaningful exchange—political, economic, and social—with the rest of Palestine, was crucial.

Israel's strategy proved to be prescient. Without Gaza, the national collective has been diminished, if not destroyed. Without Gaza, the geographic basis of a Palestinian economy has ceased to exist, and with it any possibility of a viable state. This reality was affirmed by Israel's Minister of Education, Naftali Bennett, who years ago concluded that the "idea that a Palestinian state will be formed in the land of Israel has come to a dead end . . . Never in the annals of Israel have so many people expended so much energy on something so futile."[3]

Invalidating Gaza's place in Palestine, and the rights that naturally emanate from this, has been achieved through a number of Israeli policies, prominent among them the transformation of Gaza from a political issue into a humanitarian problem. The struggle between political claims and humanitarian needs has become acute and is expressed

1. Dina Matar, "Gaza: Image Normalization," in Helga Tawil-Souri and Dina Matar (eds.) *Gaza as Metaphor* (London: Hurst and Company, 2016).

2. Edward Said, *After the Last Sky: Palestinian Lives* (London: Vintage, 1986), 41–42, quoted in Matar, "Gaza: Image as Normalization," 182–83.

3. Barak Ravid and John Khoury, "Idea of a Two-State Solution Has Reached 'Dead-End,' Bennett Says," *Haaretz*, June 17, 2013; see also Sara Roy, "Forward," in *Decolonizing Palestinian Political Economy: De-development and Beyond*, eds. Mandy Turner and Omar Shweiki (London: Palgrave/Macmillan, 2014).

by "the consistently profound and expanding need of the population on the one hand [primarily due to Israel's blockade of Gaza's economy, now in its thirteenth year], and the deliberate use of humanitarian aid to frustrate or achieve specific political ends, including the prolongation of conflict and suffering, on the other."[4]

A senior official at the Israeli human rights organization, GISHA, which monitors the Gaza Strip, captured the core of Israel's approach to Gaza: "In the rest of the world we try to bring people up to the humanitarian standard. Gaza is the only place where we're trying to push them down—to keep them at the lowest possible indicators."[5] Gazans are reduced from a people with political and economic rights and nationalist claims into charity cases in constant need of sustenance (which is provided by a compliant and complicit international community). In this way, Israel creates and maintains a humanitarian problem in order to manage a political one. Gaza is not only isolated but also made irrelevant and expendable; human life is wholly vulnerable without, in effect, any legal or juridical status, recourse, or appeal—reduced to what the Italian philosopher Giorgio Agamben defined as a state of exception—while Israel remains distanced from the violence it inflicts. In this state of exception, Gazans are rendered "unnameable" in Agamben's terminology, except for their biological needs. They cease to inhabit space that is animate and resonant, or endowed with any meaning or potential.

In his poem "Silence for Gaza," Mahmoud Darwish rejects any notion of Gaza's inconsequence. Rather,

he describes Gaza's power and significance when he writes:

> [Gaza] is not the most elegant or the biggest, but it equals the history of an entire homeland, because it is more ugly, impoverished, miserable, and vicious in the eyes of enemies. Because it is the most capable, among us, of disturbing the enemy's mood and his comfort... Enemies might triumph over Gaza ... They might break its bones ... But it will not repeat lies and say "Yes" to invaders. It will continue to explode. It is neither death, nor suicide. It is Gaza's way of declaring that it deserves to live.[6]

The collection of works that follows is inspired by, and itself embraces, Gaza's declaration of life. *Open Gaza* rejects Gaza's state of exception, insisting instead on its rightful and normal place in the world, and envisions real ways of securing that place by engaging the potential that resides in Gaza. Some authors consider Gaza's oppression, providing a powerful and compelling examination of the challenges that must be addressed. Others consider these challenges through the discourses of architecture, planning, and environment, where space can embody Palestinian aspirations and dreams. They envision possibility and meaningful change that is predicated, of course, on peace (and the demilitarization of space), human rights, and the end of division and separation, where physical borders are no longer determinative.

The ideas presented here do not emerge from "outside the box" but from the *absence* of a box.

4. Sara Roy, "Humanitarianism in Gaza: What Not to Do" (panel, The Syrian Humanitarian Crisis: What is to be Done?, Middle East Policy Council Capitol Hill Conference, April 21, 2015); see edited transcript in: Sara Roy, et al., "The Syrian Humanitarian Crisis: What is to be Done?" *Middle East Policy* 22, no. 2 (Summer 2015), which provides a more detailed examination of the role of humanitarianism in Gaza.

5. Roy, "Humanitarianism in Gaza."

6. Henry Norr, "Mahmoud Darwish: 'Silence for Gaza,'" *Mondoweiss*, November 24, 2012.

Gaza's capabilities are real and its potential realizable. In the practical and energizing ideas found in this volume, Gaza's well-being—and that of the region as a whole—lies in inclusion and in the promise that such inclusion embodies, which, as is argued, is truly worth pursuing.

WORKS CITED

Matar, Dina. "Gaza: Image Normalization." In *Gaza as Metaphor*, edited by Helga Tawil-Souri and Dina Matar. London: Hurst & Co, 2016.

Norr, Henry. "Mahmoud Darwish: 'Silence for Gaza.'" *Mondoweiss*, November 24, 2012.

Ravid, Barak, and John Khoury. "Idea of a Two-State Solution Has Reached 'Dead-End,' Bennett Says." *Haaretz*, June 17, 2013.

Roy, Sara. "Forward." In *Decolonizing Palestinian Political Economy: De-development and Beyond*, edited by Mandy Turner and Omar Shweiki. London: Palgrave/Macmillan, 2014.

Roy, Sara. "Humanitarianism in Gaza: What Not to Do." Panel, The Syrian Humanitarian Crisis: What is to be Done?, Middle East Policy Council Capitol Hill Conference, April 21, 2015.

Roy, Sara, Karen AbuZayd, Denis J. Sullivan, and Susan M. Akram. "The Syrian Humanitarian Crisis: What is to be Done?" *Middle East Policy* 22, no. 2 (Summer 2015): 1-29.

Said, Edward. *After the Last Sky: Palestinian Lives*. London: Vintage, 1986.

INTRODUCTION

Terreform

Michael Sorkin
Deen Sharp

At the Fun Time beach café located on the Khan Younis seafront in Gaza, a small group of Palestinian men were watching the 2014 World Cup semifinal between the Netherlands and Argentina. Bilal al-Astal and the soccer fans gathered with him were not given the chance to find out which team would proceed to the global spectacle of the World Cup final. As al-Astal stated in his testimony to the Israeli NGO B'Tselem:

> We watched the first half of the match together. We drank tea and coffee and there was a relaxed mood. We didn't hear any airplanes nearby. Suddenly, there was a loud explosion. By the time I realized what was happening, I found myself buried under a pile of sand and dirt.[1]

Such is the nature of daily life for Gazans: a schizophrenic rift between simple enjoyments that are routine for most of us and sudden eruptions of lethal violence from above. Urbanity instantaneously turns to terror.

The Gaza Strip is one of the most beleaguered environments on earth. Crammed into a space of 139 square miles (360 square kilometers), 1.8 million people live under siege in conditions that continue to plummet to ever more unimaginable depths of degradation and despair. In 2014, Operation Protective Edge (OPE), the third major Israeli assault on Gaza in six years, brought destruction on a scale that shocked both residents and long-time observers. As Sara Roy, who has worked for over thirty years on and in Gaza, wrote shortly after the end of OPE: "I can say without hesitation that I have never

seen the kind of human, physical, and psychological destruction that I see there today."[2] OPE only accelerated the conclusions of an infamous UN report published in 2012 that questioned whether Gaza would still be a "livable place" by 2020.[3]

The violence unleashed by Israel during OPE provided the impetus for Terreform to think about the sorts of productive interventions that might result from bringing together an eclectic group of designers, environmentalists, planners, activists, and scholars—from Palestine and Israel, the US, the UK, India, and elsewhere. Our aim was not simply to denounce or "deconstruct" the literal deconstruction of Gaza by remorseless bombing and blockade, but to imagine and celebrate the spaces of steadfastness and even hope. As firm believers in the "right to the city," we approach Gaza not for its scenographic horror but always as authentically urban, in defense of what we see as a critical avenue of resistance: imagining a better place for its citizens, one in which gathering in a café or taking a dip in the sea no longer brings the constant threat of sudden death.

We are not Panglossian, naively optimistic, and this volume firmly rejects the immiserization of Gazans. It does so by insisting on the particularity of alternatives, by seeing Gazans as people filled with aspiration, not as statistics—subjects to be destroyed—or the numbed inhabitants of a completely bare life. Gaza and Palestine are more than occupied territories under siege, and existence there is not defined solely by Israeli domination. The projects and essays in this volume engage Gaza *beyond* the malign

1. B'Tselem, "Bilal al-Astal Recounts Bombing That Killed 9 in Gazan Café, Where He and Others Were Watching a World Cup Match," July 15, 2014.

2. Sara Roy, *The Gaza Strip: The Political Economy of De-Development.* 3rd ed. (Washington, DC: Institute for Palestine Studies, 2016).

3. United Nations Country Team in the Occupied Palestinian Territory, "Gaza in 2020: A Livable Place?" (UNRWA, August 2012).

logic of bombing and blockade. They consider how life could be improved in Gaza *within* the limitations imposed by Israeli malevolence but also reach beyond this framework of endless war to imagine Gaza in a future *without* conflict.

While the Israeli siege aspires to control the minutest details of Gazans' everyday lives, down to the toothpaste they can or cannot use, the people of Gaza still dream, fantasize, and live in ways that lie outside the coercive and seemingly overwhelming logics of the Israel-Palestine conflict. As Atef Abu Saif writes in his diary, even in the context of a mere twelve-hour truce during OPE, city life quickly returned to the streets and people went about their daily lives: "People in their thousands on the street, buying food, moving from one place to another; the shops open, kids playing in the streets. It is a city that has poured itself out into a few moments of peace."[4]

The cover of this book articulates our intent, as editors, to both illuminate the Israeli siege and thwart its imposed logic. It shows a member of the Parkour group in Gaza founded by Mohammed Aljakhabir and Ahmad Matar in 2007 in the Khan Younis refugee camp. Parkour has provided an important set of practices through which Gazan youth can escape the oppression of the occupation. Parkour is, Matar has said, "the only thing that I could do, and the only thing that helped me to keep hope that the future is coming, and that something will happen for me . . . For us in Gaza, we practiced Parkour to feel our freedom. Because it's the sport that we can fly, we can jump over the obstacles, there is nothing [that] can stop us."[5] *Open Gaza* illuminates the incredible energy and ingenuity of the inhabitants of Gaza that is being so brutally stultified by the Israeli occupation. But it is also important to stress that both Aljakhabir and Matar have escaped the occupation, with many other members of the Parkour movement, by leaving Gaza. The cover of this book also marks the simultaneous presence of hope and its absence, or what the Palestinian poet Mahmoud Darwish called the "presence of absence."[6]

Open Gaza reassembles many members of a cohort that contributed to two earlier volumes: *The Next Jerusalem: Sharing the Divided City* (2002)[7] and *Against the Wall* (2005).[8] Although these books track a rapid descent from the myopic optimism that followed the Oslo agreement to the agenda of repression and apartheid concealed behind its false promise, both— like the present volume—engage authors from inside the space of conflict and from outside. These assemblies of Palestinians, Israelis, and "others" have sought to upend the representation of Palestinians, so often obscured through the lenses of colonialism and its attendant Orientalism. These books offered not simply a riposte to mainstream depictions and analysis, but also progressive visions of a shared and open future for Palestinians and Israelis.

In the years since the publication of these earlier works, reality has, alas, been far more cruel than progressive: the arguments made in *The Next Jerusalem* and *Against the Wall* have not only gone unheeded but the violence, separation, and

4. Atef Abu Saif, "Life under Fire in Gaza: The Diary of a Palestinian," *The Guardian*, July 28, 2018.

5. Sarah Illingworth, "Learning Parkour in Gaza Made Me Feel Free," *Huffington Post*, February 22, 2017.

6. Mahmoud Darwish, *In the Presence of Absence*, translated by Sinan Antoon (New York: Archipelago, 2011).

7. Michael Sorkin, ed., *The Next Jerusalem: Sharing the Divided City* (New York: Monacelli Press, 2002).

8. Michael Sorkin, ed., *Against the Wall: Israel's Barrier to Peace* (New York: The New Press, 2005).

oppression that they described have only intensified. Calls to tear down the wall have been met with the construction of more walls, trenches, and wires. In Gaza, where hundreds have been shot dead for approaching its incarcerating edge, the building of divides has been particularly intensive. In August 2018, the Israeli Ministry of Defense released new images of a two-hundred-meter-long sea barrier designed to further blockade Gaza, consisting of three layers: a fifty-meter-wide sea-level platform made of armored stone, a six-meter-high barbed-wire fence, and an additional wall to surround the barrier itself. Israel is building walls upon walls in its efforts to seal off Gaza from the world, and we denounce not simply these constructions but also the cohort of "professionals"—engineers, architects, planners, and apologetic academics—which enables and defends them.

The ever-expanding consequences of the blockade for Palestinian life have been profound, and the siege of Gaza has resulted in extremes of poverty, humiliation, injury, murder, and what Sara Roy has termed "de-development." In this volume, Tareq Baconi writes that the Israeli blockade of Gaza is not merely about containment, but about terrorizing a population into submission. To a substantial extent, this strategy is working. The stresses imposed by the siege— and the petty crime, kidnappings, and domestic violence that have become normalized as a result—all work to tear the Palestinian social fabric apart. But Baconi argues that Israel's enclosure of Gaza has failed to completely dominate the more

emotional, metaphysical realm, nor has it succeed in destroying the solidarity of citizens under siege (and, in this way, Gaza reproduces the unexpected stiffening of resolve during the bombing campaigns and sieges of the Second World War or Vietnam). Indeed, the very familiarity of the daily horrors that occur in the Strip breaks the blockade and carries the cause of Gaza to the broader world. Protests in support of Gaza in Istanbul, San Diego, Oslo, and Osaka bind the territory to a broader humanity—a glimmer of hope in an otherwise desolate context. No matter how high the fence or unrelenting the systems of control, Gaza cannot be sealed off from the world. Despite the risks in even the most basic everyday acts—like watching a soccer match on TV at the beach—Gazans find ways to be in the world, to be part of its cultures of normality. *Open Gaza* celebrates the tenacity revealed in the heroic pursuit of what, for most of us, seems simply banal.

Like its contributors, the work in this volume is surely eclectic and does not aspire to any version of a "complete" picture; an acknowledgment that no single discourse is adequate to the urban, and certainly not to Gaza's complexities. Engaging the tools of architecture and planning, the social sciences, environmentalism, and critical theory, it rises in defense of expansiveness, of freedom of thought and imagination, and proudly celebrates Gaza's courage and positive capability. The tunnels, for instance, that have been built in the Strip in an attempt to circumvent the blockade articulate the ingenuity and steadfastness of Gaza's inhabitants. Dramatic images of cows, fridges, and even full-sized SUVs being smuggled through these subterranean passages have circulated around the global mediascape. A chapter in this book (authored under a pseudonym— which reminds us of the constant danger that accompanies being in and writing about Gaza) takes us into tunnels between Gaza and Egypt. The author and illustrator depict the sophisticated engineering and complex sociopolitical organization required to keep them operating, as well as the perverse routines—the smuggler's Expedia—needed to negotiate them.

The tunnels have been particularly critical for the smuggling of basic construction materials, such as steel and cement, that have otherwise been banned from Gaza by the blockade. Several contributors describe the extensive lengths to which Israel has gone to ensure that Gaza's reconstruction is interrupted and controlled. The Gaza Reconstruction Mechanism (GRM), a tripartite agreement between the Palestinian Authority, the Israeli government, and the United Nations, was introduced in 2014 following the destruction caused by OPE. The contributions by the Royal College of Art and Pietro Stefanini argue, however, that far from facilitating reconstruction, the GRM has entrenched the blockade of Gaza and allowed Israel to control what can be built, as well as how, when, and where. This reinforces the sick circular economy of destruction and reconstruction that continuously engorges arms makers and contractors.

The GRM also introduced a centralized database system to collect microdata from every corner of Gaza. Francesco Sebregondi argues that the GRM has effectively turned Gaza into a version of the latest technocratic wet dream, the "smart city." While the "smart" technology utilized in the GRM is relatively rudimentary, it nonetheless offers us an insight into how the operation of smart cities—in which we *all* increasingly live—can be a dominating and oppressive technology of power. The deployment of these tools and techniques in Gaza powerfully illuminates just how problematic the questions of who manages and oversees the smart city and who controls the data it harvests really are. It also dramatically returns the smart city to its military point of origin, to the electronic battlefield and "network-centric" warfare. In this sense, Gaza is not unique but is the embodiment *in extremis* of the new normal for cities around the globe.

Beyond its analytical pieces on Gaza's predicament and history, this volume also offers a series of more speculative interventions that, while grounded in Gaza's particularities, take flight—like the kids of Parkour— to suggest directions in which a reimagined Gaza might grow and prosper. While these visionary forays offer strategies for wisely deploying resources in line with sustainable best practices, our objective is not to elaborate a model that obliges Gaza to "live within its means" but to unpack ideas about both limits and possibilities. These schemes include a blueprint for a solar-powered Gaza from Chris Mackey and Rafi Segal, which proposes a distributed energy infrastructure that could constitute a protective solar dome.

Alberto Foyo and Postopia imagine Gaza's potential to develop a fabric of architecture and agriculture that can help heal "Gaza's burned skin," while Romi Khosla proposes the construction of a *Nakba* memorial to act as a place of dialogue and reconciliation. Other architectural and urbanist propositions envision new ways in which to reread and redraw Gaza's urban fabric. Helga Tawil-Souri proposes an Internet Pigeon Network (IPN) to create a self-reliant, Israel-free means of sending and receiving data in Gaza. This IPN, Tawil-Souri argues, would offer Gazans the ability to control their own communications infrastructure and creatively embrace the "low-technologization" that has been imposed on them by the Israeli blockade, forcing them to survive on an "ecological footprint" that is less than one-tenth of the world's average.

Embedded in these imaginative pitches for Gaza are arguments about how this beleaguered place can reclaim its independence and dignity through the agency of space. It was the fatal delusion of modernist architecture and planning that their spatial practices could *by themselves* transform the social and political realms. We are under no such illusions. Nor do we have the slightest doubt that substantive change can only occur if Israel's boot is lifted from Gazan throats and Palestinian national aspirations are realized. We take special, dispirited note of the insanity of two current, externally proposed extraterritorial "solutions" to Gaza's problems: the periodically mooted Israeli project to build an island in the Mediterranean three miles offshore—connected to Gaza via a tenuous bridge—to house an easily controlled airport, seaport, electric plant, and logistics hub; and the Trump-Kushner plan to employ Gazans as laborers in a Special Economic Zone under Egyptian sovereignty deep in the Sinai.

Both resemble the situation in the American South not so long ago, where male descendants of freed slaves were imprisoned by the state in huge numbers and then hired out by their jailers to work in the very same cotton fields their ancestors cultivated as chattel.

These absurd declarations of a willingness to spend billions to "improve" the situation in Gaza as long as they do not actually have to be spent *in* Gaza constitute the kind of colonial villainy this volume vehemently opposes. Gaza needs a seaport, an airport, a robust source of energy, and a vibrant and diversified economy *on its own territory*. For this to happen, the Israeli siege on Gaza must end. Gazans—and all Palestinians—must be given control over the social, political, and economic resources that frame their own lives. Gaza's "de-development" will continue as long as Israel represses Palestinian sovereignty and autonomy. While it seems today that we have never been further from any possibility of Palestinians being able to truly rule their own lives, or further from a durable peace for Gaza, this absence makes this volume—and every other expansive assertion of Gaza's humanity—all the more urgent and necessary.

Open Gaza Now!

Michael Sorkin and Deen Sharp
New York City, Terreform, 2020

GAZA'S SKIN

Tareq Baconi

To say that Gaza is an "open-air prison" is to bandy about a cliché. Perhaps, like all hackneyed metaphors, this platitude captures some truthful *sense* of Gaza, yet remains far from adequate as a descriptor of the intricately manufactured ecosystem that has been created in this space.

Imagining Gaza as a prison does convey the essence of tortured resignation at one's inability to leave, at being locked in a confined space against one's will. It is hard to overcome the feeling of imprisonment in Gaza. Even standing on the shores here and looking out across the immense blue of the Mediterranean conjures up claustrophobia, not awe at the vast horizon of the planet.

There is no vastness here. There are restrictions, limitations, walls. There are barriers and confined spaces. But this imagery is where the metaphor of incarceration ends and the suffering in Gaza begins. The blockade of Gaza—officially in place since 2007, unofficially since much longer—is not designed solely for containment. On this stretch of land, a modest 365 square kilometers, close to two million Palestinians are starved, bombarded, surveilled, eviscerated, and generally terrorized into submission.

The Israeli architect and thinker Eyal Weizman has argued that the Gaza Strip is a site of experimentation.[1] The experiment revolves around how to conclusively pacify an unruly collection of people, to force them to acquiesce to their fate, to numb their survivalist instincts. From phosphorus bombs to drone attacks, from digital occupation to traditional spying, from humanitarianism to legalistic manipulations, the Gaza Strip has become the canvas on which to develop, test, and monitor different techniques of suppression.

It is on this strip of land that the notion of "extrajudicial killings" successfully transitioned from the gray area of customary international law to the "targeted assassinations" that are central to America's "War on Terror."[2] Within the context of Gaza, algorithms were built to compute and quantify the cost of human life in order to outline, to the last soul, the limits of proportional (read: "legitimate") warfare. It is here that databases were built to measure the caloric intake of Gaza's imprisoned population, to elucidate the fine line between annihilation and starvation.[3] This is where Israel perfected the art of constructing and managing humanitarian catastrophes.[4]

Over the course of the last five decades of Israel's occupation, Gaza has been transformed into a tightly controlled laboratory, precisely engineered to study the science of domination. Central to this transformation is "the blockade," a basic-sounding intervention that fails to adequately communicate the sprawling infrastructure of oppression that has been constructed on Gaza's territory.

The blockade's main function is to regulate Gaza's environment and sustain it as a detached and autonomous ecosystem. The fundamentals of such regulation are basic, rooted in the laws of physics: what comes in must be equal to what goes out. Input and output must be stringently measured and controlled to shape the evolution of any space that is cordoned off. One needs to

1. Eyal Weizman, *The Least of All Possible Evils: Humanitarian Violence from Arendt to Gaza* (London: Verso, 2011).

2. Antonio Cassese, "Expert Opinion on Whether Israel's Targeted Killings of Palestinian Terrorists is Consonant with International Humanitarian Law," Supreme Court of Israel: The Public Committee against Torture et al. v. The Government of Israel et al., HCJ 769/02 (2003); Nils Melzer, *Targeted Killing in International Law* (Oxford: Oxford University Press, 2008); and Mark V. Vlasic, "Assassination and Targeted Killing: A Historical and Post–Bin Laden Legal Analysis," *Georgetown Journal of International Law* 43 (2012): 259–333.

3. Coordination of Government Activities in the Territories (COGAT), "Food Consumption in the Gaza Strip – Red Lines," trans. Gisha: Legal Center for Freedom of Movement (slide presentation, Jerusalem, 2008).

4. Ilana Feldman, "Gaza's Humanitarianism Problem," *Journal of Palestine Studies* 38, no. 3 (2009): 22–37; see also Avi Shlaim, "How Israel Brought Gaza to the Brink of a Humanitarian Catastrophe," *The Guardian*, January 7, 2009.

look no further than the skin on their fingers, stretched over bones and muscles, to comprehend the intuitive complexity of an enclosure that regulates systems. Impervious and multilayered, our skin is a protective membrane that is deceptively simple in its functions, yet highly intricate.

Gaza's blockade similarly appears quite basic, its image best encapsulated by the domineering fence that has been erected around the imagined periphery that separates the Gaza Strip from Israel. This structure interweaves the traditional building blocks of prison complexes, including wires and metal gates, with highly digitized systems of control.[5]

But in reality, Gaza's enclosure is more complex, and it plays out through three different mediums: the physical, the conceptual, and the emotional. These mediums are not mutually exclusive, rather interconnected and interdependent. Together, they form a maze of restrictions that sustains Gaza's distinct habitat.

The physical medium, being the only tangible manifestation of Gaza's enclosure, is perhaps the easiest to visualize. Gaza's urban space, like any other, stretches to include the underground, the skies, and the intangible electromagnetic waves vibrating throughout the Strip. We interact mainly and predominantly with the surface above ground. One can almost imagine that a skin-like membrane has been pulled out from the corner of historic Palestine on the edge of the Sinai Peninsula, like a piece of cling film, and wrapped over Gaza's landscape.

As with any membrane, Gaza's skin operates predominantly as a barrier, a gatekeeper of sorts. While skins typically protect the integrity of the ecosystems they ensconce, this is not the case in the Gaza Strip, where the function of the membrane is to manage Gaza's internal environment in accordance with well-defined metrics. The membrane's porous nature is carefully overseen by Israeli "civil administrators," who engineer its selectivity to ensure optimal conditions within Gaza. Items such as flour and toothpaste are impurities that must be prevented from crossing into the quarantined space. Cement, steel, and other construction material must also be stringently regulated to ensure that Gaza's habitat is sufficiently sterilized. For break-even survival, we now know that 2,207 calories have to be injected through the membrane for each adult male in the Strip. Slightly fewer calories are needed for each adult female.[6]

Alongside this measured inflow, fundamental barrier functions dictate that outflow must be carefully planned, if not prevented. The clinical sterility of this process of outflow can be jarring. I recall the first time I walked out of the manufactured ecosystem of the Gaza Strip. Red blinking lights and loudspeakers direct the trickle of travelers exiting through a dizzying maze. Long corridors are interspersed with bare white rooms, furnished with cold steel tables over which Palestinians are forced to shed their clothes. Israeli civil administrators look down at these naked subjects through bulletproof glass cubicles located one floor above, as if from a microscope. Human interaction has been efficiently scrubbed and communication reduced to blinking lights and automated instructions.

The membrane's key function is to

5. Helga Tawil-Souri, "Digital Occupation: Gaza's High-Tech Enclosure," *Journal of Palestine Studies* 41, no. 2 (Winter 2012): 27–43.

6. "WikiLeaks: Israel Aimed to Keep Gaza Economy on Brink of Collapse," *Haaretz*, January 5, 2011.

keep Gazans in Gaza. So these exits are only, if ever, used in exceptional circumstances. For the past decade, a miniscule fraction of the two million imprisoned Palestinians have been allowed out. Gaza's landscape is now littered with young students clutching unstamped visas and crumpled university admission letters, tumors expanding in cancer patients, and loved ones dreaming of hugging significant others who have somehow left this cell. An ecosystem of despair and agony, of heartache and broken dreams, has been skillfully built.

While crossing the "border" between Gaza and Israel, the engineer in me could not help but marvel at the planning and execution of this system of enclosure, the mechanics of which stretch the limits of both legality and humanity. The feat of engineering underpinning Gaza's exceptional existence today is incredible; the financial, political, and technological investments that support this man-made ecosystem are staggering.

The brilliance of the underlying foundation is even more striking because it often goes unnoticed. As I stood opposite an Israeli security agent manning the last station before I was to "reenter" Israel, Hannah Arendt's "banality of evil" floated through my mind. I wondered if the guard reviewing my permit understood the scale of the machinery she was co-administering. I speculated about how many guards, like her, on how many levels and spheres of influence, were actively sustaining Gaza's inhumane ecosystem.

The processes underpinning Gaza's enclosure were, like our skin, deceptively simple. Sitting in her cubicle, the guard's assignment was straightforward enough: to ensure that I had the right permit to leave Gaza and enter Israel. As she signed me in, the vast machinery of Gaza's imprisonment was efficiently distilled into the most legitimate of actions. Yet the scaffolding sprawling underneath the surface that defined this guard's basic job was expansive and significantly more malicious.

Pulling the membrane over Gaza was merely a first step, one that has been perfected into a frightening science. So has the quest for supremacy over Gaza's skies, teeming as they are with drones and satellites that have exposed its most private parts. The electromagnetic field has been thoroughly crippled, if not defeated. As the membrane captures shipments of fuel before they can cross the fence, electric generators grind to a halt. Computers flicker, TV screens black out, cell phones lose their signal, meat rots in warm refrigerators, dialysis machines stop working, and tenants are confined to their high-rise apartments.

It is in the subterranean, however, where battles rage inconclusively. Early cracks in Gaza's enclosure began emerging when, horrifically and almost predictably, the imprisoned subjects seized on their most basic instincts to mitigate their imprisonment. Like dogs in a pen, Palestinians in Gaza began burrowing into the earth. Chunks of mud and soil flew up as deep caves snaked for miles below the earth's surface. As the membrane was tucked into Gaza's corners, frantic digging could be heard throughout the land. Tunnels burst out from this quarantined space as Palestinians fought for a modicum of agency in managing their ecosystem.

Ingenuous and utterly human in their survivalist impulse, the tunnels became Gaza's last grasp for control, the desperate final breath of protest against subjugation. Whatever the membrane held back, the tunnels sucked in. Construction material, fuel, donkeys, and buckets of KFC traversed this shadowy world into Gaza. The scientific measurement of Gaza's indicators by Israeli "civil administrators" was offset by uncontrollable inflows and outflows elsewhere, contaminating the habitat that was being regulated. The valves of Gaza's controlled ecosystem had moved underground.

Overseers of this experiment swiftly moved to deal with these dangerous leaks. Bombs and explosive devices were dropped above the tunnels to precipitate their collapse. Raw sewage and water were propelled into their entrances to drown their occupants. Tractors razed tunnel exits. Engineers began designing large steel walls that could be sunk into the ground to extend Gaza's surface skin downwards.

For all their innovative brilliance, these tools remain quite ineffective on their own. Built infrastructure is rarely disconnected from the world around it. For Gaza's enclosure to be complete, the ultimate battle lies not in the realm of the physical, but rather in the conceptual, the second medium through which the blockade operates. This is where the philosophy of the membrane is formulated.

I heard a story in Gaza. A congregant in a synagogue goes to his rabbi to complain about his wife. The man says that she is a pain, constantly nagging, constantly asking for more space in their modest two-bedroom home where they are raising three kids. The rabbi nods sympathetically.

"Bring in the goat from the outside fields," he says.

The man looks at him quizzically, but obeys. The episode repeats itself weekly.

"Bring in the cows."

"The chickens."

"The donkey."

By the end of the month, the congregant is near his wits' end. "Now," says the rabbi, "take the animals out and ask your wife how she feels."

People in Gaza have been, like the congregant's wife, forcefully socialized into lowering expectations. But it is outside of Gaza where the power of shifting perceptions has been most impactful. It is on the international stage that the logic underpinning the physical manifestation of Gaza's enclosure has been carefully crafted, over the course of many decades.

As early as the 1950s, Israel began laying the groundwork for Gaza's isolation, portraying the Strip as being home to an unruly population of *Fedayeen*.[7] Raids, incursions, enclosures, and massacres intermittently paved the way for quashing Gaza's fiery spirits. Now, under Hamas, Gaza has morphed into a "terrorist haven" that similarly merits an iron fist.

To guard Western civilization against the scourge of Islamism, Israel has been forced into undignified and uncivilized behavior to defeat the terrorist enclave on its doorstep, or so the narrative goes. Such discursive manipulation serves predetermined political goals to colonize Palestinian territories and demographically engineer Israel's Jewish majority. But

7. Jean-Pierre Filiu, "The Twelve Wars on Gaza," *Journal for Palestine Studies* 44, no. 1 (Autumn 2014): 53.

with (almost embarrassingly) simple rhetorical reconceptualization, Gaza's isolation becomes a necessary and unfortunate responsibility, grudgingly assumed by a civilized nation.

Such rhetorical engineering is central to sustaining Gaza's eco-system as a distinct and dangerous environment. Only with the effective framing of Gaza as an anomalous space filled with subhumans can Israel's domination be tolerated.

The way in which this process of reconceptualization unfolds is clear to see. Israel's Minister of Justice refers to newborn babies in Gaza as "snakes" and "vermin" that have to be quashed.[8] Bombs exploding over Gaza become "fireworks" that can be enjoyed from Israel's nearby Kobi Hill, a viewing point within Israel replete with sofas and popcorn.[9] Children playing soccer on the beach in Gaza are "Hamas operatives."[10] Gaza's men are primitives who seek death to satisfy their animalistic urges to copulate with virgins in heaven. Tunnels, perhaps the rawest indication of human survivalist instincts, become "terror tunnels," a maddening phenomenon, proof of the wildness and brutality of Gaza's savages.

Gazans cannot be human. Sitting on the outside, we cannot see ourselves reflected in the eyes of the people of Gaza. How else would we tolerate the systems of experimentation and sterilization unfolding over the Strip? Dehumanization has sustained the ongoing processes of containment necessary to cordon off the Gaza Strip. As Gazans protest their imprisonment, we sanction the deafening force unleashed over its skies, both physically and rhetorically. We watch as a full military arsenal,

regionally unparalleled in its sophistication, is let loose over a population that fights for survival by building primitive weapons in backyards.

The pacification of Gazans and the battle to break their spirit remains inconclusive, but the conditioning of Gaza's broader environment has been a resounding success. Now the US, the world's superpower, actively reinforces and benefits from this experimental canvas, building iron domes and tunnel-seeking technology to hermetically seal off this strip of land.

There is one medium, the third, which remains unconquered. This is the emotional, or the metaphysical realm, from which the almost silent whisper of doubt bubbles up, emerging from the deepest recesses of someone's mind as they think of Gaza. A single question floats, unperturbed, through one's core: the resonance of a shared humanity that persists against all odds. Arendt's words come to mind again:

> *Acceptance of lesser evils is consciously used in conditioning government officials as well as the population at large to the acceptance of evil as such . . . Politically, the weakness of the argument has always been that those who choose the lesser evil forget very quickly that they chose evil.*[11]

Does everyone forget? One can often detect a certain uneasiness when talking about Gaza, particularly when speaking with individuals who are not directly implicated in the machinations on the ground. They appear to have a gut feeling that

8. William McGowan, "The member of Knesset who called for genocide – against the mothers of the 'snakes,'" *Mondoweiss*, August 2, 2014.

9. Robert Mackey, "Israelis Watch Bombs Drop on Gaza From Front-Row Seats," *New York Times*, July 14, 2014. Similar scenes happened in 2009, as depicted in the Israeli documentary *Matador hamilchama (The War Matador)*, dir. Avner Faingulernt and Macabit Abramson, J.M.T. Film, 2011, film.

10. Peter Beaumont, "Israel Exonerates Itself over Gaza Beach Killings of Four Children Last Year," *The Guardian*, June 11, 2015.

11. Hannah Arendt (1964), quoted in Weizman, *Least of All Possible Evils*, 27.

something is not quite right; a whiff of rot. There is often an overeager assertion of denunciation. "It's like a ghetto! It's worse than a ghetto! How can they do that?" Because for all the energy invested in manipulating frames of mind, what Arendt refers to as conditioning, empathy remains an indefatigable force and evil a largely perceptible presence, regardless of the clothing it dons.

Despite its effective policing of the physical world, Gaza's membrane has been far less successful in dominating the realm of the abstract, that world just beyond the laws of physics. This is where the enigmatic tissue that binds us in some form of shared humanity lives on. Efforts to conquer the metaphysical through domination of the physical and the conceptual persist. Israel's Prime Minister understands this battlefield well. As pictures of blood-soaked children's limbs dominated the airwaves in 2014, Netanyahu blamed Hamas for telegenic manipulation.[12] These images cut through propaganda with greater ease than anything else might have. Their power is evident in the attempts by Gaza's administrators to ensure the membrane's impermeability to journalists and investigators, for untold stories do not have any morals to share, and what people cannot see they swiftly forget.

There are signs that severing Gaza from the airwaves has had some success in limiting the connectivity of this metaphysical plane. Gaza's narrative is so tightly woven that even West Bankers are aware of only a semblance of the horrors that reside within that strip of land. Still, Gaza's regulated ecosystem is bound to the planet by a fluid of humanity that the membrane is struggling to sieve out. The air, heavy with emotions, thoughts, and solidarity, cannot be barricaded out of the Gaza Strip, even as it is shrouded by its membrane.

As these forms of enclosure—the physical, conceptual, and emotional—grow and intersect, the experiment within Gaza has begun yielding results. Gaza's ecosystem is now adapting to its isolation, with time and space recalibrating to adjust to the Strip's violent removal from global connectivity.

The signs are perhaps, again, most tangible in Gaza's building blocks. The very foundation of the Strip has been sagging and decaying for decades, having been prevented from any form of investment or refurbishment.[13] Like an old woman who has slowly begun hunching over, Gaza's physical frame has given way to rapid deterioration.

There is no dignity in Gaza's aging, since it is brought about not by fleeting years but by starvation and battering. Raw sewage and excrement run down its alleyways and contaminate its once-beautiful shorelines. Instead of pride at the lifelong achievement of building homes for loved ones, fathers now weep next to shattered debris and collapsed bedrooms. Mothers age thinking about the hopeless future they've left their children and grandchildren with. The twinkling lights of Gaza's cityscapes are more often than not dulled and muted, with the Strip lying in pitch-black darkness. Like coarse make-up over painful bruises, colorful cloths hang where apartment walls once stood, as Gazans fight for some privacy and the illusion of normalcy. These efforts fail to hide the brokenness just below the surface.

All aging entails a reversal of

12. Ben Lynfield, "Israel–Gaza Conflict: Netanyahu Says Hamas Using Rising Death Toll to Make Israel Look Bad," *The Independent*, July 20, 2014.

13. Sara Roy, *The Gaza Strip: The Political Economy of De-development* (Washington, DC: Institute for Palestine Studies, 1995).

time, back to childlike behavior. This is true for Gaza as well, where the membrane's efforts to isolate this land have forced it to return to the mechanical basics of life. Cars are now often replaced with carts and donkeys. Rather than drinking water coming from taps, there are contaminated wells in towns. Instead of electric respirators, there are nurses who manually pump oxygen into the lungs of babies.

And the results are severe, not only for objects. Alongside infrastructural de-development, there has been a less tangible but no less present process of human degradation. As Gazans' hierarchy of needs shifts disproportionately toward shelter, food, and basic survival, the ingredients of social cohesion are eroding. Domestic suspicions, bitterness, and resentment are often aggravated by design. While walking through the rubble where neighborhoods once stood, a solitary building that remained standing was pointed out to me.

"Why is that building not on the ground?"

"Who lives there?"

"Why did the Israelis spare them?"

"Are they collaborators?"

In a tight-knit Palestinian society, invisible walls are rising. Just as Gaza's infrastructure transforms under the weight of isolation, its communal fabric is also morphing. Extreme poverty, hunger, loss of dignity, grief, and claustrophobia are all fundamentally restructuring the tenets of humanity in this place. Domestic violence is on the rise as walls move ever more aggressively into people's lives, imprisoning them in loveless, dreamless, and often violent marriages. Petty crime

and kidnappings, drug use and prostitution, and normalized violence are expanding within Gaza as a horrified society looks on, trying to make sense of these alien signs of moral degradation.

These are mere symptoms of what is happening within each individual's mind. I recall a tear-filled conversation with a human-rights advocate at a restaurant on one of Gaza's piers.

"People are now ashamed of grief," she told me, "they feel they no longer have the right to mourn."

How can one mourn a father or a brother murdered by Israeli bombs when entire families are wiped out just down the street? What right do they have to proclaim their grief for tragedies that are dwarfed, made almost negligible, when compared to others? The hierarchy of suffering has become so extreme, so unimaginable, that the right to mourn is often a luxury. There is shame in pained loss. Everyone has paid a price so staggering that tears are treasonous. They betray weakness and doubt— that perhaps the agony required for liberation from such a merciless foe might just be too much to bear.

Self-conscious grief is perhaps the most intimate of signs that the social fabric in Gaza is being re-engineered under pressure. But also, is there a more vivid example of self-censorship, of erecting walls within one's mind? The systems of enclosure are not only rising on the periphery of Gaza's terrain—they are also taking root among the thoughts of its people.

And this is irreversible. A growing generation of children is already being traumatically socialized within this siloed world, through bombs and missiles. Kids below the age of ten have lived through three military assaults that have devastated their surroundings. In the last assault on Gaza in 2014, more than 550 children were slaughtered. Little boys told me they lost more than half of their classmates that summer. I wondered how many wet bedsheets were being washed in Gaza every morning.

Even for other Palestinians, Gazans now command a particularly distinct and evocative form of Palestinian-ness. Gaza is surrounded by a special aura, held apart both as a site of incredible steadfastness and a reminder of overwhelming sadness. Somehow, even in acknowledging Gaza's humanity, we now inadvertently reinforce its separateness.

These emotional walls, rather than the physical ones, constitute perhaps the most resounding success of the experiment that is Gaza. What power can be derived from slowly and systematically altering a whole people's mental make-up! The membrane has been so effective that even Gazans who manage to leave remain separate from the rest of the world's population. Beyond Gaza's ecosystem, the membrane sticks to them incessantly in the form of guilt at abandoning a drowning population, of deathly cynicism, having seen what humanity is capable of. I imagine that every Gazan who transcends this ecosystem remains tethered to its land. It is as if the suffocating imprisonment of one's mind persists, with Gaza's membrane sticking like skin to the exiled body.

As these transformations take root on every level within Gaza, a peculiar thing has happened. Gaza's manufactured ecosystem has produced a space that acts as a microcosm of our time. Gaza is today a site where the "isms" shaping and reshaping our contemporary world order are condensed into a small and overcrowded place.

Terrorism and Islamism. Nationalism and colonialism. Western imperialism. Capitalism and neoliberalism. Racism. These ricochet against the inner walls enclosing the cell that is Gaza, manifesting themselves most tangibly—and lethally—on the ground. Their presence is heightened here in such a way that one can see the exact manner in which these fault lines shape our lives in less obvious, more diluted forms elsewhere.

Gaza has become the frontline of the fabricated battle between civilizations, a stage erected to play out an imagined clash between an East that denotes Islamic Terrorism and a West that proclaims Humanism. It has emerged as the underbelly of unbridled power, of Israel's domination over the Palestinians, a dynamic evocation of America's unchecked global supremacy. The length and breadth of this coastal enclave is a portrait of hegemony, its features stark and unforgiving.

Gaza is the clearest spatial manifestation of what absolute domination looks like. It is a marketplace where the true value of human life is quantified and traded. Gone is the self-conscious pretense debated in the Western hallways of power that life is equal across race, ethnicity, or nationality. In Gaza, the mask is off. Shades of human value are measured transparently and renegotiated intermittently. At last count, we know it was 1,027 Palestinians to one Israeli.[14] The tiers of human rights and the politics undergirding our humanity are

14. This is in reference to the Shalit prisoner exchange. See Ronen Bergman, "The Human Swap," *New York Times Magazine*, November 13, 2011, 34–39.

perhaps more unapologetically evident in this space than anywhere else on the planet. A focal point where all forms of constructed political correctness are dropped, Gaza has somehow inadvertently become an example of purity, of truthfulness.

In these ways, the ecosystem produced in Gaza has created what is perhaps the most honest reflection of our time. Somehow, unexpectedly, Gaza has emerged as a site of concentrated worldliness,

a place where our reality—our most basic and rawest self—is presented unvarnished, left open to be viewed in all its beauty and hideousness. In that way, for all its separateness, Gaza remains inextricably intertwined and interconnected with our world. This realization counterintuitively gives me hope. It confirms to me that the delusion that any people can be severed from the rest of humanity is just that: a delusion.

WORKS CITED

Arendt, Hannah. 1964. Quoted in Weizman, Eyal. *The Least of All Possible Evils: Humanitarian Violence from Arendt to Gaza*. London: Verso, 2011.

Baconi, Tareq. "What the Gaza Protests Portend." *The New York Review of Books*, May 15, 2018.

Beaumont, Peter. "Israel Exonerates Itself over Gaza Beach Killings of Four Children Last Year." *The Guardian*, June 11, 2015.

Cassese, Antonio. "Expert Opinion on Whether Israel's Targeted Killings of Palestinian Terrorists is Consonant with International Humanitarian Law." Supreme Court of Israel: The Public Committee against Torture et al. v. The Government of Israel et al. HCJ 769/02. 2003.

Coordination of Government Activities in the Territories (COGAT). "Food Consumption in the Gaza Strip - Red Lines." Translated by Gisha: Legal Center for Freedom of Movement. Slide presentation, Jerusalem, 2008.

Feldman, Ilana. "Gaza's Humanitarianism Problem." *Journal of Palestine Studies* 38, no. 3 (2009): 22–37.

Filiu, Jean-Pierre. "The Twelve Wars on Gaza." *Journal for Palestine Studies* 44, no. 1 (Autumn 2014): 53.

Lynfield, Ben. "Israel-Gaza Conflict: Netanyahu Says Hamas Using Rising Death Toll to Make Israel Look Bad." *The Independent*, July 20, 2014.

Mackey, Robert. "Israelis Watch Bombs Drop on Gaza From Front-Row Seats." *New York Times*, July 14, 2014.

Matador hamilchama (The War Matador). Directed by Avner Faingulernt and Macabit Abramson. J.M.T. Film, 2011, film.

McGowan, William. "The member of Knesset who called for genocide – against the mothers of the 'snakes.'" *Mondoweiss*, August 2, 2014.

Melzer, Nils. *Targeted Killing in International Law*. Oxford: Oxford University Press, 2008.

Roy, Sara. *The Gaza Strip: The Political Economy of De-development*. Washington, DC: Institute for Palestine Studies, 1995.

Rynhold, Jonathan, and Dov Waxman, "Ideological Change and Israel's Disengagement from Gaza." *Political Science Quarterly* 123, no. 1 (2008): 11–37.

Shlaim, Avi. "How Israel Brought Gaza to the Brink of a Humanitarian Catastrophe." *The Guardian*, January 7, 2009.

Tawil-Souri, Helga. "Digital Occupation: Gaza's High-Tech Enclosure." *Journal of Palestine Studies* 41, no. 2 (Winter 2012): 27–43.

Vlasic, Mark V. "Assassination and Targeted Killing: A Historical and Post-Bin Laden Legal Analysis." *Georgetown Journal of International Law* 43 (2012): 259–333.

Weizman, Eyal. *The Least of All Possible Evils: Humanitarian Violence from Arendt to Gaza*. London: Verso, 2011.

"WikiLeaks: Israel Aimed to Keep Gaza Economy on Brink of Collapse." *Haaretz*, January 5, 2011.

ARCHITECTURE OF THE EVERYDAY

Salem Al Qudwa

In the Gaza Strip, the building products that appear in the street are gray concrete blocks, built to specifications far below basic international standards. Often, construction materials are limited to what is available in the Strip. These ordinary buildings can hardly respond to Gazan communities' urgent, everyday needs and to a set of climatic conditions that demand heavy, long-term inputs of water, electricity, and resources. Even the methods used to construct these bare-bones structures fail to reflect Gaza's everyday cultural practices. The way that architecture in the Gaza Strip is evolving tends to disregard the sense of place its inhabitants have cultivated over history, leaving little room for the cohabitation of extended families, alternative environmental practices with the potential to reduce the use of natural resources, and the building process itself, which lacks responsive collaboration between the local people.

On the other hand, a new interest in the "architecture of the everyday" is emerging in the profession, making architects look to the rhythm of daily life as a means of escaping the ever-quickening cycles of consumption and fashion that have reduced architecture to a series of stylistic fads.[1] It is instructive to contemplate how this ordinary, everyday language could help improve the existing tectonic and spatial forms and realities in Gaza. In this chapter, I offer a visual analysis of the existing objects that surround Gaza's inhabitants and the buildings in which they—and I—live. This is followed by a social and physical mapping of selected areas in the Gaza Strip showing the process of construction and reflecting on it.

***

Ordinary. Banal. Quotidian. The "architecture of the everyday" makes a plea for the un-monumental and the anti-heroic.[2] In any society, buildings are generally the largest and frequently the most permanent of any human artifacts and are invested with profound meanings. In Gaza, however, we find yet another aspect of the "ordinary" that has to do with the reduction of everyday life to a bare minimum where access to fuel, electricity, and other basic needs are not free, but restricted by Israel, whose control of the Gaza Strip's theoretical borders is absolute.[3] The corrosion of these essential resources is exacerbated by the density of life in Gaza, with the Strip being the most densely populated stretch of land in the world.

Gaza is linked to the outside world through five border crossings: four with Israel and one with Egypt. All materials and goods must officially enter through the Israeli border crossings, whereas the Egyptian crossing is only for the movement of people. Access to the Mediterranean Sea is limited to three nautical miles along the Strip's coastline.[4] The area has endured difficult circumstances, such as low incomes, a high rate of unemployment, and a siege that prohibits the entry of many essential items, including construction materials.

Urban life in the Gaza Strip has been shaped by periods of growth and crisis. First are the cultural urban transformations in the Gaza Strip. Changes in the social structure and urban landscape, where spaces that were once open are becoming closed, have led to box-like buildings. The

1. Deborah Berke and Steven Harris, *Architecture of the Everyday* (Princeton, NJ: Princeton Architectural Press, 1997).

2. Ibid.

3. Sari Nusseibeh, "Gas-less in Gaza" (presentation, Human Rights and Intercultural Dialogue in the Mediterranean conference, University of Teramo, Italy, March 27–29, 2008).

4. Ahmed Muhaisen and Johan Ahlbäck, *ILO Gaza Strip Assessment: Towards Sustainable Construction and Green Jobs in the Gaza Strip* (Geneva: International Labour Organization, 2012), 4–6.

Figure 1: A typical self-built house in the Gaza Strip, where the possibilities of form are dictated by needs of the occupants, 2015.

majority of residential buildings in the Strip are known for being unfinished gray boxes of concrete and plaster, and for their use of simple building details. The unstable economic situation, lack of access to raw materials as a result of the blockade, and the shortage of building materials often force families to build lower-quality houses. Most do not look good, and appear as if they might have been built in the 1970s or 1980s. This is the impact of the new vernacular architecture in the Strip.[5]

SELF-BUILT BUILDINGS AND THE UNCERTAINTY OF PLANNING IN THE GAZA STRIP

In this dense urban area, residential buildings display a wide variety of housing and building qualities, and range from extremely solid, fully serviced concrete frame constructions to squalid, windowless shacks made of concrete blocks. Some occupants are able to mobilize enough funds to improve their dwellings to middle-class standards, while others continue living in the most basic shelters, unable to afford any improvements.

Out of necessity, buildings in the Gaza Strip are built with the bare essentials. Houses are constructed to be functionally efficient, providing shelter using the most rudimentary elements. Single and extended family houses are scattered in the Gaza Strip with a slab of living spaces raised on pilotis and a flat roof.

Early modernism had a notable influence on the region. This style filtered through to Gaza via Palestinian construction workers who worked in occupied Palestine.[6]

5. Eyal Weizman and Carola Dietrich, "Austrian Housing Project, Khan Younis," *Architektur-Aktuell*, no. 9 (2000).

6. Ibid.

Figure 2: Hollow concrete blocks with which local work crews in the Gaza Strip are well versed, 2015.

The lack of urban and regional planning and oversight of construction in the Gaza Strip are critical issues. Building licenses are granted liberally, existing land use regulations are often ignored, and the Strip lacks experience with planning in general. While the population is increasing, available land is decreasing. Occupants' lifestyles and needs dictate forms and spatial relationships (see fig. 1), rather than the willful composition of a designer, if there is a designer at all. Until the late 1980s, the architect was not only the designer, but the building process could not even go ahead without the architect's signature. Yet, building without architects is common practice. Competent, low-skilled workers are used to maintain the quality of existing buildings, while almost all houses belonging to the poor go without plastering their walls, on either the outside or the inside.

ARCHITECTURAL COMPONENTS
The geometry of buildings is dictated by the construction materials available and the topography of the landscape. To build in the most efficient way, materials have to be put together using their inherent qualities, which include size and shape. This provides the architecture with an order that is not based on conceptual ideas, but on logic and rationale.[7] Construction methods are kept simple because of a lack of technologically advanced skills. Each individual building deviates a little from a straightforward pattern of rational arrangement and construction. Another consideration is the client's budget, which generally means that the main building component is the concrete masonry unit (see fig. 2), a popular material that workers have experience with. Following typical architectural plans, workers employ poured concrete and concrete masonry units as some of their principal building materials. Blocks are then coated with a lime plaster wash in order to protect the building against dampness, and are arranged with apertures that provide screening and filter daylight into interior spaces.

7. Amanda Heal, "Building Simply: An Investigation into the Potential for Building Simply in the UK" (MPhil thesis, Cardiff University, 2010).

Figure 3: Bricks lined up in a row could be seen as similar to the grid formats of minimalist artist Carl Andre, 2007.

Figure 4: Dough circles repeated in rows, 2016.

REINVENTING EVERYDAY ART

Objects do not exist in an autonomous space that separates them from their surroundings. They exist in what sculptor Donald Judd describes as "actual space": they share a space in which the viewer's body is also located. Judd's concept challenged the idea that the presence of the artist's hand alone is enough to signify quality aesthetics. In other words, the effect of an everyday artwork in an exhibition would vanish, were no one to frame it or place it on a pedestal. The most impressive photographs are those that do not isolate everyday artworks, but rather show them in their surroundings.[8]

The reality of the arts in the Gaza Strip is that there are a limited number of exhibitions and galleries, so only a small number of people are able to see paintings and sculptures. Artists, sculptors, art experts, and critics have to receive their education abroad, in other Arab countries or in Europe. Given the dire economic situation, art has been limited to school education and a few annual exhibitions organized by associations of artists.[9] People in the Gaza Strip are constantly subjected to political instability, and ordinary citizens look to art only for its everyday utility (see fig. 3); it is thus no accident that mainly only the applied arts have been developed.

On the other hand, residential buildings in the Strip may look like disorganized groups of crowded, gray concrete boxes, but when you look beneath their outer layers, you will find all sorts of complex and human life-support systems at work, in which resourcefulness, not hopelessness, is predominant.[10] For example, ordinary Palestinian women in the Gaza Strip prepare the traditional flatbread for their families using wheat flour that they receive from humanitarian aid agencies. Baking bread at home saves hundreds of shekels in groceries every month. Women lay the dough in clean circular shapes, and repeat

8. Andreas Ruby, Angeli Sachs, and Philip Ursprung, *Minimal Architecture: From Contemporary International Style to New Strategies* (Munich: Prestel Publishing, 2003).

9. Asad Al Asad, "Contemporary Art of Palestine: Development Issues," *Art San'at*, no. 2 (2007).

10. UN-Habitat, *Quick Guide 2: Low Income Housing: Approaches to help the urban poor find adequate accommodation*, Housing the Poor in Asian Cities (UN Economic and Social Commission for Asia and the Pacific, 2008).

Figure 5: Horizontal and vertical lines, a typical security screen window, 2007.

these in rows, echoing minimal art shapes (see fig. 4). The natural light coming through the aluminum frame of the windows in each room illuminates "actual space" in the house, and the presence of metal window bars similarly points to simplicity, order, and abstraction (see fig. 5).

Applied art is the application of design and aesthetics to functional objects and objects of everyday use, whereas fine arts serve as intellectual stimulation to the viewer, and are produced or intended primarily for beauty. In industrial arts, beauty can only be part of the total meaning and is dependent on utility. For beauty is still in the realm of perception and contemplation, not of use. No matter how much of an artist a builder or a potter may be, s/he is necessarily controlled by the practical needs that houses or pots serve. The applied arts incorporate design and creative ideals into objects of utility, such as a cup, magazine, or decorative park bench. There is considerable overlap between the fields of applied and decorative arts; to some extent, they are alternative terms.[11]

The aesthetics of the raw material, the relationship of objects to actual space, the effects of natural light on street volumes, and the immediate and quick production of highly reduced building arrangements are all significant elements to consider within the visual context of the Gaza Strip. Following these basic elements, accidental sculptures that embody the forms and concepts of minimal art are primarily made from industrial materials, such as natural stone, concrete, wood, steel, aluminum, glass, and plastic. Without any intention, the objects are frequently reduced to very simple geometric shapes and are industrially produced, thus removing the artist's personal signature from the work. The works are also characterized by serial arrangements of a number of shapes in small and medium dimensions. Freestanding objects, such as metallic

tubes and wooden stacks, can be seen laid along the streets of the Gaza Strip, with their circular and rectangular ends repeated in lines, horizontally and vertically (see fig. 6). Wood pallets, stacks of plywood, rusty tubes—the concentrated presence of these formal elements of building composition forms a close link with the sculptural works of minimal art. While watching the blacksmith working metal with a hammer and anvil, and the carpenter working at his carpentry, one can see that they are making pieces of sculpture, but keeping them simple and affordable.

Moving through the streets of the Gaza Strip, one can see solid and hollow cement blocks arranged in sculptural patterns similar to those of Judd's minimalist sculpture, and cubes arranged in modular and grid formats, where each worker has his own way of geometrically ordering the boxes according to their thickness. Other static objects

Figure 6a & 6b: Stacks of construction materials, 2015.

11. Dewitt H. Parker, *The Principles Of Aesthetics* (CreateSpace Independent Publishing Platform, 2012).

include stacks of construction materials in the streets of the Gaza Strip, stacks of wood and cement bricks in a unit-bar version, and concrete exterior walls (fig. 7). Many of these works convey an aesthetic similarity to minimalist art, in which the pictorial elements no longer have any meaning beyond their own selves. Aesthetic strategies such as symmetry and repetition can be seen as well.

Figure 7: Static minimalistic objects on the streets of Gaza, 2015.

GRAY BOXES AND THE FORM-MAKING PROCESS

Thousands of Palestinians in the Gaza Strip live in moderate dwellings or poor-quality shelters that have gradually become permanent settlements. The overcrowded residential buildings are equipped with cement blocks for internal and external walls, and flat slabs of concrete roofing. For larger buildings, which have a natural tendency to be more complex than smaller buildings, it may be necessary to reduce complexity through repetition.[12] A generic form or type can be repeated to accommodate a complex residential plan. In this way, the number of different forms and building types is minimized. The same can be said for the repetitive use of building products and components in construction, which together form a simple whole.

There are buildings with no particular architectural identity or style. They are basic in geometry, simple, and gray (see fig. 8).

REHABILITATION OF LOW-INCOME HOUSING, 2011

To identify obstacles to the renovation and reconstruction of everyday buildings in the Gaza Strip, I worked at several sites there, following the customary stages of need assessment: design, procurement, and construction. These are outlined within the overall framework for the project and the work methodologies employed at the time. As project architect and coordinator, I was able to see the application of theory to real design, and then feed the project's data back into my research.

NEEDS ASSESSMENT AND SITE ATMOSPHERE

Our needs assessments revealed long waiting lists of damaged houses that belong to poor families with low social status. I visited more than two hundred individual homes to assess what conditions should be adapted to suit the needs of each family, and then drew up plans for modifications. Field visits to the area (beginning on March 15, 2007) confirmed the need for serious rehabilitation of houses located in Beit Lahia and Al Shouka (see fig. 9).

Most of these families live in scrap-built homes, without access to water and sanitation services (see fig. 10). Residents use local materials, cement, hollow blocks, and appropriate technology to rehabilitate or build their homes.

FLOOR PLANS AND FACADES

The proposed housing unit (see fig. 12) provides new views and privacy, while maintaining its connection to the rest of the household. Most existing houses are too hot in summer; because the poorly insulated, sheet metal roofs quickly heat up the interior and poor ventilation does not allow the hot air to escape. They are also too cold in winter, because cold air comes in through the openings and hot air escapes through the roof. Roof thermal masses, insulation, glass windows, and openings designed for cross ventilation assure that the indoor temperature is comfortable. New building technologies also significantly increase the durability and lifespan of concrete homes. Local materials were used to reduce costs: foundations with a thin layer of cement and a damp-proof course prevent pests from burrowing into

12. Heal, "Building Simply."

Figure 8: Repetitive use of building products and components, 2016.

Figure 9: Basic materials used for fencing in rural and marginalized areas, 2016.

Figure 10: A public toilet unit among the scrap–built homes in Al Shouka, which are without proper access to water and sanitation services, Al Shouka, 2007.

Figure 11a & 11b:
Sketch notebook and
concrete were the
media of communication
on-site, Beit Lahia, 2010.

the buildings and moisture from seeping up from the ground into the walls. Research and planning were carried out in place, and construction has been a continuous and dynamic process. Architectural drawings and plans were nowhere to be found: only basic drawings were available for the contractor. Other details were developed on-site. Concrete and a sketchbook were the media of communication (see fig. 11).

As in traditional vernacular architecture, the kitchen and bathroom are still housed in separate structures. The new buildings have three options: a bedroom with a bathroom unit, a bedroom with a kitchen unit, and a kitchen–bathroom unit (see fig. 12). However, these options double the family living area, while maintaining the same building footprint. Land is saved by adding these new units on the sites of existing, lower-utility forms of shelter. The project offers low-cost housing solutions for poor communities that are also environmentally adapted. It uses context-sensitive building materials, adopts local building techniques, and employs a participatory community approach.

PROJECT COSTS

With a tight budget, the project attempted to employ some ideas of ordinary architecture in its design and construction. Sometimes, it seems that the human aspect is forgotten in typical building projects. Deadlines, budgets, and systems seem to take up most of the architects' attention. This project, however, was built according to the architecture of necessity.

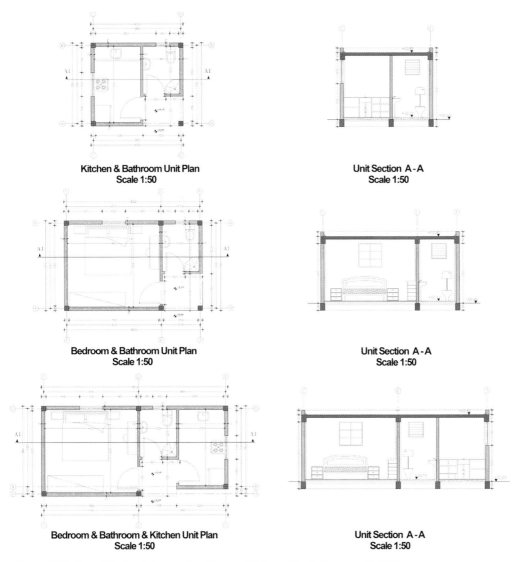

Kitchen & Bathroom Unit Plan
Scale 1:50

Unit Section A - A
Scale 1:50

Bedroom & Bathroom Unit Plan
Scale 1:50

Unit Section A - A
Scale 1:50

Bedroom & Bathroom & Kitchen Unit Plan
Scale 1:50

Unit Section A - A
Scale 1:50

Figure 12: Basic architectural plans and sections—a kitchen with a bathroom unit, 2010.

The shelters provided in this rehabilitation project for low-income families were very basic: cubes, essentially, which can be implemented anywhere in the world. This reduced the need for large amounts of expensive materials and time-consuming maintenance. Because the budget and available materials were limited, the project team was forced to concentrate on the basic needs of their clients (poor families) and create intelligent designs that made the most of existing resources, in some ways pushing them to new levels by adding more rooms. The resulting architecture reflects a pureness of form and material (fig. 13). The effort to rehabilitate the houses found in these marginalized and poor areas exceeds the pain of the imposed siege on the Strip. Simple materials are still available in local markets, and what's more, the project provided unemployed workers with hundreds of jobs. The estimated cost for the restoration of each residential unit is about $4,400 (55 percent less than the normal cost). It took just seven months to renovate seventy housing units for the first target group.

PROJECT SUSTAINABILITY

Solutions to fundamental challenges call for architecture where everything serves a purpose; architecture that

Figure 13: The project offers low-cost housing solutions for poor communities, 2010.

follows necessity. By involving the local populace in both the design and the building of their projects, architects are able to establish a framework for the mutual exchange of knowledge and skills. All materials used in the projects are collected close to the sites or purchased from local merchants.

The goal of the rehabilitation project was to improve the living conditions of the local population and to strengthen national identity, while maintaining the high level of sustainability that exists in home construction. We moved toward this goal by building three model houses for low-income families that were designed by young local architects and built by local craftsmen who were trained in modern building techniques. It is expected that these young architects will carry their knowledge and skills to other regions, and that newly trained laborers will be able to use their skills to build other modern homes in the region. The project is sustainable for two main reasons: first, it uses readily available resources (sand, aggregates, and cement); second, it saves land for agriculture by erecting single-story buildings at the same locations as preexisting shelters. I should note that despite the greater availability of the aforementioned resources, people in rural areas increasingly desire to build homes out of cement bricks, concrete, and corrugated iron sheet.

CONCLUSION

In the midst of challenging living conditions, it is important to mobilize people's aesthetic sensibilities by creating and appreciating everyday objects and activities that enhance life and human dignity. The severe restriction of resources, technology,

Figure 14: A powerful dichotomy of the imagery and the simple surroundings in the actual space, 2007.

and manpower does not necessarily lead to "hopelessness," but can be transformed against the odds into qualities of "resourcefulness" and "resilience."[13] The ideology of the everyday is about the search for the essence of the human condition, material, texture, space, and light. It requires getting down to the bones of existing construction techniques. In the Gaza Strip, the architecture of the everyday is not an alternative paradigm, but a consequence of the current availability of material resources and local expertise in building techniques and form-making processes. Palestinian architects and urban designers working in the field should seek simplicity and rediscover the valuable qualities of humble materials. The role of the architect is to envision another world, a better world.

WORKS CITED

Al Asad, Asad. "Contemporary Art of Palestine: Development Issues." *Art San'at*, no. 2 (2007).

Berke, Deborah, and Steven Harris. *Architecture of the Everyday*. Princeton, NJ: Princeton Architectural Press, 1997.

Heal, Amanda. "Building Simply: An Investigation into the Potential for Building Simply in the UK." MPhil thesis, Cardiff University, 2010.

Muhaisen, Ahmed, and Johan Ahlbäck. *ILO Gaza Strip Assessment: Towards Sustainable Construction and Green Jobs in the Gaza Strip*. Geneva: International Labour Organization, 2012.

Nusseibeh, Sari. "Gas-less in Gaza." Presentation at the Human Rights and Intercultural Dialogue in the Mediterranean conference, University of Teramo, Italy, March 27–29, 2008.

Parker, Dewitt H. *The Principles Of Aesthetics*. CreateSpace Independent Publishing Platform, 2012.

Palestinian Central Bureau of Statistics (PCBS). "Census 2017." West Bank, 2017.

Ruby, Andreas, Angeli Sachs, and Philip Ursprung. *Minimal Architecture: From Contemporary International Style to New Strategies*. Munich: Prestel Publishing, 2003.

Saito, Yuriko. *Aesthetics of the Familiar: Everyday Life and World-Making*. Oxford: Oxford University Press, 2017.

UN–Habitat. *Quick Guide 2: Low Income Housing: Approaches to help the urban poor find adequate accommodation*. Housing the Poor in Asian Cities. UN Economic and Social Commission for Asia and the Pacific, 2008.

Weizman, Eyal, and Carola Dietrich. "Austrian Housing Project, Khan Younis." *Architektur-Aktuell*, no. 9 (2000).

13. Yuriko Saito, *Aesthetics of the Familiar: Everyday Life and World-Making*, (Oxford: Oxford University Press, 2017), 18–19.

RING CITY: A METROPOLIS, NOT AN ENCLAVE

Terreform

Michael Sorkin
Damiano Cerrone
Jie Gu
Andrea Johnson
Ying Liu

Planning is a blunt instrument, too often blind to categories beyond its own. A historic critique of its physical practices confronts their frequent indifference to the social and political substrate of their operations. Indeed, "planning" in the United States—and in places that share its methods—fell into disrepute because of the dumb, often authoritarian, instrumentality with which it has been practiced: for the highways rammed through neighborhoods too disenfranchised to resist, for the "urban renewal" that wiped out rich social ecologies and replaced them with dull uniformity, for the dogmatic classification of subjects and classes and for the massive reorganization of the city via prejudicial data masquerading as "objective."

Our speculation wonders if this myopia can be turned to an advantage, if traditional planning's willful indifference can provide clarity. Gaza has been mapped—planned—by many actors with many motives. Numerous schemes and documents—Ottoman, British, Egyptian, Israeli, Palestinian, United Nations—are publicly accessible and completely confused, as Christine Boyer so carefully details in this volume. Other plans—presumably fiendish in their sensorial and operational detail—are covert, reserved for agents with authentically malign motives. This secret regime—the darkest side of the "smart city"—is surely a component of planning's instrumentalities of control but, in a familiar elision, it reveals the repressive policing that infects the very idea of the "master" plan and its top-down authority.

The plan presented here is hardly bottom up. On the contrary, it is frankly deterministic propaganda for a very particular all-at-once that seeks its conceptual and political sanction in the fact that it enjoys no power, save persuasion. Here, we argue, is one of many rational, possible, and humane ways of designing a city that grows from a known series of facts on the ground. If it has any power, it arises from both the simple logics of a set of "solutions" to conventionally understood "problems"—movement, enhancement of natural systems, distribution of cultural and public infrastructure, zoning for agricultural and industrial production, management of density, housing production, etc.—and from a single, radical observation: one thinks very differently about Gaza and its hinterlands if its political border disappears as a physical fact.

The urban development proposed here does have an obvious predicate: peace. However, it remains mute about nationality, and it would be a mistake to see this work as a vision of either Israeli or Palestinian hegemony or, for that matter, of any specific form of condominium. Of course, its implication is to reject ideas of citizenship that are either simple acts of sorting, renunciations of difference, or the surrender of self-determination. As urbanists, we feel there are many characteristics of city life that can and must be shared, however inflected by the forms, habits, and social and bioclimatic particulars of place.

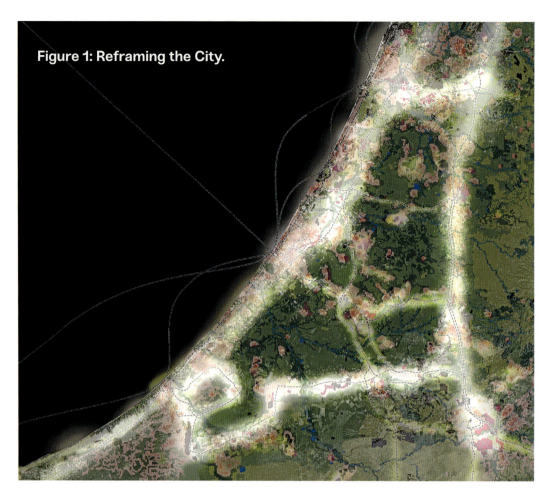

Figure 1: Reframing the City.

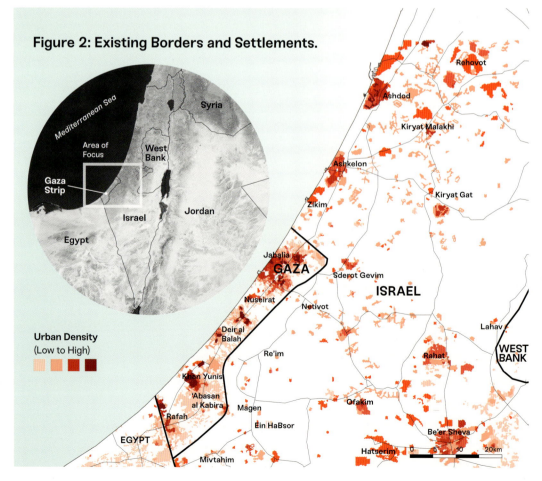

Figure 2: Existing Borders and Settlements.

REFRAMING GAZA

In its erasure of the border, this project distinguishes itself from many plans, including a well-intentioned document produced for UN Habitat by the International Society of City and Regional Planners' (ISOCARP) Urban Planning Advisory Teams in 2015.[1] The ISOCARP document is a compendium of conventional wisdom—including the participation by local actors—and, like the plan we have created, it is less important for the reasonable quality of its well-rehearsed and largely familiar specifics than for its deadpan insistence that planning in such a riven environment is actually possible. We agree that there is an urgency to such normalization, which we see as an ascription of the "right to the city" to Gaza's inhabitants. And we surely believe that the plan is a demand for political rights.

However, the ISOCARP document is also framed by the denial of a broad repertoire of such rights. From an urbanistic point of view, the boundaries imposed on Gaza are both arbitrary and cruel; the result of partition, catastrophe, invasion, occupation, expulsion, bombardment, and endless incarceration. This history of physical, economic, social, and political isolation is radically exacerbated by a dramatically enlarged population resulting from the huge influx of refugees in 1948 and the continuing presence of refugee "camps." The latter insistently retain the idea of impermanence to the huge everyday detriment of their inhabitants, maintaining them in a state of dependency and political limbo that—while rooted in the right to return, a foundational idea of justice and redress—has had misery as its main effect.

If anything has revolutionized the practice of planning in recent years, it is the idea that the city is the embodiment of multiple ecologies, including those subsumed in that tenuous category: the "natural." We now habitually understand cities in terms of their "ecological footprints," an admittedly crude heuristic that nonetheless suggests that no settlement can be thought of as simply lying within its administrative territory. All of us depend on the Amazon basin for our oxygen, the oceans for sinking our carbon, remote aquifers for our water, arable countryside for our food, and our neighbors for our culture and welfare. It is tragic that access to such vital resources—the health of nations—should be contingent on our debased systems of equity and on the stupidity of both global and local governance; a situation perhaps more legible in Gaza than anywhere on earth. In a place in which the porosity of borders is the only guarantor of water, food, building supplies, and virtually every other material component of daily life, its besieged environment can only spiral toward further desperation.

Our practice, Terreform, sees planning and design through a lens of optimism: as the possibility of improving the quality of urban life in many registers, including the formal, legal, and environmental. The failure of the ISOCARP plan is precisely the self-prevented expansiveness arising from the political delimitation of its own optimism. Its Gaza is overwhelmingly the creature of a fantasy of a particular version of Palestinian national independence and of the ongoing (if not entirely

1. ISOCARP (International Society of City and Regional Planners), "Spatial Visioning Reflections: Gaza," *Plan*, Issue 2, December 2015.

irrational) assumption of animus on the part of the powers that surround and choke it. For all its hopeful infrastructure, this Gaza remains a prison. Although the plan embodies aspirational analogies—Singapore! Switzerland! Grand Cayman!—we all know that the current reality will not support this.

Our approach is, perhaps, even more improbable in its optimistic assumptions than ISOCARP's. However, the model that informs our work is not so much a dream of the lion lying down with the lamb but of what, under "normal" circumstances, would be a basic regional approach to a continuous conurbation. It looks to, for example, the logic of Portland, Oregon (could any place be less like Gaza?) and the metropolitan governance that embraces communities in its hinterland, including towns across the border in Washington State. Paradoxically, we also look to the city's self-imposed growth boundary, which seeks not to pen its people in but to protect surrounding agricultural and green space. Such planning foregrounds cooperation, preservation, and coordination in issues of transportation, open and agricultural space, centers, institutional distribution, water conservation and management, density, and other vectors of a rational, sustainable, and shared urban condition.

The plan we propose also embodies a "Ptolemaic" model of the city, laying out a mechanism of cycles and epicycles that form an urban ring embracing the string of Gazan settlements and the Israeli, Palestinian, and Egyptian ones that fall within their gravitational field. It sits in a larger system of cities that lie on an obvious ring, including Gaza City, Beersheba, Hebron, and Jerusalem. Moreover, once the logic of convenient knitting is unleashed, myriad connections are liberated. A line forms from Beersheba to Gaza to Nicosia. Another runs along the coast from Alexandria to Latakia. The plan is about joinery, not division.

CONURBATION

Gaza's density is, for many reasons, concentrated along the Mediterranean coast. While there are persuasive arguments for hugging the water, the city is forced to deny the actuality and necessity of its hinterland and the logic of its relationships to settlements both inland and up and down the coastline, that arose from historic trade routes, access to fishing grounds, and the general hospitality of the shore. This scheme "invents" a city that is already incipient in the region and that takes the form of a polycentric ring. Instead of a linear array of urban enclaves, we propose a circular morphology—a necklace of settlement—with a green, agricultural heart functioning as both a central park and a shared resource for the production of a vital necessity: food. This ring morphology offers opportunities for the redistribution of density and population growth, ease of access to the natural environment, and a greater variety of living circumstances. While we propose to limit development to preserve fragile ecologies and to reinforce existing neighborhood patterns, we anticipate that certain locations will add density—along the seafront, around existing cores and commerce, facing green spaces, and opening onto the majestic desert.

Although we think the future of cities lies in the reduction of conventional use zoning and an increase in the compatibility of activities, we recognize that certain functions must be concentrated to multiply adjacency effects— market and craft districts offer convenience—or must be isolated because of potentially obnoxious

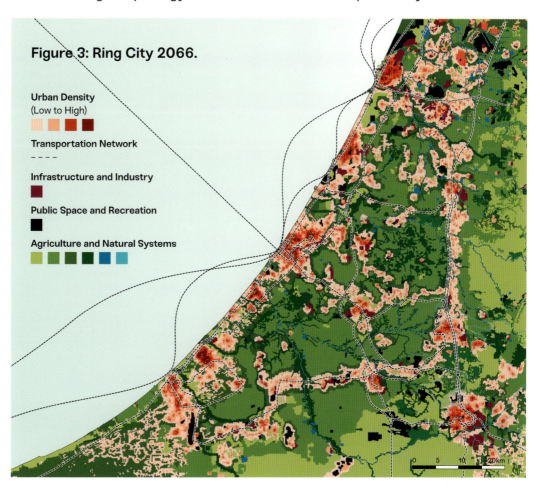

Figure 3: Ring City 2066.

Urban Density
(Low to High)

Transportation Network

Infrastructure and Industry

Public Space and Recreation

Agriculture and Natural Systems

0   5   10   20km

Figure 4: Gaza feeds itself, 2017.

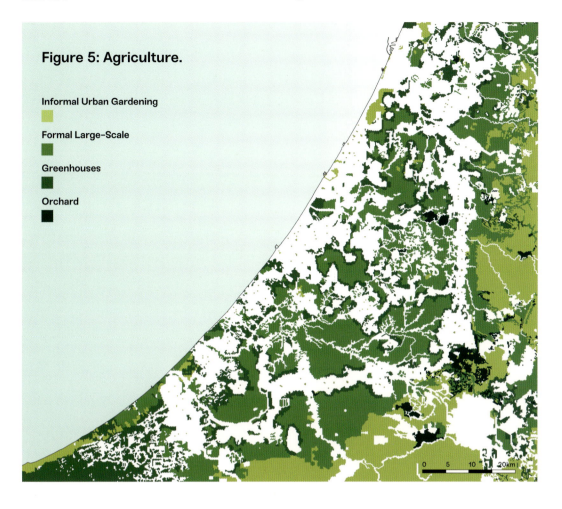

Figure 5: Agriculture.

Informal Urban Gardening

Formal Large-Scale

Greenhouses

Orchard

0   5   10   20km

consequences: an airport does not belong in a quiet residential area. We have identified locations for certain large-scale utilities, including energy production (a huge solar array), factories, an airport, a seaport, and other drivers of a city metabolism striving to provide for itself.

AGRICULTURE

If we were to legislate a zone of special privilege and protection, it would be one for farming. The Ring City celebrates its central agricultural zone and expands and protects agricultural activity in harmony with the nutritional needs of the city and the availability of the most contingent resource in the region: water. We are ambivalent, even hostile, to the large-scale desalination of seawater, knowing its enormous energy requirements and deleterious effects on the aquifer. Desalination becomes a coerced technology in a context in which water resources that should be shared regionally are usurped by the local hegemon. This is an instance in which the project of autonomy in one register forces surrender in others.

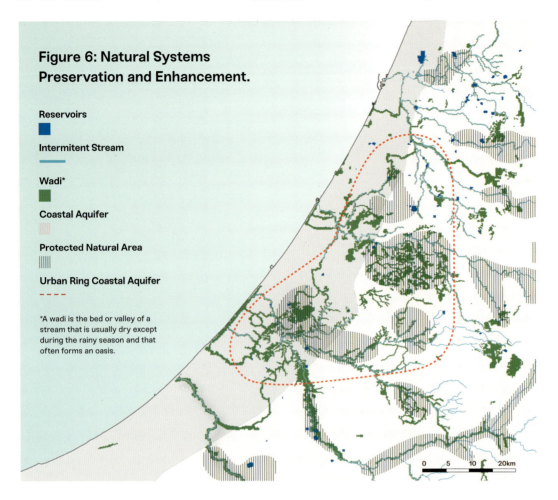

Figure 6: Natural Systems Preservation and Enhancement.

Reservoirs

Intermitent Stream

Wadi*

Coastal Aquifer

Protected Natural Area

Urban Ring Coastal Aquifer

*A wadi is the bed or valley of a stream that is usually dry except during the rainy season and that often forms an oasis.

0   5   10   20km

NATURAL SYSTEMS PRESERVATION AND ENHANCEMENT

Gaza is laced with fragilities—social, metabolic, constructed, and environmental—and is severely under-resourced in both practices and possibilities. Urgent steps to be taken include protection of the seashore, the reversal of the salinization of the aquifer, securing the length and banks of the wadis (seasonal creeks or streams), the stewarding of desert ecologies, and advancing the future of appropriate agricultural activities, from ancient olive groves, modern greenhouses, large-scale and low-water crop fields to grazing land and domestic gardens.

TRANSPORTATION

An efficient transit system is based on universal convenience and equitable access. The linearity of the densest portions of the Gaza Strip enables a double tram line to place all residents within close proximity to public means of mobility. A variety of "last mile" possibilities—including bicycles, shared cars, taxis, and enhanced pedestrian ways, would be provided at each tram stop. The system also encompasses the larger loop that forms the ring city, and this light rail would be augmented by a regional heavy-rail network extending to towns and cities in Egypt, Israel, Palestine, Jordan, Lebanon, Syria, and beyond.

Taking advantage of Gaza's proximity to the sea, we have also suggested a coastal ferry system for both local and regional transit, as well as enhancements to the port.

This would allow for travel around the Mediterranean to the innumerable cities on its shores—Haifa, Izmir, Brindisi, Marseille, Tangier—that are not under siege. The waterborne system would join the heavy rail and enhanced roadways to enable site saturation by a multi-modal logistics system.

Finally, we have suggested the conversion of the Hatzerim Military Airbase, west of Beersheba, into an international civilian airport. This more capacious site would be served by both the light- and heavy-rail systems and would be located in a more favorable acoustic environment than the now destroyed Gaza airport. Additionally, it can offer greater flexibility for expansion, cargo handling, and other ancillary facilities, including storage, manufacture, and aerospace.

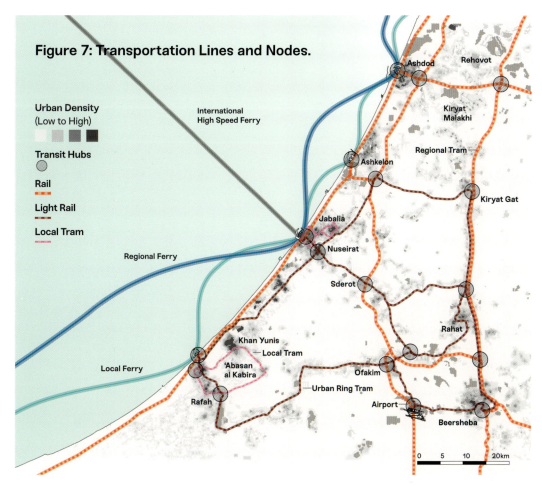

Figure 7: Transportation Lines and Nodes.

Urban Density (Low to High)

Transit Hubs

Rail

Light Rail

Local Tram

International High Speed Ferry

Regional Ferry

Local Ferry

Ashdod

Rehovot

Kiryat Malakhi

Regional Tram

Ashkelon

Kiryat Gat

Jabalia

Nuseirat

Sderot

Rahat

Khan Yunis

Local Tram

'Abasan al Kabira

Ofakim

Urban Ring Tram

Rafah

Airport

Beersheba

0 5 10 20km

Figure 8: Transportation, 2017.

CULTURAL, EDUCATIONAL, AND RECREATIONAL FACILITIES

Mapping the density of existing facilities reveals patterns of concentration and sparseness that can be read for both access and deprivation. Our solution is gestural: to harmonize the numbers of facilities with the density of populations. The placement of shared facilities is rooted in the idea of local access. We do not seek the even densities of sprawl: on the contrary, the morphology we propose is one in which the thickness of urbanity is the material condition of both sociability and sustainability. We are working at a grain where a mosque is indistinguishable from a football field but we are certain that all such facilities should be fully accessible to all who would use them. By zooming out from the familiar scale of the Strip,

we seek to use the representational valence of the map to foreground forms of subjectivity and urban desire that are shared.

We identify this most important subdivision of the city in a notional rather than specific way. Were we to actually design the future of a Ring City neighborhood, we would think about providing all needed facilities for happily living everyday life, about open space, about styles of gathering, about decent housing for all inhabitants, about services and infrastructure, about transportation and walkability. Categories that are inevitably mapped under a political frame—refugee camps, military bases, settlements—would surrender these descriptors to become mere places in the city. The striking material similarity between prosperous and tractable

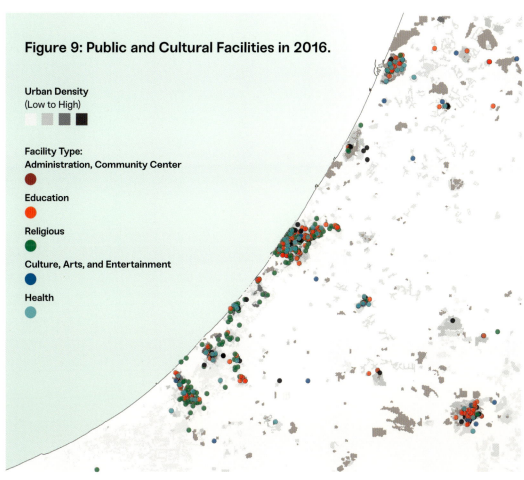

Figure 9: Public and Cultural Facilities in 2016.

Urban Density
(Low to High)

Facility Type:
Administration, Community Center

Education

Religious

Culture, Arts, and Entertainment

Health

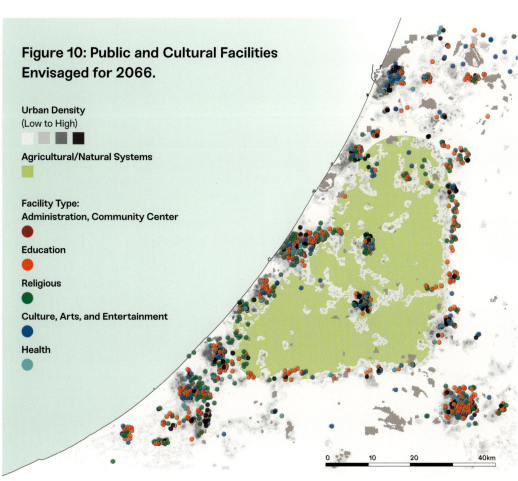

Figure 10: Public and Cultural Facilities Envisaged for 2066.

Urban Density
(Low to High)

Agricultural/Natural Systems

Facility Type:
Administration, Community Center

Education

Religious

Culture, Arts, and Entertainment

Health

0   10   20   40km

Figure 11a and 11b: Gaza
before and after the creation
of the Ring City, 2017.

Before

After

Figure 12a and 12b: Gaza before and after the creation of the Ring City, 2017.

Before

After

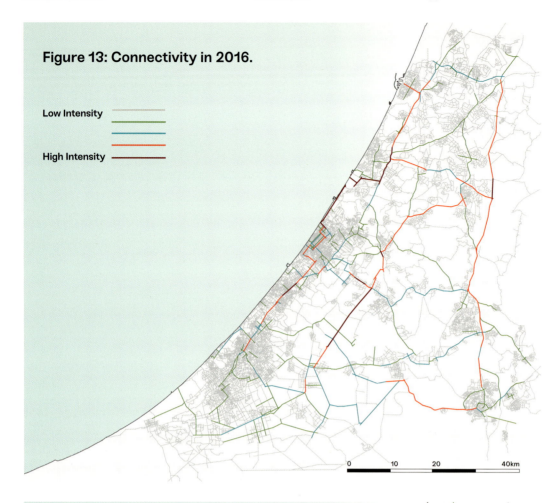

Figure 13: Connectivity in 2016.

Low Intensity

High Intensity

0   10   20   40km

A spatial syntax interaccessibility model reveals Gaza's limited interconnection. The low intensity signifies greater difficulty to reach that segment from all other segments and lesser likelihood that movement between different parts of the network will pass along that segment.

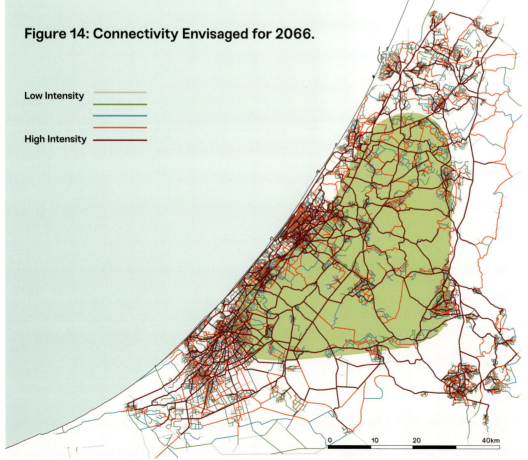

Figure 14: Connectivity Envisaged for 2066.

Low Intensity

High Intensity

0   10   20   40km

An improved street hierarchy and a plethora of public transportation options, including last mile bike and pedestrian paths, augment and distribute accessibility and connection throughout the region.

environments throughout the region suggests grounds for convergence, based on both shared and elected affinities and a common bioclimate, and a continuous topography and geology. We thus identify occurring and prospective urban structures that can be traversed in twenty minutes and house populations invested in their own neighborliness. Of course, there must be that imperative universal right to the city, and this will surely bring about changes, including dramatic ones. This right—in its classic articulation by Henri Lefebvre, David Harvey, and others—is fundamental and to be understood not simply in terms of freedom of movement, safety from surveillance, or access to services but, crucially, in the right to imagine and demand a city that is most deeply rooted in individual dreams and desires.

CONNECTIVITY

A spatial syntax model—used to analyze street and path segments and their inter-accessibility within the network—reveals Gaza's limited interconnections. The low intensity of connectivity shown in figure 13 signifies greater difficulty reaching that segment from all other segments and less likelihood that movement between different parts of the network will pass along that segment.

We have enhanced and extended the pattern of roadways to increase ease of movement and mobility choices in the city, and strategically located uses that are contingent on high levels of traffic and access. An improved street and pathway hierarchy and an abundance of public transportation options augment and distribute accessibility and connection throughout the region.

ECOLOGICAL FOOTPRINT

A simple Ecological Footprint (EF) calculation is imprecise until fleshed out with local particulars, but it can be a very useful medium of articulation and situation. Using Israel's current EF—6.2 global hectares (gha) per capita (i.e., the average Israeli uses 6.2 hectares to produce their resources, the largest number among nations in the OECD; Gaza's footprint is around one-tenth of this number!)—the 2016 image (see figure 15) reveals the actual "size" of Gaza when the calculus includes the full, if abstracted, extent of the territory required to provision the entire population of this newly, and otherly, understood city at the same rates of consumption currently enjoyed by Israelis.

Despite a widening gap between the EF and regional biocapacity, we believe that the use of rational appropriate technologies can shrink environmental demand even as expectations for the quality of life are raised. If resource demands were reduced to meet the biologically productive area available in the region, the EF would shrink to twenty-seven times the area of its current political boundary, shown as the smallest footprint on our 2066 plan (when Israel/Palestine is projected to be one of the densest places on the planet). This would—again at current Israeli rates of consumption—only support 161,000 people, well under one-tenth the current population of Gaza.

It is unrealistic, however, that Palestine or Israel could ever operate in an ecological reserve, given their high population densities and harsh climate, marked by water scarcity and limited fertile land. We have therefore

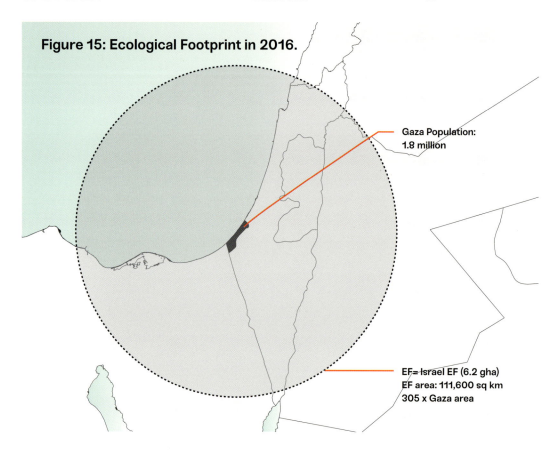

Figure 15: Ecological Footprint in 2016.

Gaza Population:
1.8 million

EF= Israel EF (6.2 gha)
EF area: 111,600 sq km
305 x Gaza area

Ecological Footprint (EF) measures the land and water area a population requires to produce the resources it consumes and absorb the carbon dioxide emissions it generates. A population whose EF is higher than its biocapacity, defined as the biologically productive area required to generate an ongoing supply of renewable resources, must import biocapacity through trade. Israel has an ecological deficit of –5.9 global hectares per capita (gha) and a low biocapacity at .4 gha (compared to the world average of 1.7, the US' 3.8, and Brazil's 9.1), due to water scarcity and limited fertile land. As consumption increases and land availability shrinks, the gap between supply and demand, or biocapacity and EF, widens.

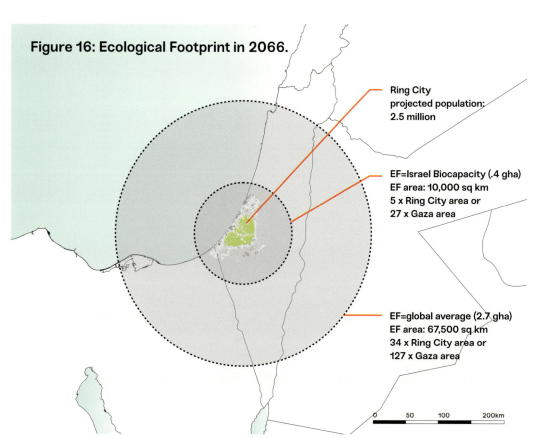

Figure 16: Ecological Footprint in 2066.

Ring City
projected population:
2.5 million

EF=Israel Biocapacity (.4 gha)
EF area: 10,000 sq km
5 x Ring City area or
27 x Gaza area

EF=global average (2.7 gha)
EF area: 67,500 sq km
34 x Ring City area or
127 x Gaza area

0   50   100   200km

To visualize Gaza's EF if every resident consumed at the Israeli level of 6.2 gha (i.e., the average person requires 6.2 hectares to produce their resources), Gaza's EF would encompass an area 305 times its actual size.

This proposal suggests that through renewable energy production, an efficient transport system, desalination of the aquifer, reduction of waste, local processing, and protection of natural resources and agriculture land it is possible to significantly reduce the EF while increasing biocapacity.

An extreme scenario, utilizing an EF equivalent to Israel's biocapacity of .4 gha, would drastically shrink the Ring City's footprint to five times its actual size. Accepting, however, the region's unlikelihood of ever operating in ecological reserve due to its high population density and harsh climate, we consider a more realistic EF equivalent to the world average of 2.7 gha. This scenario almost cuts in half the current footprint and would allow for a comfortable standard of living, but would drastically reduce the cumulative impacts of human activities on natural systems and permit greater degree of self-sufficiency in the region.

also shown the dimensions of a footprint for the proposed Ring City at a population of 2.5 million, based on a somewhat different perspective. This has been calculated not at Israeli rates but at the current world average of 2.7 gha, which would cut the current footprint almost in half, even accounting for population increases. This scenario would provide a comfortable standard of living, but drastically reduce the cumulative impacts of human activities on natural systems and allow for a greater degree of regional autonomy and equity.

While recognizing that EF calculations are fuzzy, fraught, and reductive, they can, nevertheless, be revelatory. To begin, they measure inequality with great precision and map embedded global injustice at every scale. Gaza, walled from its sustaining hinterland and obliged to beg, fight, or smuggle to maintain its cruel subsistence, is fundamentally unsustainable within its cruel and murderous walls. To a planner operating with justice—both local and planetary—as a basis for design, this

calculus obliges the infusion of the procedures of physical distribution with an ethical standard. While mathematical formulas for human equality are perilous things, especially when it comes to the recognition and defense of meaningful difference, the idea of equalizing access to both sustenance and opportunity is at the vital center of what it means to plan.

This proposal stages a confrontation between representation and justice. In an environment that lives in a permanent state of exception, the tools of "normal" planning suggest not only the degree to which human rights—including the right to the city—are impossible under the carceral regime that governs Gaza, but also that a literal reframing of the situation points to an imperative political logic towards which urban and environmental design arc. Strategies and styles of redress directed to the situation on the ground in Gaza—however urgent in the immediate term—also have the effect of reifying a nightmare. A few calories added to the prison meal will not hasten the breakout.

FOUR TUNNELS

Bint al-Sirhid*

*Pseudonym

Egyptian officials at the Rafah border crossing turned me away twice—first in 2013 and then in 2014—leaving me with no option but to go underground. Visiting relatives in Gaza is no easy task, and it gets more and more difficult with each passing year. It is nearly impossible if you do not have a *hawiyya*, the Israeli-issued ID card that contains your bio-data and designates where you are and are not allowed to go. Since I do not possess this document, there was essentially no way that Israel would approve a visit through the Erez crossing. After having made the onerous journey from Cairo across the Suez Canal and through northern Sinai, and after coming close to Gaza, turning back was inconceivable. Hence, I took the alternative route to enter and exit Gaza during my two visits. By now, I have been through a total of four tunnels, each one more precarious than the previous. This account describes what it was like.

TUNNEL 1:
A VERY IMPORTANT TUNNEL (VIT)
It was August 2013, and a military coup had just overthrown Egyptian President Mohammed Morsi of the Muslim Brotherhood.[1] Because of the chaos, my travel companion and I did not linger in Cairo and headed straight for the border. The Suez Canal Bridge had been closed to contain the fighting between the Egyptian military and local rebel groups in North Sinai, thus adding several hot, dusty hours to our journey as we were forced to cross by a crowded ferry instead. When we finally reached the Rafah border crossing, we were denied entry for not having a *hawiyya* for Gaza, despite the fact we both have many relatives there. Our pleading

and arguing with the Egyptian military fell on deaf ears, so we headed back to al-Arish, a North Sinai city on the Mediterranean coast located an hour from the border.

I had heard so much about al-Arish being a vibrant city, and while it was indeed a beautiful seaside town, it seemed more like a ghost town during our visit. The battles between local rebel groups and the Egyptian military had clearly taken a toll on the locals, who were mostly staying indoors. The atmosphere was eerie and discomfiting, so we did not want to stay long. We called an uncle in Gaza and explained the situation; he took down our personal details and told us to have our things ready within an hour. We were skeptical, but sure enough a car had been arranged to pick us up and take us back to the border. This time, however, we were taken to a residential area.

We arrived at a patch of land surrounded by blocks of apartment buildings. Next to a concrete wall was a large opening in the sand, with people standing around helping others enter and exit the hole with their luggage. There was no time to hesitate; we were ushered along as someone took our bags and guided us underground. We walked into the hole—upright most of the way—and despite our nervousness, we sauntered along, admiring the handiwork of the tunnel construction. Maybe this was one of the "VIP" tunnels I had heard so much about. We walked comfortably most of the way down a long, slow descent. The sides and top of the tunnel were covered with wooden framing, probably to reinforce the integrity of the walls, which consisted mostly of dense, dark clay — quite different

1. Mohammad Morsi of the Muslim Brotherhood won Egypt's elections in 2012, following the revolution and overthrow of former president Hosni Mubarak. In 2013, Morsi was ousted by a military coup, and General Abdel Fattah el-Sisi has been president ever since.

from the sand at the surface. Plenty of lighting was strung throughout, the air was cool and fresher than I would have expected, and had an earthy smell.

After about five minutes of walking, the tunnel opened up into a cavernous room that seemed like a small underground warehouse; there were several other people and quite a bit of commotion. A motorcycle-drawn "tuk-tuk" pulled up to us, and two young men, who turned out to be cousins, took our bags and helped us aboard. They drove us up and out of the tunnel, and once above ground, it was as if we had arrived in a different world. This side was an industrial zone buzzing with activity, quite unlike the more secretive Egyptian side. Several other tunnels were operating around us with semitrucks driving to and fro to pick up the delivered supplies—gas canisters, construction materials, merchandise, and other goods—all within view of the Egyptian border watchtower. We were picked up by our relatives and taken out of the industrial zone, heading toward town. On the way out of the tunnel complex, we stopped at the exit to submit some paperwork to the guards. Use of the tunnels required official government-issued permits.

TUNNEL 2:
THE MERCHANDISE TUNNEL
The departure date for our return home from Gaza happened to fall on Eid, the post–Ramadan holiday. This meant that all of the tunnels were also on holiday, posing a problem for our timely arrival in Cairo to catch our flight. The tunnels are privately owned but they are managed, secured, and taxed by the local (Hamas) government; our uncles called several tunnel owners to find

someone available to let us through. Eventually, one owner agreed to operate the tunnel for us, but at a slightly higher price. On the way in we had paid fifty dollars, and on the way out it would be one hundred dollars. Missing our flight in Cairo would have been much more costly, so we went ahead with it. The local officials also made a special arrangement, at our uncle's insistence, to have someone meet us at the offices of the tunnel authorities in order to issue us the permit. Even here, bureaucracy could not be circumvented, and as we waited in the office for the paperwork, I perused the files that had accumulated on its shelves. Each tunnel was represented by a labeled folder, named after its owner: tunnel Abu so-and-so and tunnel Abu so-and-so.[2] While we waited, the officials explained that some tunnels have one owner, some have a group of investors, and many have made fortunes.

Once the permits were ready, we drove to the deserted industrial tunnel zone. I noticed an Egyptian military watchtower on the other side of the border fence, with a plain view of all things happening on our side. Our tunnel this time was not a "VIP" tunnel like the last one, but one used for merchandise. We had to stand on a circular platform that lowered us down, down, down, more than a hundred feet, until we reached a larger cavity in the ground. The tunnel was traversed by a sled-like contraption that they call a *shayyatah*, a large bright-blue plastic barrel cut in half. The barrel is laid on its side to slide across the smooth ground surface as it transports materials through the tunnel more efficiently via a trolley or pulley

2. *Abu* means "father of" in Arabic; a common way to refer to men in the area is by the name of their eldest child, e.g., "Abu Ali," "Abu Rami."

Figure 1: A Very Important Tunnel, Illustration by Anas Awad, 2018.

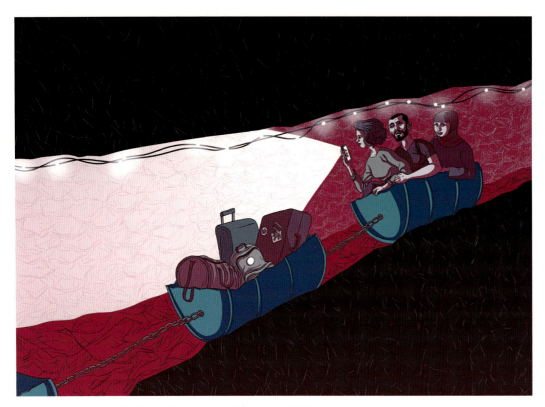

Figure 2: The Merchandise Tunnel, Illustration by Anas Awad, 2018.

system. We got into the *shayyatah* and sat down behind our luggage.

The men operating the tunnel insisted that I film since we were in an in-between area, out of both border authorities' sights. So I took my camera out and we were off, being pulled through the tunnel by a chain connected to the front of the *shayyatah*. The sides of the tunnel walls were smooth in some sections and rocky in others, not quite as refined as the VIP tunnel, and again the earth resembled densely packed clay with some sandy sections fortified with wood. As in the other tunnel, there was lighting strung throughout, and the air was much cooler and earthier than above ground. We were whizzing along for several minutes, as if on a roller coaster, when suddenly the *shayyatah* stopped. It jerked forward a few times then stopped again. My nerves began to get the best of me as we sat looking toward the end

of the tunnel for any movement. I wondered if the Egyptian authorities on the other side had discovered us. The tunnel operator tried to yell to someone at the other end but to no avail, and then he left us and walked hunched over to the end of the tunnel. About ten minutes later, he returned and told us the motor had gone out and that it was just a short walk to the other end. The guys took our bags, and we clumsily made our way through. Once we reached the opening, there was a makeshift ladder for climbing out, which was short but challenging. As we gracelessly ascended, the sides became sandier and sandier. Once outside, we found ourselves in the open, sandy courtyard of a home. The mouth of the tunnel was hidden under the shade of a tree and equipped with a rubber flap, which was used to close the opening. This flap was covered with sand, sprinkled with water from a hose, and like magic, it disappeared as if it had never been there. We were told to go to the wash basin in the corner of the courtyard and to rinse the dirt from our clothes. We were then loaded into a car in the alleyway, which took us through the winding streets of the unknown Rafah neighborhood we were in, and soon after, we were on the main road to Cairo.

TUNNEL 3:
THE DEMOLISHED TUNNEL

The next year I traveled to Gaza on my own after the bombs stopped: Israel's Operation Protective Edge had killed over 2,100 Palestinians and wounded thousands more. Thankfully, none of my relatives were hurt, but some had their homes destroyed. I wanted to go check on them after what they had just endured, especially since they were feeling so isolated. The road from Cairo to Rafah was much more difficult than before, particularly after crossing the Suez Canal by ferry. Military convoys were everywhere, stopping everyone at checkpoints for hours at a time, and randomly shooting their guns into the air. The battles between the Egyptian military and local rebel groups had become much more deadly, and when I finally reached the Egyptian side of Rafah, it became clear that it was a city under siege.

I was turned away at the border once again, despite my relatives' attempts to bribe the right Egyptian officials in order to let me through. No *hawiyya*, no way—and my American passport was of no help. After several attempts at crossing the border, the taxi driver took me to his family home, and his mother and sisters took me in as if I were one of their own. Their

flat was on the ground floor, and the top floor of the eight-story building had been turned into a military base. Rows of tanks were parked outside. Everyone moved about the neighborhood carefully, afraid to alarm any of the trigger-happy soldiers. The entire town was under curfew in the evenings; no one was allowed to leave their neighborhoods or drive their cars around after sundown.

"We watched the war on Gaza, and now Gaza is watching the war on us," one of the sisters told me as they showed me all the homes that were destroyed over the past few weeks. Even the beach was declared a military zone, and residents could no longer reach it, but the sisters pointed to it from afar. After each outing, we had to wait for clearance from the Egyptian soldiers before we could return to their apartment building. The atmosphere was tense, and everyone was trying to keep a low profile.

The family insisted on feeding me several meals: fried chicken, *daggah* (a spicy salad, well known in Gaza), *malfouf* (stuffed cabbage). They even took me out for ice cream and *barrad*, a yellow, slushy drink. I was intrigued by how the similarities with the other side had persisted, despite decades of being split by the border. I tried to eat enough to be polite, but was too nervous to have an appetite, knowing that my relatives on the other side were working full-time to find a tunnel to bring me through. I did not have the heart to admit to them that I was too afraid. The host family begged me not to put myself at risk, offering to let me stay as long as I wished. But when it became clear that I had made up my mind to cross, they arranged for me to arrive safely to find the smuggler, whom I was instructed to meet on the outskirts of town in the evening. This posed a problem: how was I going to get past the checkpoints, especially since it was now after dark?

Two of the sisters had it figured out. All three of us were dressed in black *abayahs* and hijabs; we were indistinguishable from each other. I had already been dressing this way the entire time in North Sinai so as not to draw attention to myself, and it was especially important while in Rafah—there is no other way in which I would have been able to do what happened next. We went out for an evening stroll to check the scene, and once everything seemed fine, we decided to go for it. "Let me speak to the soldiers," the older sister said to me, "they will recognize your accent is not from here." We walked down the main road that leaves the town, and as we approached the checkpoint, which was elevated and covered in camouflage colors, she told me: "They are afraid of us women wearing the *niqab*, they have no way of knowing who we are." She was the only one of the three of us with her face covered, and when she told the soldiers that they were just going out for a few minutes to walk me to my home, they waved us through. Once we passed the checkpoint, there was no turning back for me. Sensing my extreme nervousness, she said to me, "Now you have to be like the men."

I tried to calm my breathing and my racing heart, and eventually we were met by the smuggler. The sisters hugged me and made me promise I would call as soon as I made it, and I left to follow the man. We walked for what seemed forever, through sandy orchards of olive and fruit trees, under a full moon that illuminated the way. I asked him, "Aren't you nervous?" He curtly answered that yes, of course he was. Every so often we were met by other men standing on corners who indicated to the smuggler that the path was clear; eventually we arrived at a motorbike. I did not have time to think, and hopped on behind him as he drove us to the next meeting point. There, I was handed off to a family out for a walk—a father, mother, and four kids—and I slipped in among them as if I were part of the clan. We made small talk and walked to the back of a home, where I was told to wait until they called me.

I meditated on the full moon and tried to calm my breathing. A few minutes later, they called me to cross the yard to a demolished home— demolished by the Egyptian military, allegedly to stop tunnel activity. I crawled through an opening in the rubble behind one of the men, and we stood up inside a void surrounded by the wreckage. He lifted several stones from the ground, revealing an opening and my sweaty cousin below, who scolded me, "I've been waiting an hour for you!" I tried to explain that it was not exactly in my hands as they lowered me down, and once in the tunnel, we turned into excited children, each sharing what happened on each of our sides and taking several selfies. We hopped into a *shayyatah* and took off along a motorized track. He explained that they had repaired this tunnel just for me, as we whisked by the smooth, dark clay walls. The tunnel had less lighting than the ones before, so my cousin handed me a flashlight to hold while we zipped along.

Figure 3: The Demolished Tunnel, Illustration by Anas Awad, 2018.

This tunnel had several motorized *shayyatah* tracks, one for each segment. Every time we changed to the next one, another young man would hop in with us. One of them banged on the wooden framing as we passed it and reported that he had just repaired it today, clearly proud of his work. As the last *shayyatah* started to make an ascent up the tunnel with, by now, the four of us, a man in a white cap with a flashlight shone a light on us from the opening. "Go back, go back!" my cousin shouted. I was confused, and more importantly, I was not interested in going back anywhere. In any case, it was already too late. We were caught, and as we emerged from the tunnel, several men stood around listening to a skinny man with light-colored, shaggy hair, who was yelling and gesturing wildly with his arms.

One of the men told me that they needed to search my bag, which was fine with me; I was just glad to have arrived in one piece. I voluntarily handed it over, but they were too shy to conduct a search. Instead, they led me to a seating area with cushions on the ground and told me to relax while they sorted things out. Whatever the problem was did not phase me; I was relieved to be out of the danger zone of the other side of the border. It turned out that they were Hamas officials, and it seemed my cousin and the owner had not acquired the proper permits. My cousin claimed the tunnel office's printer was broken (which turned out to be true) and that they could not issue a paper permit. Anyway, my cousin and the owner ended up spending the night detained, and in the morning, my uncle and I returned to the tunnel administration officers for my "interrogation." As I sat at the officer's desk, he seemed too shy to ask me too many questions, and the other officer filling out some paperwork about me hardly wrote anything down. They seemed more curious and intrigued; I guess they did not get visitors very often anymore. The first officer explained that they worry about people smuggling large amounts of money and weapons for illegal purposes, and that they just wanted to verify my identity. My uncle vouched for my cousin and me, and we all left, trying to cheer my cousin up on the way home.

TUNNEL 4: THE SPINNING TUNNEL

The last time I left Gaza proved to be the most traumatic. When I arrived in Gaza, I had not given much thought to getting back out. But the situation deteriorated in a short time span—less than ten days—and I found myself back with my cousin in Rafah, waiting for news of a possible tunnel to get me back across. From my cousin's flat I could see the Egyptian side, which looked like a vast wasteland. "There were homes there," he told me, explaining that the ongoing house demolitions, air strikes, and explosions on that side were more intensive than the recent Israeli bombardment of Gaza. My cousin's windows had been shattered several times. I thought of the family on the other side who had helped me, and wondered how long before they, too, would be displaced. Finding a tunnel for my exit was difficult, and we had a few disappointing false starts. "Why don't you stay awhile? Maybe in a few weeks things will settle down," my cousin suggested. Was he giving up? I began to get a taste for what it means to be trapped in Gaza, and it must have shown on my face as the anxiety mounted. My cousin took one long, hard look at me and changed his mind, "I swear we will drill a way out if we have to."

He left to make more inquiries, and I was relieved, but felt a little guilty for pressuring him. His wife did not seem concerned, and tried to distract me by doing my hair and makeup. I tried to play along, despite my nervousness. After several hours, my cousin came home, and suddenly there was no time to spare. I was rushed out of the flat, loaded into his friend's car, and brought to the seemingly deserted industrial area as the sun was setting. Apparently, a tunnel owner from the other side had come over to have dinner with relatives on this side, and was on his way back. He had agreed to take me for a hefty fee of $500.

Before we entered the tunnel area, we spoke to the guards at the gate, who were already expecting us and apologized for the inconvenience of the broken printer, as they called their boss to confirm our arrival. We were led to an abandoned, half-built concrete structure and waited as if we were hiding—from whom, I did not quite understand. A man came to meet my cousin, and after they conversed around the corner, my cousin called me to walk with them. We were led to a sandy patch of ground, sat at the base of several palm trees, and waited. "I swear, smuggling just brings trouble," my cousin said. He used to be very active in the tunnel business and claims to have been the first to bring in whole cars, unlike before, when they were disassembled and reassembled on arrival. Once he built the first tunnel big enough for cars to drive through, the demand skyrocketed. "But I decided to quit once the cars began

to arrive with bloodstains inside," he said, explaining that the high prices resulted in deadly carjackings on the other side. "I'm telling you, smuggling brings trouble. After that, I said no more. Except for you."

I decided then and there that if I got out of this situation in one piece, it would be the last time. A man walked over to us, and my cousin explained that the tunnel location was so secretive that even he could not come with me. He reassured me as we said our goodbyes, and I followed the guy over to a large, tent-like canopy over the tunnel construction site. They invited me to sit down, and gave me cookies and a soft drink while I waited. The tunnel opening was very wide, surrounded by several beams that ran up from the ground and met over it in the middle, like an apex. At the top was a pulley system with a chain that lifted large, blue buckets filled with dirt from below, and as the buckets came up, a worker rolled a wooden platform over the opening. The buckets were dropped onto it, the platform was rolled back, the buckets emptied outside of the tent, and then thrown back down into the tunnel after the worker yelled down to make sure it was clear. This continued for a while before I asked someone I assumed was the boss— maybe because he was heavyset and not working—"Don't the Egyptians see you?" I pointed to the border watchtower that was in plain view. "Yes," he said, "but they have no idea which way we are going."

My phone was constantly ringing. It seemed as if every single one of my relatives in Gaza—and there are *many*—was checking on my whereabouts, and I repeatedly explained that the owner had not

Figure 4: The Spinning Tunnel, Illustration by Anas Awad, 2018.

yet arrived. Finally, during one of my explanations over the phone, the boss man walked over to me and said, "I'm the owner." I quickly hung up and apologized. He pulled up a chair and began apologizing *to me* for the situation and explained the occupation and the siege, and that they had no choice, that they needed to do this to survive. I told him that he did not need to explain and he certainly did not need to apologize.

Eventually a well-dressed young man, perhaps in his twenties, showed up. He turned out to be the co-owner from the other side who had come over for dinner. The worker and the boss man rigged a swing-like seat to the pulley. The co-owner sat in the seat and they lowered him down. Then they called me over. "I'm going down like that?" I asked. They laughed and said, "Do not be afraid." They yelled down to someone in the tunnel who they called "El Seeny," which means the Chinese man, to catch me as I came down. They helped me into the seat, put my bag in my lap, and told me that if the seat started spinning, to stop the spin by sticking my feet out and onto the walls. I was lowered down, down, and down, and someone from below yelled to the guys above ground to slow down.

"El Seeny" was a tiny guy with distinctive features; he caught me and prevented me from hitting the ground, and then we were off. The boss was coming down the opening after me; the co-owner was already heading down the tunnel. I was determined to stay close behind "El Seeny." We had to walk with our feet wedged toward the sides of the tunnel to avoid the depression in the middle that was meant for a *shayyatah* track, but it was a small stream of water at

that time. The tunnel was still under construction, but we managed to walk upright for the first section. Most of the tunnel walls were clay, like the other tunnels, but there were no wooden reinforcements on the sandy parts yet. I tried not to think too much about that, and to just keep moving. A few minutes later, the opening became smaller and we had to walk hunched over. The boss man was huffing and puffing behind me and insisting we take a break, but "El Seeny" was restless and did not stop for long. I continued behind him when suddenly the lights went out.

I gasped, and they all reassured me that everything was fine. We all took our cell phones out to light our way. After a few minutes, my light shone on what looked like a wormhole to nowhere. I felt a wave of claustrophobia and a hint of panic, but then "El Seeny" got on his hands and knees and crawled into it. I did not give myself a chance to think, got on my hands and knees, and just kept moving as close behind him as possible. We were all getting covered in dirt, but this section only lasted for a few minutes before it became wide enough to walk again. We had reached the opening on the other side, which was a steep incline with a thick plastic sheet on the bottom and a rope for pulling ourselves up. The co-owner had just finished pulling himself up and "El Seeny" was going up behind him. He looked at me skeptically and asked if I needed help. I told him not to worry and grabbed onto the rope, with the boss man giving me instructions from behind to prop myself up with my feet on the sides. Thanks to my combat boots and my half-decent fitness, I made my way up.

Halfway through, I stopped to take a rest, but the boss was still moving up behind me, unaware that I had stopped, when his head ran straight into my ass. "That's it, we are all going to hell," he said. We had a quick laugh and continued up until the incline became level. We had reached the opening, but the boss asked me to wait a few minutes. He went up to talk to the co-owner, who was asking questions about what he was supposed to do with me. I could not hear the entire conversation, but heard the boss man say, "She comes from a good family, make sure she is safe." He came back to wish me well, assured me everything was fine, and again apologized for putting me through such conditions.

I started to climb out of the opening, which was surrounded by young guys trying to help me, but I managed to pull myself up. We were in a small, dark alleyway surrounded by homes, and I followed the co-owner to a garage. We hid inside and waited for a car, and I called the family that had taken care of me. The brother answered and I put him on the phone with the co-owner. I could hear the brother's sweet voice turn coarse through the speaker as he said, "I don't know you and I don't want to know you. We just want her back with us safely." Due to the curfew, however, there was no way to reach their neighborhood. They agreed that I would stay with the co-owner's family and that he would drop me off first thing in the morning. We were loaded into a car, and I was told to lie down on the back seat—perhaps so I would not see where we were going. We arrived at a large, fancy villa, and the co-owner told me his mother and sister would take care of me. Despite the large, modern home, it was evident that they were still traditional in their ways: all the furnishings were floor cushions and low tables for eating. The mother kindly insisted that I take a shower, and she took my clothes and hand-washed them. I emerged from the bathroom to find a spread of food waiting for me. Humbled by their generosity, I ate enough to be polite, had a pleasant conversation with them, and then excused myself for bed, as I was overtaken by exhaustion. Early the next morning, the mother and the co-owner woke me to leave, and the mother told me to cover my face so that no one would see me. We arrived behind a building, and a few minutes later, the family came to get me. I was taken to their home and reunited with the sisters. They all expressed relief at my safe arrival and celebrated it with a huge breakfast they had prepared.

THE TUNNELS IN CONTEXT

After the 1967 war, during which the Israeli army decimated the grounded Egyptian air force in a "preemptive strike," Israel occupied the Sinai Peninsula, the Gaza Strip, and the West Bank. This act, and the subsequent 1978 Camp David Accords, which dictated the limits of the Egyptian military presence in the Sinai and installed an international force on the Egyptian side,[3] showed that the Egyptian state had (and continues to have) a precarious hold on the Sinai Peninsula. Israel did not complete its military pullout until 1982, after which it maintained control of the Gaza Strip and split the town of Rafah in two with the new, militarized border. Residents of Rafah found themselves separated from their relatives. According to most

3. The Multinational Force & Observers were set up as an armed peacekeeping group by the Camp David Accords of 1979. For more information, see their website at www. mfo.org.

accounts the tunneling began in this period. Israel had a near-complete hold of the Gaza Strip, as it still maintained its military occupation and the presence of several Jewish settlements. However, local kinship ties proved strong, and the tunneling and the resistance to the occupation continued. Israeli reprisals were severe and included the razing of thousands of homes, predominantly in the Rafah area.[4]

In 2005, Israeli rule over Gaza transformed from direct to indirect military occupation: the Jewish settlements were removed and the enclosure of Gaza was ensured through an external siege, instead. Israel restricted all sea access and land crossings, with the exception of the crossing on the Egyptian side. This was what Israel called "disengagement." A few years later, when Hamas came to power, the screws were tightened even more. This suffocating regime led to the proliferation of the tunnels, which became what many described as the lungs through which Gaza breathed.

The tunnel world changed dramatically from a localized, underground realm of petty border smuggling activities among large family clans to a large-scale industry, importing everything imaginable for daily consumption. Hamas even created a government ministry to manage and regulate the tunnels. They became more and more lucrative, benefiting those involved and creating many millionaires in the process. The Egyptian government turned a blind eye to all this, and several residents on the Sinai side managed to reap the financial rewards of working in the tunnel trade industry and supplying Gaza's

population with goods. Contrary to popular imagination, Gaza has its wealthy classes like any other society, and like any other society, the mainstream—and especially the younger generation—likes to consume the latest technologies and other goods. According to some reports, suppliers on the Sinai side of the tunnels turned enormous profits.[5] This was not without consequences; local scholars were alarmed about the social effects of these quick riches in highly abnormal conditions and the potential for corruption.[6]

The events in Egypt—the 2011 revolution and overthrow of Hosni Mubarak, and the 2012 election of Mohammad Morsi of the Muslim Brotherhood and his subsequent military overthrow in 2013—once again confirmed Gaza's dependency on Egypt. Morsi had opened the Rafah border, but after Abdel Fattah el-Sisi came to power, it was closed completely, and the tunnels were no longer tolerated. It was a few months after this happened that my first trip to Gaza occurred. We had been hearing that the border was open a few months prior, while Morsi was still in power, and even though things were unclear after his overthrow, we decided to give it a try. It did not become evident until much later that a rebellion against the heavy-handed Egyptian military was brewing in the northern Sinai.

The government-controlled mainstream media of Egypt blamed Hamas and the tunnels for local rebels' attacks on the military in North Sinai. Anti-Palestinian sentiment began to rise among the Egyptian population, along with the anti-Muslim Brotherhood campaign of el-Sisi, conflating the

4. Human Rights Watch, *Razing Rafah: Mass Home Demolitions in the Gaza Strip.* (Human Rights Watch, 2004).

5. Mohannad Sabry, *Sinai: Egypt's Linchpin, Gaza's Lifeline, Israel's Nightmare* (Cairo: The American University in Cairo Press, 2015).

6. Wafiq El-Agha and Sameer Abu-Mudallah, "The Economy of the Gaza Tunnels: A National Necessity or a Social and Economic Catastrophe?" *Journal of the Al-Azhar University in Gaza* 13, no.1 (2011): 1147–82. See also: Nicolas Pelham, "Gaza's Tunnel Phenomenon: The Unintended Dynamics of Israel's Siege," *Journal of Palestine Studies* 41, no. 6 (July *2012*).

Muslim Brotherhood, Hamas, and the Palestinians. After the Israeli bombardment of Gaza in 2014, during which el-Sisi refused to open the Rafah border, Egypt waged its own campaign against North Sinai, leveling entire neighborhoods in Rafah in the name of combating terrorism. This was the world I unwittingly stepped into during my second visit in 2014, when I met residents of the Egyptian side of Rafah for the first time. The entire area was under a media and telecommunications blackout—no journalists were allowed to report there, phone and internet only functioned part of the time, and, as things deteriorated further over the next couple of years, power and water cuts became normalized.

Sadly for Rafah's residents, the past few years have seen even more deterioration. In late 2014, the emergence of ISIS in Rafah and the continued Egyptian military heavy-handedness has left locals trapped in a seemingly endless battle that has created further destruction, with no clear end in sight. The border crossing with Gaza has remained closed for the most part, and the border tunnel activity is essentially over. Hamas has even created a buffer zone on the Gaza side of the border, and is in the process of handing over administrative power to the Palestinian Authority. It remains to be seen if these actions will bring any sense of normalcy to Gaza, North Sinai, and especially Rafah and the border region.

WORKS CITED

El-Agha, Wafiq, and Sameer Abu-Mudallah. "The Economy of the Gaza Tunnels: A National Necessity or a Social and Economic Catastrophe?" *Journal of the Al-Azhar University in Gaza* 13, no. 1 (2011): 1147–82.

Human Rights Watch. "Razing Rafah: Mass Home Demolitions in the Gaza Strip," (Human Rights Watch, 2004).

Pelham, Nicolas. "Gaza's Tunnel Phenomenon: The Unintended Dynamics of Israel's Siege," *Journal of Palestine Studies* 41, no. 4 (July, 2012): 6–31.

Sabry, Mohannad. *Sinai: Egypt's Linchpin, Gaza's Lifeline, Israel's Nightmare.* (Cairo: The American University in Cairo Press, 2015).

THE QATAN CENTER FOR CHILDREN

Omar Yousef

All images from Omar Yousef.

Translated from the Arabic
by Deen Sharp.

The Qatan Center for Children is an important educational and architectural landmark in the heart of Gaza. The project is distinguished by its design, implementation, and operation. The design—chosen in an architectural competition—was executed following a tour of projects in the United Kingdom, during which buildings were visited that embodied architectural ideas for similar educational and cultural processes. These were studied and integrated into the Center's architecture and organization.

The Qatan Center is a successful example of cooperation between the client, designer, construction supervisor, and workers. This partnership produced a building that is not only an important educational center but represents an island of hope and creativity in a context of war. Ironically—and sadly—the Israeli siege on Gaza has prevented me, the Center's architect, from visiting the completed work and participating in the remarkable, optimistic qualities of the building in its daily life. A cruel absurdity.

Bringing the Center to completion was not an easy experience, but it was an exciting challenge and demanded great effort. The programmatic requirements were rich and varied and the site was comparatively small, which presented difficulties since the building was required to consist of a single story only. To solve the problem, we pushed the building envelope to the boundaries of the site and focused on life within it. After multiple attempts, we finally developed the idea of a *Bazaar of Knowledge and Fun-tazy*. The building is organized like a souk, formed around a principal axis that acts as a distributor for many different activities. This interior allée is filled with light and crowned by domes and arches that form distinctive accents along this main street of the bazaar.

This variegated architectural fabric shapes the building with a series of elements derived from traditional Palestinian architecture.

Cultural Heritage

Architecture Today

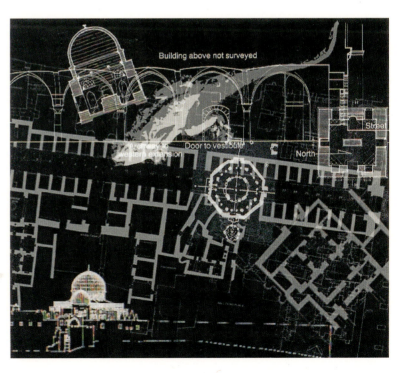

However, we have revived these design principles with dimensions, shapes, and technologies that match contemporary needs and requirements. As part of this dialogue between heritage and modernity, we have created an architectural conversation rather than simply decoratively replicating historic elements, a common practice in many contemporary Palestinian buildings. Although the Center was deeply inspired by historic forms and character, the result is legibly different from its primal sources, yet rich with reminiscence and affect. The domes and arches have distinctive cylindrical sections that act as overhead contours of light, forming familiar artistic rhythms. The internal courtyard is half-pear-shaped to accommodate an amphitheater for a storyteller and to provide a smooth transition between the different vectors of activity.

The combined principles that guided our vision had many sources. We were, for example, inspired by the appearance of the vertical slots that allowed archers to shoot from the walls of Jerusalem—and other fortresses and castles of the era—but we used this form not for defense against invaders but to modulate light. We developed a horizontal variation that protects the library from the sun while also providing panoramic vistas for the children inside. Color also played an important role in the visual composition of the Center, and we used sandstone yellow for its principal walls, blue for secondary walls, and a harmonized green in the aluminum trim, with planes of white to link them all together.

The design was intended to provide all corners of the Center with privacy while maintaining the principle of flexibility in the architectural space to facilitate its many—and changing—interactive artistic and cultural activities. The building became a box of wonder, arousing the curiosity of children, pulling them into a magical journey of symbols and puzzles. The Center is the beginning of a road, leading to the worlds of research, experimentation, learning, and dialogue, allowing children to soar beyond the prison of Gaza.

We were especially proud to see the image of the Center on the cover of *Al-Omran* magazine in 2006, under the title "a masterpiece of Palestinian art," but we were not totally convinced by the success of the building until we read the comment by Professor Manal Issa on Facebook:

> *The splendor of the Center is in its design and in every corner of it, its colors, its arches, its proportions, and its space; a wonderful piece of architecture, a home for the laughter of hearts and eyes, the glow, the children, the girls and boys together, a place for people … a space for freedom.*

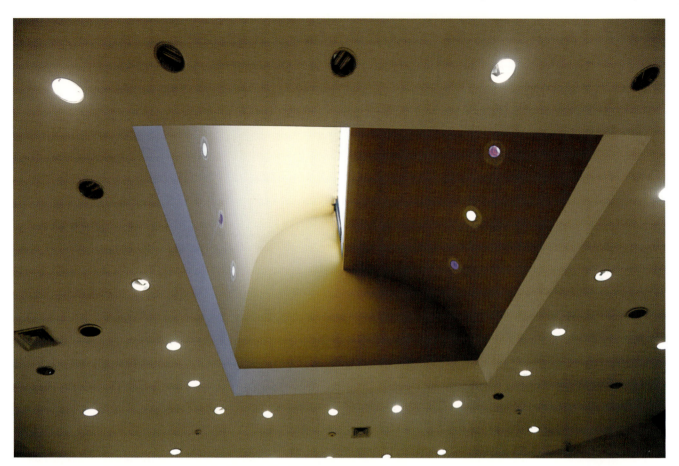

TIMELESS GAZA

Mahdi Sabbagh and Meghan McAllister

GAZA AS CONTAINER

Gaza is "developing" in a contained environment: a petri dish where the population has one of the highest growth rates in the world, while the declining economy fluctuates based on artificially imposed variations of border control, siege, war, and ceasefire. Making sense of urbanization in the Gaza Strip requires reckoning with Israel's varied mechanisms of control, all designed to limit the flow of both bodies and goods.

Nevertheless, traces of an open, connected, and expanded past can be found in the Gaza Strip and its nearby territories. Archaeological remnants of spice trade towns between Petra and Gaza remind us of Gaza's centrality in an ancient trading network. Defunct British railway lines imply a past where the Strip was not a Strip at all, but part of a network of regional cities. The Salah al-Din Road, which connects the Gaza Strip from north to south, is evidence of ancient aspirations of providing continuous mobility along the Mediterranean coast, as are the archaeological remnants of Via Maris, the Roman trading line. Late twentieth and twenty-first century infrastructure—such as the bombed airport, a besieged seaport, and rapidly built tunnels—represent a contemporary Palestinian Gaza that strives to exist as a networked city in continuity with its past.

Using a cartographic illustration of the trade and commerce routes that have shaped Gaza historically, we suggest a different reading of its present urban character and its future possibilities—one that brings the Strip's inherent connectivity to the forefront.

HISTORIC GAZA

Composed of twenty-six sheets—each 58.4 x 68.7 cm—the 1880 *Map of Western Palestine* (see pages 88–89) provides detailed survey information, including locations of towns, villages, wooded areas, orchards, palms, sand dunes, marshlands, aqueducts, bridges, cisterns, springs, ruins, historic mosques, churches, and tombs. The intricacy of this pastoral landscape drew us into the map and became a point of departure for envisioning a liberated Gaza. It was easy for the mind to wander and imagine what it was like to travel from one town to another, or to identify an area based on the trees it contained, or on its proximity to a mosque or tomb.

On this map, Gaza is seen not only as a city or a territory, but as an entire environment. It is surrounded by orchards and sand dunes, framed by folds, turns, and wadis in the landscape, neighbored by smaller towns, villages, and Bedouin tribes. The prominence of wadis suggests that water was both vital and abundant, a reminder that Gaza is part of the Fertile Crescent. A network of paths and roads emanate from Gaza, leading toward the lesser-explored[1] Bedouin-controlled territory in the Naqab desert. Gaza appears as a settlement possessing significant density, with thicker lines depicting its built-up areas and planted lands in an otherwise lightly drawn web of paths, roads, and telegraph lines. The thickness of line-weights inscribed in Gaza's landscape matches any other town on the map. Gaza is represented as a coastal destination, a strategic city, or a stop en route to another destination.

1. Lesser explored by the British at the time.

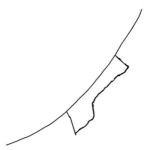

CONTAINER GAZA (PRESENT DAY)

In the public imagination, Gaza is defined by its border walls: a violent and artificial container for one of the most densely populated areas in the world. Mapping Gaza by drawing the border as a dark line has almost become a banal trope that does not capture the experienced physical width of the border condition's psychosocial weight.

WATERWAYS (PRE-1880–PRESENT)

The presence of *wadis*, valleys often with seasonal streams, threads through all the historic maps of Southern Palestine that we collected. It reminds us of how integral water access was to the growth and spread of settlements and villages, as well as the trade networks between them. The wadis are also a reminder of how natural ecosystems typically extend much further than artificially imposed political borders. The watersheds connect Gaza to its hinterlands, which once supplied urban residents with an abundance of agricultural goods.

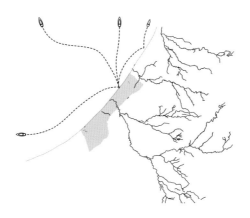

Gaza's location on the coast connected it to other cities around the Mediterranean, and made it the primary port for many major trade routes inland, including the ancient Nabataean Incense Road. Goods such as frankincense and myrrh would arrive from Southern Arabia (present-day Yemen and Oman) to the port of Gaza, where they would access ships, to eventually reach markets beyond the sea.

ROADS AND PATHS (1880–1925)

Some major routes through Gaza remained in use centuries later, such as the Salah al-Din Road (shown in bold) that runs parallel to the coast through the center of Gaza City. The Road to Beersheba (also shown in bold) was once a major road, having been paved by 1925. A web of smaller paths or "tracks" is prevalent in all the historic maps that we found. Despite being unfit for wheeled traffic, these paths appear integral to the landscape; like wrinkles, they are traces of time and culture, lacing together various villages and Bedouin lands.

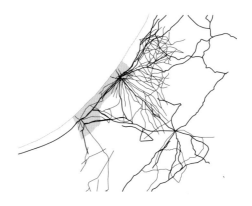

RAILWAYS (1918–PRESENT)
AND AIRWAYS (1935–2001)

Built prior to 1918, a standard-gauge railway connects Gaza to Egypt in the south and Lydda (Lydd) in central Palestine. An offshoot links Rafah to Beersheba, further connecting Gaza. Both rail lines were built by the EEF (Egyptian Expeditionary Force) and still exist today, but are not in operation.

The thought of a functioning airport for the population of the Gaza Strip is today nothing but a fantasy. But Gaza was connected to the airways since the early 1930s, while under British Mandate. For instance, Imperial Airways (today British Airways) flew to and from Gaza. It was connected to Lydd airport in Palestine, as well as Greece, Iraq, Persia, and India.

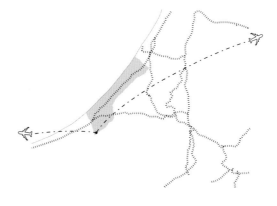

Under the Palestinian Authority, Gaza built its own international airport in 1998, its inauguration heavily televised and attended by Yasser Arafat and the Clintons. The airport functioned for two years, with flights to Amman, Istanbul, Larnaca, Cairo, Dubai, and Doha, among other cities. During the Second Intifada, the airport was bombed by the Israeli forces and then gradually reduced to rubble.

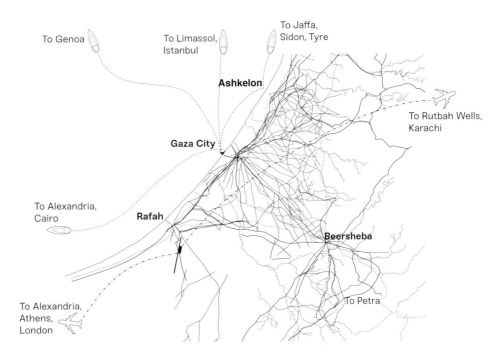

To Genoa

To Limassol,
Istanbul

To Jaffa,
Sidon, Tyre

Ashkelon

To Rutbah Wells,
Karachi

Gaza City

To Alexandria,
Cairo

Rafah

Beersheba

To Petra

To Alexandria,
Athens,
London

Layered together, Gaza's historic trade, transportation, and water networks demonstrate its inherent capability to be a regional urban hub.

After becoming absorbed in this map, we wanted to learn more about the people who drew the elaborate markings. Whoever had counted the wells, wadis, and orchards must have seen them as important enough for their map to be preserved with high quality. It was interesting to imagine a context in which certain powers recognized the existing villages with such detail and reverence.

Produced in London in 1880, the *Map of Western Palestine* was part of a larger British cartography project aimed at providing a comprehensive geo-spatial survey of land in Palestine. It was based on surveys conducted between 1872 and 1877 for the Palestine Exploration Fund (PEF).[2] The authors of the survey were Claude Reignier Conder and none other than the young H. H. Kitchener, future British Secretary of State for War. Both were officers in the Royal Corps of Engineers. Only twenty-four years old at the time, Kitchener worked on the survey from 1874 to

1877, only briefly returning to London after an incident in Safed in 1875 when he and Conder were attacked by locals. Conder suffered from a severe head injury, and Kitchener returned to Palestine without him to carry out the rest of the survey.[3]

To our delight, in addition to a set of twenty-six highly detailed maps, the survey also included nine volumes of extensive writings. This enabled us not only to imagine how the authors created the maps, but also to read their notes on all aspects of Palestine, from topography, hydrography, and archaeology, to flora and fauna. Their observations on Gaza itself painted an elaborate picture, almost jarring in contrast to the city we know today:

Ghŭzzeh-GAZA (Ow.)—The capital of the district; is a town principally of mud houses, but with mosques and other buildings well built of stone. It stands on an isolated hill in the plain, rising 180 feet above the

2. Still active today, the PEF is a British society that was created specifically for the study of the Levant. The original mission statement of the PEF was "to promote research into the archaeology and history, manners and customs and culture, topography, geology and natural sciences of biblical Palestine and the Levant." Its nineteenth century surveys were conducted by officers in the Royal Engineers, and are recognized as a combination of military intelligence gathering and archaeological expedition.

3. H. H. Kitchener, "The Safed Attack," *Palestinian Exploration Quarterly* 7, no. 4 (1875): 195–99.

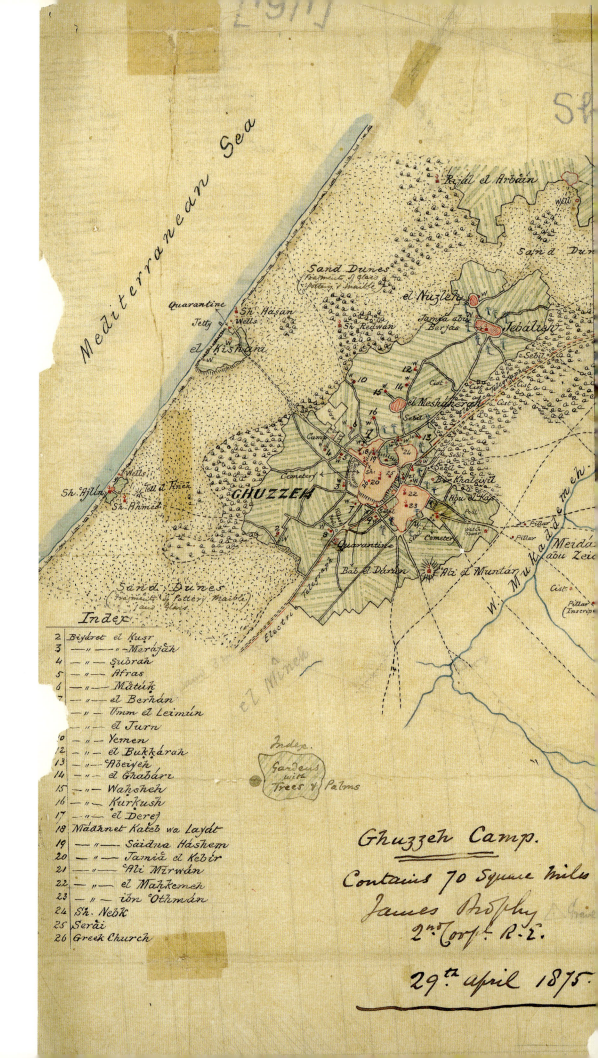

[1911]

Mediterranean Sea

Rijál el Arbaín

Well

Sand Dun

Sand Dunes
Fragments of glass,
pottery, & marble

el Nuzleh

Quarantine
Jetty
Sh. Hasan
Wells
Sh. Redwan

Jamiá abu
Berjás

Jebalieh

Sebil

el Kishani

W
10
15   14
12
W

Cist

el Meshaherah

16
Sebil

Camp
8
4 15
18
19
7
24
W
13
W   Cist

Sh: 25
3   20
W

Bir Khaleiyil

Sebil

Abu el Kas

Tell el Fineh

GHUZZEH

Cemetery
W
22
23

Peat

Sh. Ajlin
Wells
Sh. Ahmed

7
9
W
2
9
W

Soul
Cemetery

Watch
Tower

Pillar

Pillar

Meidá
Abu Zei

Quarantine

Telegraph

W. Mukaddemeh

Cist:

Bab el Darún

ᶜAli el Muntar

Pillar
(Inscrip:

Electri

el Mineh

Index
2	Biyáret el Kuṣr
3	— " — " Merdjáh
4	— " Ṣubrah
5	— " Afras
6	— " Matúḥ
7	— " el Berhán
	— " Umm el Leimún
	— " el Turn
10	— " Yemen
12	— " el Bukkárah
13	— " ᶜAbeiyeh
14	— " el Ghabári
15	— " Wahsheh
16	— " Kurkush
17	— " el Derej
18	Madhnet Kateb wa Laydt
19	— " Saidna Háshem
20	— " Jamiá el Kebír
21	— " ᶜAli Mirwán
22	— " el Mahkemeh
23	— " ibn ᶜOthmán
24	Sh. Nebk
25	Serai
26	Greek Church

Index.
Gardens
with
Trees & Palms

Ghuzzeh Camp.

Contains 70 Square Miles

James Brophy
2ⁿᵈ Corpˡ: R.E.

29ᵗʰ April 1875.

19

19

20

W. Sûfieh

Beit Hanûn
S.W. Cist.
Pool
Cist.

Cist.

Cist.

el Hatîy

Tuweil el Shair

Kh. Umm Tâbûn
Cisterns

Kh. Nejed

Tor Dimreh

W. el Hesi

Nejed
Cist.
Pool

Well

Kh. Telemeh
Cisterns
Bir Telemeh
Cist.

W. el Raml

Hûj

Kh. Hûj
Nebi Hûj

Cist. Beit Dirdis

Tell
Tûlûl el Tell
omrah

Kh. Lisn

W. el Homrah

Kh. Kûfieh
Cist.

W. Fâcilis

Kh. el Umm Harregah
near here

Kh. el Bîr

R

Cisterns

Kh. el Reseim
Cisterns

Kh. el Resm
Cisterns

Kh. Heráb Diab
Cisterns only

White Mound

sea, and some 100 feet above the surrounding flat ground. The place is divided into four Hâret, or quarters, occupying about 3/4 mile either way. . . .

The water supply is from good wells of sweet water in the town and in the surrounding gardens. The name of 15 of these wells (all marked on the Plan as B) were collected, but are unimportant.

Fine gardens surround Gaza, stretching 4 miles north and south, and 2 ½ east and west. There are many palms in these, and fine olive-groves exist beyond them on the west and north. The avenue of ancient trees along the north road, stretching for 4 miles, is the most remarkable characteristic of the town. . . .

There is a bazaar in the town, and soap is manufactured, as well as a peculiar black pottery. The potteries are west of the town. Cotton is sometimes grown, and dates, figs, olives, lentils, apricots and mulberries, melons and cucumbers, are grown in the gardens. The town has the reputation of being very healthy, probably from its dry and elevated position.

The population is said to be at the present day 18,000 souls, of whom some 200 are Greek Orthodox Christians. The Samaritans had a synagogue in Gaza about a century ago.

The remains of the ancient walls seem to be represented by the great mounds on the hill, visible on the east and south beyond the houses. The houses on the hill are the best

built, being of stone, and many ancient fragments are here used up in the walls.[4]

If Condor or Kitchener visited Gaza today, they would likely be shocked. Once "good wells of sweet water" are now limited to two hours of public access per day.[5] Gaza's "reputation of being very healthy" contrasts with today's medical facilities overwhelmed and struggling to operate.[6] But it is invigorating to discover and remind ourselves that this Gaza, with a supple and rich landscape, did exist.

We read excitement and awe in these memoirs, and just as it is also difficult to reconcile these descriptions with today's conditions, it is challenging to reconcile the tone of these memoirs with our knowledge of the authors' future roles in colonial violence.[7] This conundrum was a reminder of how often maps and surveys themselves become violent tools for political or military domination.

We realize that we should approach all maps with some skepticism; it is crucial to recognize the context in which they were made. Maps cannot avoid political bias in the same way that they cannot avoid creating an impression of "fact." They are always making an argument about a place's past as well as its potential future.[8] Even if a map claims to solely focus on landscape, topography, or ecology, the territory—now rendered and measured—will appear as if it is there for the taking. In this case, the map could render the area comprehensible and quantifiable to capitalist and expansionist outsiders, namely agents of the British Empire.

4. C.R. Conder, R.E., and Capt. H.H. Kitchener, *The Survey of Western Palestine: Memoirs of the Topography, Orography, Hydrography, and Archaeology, Volume II: Judaea* (London: The Committee of the Palestine Exploration Fund, 1881), 234–35.

5. Wissam Nassar, "In Pictures: Gaza Water Crisis Worsens," Al Jazeera, May 12, 2014.

6. Human Rights Watch, "Israel: Apparent War Crimes in Gaza," June 19, 2018.

7. Kitchener, specifically, would later be given credit for securing British control of the Sudan, for which he was made Lord Kitchener of Khartoum, see Tony Bunting, "Battle of Omdurman," Encyclopedia Britannica, August 6, 2018.

8. There has been much scholarly discussion on this topic. See J. B. Harley, "Deconstructing the Map," *Cartografica* 26, no. 2 (1989): 1–20.

Put another way, it is precisely the map's romanticization of Palestine that makes it an ominous precursor to future violence. Once Palestine has been mapped, new towns can be planned on its lands, undesirable towns can be omitted, depopulated, and replaced, and the landscape can be divided and reconfigured.

The Survey of Western Palestine itself became the basis for numerous military maps during the First World War, and effectively delineated the modern political borders of the region.[9] For example, the modern border between Israel and Lebanon is established at the point in upper Galilee where the Conder and Kitchener survey stops.[10]

Ironically this romantic image of Palestine created by the British *Survey of Western Palestine* could now powerfully resonate with the Palestinian psyche: it represents Palestine pre–Nakba, and shows that the land was far from a *tabula rasa*. This map recorded a moment in time when a network of Palestinian towns was recognized. The map can be used as both a weapon of colonization and an object capable of influencing a more equitable future.

We found that other colonial mapping projects from the 1826–1927 period do not illustrate the Palestinian towns in such a deliberate and detailed manner, but do echo the claim that Gaza is a convergence of multiple networks—an inevitable city. All routes pass through Gaza: coastal routes from Africa to the Middle East to Europe, and desert routes connecting the Arabian Peninsula and Palestine's hinterland to the Mediterranean. In addition to these intercontinental routes, a more localized intercity network appears: Gaza, Rafah,

Beersheba, and Ashkelon (then Majdal Asqalan) formed a network of trade and mobility in Southern Palestine. At a smaller scale, a prolific web of unpaved "tracks" connects Gaza to inland rural villages and a network of Bedouin communities.

Almost every early twentieth century British map of Palestine that we uncovered revealed how crucial Gaza was to multiple military forays during the First World War. Perhaps due to the presence of the British military, Gaza also became part of Imperial Airways' (now British Airways) early international network. In 1929, Imperial Airways inaugurated its first civilian flight service from London to Karachi, incorporating Gaza as one of the stops along the way.[11] Historic photographs of Gaza's airport attest to a short-lived optimism about the future.

A historically connected Gaza is also present in the popular memory and mythology of the city. The knowledge, for instance, that the route from Petra to Gaza was significant to the ancient Incense Road leaves us to ponder and speculate on the implications of such commerce.[12] Gaza's port was once a major node connecting East to West: goods from the East could access European markets via Mediterranean shipping routes and vice versa. Some archaeological evidence has begun to reveal the material aspects of such trade.[13] Similarly, the existence of the Via Maris and Salah al-Din Road, often drawn as rough lines on a regional map (because the specific locations of their respective paths have yet to be entirely uncovered), imply that one might have traveled uninterrupted along the line all the way from Syria to Egypt.

9. "During the First World War the PEF map was repeatedly revised and updated, and various versions, in several formats and different scales, were published by the Survey of Egypt on behalf of the British War Office. Both the British and the Germans had recourse to it in the preparation of new campaign maps, and after the war the PEF supplied these maps to the administration of the occupied territories in Palestine for various purposes." Dov Gavish, T*he Survey of Palestine under the British Mandate: 1920–1948* (London: Routledge Curzon Studies in Middle Eastern History, 2005), 10.

10. Neil Asher Silberman, *Digging for God and Country: Exploration, Archaeology and the Secret Struggle for the Holy Land, 1799–1917* (New York: Alfred A. Knopf, 1982).

11. The route was London (Croydon)–Paris–Basle by Argosy (by air), Basle–Genoa (by train), Genoa–Rome (Ostia)–Naples–Corfu–Athens–Suda Bay (Crete)–Tobruk–Alexandria by Calcutta (by flying boat), Alexandria–Gaza–Rutbah Wells–Baghdad–Basra–Bushire–Lingeh–Jask–Gwadar–Karachi by DH66 Hercules. "History and Heritage," British Airways, accessed April 15, 2017.

12. I. E. S. Edwards et al., eds., *The Cambridge Ancient History* (Cambridge: Cambridge University Press, 1969), 330.

13. Philipe Bohstrom, "Wealthy 3,600-Year-Old Trading Hub Found in Gaza," *Haaretz*, May 20, 2016.

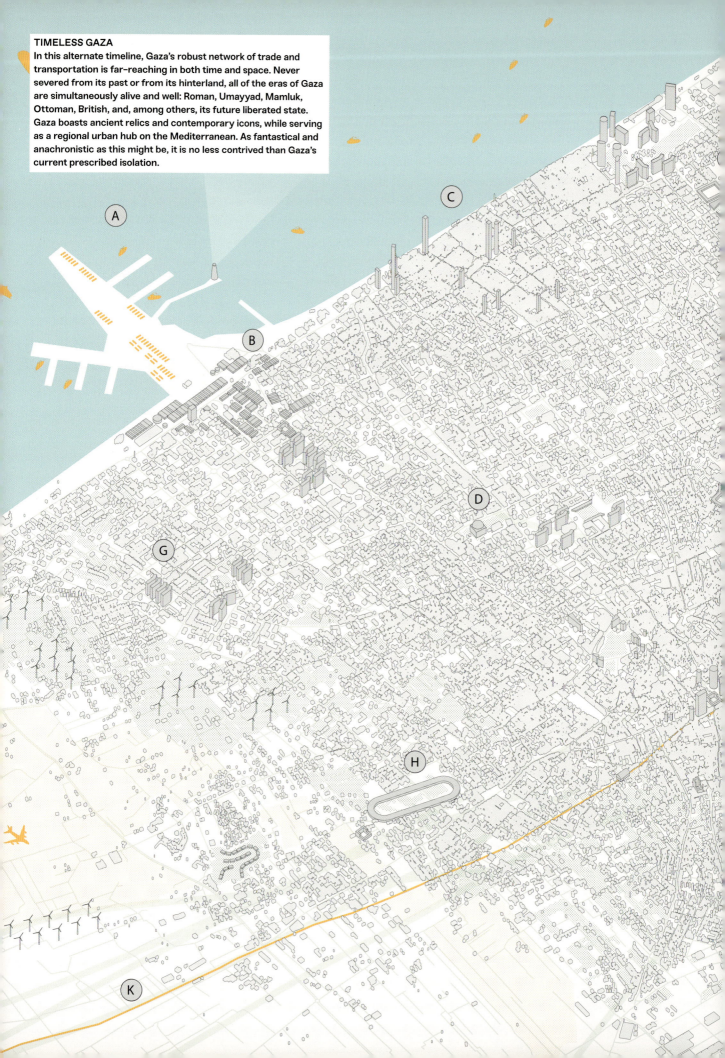

TIMELESS GAZA

In this alternate timeline, Gaza's robust network of trade and transportation is far-reaching in both time and space. Never severed from its past or from its hinterland, all of the eras of Gaza are simultaneously alive and well: Roman, Umayyad, Mamluk, Ottoman, British, and, among others, its future liberated state. Gaza boasts ancient relics and contemporary icons, while serving as a regional urban hub on the Mediterranean. As fantastical and anachronistic as this might be, it is no less contrived than Gaza's current prescribed isolation.

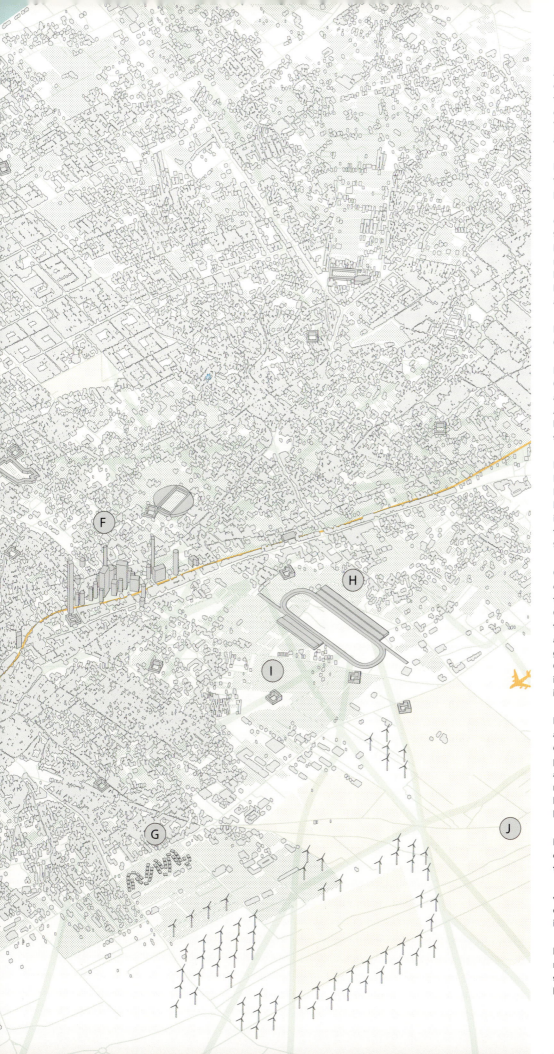

A. Commercial port connecting Gaza to global trade and commuter connection to Algeciras, Valencia, Barcelona, Genoa, Alexandria, and Haifa.

B. Industrial Zone, accessible to local residents and to the port.

C. The compact fabric of the Shati Refugee Camp remains, but it is imagined as a dense neighborhood, desirable because of its proximity to the beach and to jobs and schools across Gaza.

D. The Temple of Marnas, the Gazan God of rain and grain.

E. University Campus and Cultural Institution named after the once prominent Al-Meshal Cultural Center, bombed by Israel in the summer of 2018.

F. Gaza's Central Business District located on Salah el Deen and easily accessible locally through street infrastructure and regionally through a train line running on Salah el Deen road.

G. With access to world construction materials, techniques, and standards Gaza adapts to the expected typologies of housing such as high-rise housing and gated suburban communities. Connected to the world, it is also not immune to global inequality.

H. World-class sports amenities and other spaces of outdoors leisure are prevalent, including a Roman arena and Mamluk horse racing grounds. With no border zone, Gaza does not have a density problem.

I. Mamluk-era caravansaries continue Gaza's lively tradition of trade.

J. Gaza's expansive citrus and olive tree groves grow deep into its hinterland.

K. Salah el Deen road is a multilane artery, with high-speed light rail, bus lines, and bicycle lanes.

TIMELESS GAZA

To illustrate the absurdity of the container-like conditions within Gaza today, we juxtapose them with another plan that we call *Timeless Gaza*. This plan imagines a city whose historic networks were never severed. If a pre-1948 or pre-1967 Gaza is to be brought back, why not also resuscitate elements from the Gaza of the Bronze, Hellenistic, Roman, or medieval Islamic ages? Such a Gaza would have a port vital to regional trade, architectural and social infrastructure to support such trade, a magnificent circular temple to the Gazan god of rain and grain, Marnas, along with the prominent caravansaries and souks that once populated the city. To further push the idea of historical continuity with the present day further, we combine these relics with elements of an imagined contemporary capitalist city: a Central Business District, economic zones, suburban sprawl, gated communities, and of course a modern seaport and airport.

We use the medium of a map in a deliberate way: if maps were historically used as tools of domination, they offer the perfect rhetorical device for resistance. Through this mash-up of history presented "as fact," we critique the artificial severing of Gaza from its networked past, as well as the potential pitfalls of urban and architectural tropes under free-market capitalism. Our experiment with *Timeless Gaza* provokes the question: what is progress? Are there other, better lessons to learn from the past as Gaza moves forward? With Gaza's liberation as the ultimate goal, what else can we call for? Can Gazans demand recognition of their city as a powerful regional player?

Today, Gaza's rich cultural history is more of a footnote to its occupation. Gaza is seen as an ahistorical product of ongoing political conflict. Not only is Gaza's pre-1967 history forgotten, but its post-1967 "living" history is also often overshadowed. *Timeless Gaza*, on the other hand, is not ahistorical, but rather lives with all of its histories actively present.

In addition to multiple pasts, our maps suggest multiple futures. History provides Gaza with an inventory from which it can draw to revive or combine various infrastructures of mobility and trade. What if Gaza's former networks of trade and mobility were in use today? Imagine a city that remained a destination within an open network. What if Via Maris were still active, and what if Bedouin land tenures between Gaza and Beersheba were restored to facilitate the movement of humans, goods, and fauna? This Gaza is not imagined as merely spilling into the farmlands across the border; rather, the farmlands become part of Gaza, as its economic and cultural field expands organically in every direction. Dynamic trade and communication flows would contrast with today's isolated and controlled points of import/export. *Timeless Gaza* emerges from this network, and imagines a place, in both the past and the future, that is no longer defined by perimeter forces. *Timeless Gaza* imagines a place where the hegemony of the border might in many respects appear stranger than fiction.

WORKS CITED

Bohstrom, Philipe. "Wealthy 3,600-Year-Old Trading Hub Found in Gaza." *Haaretz*, May 20, 2016.

Bunting, Tony. "Battle of Omdurman." Encyclopedia Britannica, August 6, 2018.

Conder, C.R., R.E., and Capt. H.H. Kitchener. *The Survey of Western Palestine: Memoirs of the Topography, Orography, Hydrography, and Archaeology, Volume II: Judaea*. London: The Committee of the Palestine Exploration Fund, 1881.

Edwards, I. E. S., C.J. Gadd, N.G.L. Hammond, and E. Sollberger, editors. *The Cambridge Ancient History*. Cambridge: Cambridge University Press, 1969.

Gavish, Dov. *The Survey of Palestine under the British Mandate: 1920–1948*. London: Routledge Curzon Studies in Middle Eastern History, 2005.

Harley, J. B. "Deconstructing the Map." *Cartografica* 26, no. 2 (1989): 1–20.

"History and Heritage." British Airways, accessed April 15, 2017.

Human Rights Watch. "Israel: Apparent War Crimes in Gaza." June 19, 2018.

Kitchener, H. H. "The Safed Attack." *Palestinian Exploration Quarterly* 7, no. 4 (1875): 195–199.

Nassar, Wissam. "In Pictures: Gaza Water Crisis Worsens." *Al Jazeera*, May 12, 2014.

Silberman, Neil Asher. *Digging for God and Country: Exploration, Archaeology and the Secret Struggle for the Holy Land, 1799–1917*. New York: Alfred A. Knopf, 1982.

MAPS REFERENCED

Rafah-Gaza-Beersheba area [map]. 1917. Scale ca. 1:100,000. Sheet 1 of 2. Cairo: (British) War Office.

Map of northern Sinai and Palestine [map]. 1918. Scale 1:500,000. Inset: Defences around Gaza. Scale 1:80,000. Melbourne: A.J. Mullett, Government Printer Melbourne.

Great Britain Committee of Imperial Defence Historical Section. *Military operations in Egypt and Palestine* [map]. 1925. Scale 1:250,000. Taunton, England: Ordnance Survey.

Conder, C. R., and H. H. Kitchener. *Map of Western Palestine* [map]. 1880. Scale 1:63,360. Sheet 19 of 26. London: Committee of the Palestine Exploration Fund.

ABSURD–CITY, SUBVER–CITY

Yara Sharif and Nasser Golzari
Palestine Regeneration Team (PART)

Absurd-City, Subver-City is a continuation of our journey as NG Architects and the Palestine Regeneration Team (PART) across invisible and uncertain landscapes.[1] Through what we call "Moments of Possibilities," we engage in conceptual discussions by using different mediums, such as drawings and design, to redraw the map of the land and expose its hidden, dynamic topography. In this chapter, we share some design ideas and projects that surfaced as a result of our research and practice in the city of Gaza.

Trying to narrate Palestine and its landscape has always been a challenge. The land has often been defined through somebody else's lens, narrated through somebody else's language and text, and drawn through somebody else's map. And yet, these endless images, narratives, and maps can be so distant from one's own encounter with the land—especially as Palestinians. The narratives tend to be incomplete. Throughout history, either the Palestinians have been left out of the picturesque setting—as if they would have disturbed the scenes—or the descriptions seem to be made to meet a certain agenda.

Critical cartographers often question this perpetuation of power through maps and drawings: they argue that there is no such thing as a neutral, or an "innocent" map. Instead, we are left with just another form of occupation through imagination, whereby some cities and communities are excluded from the landscape. Edward Said best summed this up in 1995, following the Oslo peace agreement that drew the current map of fragmented Palestine:

In the history of colonial invasion, maps are always first drawn by the victors, since maps are instruments of conquest; once projected, they are then implemented. Geography is therefore the art of war but can also be the art of resistance if there is a counter-map and a counter-strategy.[2]

Gaza is surely one of those extreme cases where the exclusionary representation of the context, not only through maps but also images and text, renders its current spatial and sociocultural identity absent from today's common global narrative. With a constant process of selective "cutting and pasting," of maps, land, and imagery the physical and, most importantly, mental map of the city is distorted and confusing. The graphic cutting and pasting often renders the city merely as ruins while excluding the social layers and the daily forms of soft resistance that shape it. Moreover, the physical siege that started in 2001, the military destruction of the city in 2009 and 2014, the economic blockade, and the tactical methods of resilience and survival that emerged as a result have all changed the urban morphology of the city with new layers, all of which call for new means of mapping and narration.

Stemming from this need for an alternative discourse to challenge the distorted reality, *Absurd-City, Subver-City* is a way to reread and reconstruct Palestine and Gaza's maps, while stripping them of the dominant power of lines; a way to bring forward the absent Palestinian narrative of everyday life with its

1. The Palestinian Regeneration Team (PART) is a design-led research group that aims to search for creative and responsive spatial possibilities in Palestine in order to heal the fractured landscape. It is co-founded by Yara Sharif, Nasser Golzari, and Murray Fraser. As an interdisciplinary team of architects, spatial designers, academics, and artists, we are involved in a wide range of both speculative and live design projects in Palestine, the Middle East, and beyond. We intend to cultivate possibilities for change from within, while also provoking a critical form of spatial practice that questions—theoretically and practically—the spatial and socioeconomic potentials of Palestine and beyond. PART works on self-help housing strategies, revitalization plans, and prototype "green" buildings that celebrate and build upon everyday cultural practices. More information about PART's projects can be found at http://www.palestineregenerationproject.com.

2. Edward Said, *The Politics of Dispossession: The Struggle for Palestinian Self-Determination, 1969–1994* (New York: Vintage Books, 1994), 416.

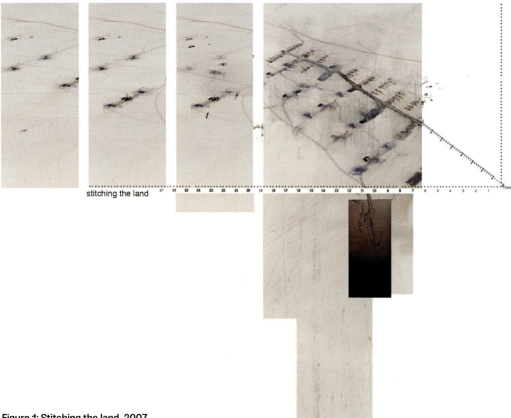

stitching the land

Figure 1: Stitching the land, 2007.

resilient nature, and expose new spatial possibilities to heal, empower, and suture the fragmented landscape. Our interventions propose spatial scenarios through what we call "matrixes," which can begin to stitch the fragmented spaces together (see figure 1). These matrixes are applied at different scales; if crisscrossed, they might create the counter-map and alternative strategy that Said has always been calling for.

In *Absurd-City*, we have specifically been exploring alternative ways to reread and redraw Gaza's urban fabric and living conditions, taking into account the relationship between people, space, and time. Navigating between text, maps, and images, we try to reveal some of the missing sociocultural and spatial layers that define the city, a means to unpack the absurdity of today from the locals' point of view. As Yara

Sharif noted in her book *Architecture of Resistance*:

Between zooming in and out, I am struck to realize that my Palestine seen from an inside lens is very different to that from outside. From an outsider's perspective, the signs all clearly seem to be there: the Separation Wall, the contested map, the confusing landscape, the uncertainty of where Palestinian space starts or ends. When viewed from the inside however, it is not that these signs are less obvious, it is just that we Palestinians have to live with them in every single detail in our daily life. This is probably the aspect that those from outside cannot see, since it might be too small to observe, or maybe too surreal to absorb.[3]

3. Yara Sharif, *Architecture of Resistance: Cultivating Moments of Possibility Within the Palestinian/Israeli Conflict* (London: Routledge, 2017), xv.

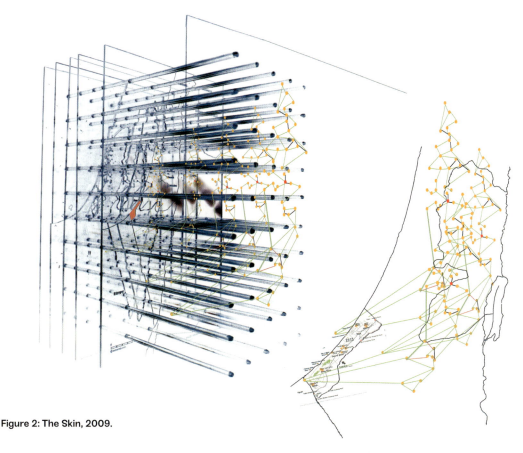

Figure 2: The Skin, 2009.

The stories portrayed in *Absurd–City*, whether they are a spatial rereading of the city, or the compiled narratives from our diaries, should be seen as fragments that complement one another and form a necessary part of the whole. They would probably not make sense if read on their own; rather, it is the accumulation of these stories that provides a closer view of what an "Absurd" condition of a city like Gaza could be.

Subver–City, on the other hand, explores spatial means of reinhabiting the city. While looking at the many challenges and constraints that exist, we try to rethink reconstruction and the domestic space of the everyday, insisting on the importance of offering propositions that build on what is already there. While doing so, we use design to question the notion of "home," especially in a fractured city with exposed skin and fabric, where the relationship between the internal

and external, the street and the room is now blurred. This reading of the city could create new typologies for inhabiting it. Emphasizing the "skin" to define what is inside, for example, and what remains of the city, is one of such approach, illustrated above (see figure 2).

Subver–City does not necessarily intend to suggest the answer to the crisis of destruction and siege; rather, we see it as part of a "process" to provoke discussion and spatial engagement. Our conceptual discussions using the media of drawings and design are aimed to reflect, question, exaggerate, and imagine while engaging with the social and spatial realities there. The interventions presented, therefore, are a combination of real and speculative ones; a navigation between reality and dream that we continuously explore in our work. Both however, are seen as a complementary part of a whole. They are consciously driven from our belief that for any Palestinian space to be nourished, one needs not only to stretch the physical space to create conditions for new possibilities, but also to enlarge the space of imagination. The interventions or "readings" aim to work at different scales. Some tackle the detailed scale of 1:1 whereby we think of possibilities to enhance the living conditions at the scale of the individual. Others approach the city from a bigger urban or regional scale, looking at what we call 1:10,000. Oscillation between scales beyond Gaza is crucial to combat the entrapment and isolation of Palestine as disconnected archipelagos and to link the city back to a broader historical and geographical imaginary.

THE ABSURD-CITY

For those who pass it without entering, the city is one thing; it is another for those who are trapped by it and never leave. There is the city where you arrive for the first time and there is another city which you leave never to return. Each deserves a different name.[4]

Trying to describe a city like Gaza is a challenge. How to reveal its absent narratives? How to read what lies beneath its resilient ruins and, most importantly, how to reconstruct it?

It might be hard to imagine, but Gaza's daily cultural practices were once an integral part of Mediterranean culture. Like many other Mediterranean coastal cities during the nineteenth century, Gaza embraced urban modernity

and contributed, along with its sister coastal cities of Jaffa, Acre, Alexandria, and Beirut, to a rich history.[5] The city has been under siege since 2001, making it one of the largest open-air prisons in modern history. The only entry and exit points to the Strip—Rafah in Egypt and Erez in Israel—have been blocked, despite a humanitarian crisis. The United Nations described this as an illegal form of collective punishment.[6] With a destroyed urban fabric, a housing deficit, a ban on reconstruction, and a lack of water, electricity, and building materials, the coastal enclave has turned into an absurd entity trying constantly to defy time and immobility.

Narrating the *Absurd-City*, as we do with the excerpts of our Gaza diaries, is a way to reinterpret the current condition and accumulate an archive for possible future scenarios.[7] It is a process of mapping and reconstructing the map, where we not only intend to document the facts on the ground, but also to imagine scenarios that can possibly happen or have already happened. This resulted in a process of cutting, stitching, drawing, and redrawing, in order to allow Gaza's hidden layers to surface and breathe—again.

In 2009—following the devastating Israeli war that left Gaza in ruins—the United Nations invited us to visit the Strip in order to explore possible options for the reconstruction along with the local community, using mainly already available materials. This was especially crucial because of the siege, as Israel had banned any international aid apart from financial assistance. Not only did they isolate the city and its community, but they also banned building materials like

4. Italo Calvino, *Invisible Cities* (San Diego, CA: Harcourt Brace Jovanovich, 1972), 125.

5. Salim Tamari, *Mountain Against the Sea: Essays on Palestinian Society and Culture* (Berkeley: University of California Press, 2008).

6. See Martine Dennis, "Who is Stopping the Reconstruction of the Gaza Strip?" *Al Jazeera*, July 7, 2016.

7. The Gaza Diaries consist of our notes and maps of the city, compiled during our visit in 2010.

Figure 3: Distorted Landscape: surface, air, and underground, 2007.

cement from entering the Strip. With the help of UN–Habitat, we started a long process of communication in order to obtain a permit to enter Gaza. Our attempts succeeded following an exhausting year of negotiations, with an authorization to cross through Rafah. A selected multidisciplinary team of experts got together following discussions with local architects in Gaza. We possessed a range of different expertise and backgrounds: rammed earth, water and sewage treatment, and self–built reconstruction.

AT THE EDGE OF THE CITY

The eight hour or so drive across the Sinai Desert from Cairo Airport to reach the Rafah border is nothing but torture faced with more torture: "Your name is not on the list," the Egyptian officer explained as we reach the crossing. Heat, dust, and rubbish are everywhere. No toilets to use, no water to drink ... We squeeze again between the crowds to show our paperwork. "Wait," the officer shouts, while

having his breakfast laid on the table: "maybe your authorization is on its way." With despair, panic, and hope for a miracle, the wait lasted over ten hours in the heat of the desert. Enough time to reflect on and watch the humiliation of the Gazans who are desperate to cross for days, if not months. The fear of not getting through grows higher after five hours of waiting ... "Use the tunnel," a young boy whispers in my ears: "$1,500 and you will be at the other end." Between shock, fear, imagination, and exhaustion, the idea of crossing through tunnels starts to sound reasonable. A shiver runs down my spine when I see the cows, sheep, and bags of food being prepared to be sent down with ropes. "Surely this is suffocating," I think to myself, before the voice of the boy breaks my line of thought: "It is not that bad, you can use the VIP tunnel if you are willing to pay more" ... "VIP WHAT?!"[8]

8. PART diary, October 2010.

The underground culture of tunnels that emerged out of the desperate need to connect Gaza to the rest of the world has expanded the boundaries of the city to another level. Invisible traces of spatial resilience grew in the voids below ground, defying the siege. With the tunnels constantly changing, appearing, and disappearing, it became difficult to draw a coherent mental map of the city and what lies beneath. In an invisible, contradictory landscape, one cannot identify who owns what, or even who is occupying what. How would one define the limits of the map?

As in the West Bank, a thin layer of urban possibilities is being born below the exhausted surface, out of pure necessity.[9] A "vertical layer," invisible and subversive, has emerged to make things happen. Within this vertical layer, one is faced with an entirely new perception of spatial comfort. Apparently, a VIP tunnel did exist between Gaza and Rafah at some point. According to local newspaper *Al-Quds*, "VIP tunnels were the latest achievement" in 2008, before the Israeli military onslaught.[10] They happen to be wide and high enough so that one does not need to bend or crawl while using them. In order to smuggle wealthy people walking upright, a VIP tunnel also offered phone lines, electricity, and the luxury of sitting areas, coupled with proper ventilation systems along the way. The stories of this underground culture are endless and surreal, from fast-food deliveries to wedding ceremonies, to scooters being dismantled and reassembled.

ENTERING GAZA

On the drive from Rafah toward the city of Gaza, one is struck by the extent of the crisis. The UN estimates that the Gaza Strip suffers from a deficit of 70,000 housing units. The shortage was initially triggered by Gaza's population increase, and plans for new construction were an attempt to address this. Not only did this construction not take place, but the Israeli assault also flattened major parts of the Strip, leaving many Gazans homeless yet again. Since then, no housing and reconstruction initiatives have been implemented, and the deficit today reflects a humanitarian disaster.

Major neighborhoods are simply left as exposed bones with tents and metal barracks emerging from the concrete rubble every now and then. Despite the difficulties and the sheer despair, clotheslines, hanging fabrics, and playing children soften the scene, turning these "non-places" into a real place. The sandy alleyways—or what is left of them—are packed with chairs, sofas, and mattresses, alongside scooters and three-wheeled, donkey-driven carts; all of these extend the domestic space beyond its conventional confines to give the street a new role.

Today we visited one neighborhood in Shujaiyah along with Ahmad and Salem: local architects and friends. A rug laid carefully in the middle of nowhere, suggesting a space of worship. We take our shoes off ... as we step in, we are faced with an unfamiliar world they call home surrounded by concrete columns and reconstruction

9. Passing through sewage pipes connecting Jerusalem with the rest of the West Bank is one example of the resilient tactics used by Palestinians to connect their fragmented geography. These invisible and ephemeral practices appear and disappear, in constant defiance of borderlines.

10. "Tunnel between Egypt and Gaza for VIPs only," *Al-Quds*, December 27, 2008. See also Avi Issacharoff, "'VIP tunnel' smuggling wealthy Gazans into Egypt," *Haaretz*, December 25, 2008.

bars. Not sure whether we are indoors or actually outdoors, but the notion of home with its familiarity and intimacy is contradicted with sudden cuts through the walls overlooking the main busy road ..."I cannot sleep in my room anymore," fourteen-year-old Ola whispers in an informal conversation while having lunch together. "I'm literally on the street with no sense of privacy... We sleep on the ground without even blankets ... How long is this temporality going to last?"[11]

In what we call the *Absurd-City,* domestic spaces have become exposed: the relationship between the internal and the external is distorted. Gaza City is no longer dwelled in, in a conventional sense; instead, the link between the street, the block, the room, and the living room is blurred. One roams through ruins and finds an absence of skin, apparently vacant voids, and frozen objects, uncertain of whether one is at the scale of a city or the scale of a room. In order to read the city, one cannot ignore the fragile, intimate objects that were left behind, or those that disappeared with the systematic erasure of intimacy with the surroundings.

THE SEA: A THEATER OF THE ABSURD

For those who are familiar with Gaza, the sea has always been a key part of its cultural and social practice. Little huts made of bamboo and fabric, vendors selling grilled corn and ice cream, and a beach packed with families: probably all of these are familiar scenes in other coastal cities, except for that half-sinking

military ship in the middle of the water. The ship is a leftover artifact from the British Mandate to remind the city of its history and add fun to children's imaginative play. Today, the ship and the magic of the sea are overshadowed by Israeli navy ships—known in Gaza as *Tarrad*—another reminder of the intensified siege. Not only does the Israeli maritime blockade deny Gaza its right to a seaport, but it also restricts fishermen to a stretch of just three nautical miles, which severely limits their catch. Despite several attempts by international activists to challenge the blockade, no one has actually been able to access Gaza via the sea: the Israeli navy intercepts any boats in international waters before they even get close to the shore. All attempts have been subjugated, and Israel's breach of human rights is simply ignored.

In the *Absurd-City*, Gazans have cultivated new attitudes toward the intensification of the siege with creative—and very often subversive—measures to help them survive and resist. Not only do they defy immobility, but destruction as well. Consequently, some reconstruction attempts are taking place using the rubble and other available materials in the absence of cement. Recycled metal, crushed concrete bricks, earth blocks, and even cooking oil are reappropriated with a creative edge to help Gazans survive and resist.

The intensification of the siege, the population increase, and the destruction did not leave any alternative but to occupy the margins and voids of the city. Therefore, what appears to be silent, inactive, or absent conceals layers of life, hope,

11. PART Diary, October 23, 2010.

Figure 4: Exploded notion of home, 2015.

and resistance. The question remains: how permanent is this temporality?

SUBVER-CITY

While shedding light on some of these moments of absurdity, we suggest alternative means for inhabiting the city, its voids, its leftover spaces, and its dynamic pockets. We operate at two different scales in order to create the *Subver-City*: a larger urban scale, which challenges the city's fragmentation, and a smaller microscale of the room and the block.

In imagining *Subver-City*, we try to explore whether spatial alternatives can be offered to heal Gaza, and whether a new geography emerging from the city and the sea can be created to mend its fractured landscape. For any kind of intervention to be sustainable, it may need initially to build on Palestinians' subversive—and at times invisible—practices of everyday life that counteract the absurd conditions. Through subversive acts, the "street," with its formal and informal network, has managed to create change on the ground that architects and planners have so far failed to achieve.[12] We see subversion as a means to use the creative potential of the locals, while we also question the current role of architects, planners, spatial designers, and other professionals within the complex political and economic structure of Gaza.

Subver-City's design approach has two components. The first is speculative: we try to explore Gaza on the 1:10,000 scale and stitch it back into its bigger urban context using a "conceptual space." The latter acts as a large umbrella that stretches and organizes the interventions, the "moments of possibilities." The other component is the "live project," whereby we test design interventions at the 1:1 scale, building on the conceptual spaces and the daily creative practices of survival that we've explored.

With the changing relationship between the street, the block, and the living room, a new perspective on everyday life is formed that warrants an alternative view of the city, a new reading where the domestic space versus the space of reproduction (live/work) needs to be redefined. How to rethink the common space of the everyday when it becomes an insidious sphere in Gaza, where dwellings are in a state of permanent "uprootedness"? Inhabiting the city in this case probably needs to challenge the cliché of what home is in its intimacy, familiarity, and privacy. In order to tackle this, two concepts emerged to navigate between the different scales of the *Subver-City:* Green Stitching, which forms the urban spine for the interventions, and the Learning Room typology, in its different functions and forms, which we will explain further.

GREEN STITCHING

After the devastating war on Gaza in 2008—09, which left so much of the Strip in ruins, we took up the challenge of trying to think how Gazans, with their remarkable capacity for survival and their long-standing agricultural and construction skills, could rebuild their houses. The work, centered on Gaza City, began by exploring creative ways to stitch the fragmented neighborhoods together and to rebuild them using speculative and pragmatic means. We especially focused on key neighborhoods' needs

12. Sharif, *Architecture of Resistance*; see also Reema Hammami, "On the Importance of Thugs: The Moral Economy of a Checkpoint," *MERIP* 34 (2004): 26–34. Reema Hammami, in her writings on the Surda and Qalandia checkpoints, has referred to the role and importance of informal networks in the absence of a formal structure.

for coherent and sustainable urban strategies, which would empower local communities and build on their existing potentials. This need was envisioned during a series of joint workshops, from which the concept of "Green Stitching" gradually emerged.[13]

Existing initiatives by the local community were identified and built upon as potential collective means for changing the skin of the city. Starting from the well-known Salah al-Deen Road that cuts through Gaza from north to south, we crossed the Shujaiyah suburb with its neighborhoods, one of the densely populated sites that were deeply affected by the war. Green rooftops with fruits and vegetables, small gardens at the street level, and extended vine trees stretching to shade the elevated summer rooms were creating dynamic urban pockets within the voids across the city. These were seen as potentials to be protected and celebrated as a starting point.

This idea of starting from the "green" was a response to the passion for farming that Gazans possess, with their expertise in agriculture and greenhouses. This passion can be emerged at a smaller scale. Arij, one of the locals who invited us for tea in her rooftop garden, reflected on the absurd reality of farming in the city. In the conversation, she explained:

My family was all farmers. We used to export oranges, tomatoes, and strawberries outside Gaza. Today our tomatoes are left to rot at the edges of the road, amongst many other trucks of fruits and vegetables banned from escaping Gaza. Instead, we watch the trucks of Israeli tomato puree cans packed at Erez crossing waiting to enter the city.

Within Green Stitching, the "common spaces of the everyday" that were identified during our mapping exercise were seen as a means to link together "moments of possibilities." The stitching crossed the city via different nodes, to reveal, celebrate, and mark these moments of possibilities with their formal and informal nature. They stretched from the sea to the dense urban fabric of the city, and from domestic spaces to the farm and beyond.

THE LEARNING ROOM

To link the two scales of the *Subver-City* together, a new typology is being developed at the 1:1 scale called the Learning Room. With its different forms, the Learning Room is envisaged as moving between urban pockets across the city, a tool manifesting the Green Stitching.[14] The Learning Room widens the notion of home to include the scale of the street and the neighborhood. All are seen as spaces of slow change and spatial invention.

The Learning Room as a Threshold

Taking advantage of the current blurred boundaries between the street, the block, and the room, we expect the "Green Learning Room" to act as a threshold between private and public space. In this case, a school is selected as a testing ground to host the Learning Room. The Learning Room offers Gaza's residents options to engage in "self-help," hinting at possible alternative

13. Workshops were held to address the issue of resources in the Gaza Strip and to promote more sustainable and appropriate forms of building technology, such as low-energy design, reduced water consumption, recycling, etc. Through what was termed "the Green Gaza Coalition," a group of experts and specialists in construction, NGOs, local builders, contractors, women representatives, and many others was formed in partnership with UN-Habitat.

14. The Learning Room typology is a follow-up to the process that we started back in 2010, when we were able to enter Gaza City and work with the local community, resulting in what we initially termed the "Green Gaza Lab," or simply the "Green Learning Room."

Figure 5: Proposed strategy to stitch Gaza's
neighborhoods, 2015.

forms of reconstruction that will make them self-sufficient and thus enhance the community's living conditions.

The Learning Room is to be, in effect, a community laboratory, as part of Gaza's reconstruction scheme, with the goal of ensuring that all new construction is based on an integrated strategy. It is intended as an interface between the public space of the school building and the more private space of the residential units around. It seeks to provide a collective drop-in space for families who possess only a basic knowledge of construction, as well as for builders and other skilled workers wishing to learn about new techniques of self-help construction. All users would thus be experimenting with and sharing low-energy and low-waste systems, and participating in creating full-size demonstration models, on display in the Learning Room, to help them rebuild their homes. By doing so, Gazans would be exposed to simple hybrid building techniques able to provide better environmental qualities, with ideas drawn once more from everyday habits, cultural practices, and local building practices.

The Learning Room Collective: 6.6.2 Typology

As reluctant as we are to enforce a conventional design intervention on a complex site like Gaza, we insist on the importance of offering propositions that build on what already exists, to reveal the potentials of the site and take advantage of the current spatial absurdity with its blurred edges between private/public and indoor/outdoor. Subsequently, the proposal for the 6.6.2 Collective[15] tries to celebrate local initiatives while challenging the reconstruction projects put forward by some funders, who do not refer to the role of the street or the collective. Many of the reconstruction projects we critique offer highly dense high rise units with little consideration for environmental, social needs, or cultural practices.

In response, the proposed 6.6.2 Collective is a modular system composed of "Start-up Units." These are living units of thirty-seven to forty square meters, meant to accommodate newlywed couples. This space is extended by a collective service core of over thirteen square meters. The proposal facilitates the expansion of the unit/house, to accommodate one- and two-bed flats. Modules can be joined together with additional platforms to offer larger units for extended families within the plot. This also allows for shared, elevated, and semi-private courtyards and garden spaces. The extendable module is an interpretation of the traditional living style and current sociocultural practice in Gaza, with its strong family units. The proposal is an alternative to the current existing building regulations, challenges the current setbacks for plots, and offers a solution where more shared and open spaces can be realized. In this approach, families extend "back to back," with more space for shared gardens, as opposed to central buildings with setbacks on the edge.

The method of construction is hybrid, combining a post-and-beam structured frame system. In addition, load-bearing rammed-earth spine walls take some of the key loads. This is based on a 600 x 600 mm grid system, easy to handle by self-builders and families. The aim is to use the earth and materials available in Gaza, without relying on cement.

15. The 6.6.2 Collective typology was designed and shortlisted as part of the Grand Designs/ National Custom & Self-Build Association's Competition in 2015, and was exhibited at that year's Grand Designs Live show in Birmingham as a manifestation of low-cost self-build typology. The design of the room is reappropriated, going beyond Gaza to reach all of Palestine and other contexts. The principles originally developed for Gaza, namely those of "stitching" and "empowering," are needed in other countries—with very different political and socio-economic conditions, including Britain—as well. Wealth and opportunity inequalities regrettably afflict all societies, as do the urgent problems caused by human-made crisis and by climate change. Thus, the design process that PART deploys as part of its urban and environmental strategies is relevant to architects across the world, suggesting fertile areas for research and projects in the future.

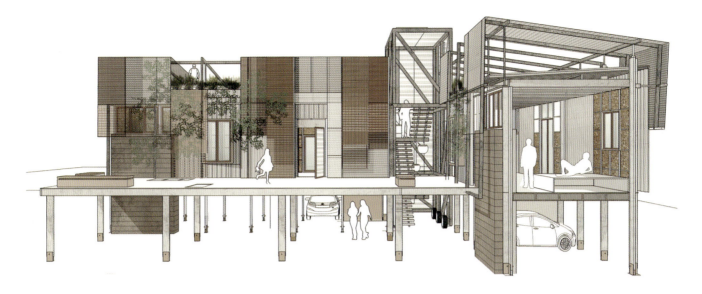

Figure 6: Learning Room clusters, 2016.

Seasonal Skin: The outer wall of the room has a multi-breathable skin, with three different layers. The inner skin (the 6.6.2 insulated box) provides the main thermal mass of the building. The second skin is made of corrugated metal (commonly available in Gaza), provides the main waterproofing element, and acts as the gray water collector. The third skin, on the other hand, is an additional protective "cloth" for the building. It is the main component of our seasonal ventilation and cooling strategy. In addition, it provides protection for the "clip–on," passive components on the walls and roofs. The material of the cloth varies from one context to another, to respond to the construction method, climate, character, and identity of the place. It can incorporate bamboo or palm leaves, which are commonly used in Gaza.[16]

Testing and making: In order to test out some of the components and principles mentioned above, we brought our projects to the West Bank.[17] Some of it was realized in the Eco Kitchen scheme in Beit Iksa village, which won the 2014 Holcim Commendation Award for Sustainable Construction.[18]

The Learning Room as a Parasite
With the city fabric left in bones, the "Learning Room as a Parasite" rereads the city and stitches its fabric back together, offering an ephemeral space to dwell. In this sense, the Room, or the lab, puts emphasis on the "skin," to define what is inside and what remained from the city.

The skin is a hybrid of existing materials and objects available on–site: a curtain–like layer to contain the ephemeral inner space and offer conditions that can awaken the sleeping city. Using the notion of

16. The bamboo furniture-making tradition was brought from Jaffa and thrived in Gaza for a while. With the blockade, however, people have mainly relied on recycling existing bamboo and bringing new material through the tunnels before the existing bamboo would be destroyed.

17. See Nasser Golzari, "Cultivating Possibilities," in *Reclaiming Space: The 50 Villages Project in Rural Palestine*, eds. Khaldun Bshara and Saud Amiry (Ramallah: Riwaq, 2015), 45–69.

18. "Adaptive Reuse: Women's centre and playground," Lafarge Holcim Foundation, June 29, 2015,

GREEN LEARNING ROOM

01. Rammed Earth
02. Wire Mesh Screen
03. Bamboo Screen
04. Service Core
05. Reinforced Bar Framework
06. 1st Skin Insulated Sterlin Board
07. 2nd Skin Corrugated Aluminum
08. 3rd Skin, Interchangeable Skin:
    *Corrugated Aluminum, Wire Mesh,
    Timber Screen*

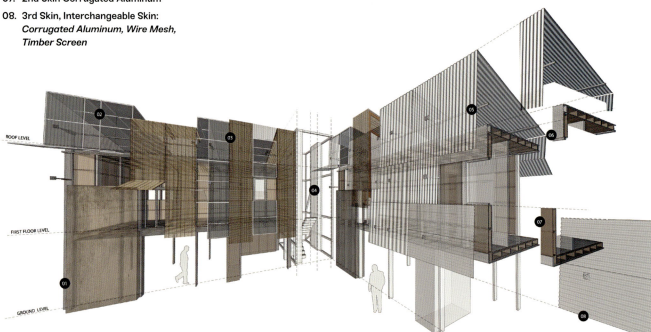

Figure 7: Green Learning Room, 2016.

A mobile "service core" provides necessary temporary services—such as passive cooling, heating, and gray water filtration—connected directly to the kitchen unit and garden. Shared between neighborhoods or clusters of units, the core offers environmental possibilities, inspired by daily practices, to address urgent basic needs such as water, electricity, and heating. The service core is mobile and can be shared depending on need and availability.

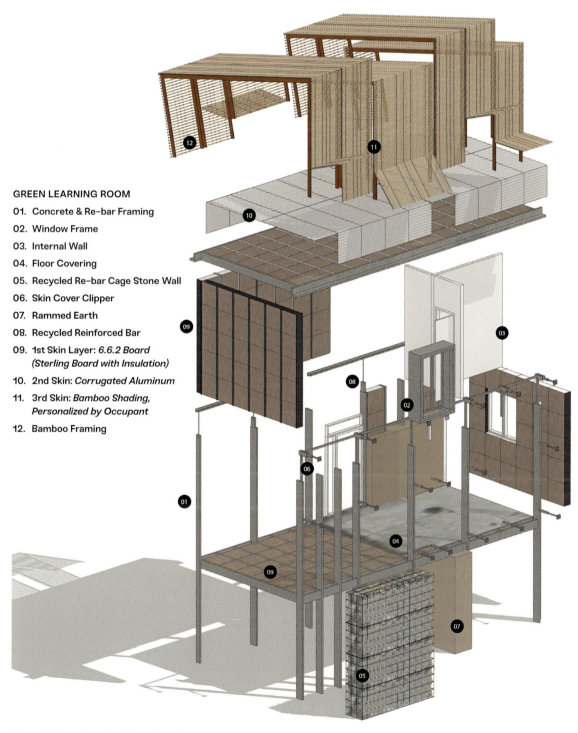

GREEN LEARNING ROOM

01. Concrete & Re–bar Framing
02. Window Frame
03. Internal Wall
04. Floor Covering
05. Recycled Re–bar Cage Stone Wall
06. Skin Cover Clipper
07. Rammed Earth
08. Recycled Reinforced Bar
09. 1st Skin Layer: *6.6.2 Board
    (Sterling Board with Insulation)*
10. 2nd Skin: *Corrugated Aluminum*
11. 3rd Skin: *Bamboo Shading,
    Personalized by Occupant*
12. Bamboo Framing

Figure 8: Green Learning Room, 2016.

Figure 9: Testing and making, 2016.

"scaffolding" as a structural base, construction rebars are collected and recycled to form the basis of the parasitic structure and stitch the different rooms together.

Putting the emphasis on the skin rather than the core of the room is our response to—or maybe questioning of—the notion of home, dwelling, and resilience within such a complex and historically layered context. A home cannot be stripped of the objects and memory traces that have accumulated over time. Most of these objects are currently absent or dislocated within the resilient city.

The term resilience is often associated with positive properties that suggest a community or a space immune to trauma, constantly bouncing back.[19] The term is rather incomplete, as resilience could refer to adjustment, but also to the suppression of memory and trauma during one's battle to survive. During that process, much is lost, and much is also being told that we cannot overlook.[20]

When reflecting on post–socialist Warsaw, Mark Dorrian questioned the Resilient City in a way that strongly resonates with our approach.

He argues:

While trauma may not change the object as such, knowledge of the trauma is often enough to alter it . . . It is the very possibility of an object to embody multiple stages and conditions of interpretation that makes it exciting as a design tool. Rather than simply looking at physical resilience, then the inquiry is also directed to how alterable an object is while maintaining the qualities that define it. It is in these qualities that we may find resilience.[21]

Like Dorrian, we value the importance of reading the existing void space with its leftovers and artifacts as key witnesses of passing time. These historically layered objects cannot be wiped out. Instead, they are overlaid with interventions consciously placed at the outer skin to draw attention to the inner core and inject life into the voids that are currently being utilized. These same void spaces, with their remains and traces, narrate the city and accumulate an archive of scenarios that have happened and could

19. "Resilience," Oxford Living Dictionaries, accessed January 13, 2017.

20. Mark Dorrian, "Introduction," in *Pamphlet Architecture 32: Resilience*, eds. James Craig and Mark Ozga-Lawn (Princeton, NJ: Princeton Architectural Press, 2012), 10.

21. Dorrian, *Pamphlet Architecture*, 10.

potentially happen. This process of narration and accumulation has been facilitated through the design of the "parasitic" Learning Room.

The interventions, with their different typologies and design approaches, lay bare the subjects of aesthetics, dwelling, and intimacy. The Learning Room, for example, is not a space for "feather pillows and throws." Instead, it is a space for production; a space that disrupts commercial complacency and shakes up any conventional association with home.

The room, in its mobility and ephemeral characteristics, tries to question and respond to an exposed threshold between private and public. It offers collective experimentation and camouflaging between the ruins and adds a temporary invisible and subversive layer to the city, while empowering families. The mobile Learning Room is seen as an alternative to the centralized system of power; a lab in a constant process of production and change, dressed up differently depending on needs and the availability of materials. Power is distributed horizontally, with less vulnerability to "state" control.

SPECULATING ABOUT THE SUBVER-CITY: EXPLORING GAZA FROM THE "OUTSIDE"

Striving to create a closer link between our practice, research, and academic activities, the following work by our postgraduate design studio (DS22) offers a complementary perspective on *Absurd–City, Subver–City*, while combining the act of practice with speculation and reality with dream. The work is an essential part of the accumulation of matrixes

of possibilities mentioned earlier that can be later put together for greater effect, while on the other hand they help to break the constraints and isolation of thought and push the boundaries further for Palestinians.

THE RIGHT TO THE CITY

Gaza is one of the sites where the play between the real and the speculative has manifested itself through design projects. With our aim of broadening the matrix of spatial possibilities, a new dialogue and relationship emerges between mapping, testing, and making other different moments of possibility on the ground. All seek to create cumulative conditions born from everyday practices, leading to spatial possibility. By zooming in and zooming out in such ways, a space is left to imagine, question, and break boundaries, whether in physical space or in the space of the imagination.

Notwithstanding the sensitive issue of ethics that is present in live and speculative projects and when working in different contexts, one needs to be aware of the temptation to impose one's personal agenda on a place. Therefore, no idea is sustainable without living up to the community's aspirations, respecting and engaging with their cultural practices and needs. However, these aspirations and needs cannot be seen in isolation from the sociopolitical conditions of Palestine, and indeed the bigger global context of capitalism.

For example, a strategic method used by Israeli authorities to push families out consists of generating a lack of fair access to resources. As summed up by Erik Swyngedouw,

Figure 10: Gazagram: The Finite City.
Andreas Christodoulou, 2016.

The Finite City navigates between the virtual and
the physical to create a space of gathering and
imagination. Gazagram is a proposed fictional app
that uses triggers within "community centers"
to project augmented reality exhibitions. It takes
inspiration from Gazans' passion for smartphones,
social media, and the internet, which allows them
to connect with and learn from a world they cannot
physically access. The project reflects on the
entrapment of the Gazans, many of whom have never
been able to get out even to see the West Bank.

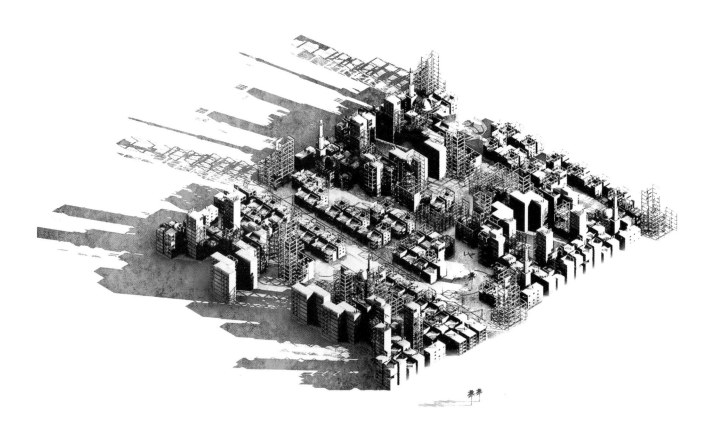

Figure 11: Resurrection from the Rubble.
John Wildsmith, 2017.

Exploring and Renewing the Edge Condition of Gaza.
Blurring boundaries between public and private space
within housing could present a new typology, which seeks
to alter the definition of the streetscape. The proposed
strategic plan takes the form of development corridors
that run all the way down the coast of Gaza, where a
deployable device is built and used wherever necessary.
The device will take the shape of a mobile workshop that
can move through the city, latching on to the existing
fabric to extend the livable space and services. Starting
from the sea, the device will be built by local fishermen,
growing through the city reforming and revitalizing the
urban fabric as it meanders inland.

Figure 12: Agrarian Arcadia. Dean Robson, 2015.

Agrarian Arcadia is an imagined scenario that subverts the borders around Gaza. It is a polemic against the shifting buffer and no-go zones, which in 2014 covered over 40 percent of the area of the Gaza Strip. In order to subvert the siege, the focus is on empowerment via self-sustainability, with special attention placed on the security of food and water resources.

   By reclaiming the agricultural lands that are within these high-risk zones, the short-term reliance on the border is eased while an epic strategy is proposed. The project's ambition is therefore to imagine a new collective socialist structure that contrasts current constraints. These mechanical fields become a palimpsest for the polemic, reflecting the tenacity of Palestinian people.

a fair distribution of resources would be crucial to protecting the community's homes and above all their right to the city: "The question of urban sustainability is not just about achieving sound, ecological and environmental conditions, but first and foremost about social struggle for access and control to the city itself."[22] Within such a context of political repression and extreme poverty in occupied Palestine, equitable and inclusive modes of spatial production require a responsive architecture. Sustainability in this context should be seen more as a means to empower the marginalized, rather than to create dependency.

The design interventions, therefore might not hold the answer to the Palestinian, or indeed the global environmental and economic crisis and its consequent social effects; however, it does suggest that there is an urgent need to start with small changes. Hopefully, by incorporating and stressing the significance of the everyday practices with all their details, we can challenge and move away from the generic, single-minded, market-driven capitalist economy, offering an alternative collective system that can give equal access to resources and a right to the city, while also maintaining the resilient social structure of the community.

22. Erik Swyngedouw, *Social Power and the Urbanization of Water: Flows of Power* (Oxford: Oxford University Press, 2004).

WORKS CITED

"Adaptive Reuse: Women's centre and playground." Lafarge Holcim Foundation, June 29, 2015,

Calvino, Italo. *Invisible Cities*. New York: Harcourt Brace Jovanovich, 1972.

Dennis, Martine. "Who is Stopping the Reconstruction of the Gaza Strip?" *Al Jazeera*, July 7, 2016.

Dorrian, Mark. "Introduction." In *Pamphlet Architecture 32: Resilience*, edited by James Craig and Mark Ozga-Lawn. Princeton, NJ: Princeton Architectural Press, 2012.

"Gaza Situation Report 149." United Nations Relief and Works Agency, June 23, 2016.

Golzari, Nasser. "Cultivating Possibilities." In *Reclaiming Space: The 50 Villages Project in Rural Palestine*, edited by Khaldun Bshara and Saud Amiry. Ramallah: Riwaq, 2015.

Golzari, Nasser and Yara Sharif. "Cultivating Spatial Possibilities in Palestine: Searching for Sub/Urban Bridges in Beit Iksa, Jerusalem." In *The Social Re-Production of Architecture: Politics and Action in Contemporary Practice*, edited by Doina Petrescu and Kim Trogal. London: Routledge, 2017.

———. "Reclaiming Space and Identity: Heritage-led Regeneration in Palestine." *The Journal of Architecture* 16, no. 1 (2011): 121–44.

Hammami, Reema. "On the Importance of Thugs: The Moral Economy of a Checkpoint." *MERIP Middle East Report* 34 (2004): 26–34.

———. "Qalandiya: Jerusalem's Tora Bora and the Frontiers of Global Inequity." *Jerusalem Quarterly*, no. 41 (Spring 2010): 29–51.

"Home." Palestine Regeneration Project, accessed February 13, 2019.

Issacharoff, Avi. "'VIP tunnel' smuggling wealthy Gazans into Egypt." *Haaretz*, December 25, 2008.

"Resilience." Oxford Living Dictionaries, accessed January 13, 2017.

Said, Edward. *The Politics of Disposession: The Struggle for Palestinian Self-Determination, 1969–1994*. New York: Vintage Books, 1994.

Sharif, Yara. *Architecture of Resistance: Cultivating Moments of Possibility Within the Palestinian/Israeli Conflict*. London: Routledge, 2017.

Swyngedouw, Erik. *Social Power and the Urbanization of Water: Flows of Power*. Oxford: Oxford University Press, 2004.

Swyngedouw, Erik, Nik Heynen, and Maria Kaika, eds. *In the Nature of Cities: Urban political ecology and the politics of urban metabolism*. London: Routledge, 2006.

Tamari, Salim. *Mountain Against the Sea: Essays on Palestinian Society and Culture*. Berkeley: University of California Press, 2008.

"Tunnel between Egypt and Gaza for VIPs only." *Al-Quds*, December 27, 2008.

PLANNING RUINATION

M. Christine Boyer

We do not live in a kind of void, inside of which we could place individuals and things . . . we live inside a set of relations that delineates sites which are irreducible to one another and absolutely not superimposable to one another.
—Michel Foucault, *Of Other Spaces*[1]

1. Michel Foucault, "Of Other Spaces," *Diacritics* 16, no. 1 (Spring 1986): 22–27, 23.

I THE PRECARIAT

Israel has never had definitive plans for the Gaza Strip's future, except to maintain a perpetually precarious situation for its people, characterized by unforeseeable events and uncertainties.[2] Perhaps it hopes that the Palestinians will simply go away. Without a planning framework, there has been little to direct foreign humanitarian aid toward any but short-term projects. There are no land-use plans to guide the physical development of Gaza's cities; most of the housing in refugee camps is of the site-and-service variety: constructions are informal with inadequate infrastructure and services.

How can planners contribute to the improvement of the Gaza Strip without accurate census data (a true count of the Palestinian population), adequate planning expertise and personnel, and consistent land use regulations? A land survey was frozen in 2006, meaning that 70 percent of privately held land is not registered, 30 percent is not even mapped, while only 10 percent of all land transactions are recorded. In this informal system, how can Gaza be expected to allocate the necessary infrastructure, settle property disputes, guarantee a flow of money and materials, and secure the welfare of its population?

In Israel, there are three levels of land-use planning: district outline plans for urban development; local outline plans for the internal structure of settlements, with tools for planning and the approval of plans; and national level plans to oversee the process of district and local planning. However, none of this pertains to the Gaza Strip. Israel is well aware

of the lack of proper planning for its occupied territories.[3] But one of the ways in which Israel controls the West Bank and the Gaza Strip is precisely through unnoticed lack of land-use planning.[4]

In Gaza an ever-enlarging stream of threats—military, economic, climate, ecological, social, political, hygienic, medical, and nutritional—all blur into one another. To exercise control over a population and eliminate these hazards, knowledge should be rationalized—concepts delineated, objects and borders described, and procedures specified. This demands political rationality: governmental intervention that deploys such knowledge and control should be enfolded in rational policies, institutions, laws, and regulations.[5] Such a necessary background, ensuring a rational planning process for the betterment of people and land in the Gaza Strip, does not exist. How, we might ask, did this inverted situation of planned ruination and insecurity come about?

WHO OWNS THE LAND?

The usual story about the Gaza Strip is about impoverishment, suffocation, and constant siege by Israel. Yet, Gaza isn't exactly what it seems. Do you want a Mercedes Benz, guns, cement, Belgian chocolate, or a double-door fridge that dispenses ice cubes? These can all be obtained via tunnels dug underneath the southern border between Gaza and the Egyptian Sinai. Even Kentucky Fried Chicken (KFC) has door-to-door service, although the route is rather circuitous. First, place an order by making an international phone call, then make a payment by wire transfer, hire an Egyptian taxi

2. Juan Cole, "Creepy Israeli Planning for Palestinian Food Insecurity in Gaza Revealed," *Informed Comment*, October 18, 2012; Nigel Parsons and Mark Salter, "Israeli Biopolitics: Closure, Territorialisation and Governmentality in the Occupied Palestinian Territories," *Geopolitics* 13 (2008): 714.

3. Nurit Alfasi, "Doomed to Informality: Familial Versus Modern Planning in Arab Towns in Israel," *Planning Theory & Practice* 15, no. 2 (2014).

4. Rami S. Abdulhadi, "Land Use Planning in the Occupied Palestinian Territories," *Institute for Palestine Studies* 19 (2006).

5. Thomas Lemke, "The Birth of Bio-politics: Michel Foucault's lecture at the Collège de France on Neoliberal Governmentality," *Economy and Society* 30, no. 2 (May 2001): 190–207.

driver to pick up the order in the Sinai and transfer it to couriers, who deliver it through a half-mile tunnel to Gaza. Four hours later, a bucket of KFC arrives.[6]

Israel claims that the primary purpose of all tunnels in Gaza is to violate Israeli "sovereignty"; all are acts of "terrorism" against it, even though these tunnels have been a vital lifeline since the siege of 2007, supplying food, medicine, construction materials, computers, livestock, fuel, automobile parts, vehicles, and other essentials. They do supply armaments as well. Hence, under the siege, Gazans have continued to build hundreds of new tunnels, costing millions of dollars, and Israel has kept a watchful eye, perfecting its anti-tunnel efforts and erecting yet another Israeli "barrier" along the Gaza border, at a cost of over $1.1 billion.[7] The Egyptian military has flooded some tunnels to prevent, they say, terrorists from Gaza entering into Egypt; Israel, seeking ever-greater security, has stuffed others with unknown substances.

Nevertheless, tunnels continue to be built. Thousands of Gazans are employed in construction and smuggling, making the so-called "owners" of these tunnels rich. Hamas has benefited by exacting taxes and customs duties, issuing licenses, obtaining approximately a quarter of its budget from such "normal" regulatory activities.[8] In the end, the risky and dangerous business of tunnel building sustains a thriving informal economy that has replaced Gaza's formal economy almost entirely, disintegrated by years of Israeli imposed blockage, bombing, and invasion. The agricultural sector suffers from reduced access to arable land, the rising costs of agricultural inputs, and restrictions on exports, and the manufacturing sector has deteriorated as well. Thus, the tunnel entrepreneurs have become the new elite of Gaza— buying up land, building new homes, and providing new commercial services. Black market cement has become the coin of the realm. At first, traditional businessmen shunned these black marketeers, but eventually, they too joined the illicit traffickers.[9] Now, the flourishing tunnel industry keeps Gaza afloat.

In 1985, there were a dozen Gazan "big families": farmers, large landowners, and merchants. Some of these descended from the large landowning class created during the Ottoman period, including the Khayal, Abu Ramadan, Abu Khadra, Shawwa, Alami, Sourani, Husayni, and Rayyis families.[10] Others, such as the Abu Salims, apparently built their large estates with money earned from smuggling hashish during the British Mandate. Still others, such as soft drink kings Yazji and Murtaja, got rich during the relative calm of "free trade" smuggling during the late 1950s. Although these big families sold part of their holdings to Zionists before 1948, and then lost even more with the influx of refugees, by the mid-1980s, they still controlled the main industry in Gaza: agriculture. They owned and operated large citrus-export packing plants, obliging all small citrus growers to sell their products to them.

At the beginning of the Second Intifada in 2000 however, Israel began to raze citrus and olive farms across the Gaza Strip. Irrigation

6. Harriet Sherwood, "The KFC Smugglers of Gaza," *The Guardian*, May 19, 2013.

7. Daphna Their, "Starving Gaza One Tunnel at a Time," *Socialist Worker*, January 22, 2018.

8. Ibid.

9. Harriet Sherwood, "Gaza Blockade is a Blessing for the Black Economy—and for Hamas," *The Guardian*, June 5, 2010; Doron Peskin, "Hamas Got Rich as Gaza was Plunged into Poverty," *Net News*, July 15, 2014.

10. Joan Mandell, "Gaza: Israel's Soweto," *MERIP* no. 136/137 (Oct.–Dec 1985).

water was expensive, and constant military incursions forced families to leave fruit rotting on their trees, while border closures curtailed agricultural exports even further. Eventually, the flourishing citrus business declined, and with it the prestige and wealth of these large families.

Yet, amid the miseries of Gaza, a wafer-thin middle class exists. Members of the new black-market elite, numbering around six hundred, cater to their needs and whims by establishing a handful of new luxury-car dealerships, boutiques selling designer clothes, hip restaurants, rooftop cafes, and a few seaside hotels and bungalows.[11] This precarious, endangered middle class numbers at least a hundred thousand people, supporting such extraordinary enterprises as the high-end Capital Mall, which opened in February 2017.[12] This mall stands in stark contrast to the poverty of most Palestinians, and to the barrage of media stories reporting there is no money in Gaza.

A large area of urban land is owned by very few people, some living outside of Gaza, but there are few specifics of who these landowners are and whether the families still control their lands.[13] There has been a failure by the media and academics to ask fundamental questions about property ownership and its relation to land-use planning. The overwhelming issue in Gaza, however, is not about a new black market elite, nor the diminishing middle class and their preference for gaudy malls and single family housing, but the fact that two in three Palestinians in Gaza is a refugee or descendent of one, to whom Israel has denied any "right of return" to the lands from which they were expelled in 1948.[14]

On March 30, 2018, the annual commemoration of "Land Day," thousands of Palestinians congregated at the border crossings with Israel, calling their gathering the "Great March of Return." Once again, Israel labeled these demonstrators—grandchildren of the refugees of 1948—"infiltrators." "Land Day," with its evocation of dispossession, remains an annual reminder to Palestinians of their right to their expropriated lands. But the "return" that the refugees are invoking is more than physical return to lost homes and villages: "It is a cry for justice, a call for recognition of dignity and humanity amidst continuous negation of the most basic rights endured through long years of exile and inaction of the international community."[15]

The Great March of Return 2018 was in part a response to President Trump's announcement, as part of the undisclosed "deal of the century" in December of 2017, that "Jerusalem is Israel's capital." A few weeks later the US would slash funding for the United Nations Relief and Works Agency's (UNRWA) aid for Palestine refugees in the Middle East by more than 50 percent. Many families in Gaza depend on UNRWA for basic support. The protest was also propelled by the precarious situation in the Strip—especially for young people who have little access to basic needs such as housing and employment.

Since 1993, Israel has imposed closure on Gaza, restricting the movement of goods, labor, and workers between Gaza and the West Bank and between them and Israel.[16] The inevitable result has

11. William Booth, "Gaza Strip's Middle Class Enjoys Spin Classes, Fine Dining, Private Beaches," *The Washington Post*, August 23, 2015.

12. "Gazans Excited Over Territory's New Indoor Mall," *The Times of Israel*, January 23, 2017.

13. O.S. Asfour, "The Role of Land Planning Policies in Supporting Housing Affordability: The Case of Gaza Strip," *Land Use Policy* 62 (March 2017).

14. Houssem Ben Lazreg and Tesbih Habbal, "Palestinian Land Day: A universal reminder of what was stolen," *The Conversation*, April 19, 2018.

15. Frances Albanese, "Ending Seventy Years of Exile for Palestinian Refugees," *Mondoweiss*, May 10, 2018.

16. Julie Peteet, *Space and Mobility in Palestine* (Indianapolis: Indiana Press, 2017).

been economic ruination, bringing Gaza to the brink of collapse without pushing it over the edge. Fear of further impoverishment propelled activists to march toward the "fence," the complex system of earth berms, surveillance towers, barbed wire, and a one-kilometer long buffer zone erected by Israel to ensure the closure of the Strip.[17]

THE MILITARY ENCLOSURE OF THE GAZA STRIP

> "We're trapped *'min al-silik ila al-silik'* (from the fence to the fence)."
> —A common saying used by Palestinians in Gaza to refer to the Strip[18]

Today, the population of the Gaza Strip has reached two million people: 71 percent are under thirty years of age, and 70 percent are refugees. The unemployment rate is roughly 50 percent, rising to 65 percent among young people. With an estimated annual population growth rate of 2.9 percent, this makes Gaza—an area of 365 square kilometers—extremely overcrowded. Yet, there is little opportunity to build new housing and facilities to accommodate this growth. More than half the population is food insecure, and more than 80 percent depend on international aid for survival. Electricity is limited to four hours per day; clean water is contaminated with sewage. Egypt's border at Rafah is closed most of the time, leaving only the crossing at Erez, allowing a restricted number of pedestrian crossings. The Gaza Strip is an enclosed enclave on the brink of a humanitarian collapse. The UN predicts that under current conditions, the Gaza Strip will be unsustainable by 2020.[19]

THE TWELVE WARS OF GAZA

Since 1948, Israel has waged twelve wars against Gaza—invading when considered essential, controlling from afar when necessary. It began to build settlements in Gaza in 1967 as a direct means of integrating the Strip into Israel's territory, but dismantled them in 2005, when this operation was deemed unsuccessful and too costly. In 1994, Israel gave Gaza the right of self-governance through the Palestinian Authority, but after Hamas came to power in 2006, Israel was provided with a useful excuse for tightening its enclosure of Gaza.

Can history teach us how this military enclosure of the Gaza Strip came about? How were the boundaries of the enclave established? How were the lines drawn and redrawn? The southern border between Gaza and Egypt was recognized as an international border in 1906, a line drawn between the Ottoman and British Empires.[20] The Israeli–Egyptian Armistice Agreement of November 1949 established Gaza's northern and eastern borders, which were determined by the cease-fire positions of the Egyptian and Israeli armed forces at the end of battle. This temporary border was called a "separation line," and sides agreed it was not an international border. However, Israel unilaterally declared its border with Gaza to be an international border. Until recently, no one in Gaza referred to the armistice line as the "border," but instead as the "wire" or "the fence."[21]

A year before the British withdrew from Mandatory Palestine in 1948, the nascent United Nations was

17. Jehad Abusalim, "The Great March of Return: An Organizer's Perspective," *Journal of Palestine Studies* 47, no. 4 (Summer 2018).

18. Jehad Abusalim, "How Gaza came to be trapped from 'fence to fence,'" *Mondoweiss*, April 10, 2018, excerpted Helga Tawil–Souri and Dina Matar (eds.) *Gaza as Metaphor* (London: Hurst and Company, 2016).

19. Jehad Arafat, Sarah Adamczyk, and Martin Clutterbuck, "Unsettled Land: The Role of Humanitarian Organizations in Fostering Transparency and Accountability in Gaza Strip Land Administration" (paper presentation, Annual World Bank Conference on Land and Poverty: Integrating Land Governance into the Post-2015 Agenda, Washington, DC, March 24–27, 2014), 2; see also Diaa Hadid, "Gaza: U.N. Issues Warning about Gaza Condition," *New York Times*, September 2, 2015.

20. Ibid.

21. Abusalim, "Gaza, From Fence to Fence."

tasked with dividing Palestine into a Jewish and an Arab state, with a federal structure or an economic union. Before this was done, however, Jewish settlers in Palestine declared the independent state of Israel, claiming not only territory that had been assigned to the Jewish state, but that was assigned to the Arab state as well. The latter was land that had been "cleansed" of Arab residents during the spring of 1948. Called "Plan Dalet," the cleansing lasted six weeks, creating approximately 750,000 Palestinian refugees, which led to the first Arab–Israeli war. The war ended in an armistice agreement in 1949, leaving Israel in control of approximately 78 percent of pre–1948 Palestine. The remaining land consisted of two small, non-independent Palestinian entities—a "truncated Palestine"—the Gaza Strip and the West Bank, under Egyptian and Jordanian control respectively.[22]

By the end of the 1948–49 War, called the "war of independence" by the Israelis, and "the catastrophe" (*the Nakba*) by the Palestinians, some seven to eight hundred thousand Arabs fled or were expelled by military force, and over 420 Palestinian villages were demolished. Approximately three hundred thousand refugees sought safety in Gaza, which at that time had a population of about eighty thousand. Palestine suddenly disappeared as a country, a land, and even a name on the map. Arab Palestinians found their homes occupied by strangers, and themselves refugees in another's land. They now resided in eastern Palestine, renamed the "West Bank," with Jordanian citizenship, or were exiled to refugee camps in the Gaza Strip and placed under Egyptian

military rule. A Palestinian Arab was now called an "Israeli Arab," and in the West Bank and the Gaza Strip, they were called an Arab resident of the administered territories of "Judea, Samaria, and Gaza." Israelis never used the name "Palestine."[23]

The many refugee camps in Gaza, the West Bank, Jordan, Lebanon, and Syria are organized and run by the UNRWA. The debate over the 1948 "peaceful expulsion" of Palestinians—otherwise referred to as "the transfer option"—still haunts discussions about Palestinian–Israeli geopolitics.[24] The Palestinians' legal "right of return" to their homeland has been continuously denied since 1948, even though UN Mediator Count Folke Bernadotte stated in the same year: "It would be an offence against the principles of elemental justice if these innocent victims of the conflict were denied the right to return to their homes, while Jewish immigrants flow into Palestine."[25] UNRWA refers to Gaza and the West Bank as "Occupied Palestinian Territories," not as "Judea and Samaria," the Israeli terms.[26]

But what housing options existed in Gaza for the refugees? Some rented places; others found shelter in barracks, schools, or mosques; while others squatted on beaches, in orchards, and on pavements. Most longed to return to their homes and the lands they had left behind.[27] Some began to return, to water their gardens, feed their flocks, and bring back a few belongings in anticipation of a final return. The Israelis laid mines at water sources and crossroads, killing some 2,700–5,000 people trying to cross the imaginary line back to their homes. They called those refugees "infiltrators," and

22. Jaafar Alloul, "Signs of Visual Resistance in Palestine: Unsettling the Settler–Colonial Matrix," *Middle East Critique* 25, no. 1 (2016).

23. Issam Nassar, "Remapping Palestine and the Palestinians: Decolonizing and Research," *Comparative Studies of South Asia, Africa, and the Middle East* 23, no. 1 (2003).

24. Ibid, 151.

25. UN General Assembly, Progress Report of the United Nations Mediator on Palestine Submitted to the Secretary-General For Transmission to the Members of the United Nations, Doc. Al 648, September 16, 1948.

26. Alloul, "Signs of Visual Resistance."

27. Jean Pierre Filiu, *Gaza: A History* (Oxford: Oxford Univeristy Press, 2014), 71.

suggested the creation of a "buffer zone" to deter them from crossing the border.

A secret agreement established such a security zone, shrinking the Strip by two to three kilometers. Over time, Israel slowly enlarged this buffer zone, reducing the Strip by a further 20 percent.[28] As more and more refugees sought to return to their lands, a military order issued in 1953 stated clearly what would happen to them:

> The battle against infiltration in the border areas at all times of day and night will be carried out mainly by opening fire, without giving warning, on any individual or group that cannot be identified from afar by our troops as Israeli citizens and who are, at the moment they are spotted, [infiltrating] into Israeli territory.[29]

Meanwhile due to the inundation of refugees, many inhabitants of Gaza City, Khan Younis, and Rafah lost their surrounding lands (and thus agriculture) and the markets on which they depended. The Gaza district comprised 1 percent of Mandatory Palestine, but was now home to more than one quarter of Palestine's Arab population—"an involuntary Noah's Ark."[30]

Beginning in 1950, UNRWA opened eight refugee camps in Gaza, providing tents and eventually building more permanent structures. The land, however, remained the property of the United Nations, and Gazans were aware that the door had slammed shut on their right of return. Outraged by their circumstances, small groups of Palestinian resisters,

known as the fedayeen, began to cross the imaginary line to attack the occupiers of their homeland. Israelis tried to put a stop to this resistance by repeatedly attacking Gaza. In August 1953, Israel assaulted the Bureij refugee camp; in August 1955, it exploded Khan Younis's police station and attacked a Gazan railway station. Strikes by Israelis continued, as did attacks by the fedayeen.

Another attempt to root out the fedayeen took place during the Suez Campaign in October and November 1956, when Israel invaded and occupied the Gaza Strip. Large-scale raids, intrusions into private homes, and prolonged curfews were normal practice for the invaders, but the wholesale slaughters that took place in Khan Younis and Rafah were the matches that unified the fires of Gazan resistance.[31] On March 7, 1957, the Israelis withdrew from the Gaza Strip, and control returned to the Egyptians. Some normality was restored. The port of Gaza became a "free port," small Egyptian businessmen began to construct hotels along the seafront, congestion was eased in Gaza City with the new thoroughfare of Al-Wahda Street, and exports of Gaza's citrus crop to Eastern Bloc countries brought wealth to a few large-scale landowners.[32] However, the refugee camps remained, and bitterness festered.

War struck Gaza once again in June 1967, when Israel occupied the Strip, placing its 1.8 million people under direct military rule and setting up a new blockade. In hopes of removing the irritants, Israel offered financial incentives to all refugees, easing their exits to Europe or Latin America. Only a minority of Palestinians took advantage of this.

28. Salman Abu Sitta, "Gaza Strip: Lessons of History," in Tawil-Souri and Matar (eds.), *Gaza as Metaphor.*

29. Tareq Baconi, "What the Gaza Protests Portend," *New York Review of Books*, April 15, 2018.

30. Filiu, *Gaza*, 71, 72.

31. Ibid., 100, 105.

32. Ibid., 119.

Giving an extra push, Israel destroyed refugee camps.[33]

The enclosure of Gaza, as an entity separate from the West Bank, has been implemented over several decades. Until the First Intifada (1987–1991), Palestinians in Gaza could move in and out of the Strip freely. Over half of Gaza's workforce was employed in Israel as construction workers, waiters, busboys, drivers, factory hands, and farm workers. Yet, Israel kept a sharp eye on all movement and was quick to punish and suppress those it found suspicious. The Intifada began in the Jabalia camp on the outskirts of Gaza City.[34] In 1991, the "General Exit Permit" was canceled. Restrictions on the flow of people and goods caused the economy to deteriorate. After the Oslo agreement was signed in 1994, the new Palestinian Authority took over the administration of the Gaza Strip, even though Israel imposed a "full closure," restricting all attempts at movement without a hard-to-acquire permit to travel to or work inside Israel. Between 1994 and 1996, in order to improve its "security," Israel began to build an electric fence, the "Israeli–Gaza Strip barrier." When the Second Intifada erupted (2000), the barrier was largely destroyed, but Israel rebuilt it between December 2000 and June 2001. Another fortified barrier was erected on the Gaza Strip–Sinai border in 2004.

This second enclosure turned Gaza into an isolated strip, with two main, heavily militarized, border crossings: the northern Erez crossing into Israel, and the southern Rafah crossing into Egypt.[35] The Second Intifada marked the beginning of rocket attacks on Israeli border

communities, and the Israeli army responded: large areas of Rafah were flattened by Caterpillar D9 armored bulldozers in 2001. Over half of the Palestinian homes demolished by the army between 2000 and 2004 were inside the Gaza Strip.[36] The Palestinian Centre for Human Rights in Gaza has documented the deliberate destruction by the Israeli army of 20 percent of the agricultural land in the Gaza Strip: uprooting of trees, bulldozing of crops, demolition of greenhouses.[37] Still, the resistance held strong.

Another attempt at controlling Gaza placed Jewish settlements *within* it. There have long been Jewish settlements in Gaza, going back to biblical times, but Arab forces destroyed these communities in 1948. After its decisive military victory in 1967, however, Israel began to settle twenty-one communities in the Strip. While these consisted of a mere 8,500 Israeli settlers, they nevertheless grabbed at least 20–25 percent of the land—arable land with the best water sources. The settlements included roads for the exclusive use of settlers, military outposts, security zones, and checkpoints for their protection.[38]

Then, in February 2005, Israel decided to "disengage" from the Gaza Strip, dismantling all of its settlements, evacuating its settlers, and withdrawing its military: it had become too expensive to provide for their security. In addition, Israel proclaimed that it was no longer responsible for the safety and well-being of the population of Gaza and left Gaza City and other urbanized areas to be administered and policed by the new Palestinian Authority. But the disengagement plan continued to give Israel complete control over the

33. Sitta, "Gaza Strip."

34. Saree Makdisi, *Palestine Inside Out: An Everyday Occupation* (New York and London: W. W. Norton & Company, 2010), 86–87.

35. "A Costly Divide/February 15: Economic Repercussions of Separating Gaza and the West Bank" (Gaza and the West Bank position paper, GISHA—Legal Center for Freedom and Movement, February 26, 2015), 1–25, 5.

36. Makdisi, *Palestine Inside Out*, 111.

37. Ibid., 112–13.

38. Donald Macintyre, *Gaza Preparing for Dawn* (London: One World Publications, 2017), 53.

Gaza Strip's airspace and territorial waters, controls that were set up in 1967. It left Gaza with six land-border crossings. One at its southern border with Egypt (Rafah). And five others: Sufa for humanitarian aid and construction materials; Kerem Shadom for humanitarian aid (now mostly closed); Nahal Oz for oil imports; and two major exits for people, Erez and Karni.[39] These crossings are the umbilical cord that keep Gazans in a state of economic dependence. All legal trade has to be channeled via Israel, which monitors and controls the openings and closings of these crossings, trying to squeeze Gazans into a precarious existence.

Meanwhile, as Hamas continued to fire rockets and mortar bombs into Israeli towns and border settlements, Israel declared the Gaza Strip to be a "hostile entity" and imposed still tighter controls. A leaked planning document showed the idea was "to put the Palestinians on a diet but not to make them die of hunger."[40] Their "minimum basket" would be just sufficient enough to keep them from starvation.[41] About 10 percent of Gaza's children under five experience stunted growth caused by malnutrition.[42] In January 2008, Prime Minster Ehud Olmert declared: "We won't allow for a humanitarian crisis, but have no intention of making their lives easier. And the harder their lives, excluding humanitarian damage, we will not allow them to lead a pleasant life."[43]

Israel imposed a comprehensive blockade, hoping that under such pressure, Gazan civilians would halt their support for Hamas. The blockade meant that: imports of industrial, agricultural, and construction materials were severely curtailed; all exports were forbidden; the amount of fuel for power and cooking was controlled; the crossings at Karni and Rafah were closed; Palestinian movement was banned at the crossing at Erez except for a few "humanitarian cases"; fishing areas and accessible farming land were reduced; and cash deposits to banks in Gaza restricted.[44]

Israeli airstrikes and ground attacks in March 2008 led to Palestinian deaths and extensive damage to the Jabalia refugee camp. In December 2008, Israeli aircraft struck designated sites believed to be weapons depots: police stations, schools, hospitals, UN warehouses, mosques, and various government buildings. Israel warned civilians living near such targets to leave before the attacks, while Hamas asked civilians to act as human shields protecting its facilities as a "necessary evil."[45] In January 2009, Israel began a ground invasion—a twenty-two-day war called "Operation Cast Lead."

When Israel unilaterally declared a ceasefire, it had damaged or destroyed tens of thousands of homes, fifteen of Gaza's twenty-seven hospitals, forty-three of its 110 primary health care facilities, eight hundred water wells, 186 greenhouses, and nearly all of the ten thousand family farms. The damage left fifty thousand homeless, four hundred to five hundred thousand without water, and one million without electricity, and the entirety of the Gaza Strip with an acute shortage of food and medical supplies. After the war, Egypt and Israel continued the blockade. Israel called it "sanctions," while a Gazan consultant for UNRWA

39. Avi Bell and Dov Shefi, "The Mythical Post-2005 Israeli Occupation of the Gaza Strip," *Israeli Affairs* 16, no. 2 (2010): 269; Liberall, "Gaza Strip History"; Makdisi, *Palestine Inside Out*, 158.

40. Dov Weisglass. Quoted by Khalid Manzoor Butt and Anam Abid Butt, "Blockade on Gaza Strip: A Living Hell on Earth," *Journal of Political Studies* 23, no. 1 (2016): 160.

41. Trude Strand, "Tightening the Noose: The Institutionalized Impoverishment of Gaza, 2005–2010," *Journal of Palestine Studies* 43, no. 2 (Winter 2014).

42. Cole, "Creepy Israeli Planning."

43. Ehud Olmert, 2008, quoted in Strand, "Tightening the Noose," 6.

44. Butt and Butt, "Blockade on Gaza Strip," 161.

45. Mikko Joronen, "'Death comes knocking on the roof': Thanatopolitics of Ethical Killing During Operation Protective Edge in Gaza," *Antipode* 48, no. 2 (2016): 341.

claimed it was "an action outside of international law."[46]

In addition, the Israeli imposition of an enlarged buffer zone, known as the "Access Restricted Area" (ARA), its continual military engagement, and its limitation of the import of construction material considered to have "dual-use" purposes, deepened the housing and land crisis. The fifteen hundred meter–wide ARA occupies nearly 17 percent of the Gaza Strip's territory and 35 percent of its agricultural lands. In ARA areas, the Israeli Defense Force (IDF) has leveled and cleared almost all structures to a depth of three hundred meters into Gaza, and 70 percent of structures located between three to six hundred meters in.[47] The buffer zone can reach as deep as two kilometers, making the both uncertain and deadly, with its deployment of sensors, infrared cameras, drones, radar stations, and remote-controlled machine guns. It has imposed an aggressive open-fire rule on anyone caught in these zones. These no-go zones include some of the most fertile land in Gaza.[48]

In response to international pressure, some of these restrictions were loosened in 2010: the Rafah crossing was partially opened, mainly for people, not for aid; the building permit system was somewhat "streamlined;" a few imports were allowed; and commercial crossings were expanded. In addition, the gradual approval of some construction projects occurred, if they were funded by approved international agencies. All items listed as having dual civil-military use remained restricted, severely inhibiting the reconstruction

of destroyed homes and the construction of new units to house the rapidly expanding population. In addition, damaged infrastructure that would allow access to potable water was not repaired.[49]

Another war ensued: the eight-day "Operation Pillar of Defense" in November 2012 attacked fifteen hundred targets, including arms-smuggling tunnels, underground rocket launchers, and weapons storage facilities. A truce was established, but the Israeli blockade remained in force. Gaza continued to suffer from an energy crisis, limited medical supplies and equipment, reduced access to potable water, a curtailment of building material imports, and increasing poverty and unemployment.[50]

Less than two years later, Israel staged its most extensive attack against Gaza to date. In July 2014, the fifty-one-day "Operation Protective Edge" was unleashed with heavy bombing and deployment of the "Iron Dome" air-defense system, which intercepted most of the rockets that Hamas lobbed into Israel. Once again, the IDF pulverized Gaza's infrastructure, severely damaged its businesses and industries, destroyed many of its medical facilities, decimated its lone power station, and bombed at least one-third of its mosques. Above all, Israeli forces leveled eighteen thousand civilian homes, forcing some one hundred thousand Gazans into homelessness or life in yet more overcrowded conditions.[51] The war, according to UNRWA sources, killed at least 2,256 Palestinians, of whom 70 percent were civilians, and seventy-one Israelis, of whom 96 percent were soldiers.

46. Liberall, "Gaza Strip History."

47. Arafat, Adamczyk, and Clutterbuck, "Unsettled Land."

48. Elena N. Hogan, "Field Notes from Jerusalem and Gaza, 2009–2011," *Journal of Palestine Studies* 41, no. 2 (Winter 2012).

49. Butt and Butt, "Blockade on Gaza Strip," 162.

50. Ibid., 163.

51. Joronen, "'Death comes knocking on the roof.'"

Since the imposition of the blockade in 2007 and its subsequent increased restrictions, Gaza has undergone a continuous policy of what Sara Roy has called "de-development": "the deliberate, systematic deconstruction of an indigenous economy by a dominant power."[52] In spite of receiving one of the highest per capita levels of foreign aid over the last several decades, the Gaza Strip continues to experience frequent military assaults and prohibitions imposed by Israel, leaving it in a constant state of ruination. The population of the Gaza Strip serves no purpose for the Israeli government: the entire territory appears to be a "sacrifice zone" in a state of permanent liminality.[53] Israel no longer needs to employ cheap Gazan laborers. The territory's entire population is considered a surplus— composed of neither producers nor workers.[54]

II GAZA'S LAND-USE LAWS

The separate planning process, one for the Israeli settlements and the other for Palestinians, initiated in the late seventies continued under separate administrations, different standards, and with clear efforts [by the Israelis] to use physical planning as a tool in the scramble for control over space. —Meron Benvenisti[55]

Housing, land-use planning, and property rights in the Gaza Strip cannot be divorced from issues of conflict and humanitarian needs— they are inseparably linked, one superimposed on the other. The more the Gaza Strip is ruined by aerial bombardment and ground incursions, the greater the necessity to have well-defined plans to reconstruct, create a formalized real estate market, and develop economic independence. But the Gaza Strip's state of insecurity over land-use regulations actually intensifies the damage that war inflicts.

Land in Gaza is scarce, and its scarcity is exacerbated by the confiscation and enclosure of property for road building, settlements, and security buffer zones. Land use is further complicated by a non-transparent system of land administration and by Gaza's reliance on antiquated Ottoman, British Mandate, and Egyptian-era laws. This framework— governing housing, land, and property—is based on a complicated, non-transparent set of thirty distinct laws, which fail to offer security of land ownership or adequate compensation for land confiscations, whether executed by Israelis or Palestinians.

Ottoman Land Use Laws: The Ottomans introduced two laws that are still in force in the Gaza Strip. The Ottoman Land Code of 1858 classified land into five different categories: private land (*mülk*), state land (*miri*), religious endowment land (*waqf*), uncultivated or empty land without ownership (*mewat*), and land designated for public use (*metruk*), such as roads and infrastructure. The last two categories, *mewat* and *metruk* lands, no longer exist in the Gaza Strip. Approximately 50 percent of the territory is private land (*mülk*); 31 percent is state land (*miri*) and can only be privatized if disposed of by the state. This voids any consideration that long-term occupation or use of state lands centers the right of

52. Cited in Sarah Roy, *The Gaza Strip:The Political Economy ofDe-Development* (Washington, DC: Institute for Palestine Studies, 2015).

53. Smith, Ron. "Isolation Through Humanitarianism: Subaltern Geopolitics of the Siege on Gaza." *Antipode* 48, no. 3 (2016), 4.

54. Ibid.

55. Meron Benvenisti, quoted in Abdulhadi, "Land Use Planning," 51.

ownership. Less than 2 percent of the Strip is *waqf* land or religious endowment. This land cannot be transferred by legal action or acquired by long-term occupation.[56] The subsequent Ottoman Civil Code of 1861 remains the law guiding land and property rights, describing how land can be acquired and determining legitimate claims on each type of land.

These two nineteenth century Ottoman reforms attempted to establish a private land market that guaranteed the right to buy, sell, mortgage, and inherit land. They also encouraged the expansion of cultivated land in order to increase the tax base of the ever-indebted Empire. Nevertheless, the reforms met with limited success: peasant-cultivators preferred their traditional communal land tenure system (*mushaa*) over individual property ownership (*mülk*). The *mushaa* system was based on collective responsibility for plowing, harvesting, grazing, and even paying a village's taxes, on shared, not individual, ownership of land.[57] Over time, however, a new class of large landholders emerged that acquired considerable holdings from indebted peasant farmers or bought up state lands that the Ottomans were glad to sell. By the early twentieth century, 144 large estates possessed 38 percent of all arable land in Palestine.[58]

The British Mandate (1917–1949) made minor adjustments to the existing Ottoman laws. Even though the British advocated surveying and registering all land as an essential ingredient in the development of a burgeoning land market, 70 percent of village lands remained under the *mushaa* system. Yet, land continued

to be transferred to the state from cultivators who had evaded paying taxes and were deeply in debt. In Gaza, the al-Shawwa land holdings were the largest.[59] The Egyptian administration (1949–1967) continued to uphold the Ottoman and British legal systems, but added new laws that eliminated the statute of limitations for the governing authority to reclaim state and *waqf* land, and legitimized the existence and boundaries of Gaza's eight refugee camps. In 1994, the Palestinian Authority retained all land-use laws, until the time it could harmonize the overlapping and differing laws covering Gaza and the West Bank. All possibilities for such unification ceased after Hamas came to power in 2007.[60]

ACTS OF ENCLOSURE

Gary Fields defines "enclosure" as "a practice resulting in the transfer of land from one group of people to another and the establishment of exclusionary spaces on territorial landscapes."[61] With respect to Palestine, he argues that the key instrument in the transfer of land to Israeli control was the creation of state land (*miri*), because once land was transferred to the state, it could then be redistributed to Israeli settlements for security purposes.[62] In the nineteenth century, the Ottoman state owned 87 to 90 percent of all agricultural land (*miri*) in the entire Empire. Today, Jewish settlements and the infrastructure supporting them occupy about 85 percent of former Palestine.[63] Just how was this transfer—or enclosure—achieved?

In the late nineteenth century, two groups sought a homeland in

56. Arafat, Adamczyk, and Clutterbuck, "Unsettled Land."

57. Gary Fields, *Enclosure: Palestinian Landscapes in a Historical Mirror* (Oakland: University of California Press, 2017), 192.

58. Ibid, 184.

59. Today, no members of the al-Shawwa family resides in Gaza. Ibid., 195–96.

60. Arafat, Adamczyk, and Clutterbuck, "Unsettled Land."

61. Fields, *Enclosure*, 5.

62. Ibid., 15.

63. Ibid., 178.

biblical Palestine. Palestinians, a mostly agrarian society that lived on the local lands for centuries, sought self-determination, on their own or through a pan-Arab entity. As peasant-cultivators, they had the right to "use" *miri* (state) lands as long as they paid the levied taxes.[64] Zionists wanted to establish a Jewish homeland in Palestine. Their famous slogan—and false dream—of 1905 was "A Land without People, for a People without Land."[65] They believed Palestine was a neglected, barren territory that the Jews could improve through hard work. In this way, they would earn the right to own it.[66]

The League of Nations assumed responsibility for the former Ottoman Empire after World War I and set out the terms and conditions under which the British would rule over the southern part of Ottoman Syria (1923–1948). The British promised something to both groups, both the local Arabs and the Zionists. The McMahon-Hussein correspondence of 1915 and 1917 supported Arab efforts to achieve independence, while the Balfour Declaration of 1917 acknowledged the need to create a homeland for the Jewish people in Palestine.[67] In addition, the Balfour Declaration secretly made promises to ensure Jewish immigration and land acquisition for settlement in Palestine. Before this, Turkish Sultan Abdel Hamid had rebuffed such an idea, stating that "Palestine is the patrimony of Muslims and I will not sell it for the gold of the world. Let the Jews keep their millions. If the Empire is divided, maybe the Jews will get it for nothing, but only over our dead bodies."[68]

Nevertheless, support for a Zionist homeland in Palestine became official British policy, and while it protected the Palestinian population from resettlement, it said nothing about their rights to the land and to self-determination. They were to be under the authority of the Mandate until the time they "proved" capable of achieving independence.[69] The Balfour Declaration ushered in one hundred years of conflict between Arabs and Jews, even though they had previously coexisted for centuries. It failed to recognize the rights of indigenous Palestinians, merely referring to them as the non-Jewish population. On the other hand, it granted full political and civil rights to the Jewish minority and immigrants.[70]

The British Mandate authorities were preoccupied with establishing a legal basis of land-use controls and uniform standards for their application.[71] They tried to register land in all areas of Palestine and to establish a real estate market with up-to-date information, surveys, and maps, although it was unable to complete this task before 1948.[72] To this end, they established a Land Registration Department (Tabu Department) in 1920, which enacted new laws for the registration of property and real estate transactions. It required written approval, given by the Tabu, for any real estate transactions of registered property, except for the transfer of *miri* (state) lands to *mülk* (private) land.[73] Two years later, it introduced a new land category, public land, or all land held in the public interest under the supervision of the Palestinian state. It allowed the High Commissioner to grant temporary use rights or rent out these lands. This privilege was extended in 1933 to include the right

64. Alloul, "Signs of Visual Resistance."

65. Nassar, "Remapping Palestine," 149.

66. Fields, *Enclosure*, 209–10.

67. Reecia Orzeck, "Normative Geographies and the 1940 Land Transfer Regulations in Palestine," *Transactions of the British Institute of Geographers* 39 (2014): 346–59.

68. Sultan Abdel Hamid, quoted in Salman H. Abu-Sitta, *Atlas of Palestine (1917–1966)* (London: Palestine Land Society, 2010), 2.

69. Orzeck, "Normative geographies."

70. Abu-Sitta, *Atlas of Palestine*, 3.

71. Stanley Waterman, "Pre-Israeli Planning in Palestine: The Example of Acre," *Town Planning Review* 42, no. 1 (January 1971): 85–99.

72. Jehad Arafat et al., *A Guide to Housing, Land and Property Law in the Gaza Strip (October, 2015)* (Oslo: Norwegian Refugee Council [NRC], 2015), 15–16.

73. The Mandate introduced the Law of Land Transactions No. 39 in 1920. Arafat et al., *A Guide to Housing*, 15.

to change the status of *miri* (state) land to *mülk* (private) land.[74] This set an important precedent. A Jewish buyer of land could demand that the Tabu register the transferred *miri* (state) property in "his" name, voiding all previous Arab claims based on communal ownership or rights of use. Israel would subsequently use this law to avoid the appearance of confiscating Arab land, by reallocating it first to *miri* (state) and then to *mülk* (private) land. Hence the gradual enclosure of Palestinian land.

WHO HAS THE LEGAL RIGHT TO OWN THE LAND?

Conflicts over land between Palestinians and Jewish settlers erupted into violence on several occasions, leading to the 1936–39 Great Arab Revolt. A Palestinian urban merchant class demanded a halt to Jewish immigration and a stop to the transfer of land to Zionists. It demanded the British take positive steps toward ceding control of the territory to Palestinians. Instead, in 1939, the British called for the creation of a single state of Palestine within ten years, to be administered by Arabs and Jews in proportion to their numbers. They did place restrictions on Jewish immigration and limited the areas in which Jews could purchase land. They even warned that if the sale of land to Jews continued in certain areas of Palestine, a considerable landless Arab population would soon be the result.[75]

In the first post–1948 years of the new state, the national planning challenge for the Israelis consisted of "'conquering the wilderness' and creating facts on the ground."[76] Establishing new settlements was a

way of reinforcing the borders of the nascent state. As many as 300,000 Palestinians had been forced to become refugees, forbidden to return to their homes, businesses, fields, and flocks, while 78 percent of Mandatory Palestine was transferred to the state of Israel.[77] Palestinians had to prove their legal ownership of property; devoid of such documentation, their lands were simply transferred to the state.

Absentee Property Regulations were passed in 1948, an "absentee" being anyone who had left their homes and land, no matter how temporarily. Refusing to recognize the traditional descriptive manner by which Palestinians designated ownership, Israel retroactively classified all absentee properties as essential for the security or development of the state.[78] Before this land was transferred to the state it was surveyed, subdivided into plots, and made legible as gridded space. For more than fifty years, Israel kept these Arab lands under the "Custodian of Absentee Property," which could transfer these expropriated properties to a "Development Authority" that had the power to allocate the holdings to settlements, which were in the benefit of the public (i.e., Jews only).[79] From 1948 to 1953, Israel built 370 new settlements; 350 of them were on confiscated Palestinian land.[80]

Meanwhile, in 1954, the Egyptian administration requested that all unregistered land in the Gaza Strip be registered with its Property Tax Directorate. The owner of such registered land became the sole owner, but all unregistered land reverted to state land. Even today, registration of land in the Gaza Strip

74. Ibid.

75. Nine months later, the 1940 Land Transfer Regulations were published. Palestine was divided into three zones: Zone A, where the transfer of land to non-Palestinian Arabs was prohibited (63 percent of Palestinian land); Zone B, where the transfer of land from Palestinian Arabs to non-Arabs was allowed only with the approval of the High Commissioner (32 percent of Palestine); and Zone C, where land transfers were not restricted (5 percent of Palestine). The Jews protested this arrangement, claiming it introduced racial discrimination, essentially confining Jews to a ghetto without freedom of movement and settlement within their "National Home." While the British were sensitive to the Arab case, and willing to place restrictions on Jewish possession of Palestinian lands, these regulations would not survive in post-Mandate Palestine. Orzeck, "Normative Geographies."

76. "Introduction to Open Spaces" (position paper, Society for Protection of Nature in Israel), quoted in Alon Tal, "Space Matters: Historic Drivers and Turning Points in Israel's Open Space Protection Policy," *Israeli Studies* 13, no. 1 (2002): 120.

77. Fields, *Enclosure*, 236.

78. Ibid., 240.

79. Palestinian Right to Return Coalition, "Palestinians."

80. Fields, *Enclosure*, 241, 245–56.

is complicated: sometimes part, but not all of a given holding will be registered in order to avoid excessive taxation. In the Gaza Strip, an expanding population has encroached—that is, illegally occupied or appropriated for agricultural use—many designated state lands.[81] In such cases land administrators resort to two types of action: first, where occupation of state land is deemed to be unauthorized, local authorities rely on eviction and resettlement; and second, they simply expropriate land for the construction of roads previously planned but not implemented. In both cases, Gazan residents are stripped of a critical asset—land—and further impoverished.[82]

During the Six-Day War of 1967, Israel appropriated territories to the north, center, and south of its former boundaries, seizing the Gaza Strip and the West Bank. But how was this land, state or private, legally possessed? Israel classified all land in the West Bank and Gaza as located in "disputed territories," not "occupied territories." Since neither Egypt nor Jordan had been the legal sovereign of these lands prior to 1967, the Geneva Conventions—that forbid the annexation of "occupied" lands—did not protect them. In a sleight of hand, these lands became *state* lands, open for Israeli settlement. This, it was argued, was essential for the military security of the Israeli state.[83]

A Colonization Plan: A 1970 Israeli state publication entitled "Judea and Samaria: Guidelines for Regional and Physical Planning" declared "as a central objective 'the development of periphery of Samaria and Judea,

so that it may become integrated with the rest of the country.'"[84] The Allon plan of 1967, finalized in 1970, stipulated a chain of Jewish colonies along the Jordan River, the Rift Valley, and the "Judean" desert, to ensure Israel's "security." It also called for the settler colonization of the Gaza Strip's southern territory. The northern part of the Strip and the densely populated areas of the West Bank were to be part of Jordanian Palestine, ruled from Amman. While it was never approved, the Allon plan nevertheless guided the deployment of settlements in the West Bank and Gaza until 1977. Other plans were put in place, which continued to detail a comprehensive colonization plan of buffer settlements, including road networks, to further isolate Palestinian towns and villages. Part of this colonization plan included amending the planning laws in force in the West Bank and Gaza, with the objective of tightening control over Palestinian development, by centralizing planning at the national level and by widening the planning powers of Israeli authorities. It was "occupation by bureaucracy," embedding all land transactions in an entangled network of legal regulations.

As the occupying power in the West Bank and Gaza during the post–1967 period, Israel placed the issue of land-use planning under the control of the military government, which was in charge of issuing permits for industrial and economic development, as well as for the expansion of Palestinian settlements. For example, "Military Order (M. O.) 393, issued in 1970, authorized the military commander to forbid, halt, or set conditions for construction.

81. Arafat et al., *A Guide to Housing*, 16–17, 29, 33.

82. Arafat, Adamczyk, and Clutterbuck, "Unsettled Land."

83. Fields, *Enclosure*, 287–88.

84. *Judea and Samaria: Guidelines for Regional and Physical Planning* (Jerusalem: Ministry of the Interior, 1970), quoted in Abdulhadi, "Land Use Planning," 47.

Under Military Order 418, issued in March 1971, all planning authority was vested in the Higher Planning Council, which was given extensive powers to suspend any plan or license anywhere within the West Bank [and the Gaza Strip]."[85] The Order included the right to exempt any person—non-Arab that is—from the need to obtain a building permit, thus facilitating the construction of Jewish settlements.

Military Order 783 of March 1979 set up Jewish councils, which were given the right to make land-use plans and build infrastructure, roads, and settlements, even in areas where the Palestinian population outnumbered Israeli settlers.[86] In contrast, Palestinians were faced with multiple difficulties: first of all, to obtain a permit they had to receive approval from many departments (Antiquities, the Custodian of Absentee Property, the Military Governor, the information committee, taxation authorities, internal review offices, etc.); second, the legal basis for granting permits was based on outdated regional plans drawn up during the British Mandate, which no longer met the needs of the Palestinians. Thus, many simply built without permits and thus faced the threat of demolition at a future date.[87] This situation also created a dual system, under which Jews could expand their control over private property, while Arabs were contained within a static geography.[88]

Reconstructing Gaza with a Plan: Palestinians have long recognized that land-use planning is necessary for economic growth and future prosperity. Out of the 540 Palestinian settlements in the West Bank and the Gaza Strip, only about a hundred have any kind of physical plan.

Deprived of a plan, most Palestinian villages—which are actually small cities and refugee camps—are severely overcrowded. With deteriorating physical environments and insufficient infrastructure to manage water, sewage, or electricity, they lack access roads, health facilities, schools, or dignified human habitations. These cities are sprawling, haphazard developments eating up valuable open space; housing—often built without permit, plan, or designed layouts—fills interstitial areas and public spaces. The isolation of the Gaza Strip from the West Bank, and the blockade that stops the flow of goods and people, also curtails socioeconomic recovery.[89]

Under continuous siege, Gaza has suffered endless destruction in the twelve wars waged against it. To summarize: Operation Cast Lead (2008–2009) destroyed 3,481 houses, severely damaged another 2,755, and inflicted at least minor damage on 55,000. Operation Pillar of Defense (2012) destroyed or inflicted major damage on 382 housing units and minor damage on an additional 8,000 units.[90] Operation Protective Edge (2014) damaged or destroyed 26 schools, 24 medical facilities, 75,000 homes, 360 factories, the only power plant in Gaza, and one-third of Gaza's mosques.[91] How is it possible to rebuild the Gaza Strip after so much demolition, if land-use laws are antiquated, complicated, and under military control?

Israel is well aware that much of the housing in the Gaza Strip is overcrowded, unsanitary, and in need of replacement and rehabilitation. They acknowledge the years of military destruction of civilian

85. Abdulhadi, "Land Use Planning," 49.

86. Ibid., 51.

87. Ali Abdelhamid, "Urban Development and Planning in the Occupied Palestinian Territories: Impacts on Urban Form" (paper presentation, The Conference on Nordic and International Urban Morphology: Distinctive and Common Themes, Stockholm, Sweden, September 3–5, 2006).

88. Arafat et al., A Guide to Housing, 17; Amjad Alqasis, "The Ongoing Nakba: The Continuous Forcible Displacement of the Palestinian People," Mondoweiss, May 15, 2013.

89. Musallam F. Abu Helu, "Urban Sprawl in Palestinian Occupied Territories. Causes, Consequences and Future," Environment and Urbanization ASIA 3, no. 1 (2012).

90. Arafat, Adamczyk, and Clutterbuck, "Unsettled Land."

91. Joronen, "'Death comes knocking on the roof," 4.

properties. Yet, in December 1982, Israel, professing its concern with the level of concentration in Gaza's refugee camps, made it a legal offense to sell, buy, rent, mortgage, transfer, add to, or extend existing shelters or to demolish them in order to build new ones. Penalties were imposed on violators and the homes of families with members charged with security violations faced demolitions.[92] Because refugee camps were sites of military resistance, they were often subjected to forced demolition to break up their concentration, besides being placed under tight surveillance, with monitored entries and exits. Obviously, these policies, which Israel sees as deterrent action necessary for its "security," aggravate the housing crisis. Nothing seems to relieve the situation and successive Palestinian Authority governments have not helped, enacting no new land-use regulations in refugee camps. Perhaps this is intentional, since any improvement of the camps would appear to weaken refugees' claims to their right of return.

It is difficult to know how much of this tangled legal framework is relevant to development in the Gaza Strip, because accounts lump together references to planning in the "West Bank and Gaza Strip."[93] Although the Palestinian Land Authority (PLA), established by presidential decree in 2002, is currently responsible for administering land in Gaza, no law has ever specified its powers and authority. Its mandate is to protect and preserve land, property titles, and the property rights of citizens, government, and civic and official institutions by surveying plots and placing them in a land registry. However, due to high registration fees and property taxes, only about 10 percent of all land transactions are recorded. The PLA is also responsible for land demarcation, the resolution of land disputes, and the preservation and proper disposal of public lands. In place of a land market regulated by standardized laws, a robust informal land market was developed instead, trading mostly unregistered properties without proper titles or guaranteed rights. In addition, there is a confusing complex of other actors involved with land, but none of these have precisely demarcated areas of responsibility: the Ministry of Housing and Public Works, the Ministry of Finance, the Income and Property Tax Department, the Ministry of Local Government, and twenty-five local municipalities in the Gaza Strip. All of this simply exacerbates the uncertainties of land-use laws, including the inability to solve property disputes and the failure to protect and preserve property rights through surveying and registration.[94]

In 2005, as Israel withdrew its twenty-or-so settlements from what amounted to 13 percent of the Gaza Strip's land, it demolished the settlements, but designated almost all the cleared land as *miri* (state) land. In this manner, Israel retains control, rather than occupation, of the land, by rendering it impossible for Palestinians to develop it.[956] A second classification concerns the land on which the original eight refugee camps were established in the aftermath of the 1948 war. At least 38 percent of Gaza's population lives in one of these eight camps, whose boundaries have not changed

92. Ahmed Said Dahlan, "Housing Demolition and Refugee Resettlement Schemes in the Gaza Strip," *GeoJournal* 21, no. 4 (1990).

93. Abdulhadi, "Land Use Planning," 49.

94. Arafat, Adamczyk, and Clutterbuck, "Unsettled Land."

95. Ibid.

since 1948.[96] UNRWA is the sole supervising authority in these camps, but was given no jurisdiction over the use and ownership of the land.[97] The rights of refugees are limited solely to the use of the land, not to own it or pass it on as inheritance. The right of use is limited to the lifetime of the user, but over time, UNRWA has stopped tracking. After some seventy years of camp residency, an informal system of inheritance, along with a market for use rights transactions, operates here as well.[98]

Following the withdrawal of Israeli settlements in 2005, Gaza's authorities inherited an inconsistent and overlapping series of land laws, overcrowded refugee camps, long-term illegal squatting on state lands, poor infrastructure, and non-existent urban planning, all exacerbated by continual military conflict. Any reclamation of state lands and expansion of road systems threatens hundreds of families with demolition or eviction from land on which they have resided for decades. At the same time, construction on two main north–south roads and a number of internal connecting roads between local municipalities threatens private property owners with displacement. The implementation procedures for transportation plans originating in previous decades remain unclear, and land administrators tend to take advantage of the land–planning vacuum to arbitrarily confiscate private land without compensation. The potential loss of up to 25 percent of their land forecasts economic disaster for the affected landowners.[99]

The Income and Property Taxes Directorate supervises the 30 percent of the Gaza Strip that has

not been mapped. It cooperates with the PLA to register this land, determine that the ownership is correct, and that taxes owed have been paid. Land registration is a prerequisite for obtaining a (re)building permit and receiving reconstruction assistance. However, different names and classifications are often applied to unregistered land, making it impossible to determine and legally protect ownership or settle land disputes. To repeat, over 70 percent of privately-owned land in the Gaza Strip is not registered. Inhabitants of destroyed or damaged homes on unregistered land are often unable to prove that they have a legal right to their former homes, and they may have lost all documents when their homes were destroyed. They may not know where the proper boundaries of their property are located, since tradition depended on a narrative description. Additionally, because the Israelis restrict the import of equipment for aerial surveys and the use of satellite imagery, the process of mapping and registering land is severely hampered. And, with no physical plans to guide the reconstruction of destroyed neighborhoods that were constructed on unregistered lands, it cannot be guaranteed that a viable community with suitable infrastructure, public spaces, appropriate building standards, and other services will be the result. Nor can Gazan authorities promise the development of a proper land and real estate market with a formalized system of land transactions.[100]

To make things even worse, families whose homes were destroyed or damaged must navigate a

96. Ibid.

97. Arafat et al., *A Guide to Housing*, 11.

98. Ibid., 42.

99. Arafat, Adamczyk, and Clutterbuck, "Unsettled Land."

100. Elisabeth Koek, Jehad Arafat, and Martin Clutterbuck, "Rebuilding from the Rubble: Post-Conflict Land Tenure Challenges and Opportunities in the Gaza Strip" (paper presentation, 2015 World Bank Conference on Land and Poverty, Washington, DC, March 23-27, 2015).

complex process in order to even be considered for reconstruction aid. First, they must undergo a needs assessment evaluation, then they must gather all relevant data on their household: identity card numbers, GPS coordinates of their home, title deeds, registered maps, and other personal information and submit it all to a database. Israel then has forty-eight hours to reject any name on the list. This is how Israel ultimately controls the entire process of reconstruction and the de facto planning of developments: through the imposition of buffer zones, the distribution of building materials, and even the final say in the determination of who can receive aid to rebuild.[101] No wonder the reconstruction of the Gaza Strip moves at a snail's pace, since Gazans have no sovereign control over their own land!

By the end of March 2016, approximately 17 percent, or 3,000 of the 18,000 homes destroyed or severely damaged in 2014 hostilities, had been reconstructed or repaired. An estimated 75,000 people remained displaced. Another 3,700 homes were undergoing reconstruction or repair and promises for funding for the reconstruction of another 5,100 homes had been made. This left a gap for about 5,991 homes,[102] and in August 2016, about 65,000 Palestinians were classified as displaced. It was assumed that many would receive no assistance due to a lack of funding.[103]

Fast forward to 2018. Mohammed Abu Jiab, editor-in-chief of the local *Al- Eqtesadia* newspaper in Gaza, explained in February, "Today—three years into the reconstruction plan—

only 60 percent of buildings have been reconstructed, as Israel does not allow most building materials into the Gaza Strip. This has caused the construction process to break down, harming the Palestinian companies and inflicting major losses of millions of dollars on the economy."[104] The international community of donors believes the reconstruction plan needs to be reviewed, and that Israel must allow all construction materials into Gaza. Evidently, the monitoring programs that check the destination of every bag of cement, plus the bloated salaries of international experts involved in security procedures, have created a UN siege of Gaza and institutionalized the Israeli blockade.

CONCLUSION

The population of the Gaza Strip is projected to reach 2.4 million by 2023, far exceeding the sustainable capacity of the land.[105] Limited water supplies, a heavy application of pesticides and fertilizers, overgrazing, and inappropriate agricultural practices have already led to desertification, which may be irreversible in parts of the Gaza Strip.

The Israelis have been able to manipulate ancient land-use laws to their benefit in certain regions, creating a divided and unequal Arab-Jewish space.[106] The aim has been to displace the indigenous Arabs and to void any "history" not related to a Jewish past.[107]

Focusing exclusively on reconstruction is not the answer to Gaza's continued problems of precarity. The blockade must be removed, the civilian population must be given freedom of movement,

101. BADIL, "Forced Population Transfer: The Case of Palestine Discriminatory Zoning and Planning," (working paper no. 17, BADIL–Resource Center for Palestinian Residency and Refugee Rights, December 2014).

102. OCHA, "Housing, Land and Property Rights Issues Pose Further Challenges to Gaza Reconstruction," *Monthly Humanitarian Bulletin*, OCHA Occupied Palestinian Territory, March–April 2016.

103. The UN Secretary General stated that "[t]he blockade of Gaza, which entered its tenth year in 2016, continued to undermine basic human rights and economic prospects, as well as the availability of essential services, exacerbating poverty and aid dependency." "'Reconstruction in Gaza has stumbled,' acknowledged Adnan Abu Hasna, a spokesperson for UN Relief and Works Agency (UNRWA). Unfortunately, the countries who pledged billions to rebuilding the Gaza Strip have not made good on their promises.' ... In total, international donors pledged $3.5 billion towards rebuilding Gaza at the 2014 Cairo conference, but as of August 2016, just 46 percent of that support had been disbursed." UN Secretary General, August 30, 2016, quoted in "The Gaza Strip: The Humanitarian Impact of the Blockade," OCHA, November 2016.

104. Adnan Abu Amer, "Palestinians call for new reconstruction plan for Gaza," *Al-Monitor*, March 5, 2018.

105. Basheer Abuelaish and Maria Teresa Camacho Olmedo, "Scenario of land use and land cover change in the Gaza Strip using remote sensing and GIS models," *Arab Journal of Geoscience* 9, no. 274 (2016).

106. Rena Zuabi, "Land Use Planning and the Palestinian Minority in Israel: A Comparative Regional Study," *Prospect Journal of International Affairs* (2011).

107. Noam Leshem, "Repopulating the Emptiness: A spatial critique of ruination in Israel/Palestine," *Environment and Planning D: Society and Space* 31, no. 3 (2013): 527.

and planning regulations must be formalized to allow proper development of the land and to institute a land market. The refusal by both Israeli and Gazan authorities to allow land-use planning and property law to become transparent, and instead to accept the application of outdated laws going back to the Ottoman era, allows control over the land of the Gaza Strip to remain a military tactic of the Israel Defense Forces. The politics of land enclosure curtail the Strip's economic and physical development and the well-being of all of its residents. It guarantees instead the planning of ruination.

WORKS CITED

Abdelhamid, Ali. "Urban Development and Planning in the Occupied Palestinian Territories: Impacts on Urban Form." Paper presented at The Conference on Nordic and International Urban Morphology: Distinctive and Common Themes, Stockholm, Sweden, September 3–5, 2006.

Abdulhadi, Rami S. "Land Use Planning in the Occupied Palestinian Territories." *Institute for Palestine Studies* 19 (2006): 46–63.

Abu Amer, Adnan. "Palestinians call for new reconstruction plan for Gaza." *Al-Monitor*, March 5, 2018.

Abuelaish, Basheer, and Maria Teresa Camacho Olmedo. "Scenario of land use and land cover change in the Gaza Strip using remote sensing and GIS models." *Arab Journal of Geoscience* 9, no. 274 (2016): 1–15.

Abu Helu, Musallam F. "Urban Sprawl in Palestinian Occupied Territories. Causes, Consequences and Future." *Environment and Urbanization ASIA* 3, no. 1 (2012): 121–41.

Abu-Sitta, Salman. *Atlas of Palestine (1917-1966).* London: Palestine Land Society, 2010.

———. "Gaza Strip: Lessons of History." In *Gaza as Metaphor*, edited by Helga Tawil-Souri and Dina Matar. London: Hurst and Company, 2016.

Abusalim, Jehad. "How Gaza came to be trapped 'from fence to fence.'" *Mondoweiss*, April 10, 2018.

———. "The Great March of Return: An Organizer's Perspective." *Journal of Palestine Studies* 47, no. 4 (Summer 2018): 90–100.

Albanese, Frances. "Ending Seventy Years of Exile for Palestinian Refugees." *Mondoweiss*, May 10, 2018.

Alfasi, Nurit. "Doomed to Informality: Familial Versus Modern Planning in Arab Towns in Israel." *Planning Theory & Practice* 15, no. 2 (2014): 170-86.

Alloul, Jaafar. "Signs of Visual Resistance in Palestine: Unsettling the Settler-Colonial Matrix." *Middle East Critique* 25, no. 1 (2016): 23–44.

Alqasis, Amjad. "The Ongoing Nakba: The Continuous Forcible Displacement of the Palestinian People." *Mondoweiss*, May 15, 2013.

Arafat, Jehad, Sarah Adamczyk, and Martin Clutterbuck. "Unsettled Land: The Role of Humanitarian Organizations in Fostering Transparency and Accountability in Gaza Strip Land Administration." Paper presented at the Annual World Bank Conference on Land and Poverty: Integrating Land Governance into the Post-2015 Agenda, Washington, DC, March 24-27, 2014.

Arafat, Jehad, Mona Abed Al Aziz, Fatma Al Sharif, and Yaser Al Manama. "A Guide to Housing, Land and Property Law in the Gaza Strip." Oslo: Norwegian Refugee Council, 2015.

Asfour, O.S. "The Role of Land Planning Policies in Supporting Housing Affordability: The Case of Gaza Strip." *Land Use Policy* 62 (March 2017): 40–48.

Baconi, Tareq. "What the Gaza Protests Portend," *New York Review of Books*, April 15, 2018.

BADIL. "Forced Population Transfer: The Case of Palestine Discriminatory Zoning and Planning." Working paper no. 17, BADIL–Resource Center for Palestinian Residency and Refugee Rights, December 2014.

Bell, Avi, and Dov Shefi. "The Mythical Post-2005 Israeli Occupation of the Gaza Strip." *Israeli Affairs* 16, no. 2 (2010): 268–96.

Ben Lazreg, Houssem, and Tesbih Habbal. "Palestinian Land Day: A universal reminder of what was stolen." *The Conversation*, April 19, 2018.

Blumenthal, Max. *The 51 Day War: Ruin and Resistance in Gaza*. New York: Nation Books, 2015.

Booth, William. "Gaza Strip's Middle Class Enjoys Spin Classes, Fine Dining, Private Beaches." *The Washington Post*, August 23, 2015.

Butt, Khalid Manzoor, and Anam Abid Butt. "Blockade on Gaza Strip: A Living Hell on Earth." *Journal of Political Studies* 23, no. 1 (2016): 157-82.

Cole, Juan. "Creepy Israeli Planning for Palestinian Food Insecurity in Gaza Revealed." *Informed Comment*, October 18, 2012.

Dahlan, Ahmed Said. "Housing Demolition and Refugee Resettlement Schemes in the Gaza Strip." *GeoJournal* 21, no. 4 (1990): 385-95.

Fields, David. *Enclosure: Palestinian Landscapes in a Historical Mirror*. Oakland: University of California Press, 2017.

Filiu, Jean Pierre. *Gaza: A History.* Oxford: Oxford University Press, 2014.

Foucault, Michel. "Of Other Spaces." *Diacritics* 16, no. 1 (Spring 1986): 22-27.

"Gazans Excited Over Territory's New Indoor Mall." *The Times of Israel*, January 23, 2017.

GISHA—Legal Center for Freedom and Movement. "A Costly Divide | February 15: Economic Repercussions of Separating Gaza and the West Bank." Gaza and the West Bank position paper, February 26, 2015.

Hadid, Diaa. "Gaza: U.N. Issues Warning about Gaza Condition." *New York Times*, September 2, 2015.

Hogan, Elena N. "Field Notes from Jerusalem and Gaza, 2009–2011." *Journal of Palestine Studies* 41, no. 2 (Winter 2012): 99–114.

Jarrah, Sheikh. "'Autonomy' for the Gaza Strip." *Journal of Palestine Studies* 9, no. 3 (Spring 1980): 176–80.

Joronen, Mikko. "'Death comes knocking on the roof': Thanatopolitics of Ethical Killing During Operation Protective Edge in Gaza." *Antipode* 48, No. 2 (2016): 336–54.

———. "'Refusing to be a victim, refusing to be an enemy': Form-of-life as resistance in the Palestinian struggle against settler colonialism." *Political Geography* 56 (2017): 91–100.

Koek, Elisabeth, Jehad Arafat, and Martin Clutterbuck. "Rebuilding from the Rubble: Post-Conflict Land Tenure Challenges and Opportunities in the Gaza Strip." Paper presented at the 2015 World Bank Conference on Land and Poverty, Washington, DC, March 23-27, 2015.

Lemke, Thomas. "The Birth of Bio-politics: Michel Foucault's lecture at the Collège de France on Neoliberal Governmentality." *Economy and Society* 30, no. 2 (May 2001): 190-207.

Leshem, Noam. "Repopulating the Emptiness: A spatial critique of ruination in Israel/Palestine." *Environment and Planning D: Society and Space* 31, no. 3 (2013): 522-37.

Macintyre, Donald. *Gaza Preparing for Dawn*. London: One World Publications, 2017.

Makdisi, Saree. *Palestine Inside Out: An Everyday Occupation*. New York: W. W. Norton & Company, 2010.

Mandell, Joan. "Gaza: Israel's Soweto." *MERIP Reports*, no. 136/137 (Oct.-Dec 1985).

Nassar, Issam. "Remapping Palestine and the Palestinians: Decolonizing and Research." *Comparative Studies of South Asia, Africa, and the Middle East* 23, no. 1 (2003): 149-51.

OCHA. "Gaza: Two Years Since the 2014 Hostilities." OCHA, August 2016.

———. "The Gaza Strip: The Humanitarian Impact of the Blockade." OCHA, November 2016.

———. "Housing, Land and Property Rights Issues Pose Further Challenges to Gaza Reconstruction." *Monthly Humanitarian Bulletin*, OCHA Occupied Palestinian Territory, March-April 2016.

Orzeck, Reecia. "Normative Geographies and the 1940 Land Transfer Regulations in Palestine." *Transactions of the British Institute of Geographers* 39 (2014): 346–59.

Parsons, Nigel, and Mark Salter. "Israeli Biopolitics: Closure, Territorialisation and Governmentality in the Occupied Palestinian Territories." *Geopolitics* 13 (2008): 701–23.

Peskin, Doron. "Hamas Got Rich as Gaza Was Plunged into Poverty." *Net News*, July 15, 2014.

Peteet, Julie. *Space and Mobility in Palestine*. Indianapolis: Indiana Press, 2017.

Roy, Sara. *The Gaza Strip: The Political Economy of De-Development*. Washington, DC: Institute for Palestine Studies, 2015.

Sherwood, Harriet. "Gaza Blockade is a Blessing for the Black Economy—and for Hamas." *The Guardian*, June 5, 2010.

———. "The KFC Smugglers of Gaza." *The Guardian*, May 19, 2013.

Smith, Ron. "Isolation Through Humanitarianism: Subaltern Geopolitics of the Siege on Gaza." *Antipode* 48, no. 3 (2016): 1–20.

Strand, Trude. "Tightening the Noose: The Institutionalized Impoverishment of Gaza, 2005–2010." *Journal of Palestine Studies* 43, No. 2 (Winter, 2014): 6–23.

Tal, Slon. "Space Matters: Historic Drivers and Turning Points in Israel's Open Space Protection Policy." *Israeli Studies* 13, no. 1 (2002): 119–51.

Tawil-Souri, Helga, and Dina Matar, editors. *Gaza as Metaphor*. London: Hurst and Company, 2016.

Their, Daphna. "Starving Gaza One Tunnel at a Time." *Socialist Worker*, January 22, 2018.

UN General Assembly. Progress Report of the United Nations Mediator on Palestine Submitted to the Secretary-General For Transmission to the Members of the United Nations. Document Al 648, September 16, 1948.

Waterman, Stanley. "Pre-Israeli Planning in Palestine: The Example of Acre." *Town Planning Review* 42, no. 1 (January 1971): 85–99.

Zuabi, Rena. "Land Use Planning and the Palestinian Minority in Israel: A Comparative Regional Study." *Prospect Journal of International Affairs* (2011).

RE-ECOLOGIZING GAZA

Text by Fadi Shayya
Infographics by Visualizing Palestine

The following graphic works by Visualizing Palestine (VP), the first project of the Visualizing Impact collective, serve as *method* and *medium* to reconnect what the Israeli occupation persistently separates and isolates through controlling Gaza's land borders, airspace, and territorial waters. Over the years, the militarized occupation's work revealed itself as a project of attrition, what we have historically known as siege warfare. Israel's project of siege warfare 'de-ecologizes' the Gaza Strip, through obstructing and/or interrupting its ecological flows. With no shortage of such practices, the graphic works in this chapter re-narrate a few accounts. The siege isolates the Strip's physical territory to interrupt the movement of people, labor, and resources. Since 2007, an economic blockade crushed imports-exports and intensified unemployment. The siege confines Gaza's geography to obstruct its energy flows and nutrient cycles. An enviro-geological isolation leads to excessive land runoff that contaminates the aquifer underneath, and a heavily militarized border fatally terminates protestors' lives during the recent Great Return March. Around the world, we encounter traces and effects of such 'de-ecologizing' in people's stories, the work of activists, news media reports, and research outputs of non-governmental and governmental organizations.

These research-graphic works capture manifold moments of tension where Palestinians' assassinated and calorie-controlled bodies become numbers momentarily, only to re-emerge over and over again as consumable media images. Everyday practices of the occupation soldiers and settlers and the Strip's natives and refugees complicate grand narratives of state, sovereignty, territory, and authority. The occupation recruits and/or extracts environmental commons as critical resources and infrastructures.

Against the occupation's 'de-ecologizing' project, VP's work contributes to a method of 're-ecologizing' the Gaza Strip. That is to re-connect and re-establish ecological flows relevant to humans and centered around their environment. At a conceptual and discursive level, VP's 're-ecologizing' works through engaging in a collective and transdisciplinary production of research–graphic works as public, free-of-charge, sharable digital *medium* with visual-textual and print capacities. The outputs become ready to act as learning and advocacy tools for collectives and individuals across the globe. And, the production method and output medium themselves become part of a project of 're-ecologizing' Palestine through connecting professionals, advocates, enthusiasts, and the media.

The method aims to become an intervention that subverts contemporary media's production of iconic and sensationalist representations of battered Palestinians and Palestine. The visual information lens is not a pure discursive one for quantifying excess information against all sorts of *information wars* and *post–truths* against human rationality, nor is it a mere graphical one that translates dry report numbers to enticing visual consumables. While such

functions remain part and parcel of VP's work, the visual information lens differentiates the media produced and brings people and things together. These graphic works become *a medium that is more than the message,* to subvert McLuhan's notion.

It is worth noting that these graphic works are part of a larger collection of multimedia outputs concerned with localized and extensive geographies of Palestine from the territorial physicalities of the Palestinian Territories, Gaza, and the West Bank to speculative extensions of Palestine in the practices, actions, discourses, and imaginaries of individuals and collectives across polities and geographies. VP's work stacks visual storytelling over information architecture, data visualization, research, illustration, translation, and collaboration. Drawing on sources produced across professions and interests, each visual lists its sources, frames a specific time-space, translates a situation, and acknowledges its collective capacity through creative commons licensing.[1]

1. To reuse the VP's original visuals (with the proper credits, licensing, and sources), and for further information on available language versions and community engagement, you can download the visuals from the Visualizing Palestine website (visualizingpalestine.org).

GAZA WATER CONFINED & CONTAMINATED

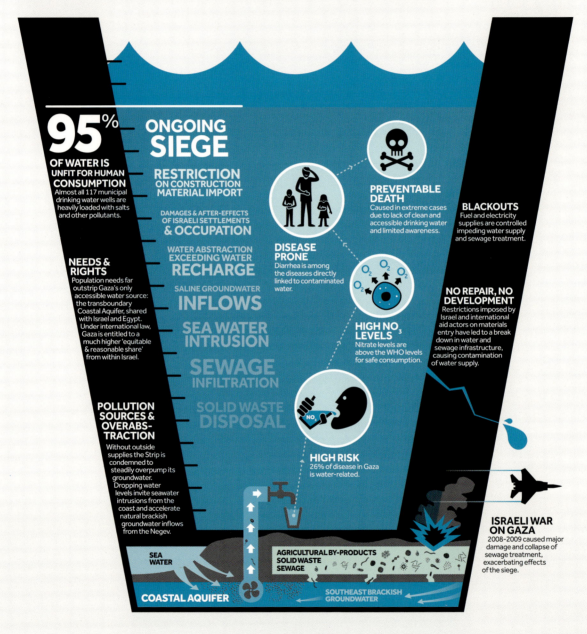

95%
OF WATER IS UNFIT FOR HUMAN CONSUMPTION
Almost all 117 municipal drinking water wells are heavily loaded with salts and other pollutants.

NEEDS & RIGHTS
Population needs far outstrip Gaza's only accessible water source: the transboundary Coastal Aquifer, shared with Israel and Egypt. Under international law, Gaza is entitled to a much higher 'equitable & reasonable share' from within Israel.

POLLUTION SOURCES & OVERABSTRACTION
Without outside supplies the Strip is condemned to steadily overpump its groundwater. Dropping water levels invite seawater intrusions from the coast and accelerate natural brackish groundwater inflows from the Negev.

ONGOING SIEGE

RESTRICTION ON CONSTRUCTION MATERIAL IMPORT

DAMAGES & AFTER-EFFECTS OF ISRAELI SETTLEMENTS & OCCUPATION

WATER ABSTRACTION EXCEEDING WATER RECHARGE

SALINE GROUNDWATER INFLOWS

SEA WATER INTRUSION

SEWAGE INFILTRATION

SOLID WASTE DISPOSAL

PREVENTABLE DEATH
Caused in extreme cases due to lack of clean and accessible drinking water and limited awareness.

DISEASE PRONE
Diarrhea is among the diseases directly linked to contaminated water.

HIGH NO$_3$ LEVELS
Nitrate levels are above the WHO levels for safe consumption.

HIGH RISK
26% of disease in Gaza is water-related.

BLACKOUTS
Fuel and electricity supplies are controlled impeding water supply and sewage treatment.

NO REPAIR, NO DEVELOPMENT
Restrictions imposed by Israel and international aid actors on materials entry have led to a break down in water and sewage infrastructure, causing contamination of water supply.

ISRAELI WAR ON GAZA
2008-2009 caused major damage and collapse of sewage treatment, exacerbating effects of the siege.

SEA WATER

AGRICULTURAL BY-PRODUCTS SOLID WASTE SEWAGE

COASTAL AQUIFER

SOUTHEAST BRACKISH GROUNDWATER

SOURCES
B'tselem, 2000, Thirsty for a Solution: The Water Shortage in the Occupied Territories and its Solution in the Final Status Agreement, p 39.
C. Messerschmid, Birzeit University, 2011, Water in Gaza: Problems and Prospects, p 3-6, 20-21.
Blue Planet and LifeSource, 2012, The Human Right to Water in Palestine, In Our Right to Water, pp 4-5.
OCHA, August 2009, Locked In: The Humanitarian Impact of Two Years of Blockade of the Gaza Strip, pp 4, 22, 23.
Save the Children and Medical Aid for Palestine, 2012, Gaza's Children: Falling Behind The effect of the blockade on child health in Gaza, pp 5, 16, 17.
Thirsting for Justice, 2003, Right to Water in oPT, pp 19, 29.
UNICEF, March 2011, Protecting Children from Unsafe Water in Gaza, pp 7, 9, 10, 16.
World Bank, 2009, Assessment of Restrictions on Palestinian Water Sector Development - West Bank and Gaza - pp 27, 29, 30 (Original source: Fieldwork interview, WHO, Gaza city, November 24).

REVISION 01
29 AUG 2012

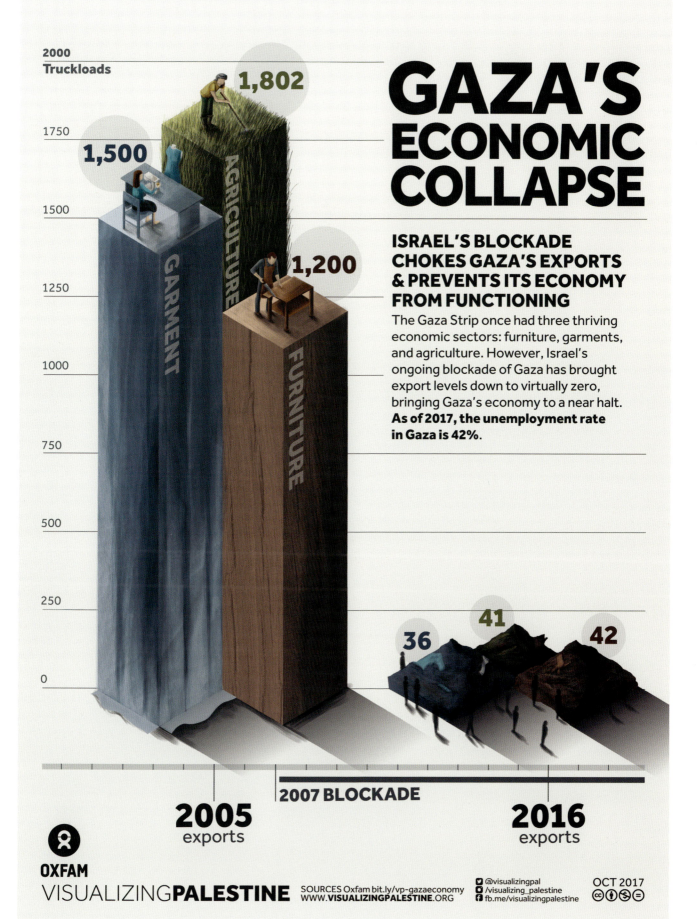

GAZA'S ECONOMIC COLLAPSE

ISRAEL'S BLOCKADE CHOKES GAZA'S EXPORTS & PREVENTS ITS ECONOMY FROM FUNCTIONING

The Gaza Strip once had three thriving economic sectors: furniture, garments, and agriculture. However, Israel's ongoing blockade of Gaza has brought export levels down to virtually zero, bringing Gaza's economy to a near halt. **As of 2017, the unemployment rate in Gaza is 42%.**

2000 Truckloads

1,802

1,500

1,200

AGRICULTURE

GARMENT

FURNITURE

1750

1500

1250

1000

750

500

250

0

36 41 42

2007 BLOCKADE

2005 exports

2016 exports

OXFAM

VISUALIZING**PALESTINE**

SOURCES Oxfam bit.ly/vp-gazaeconomy
WWW.**VISUALIZINGPALESTINE**.ORG

@visualizingpal
/visualizing_palestine
fb.me/visualizingpalestine

OCT 2017

RESTRICTED GAS RESERVES

PALESTINIANS **BARRED FROM ACCESSING OFFSHORE GAS RESERVES** WORTH

$4BN

RESTRICTED FISHING

SINCE 2007, THE ISRAELI MILITARY HAS REPEATEDLY ATTACKED PALESTINIAN FISHERMEN, **KILLING 5 AND INJURING AT LEAST 25.** THE BLOCKADE BARS THEM FROM REACHING LARGER SHOALS OF FISH, FOUND AT A **MINIMUM OF 12-15 MILES OFF GAZA.**

ISRAELI MILITARY PATROLS **RESTRICT PALESTINIANS** TO WITHIN **3 TO 6** NAUTICAL MILES OF THE COAST **DENYING ACCESS** TO GAZA'S OWN TERRITORIAL WATERS AND THE WORLD BEYOND

◄ INTERNATIONAL WATERS

9

6

VISUALIZINGPALESTINE

@visualizingpal
fb.com/visualizingpalestine

BESIEGED

THE **ECONOMIC IMPACT** OF THE **ISRAELI SIEGE ON GAZA**

DESTROYED PORTS

THE ISRAELI MILITARY **DESTROYED GAZA'S UNCOMPLETED SEAPORT IN 2002** AND ITS AIRPORT IN 2001, **PREVENTING PALESTINIANS FROM ENGAGING IN DIRECT TRADE** WITH THE OUTSIDE WORLD.

RESTRICTED ELECTRICITY

GAZA'S ONLY POWER PLANT HAS FACED REPEATED ISRAELI ATTACKS AND BLOCKED FUEL DELIVERIES. **ISRAELIS PROFIT $92M ANNUALLY** SUPPLYING ELECTRICITY TO GAZA WHILE PALESTINIANS FACE

12-16HRS
OF POWER CUTS PER DAY.

RESTRICTED LAND

PALESTINIANS **ARE BARRED FROM USING 17% OF GAZA'S LAND,** INCLUDING

35%
OF FARMLAND, DUE TO AN **ISRAELI-IMPOSED BUFFER ZONE**

SEA BLOCKADE

LAND BLOCKADE

SINCE 2007, **PALESTINIAN IMPORTS HAVE BEEN HEAVILY RESTRICTED AND EXPORTS BARRED.** ISRAELI COMPANIES PROFIT FROM A MONOPOLY ON SUPPLY OF GOODS TO GAZA MAKING

$375M
IN 2012

SINCE 2007, ISRAELI AUTHORITIES HAVE IMPOSED A DEVASTATING **LAND, AIR AND SEA BLOCKADE** ON THE GAZA STRIP, AMOUNTING TO THE ILLEGAL COLLECTIVE PUNISHMENT OF ITS 1.8 MILLION PALESTINIAN INHABITANTS. IT LEAVES THEM **ISOLATED** FROM THE WORLD, DENIED ACCESS TO THEIR OWN RESOURCES, AND FACING A **45% UNEMPLOYMENT RATE**.

3

0 NAUTICAL MILES

SOURCES
Data aggregated from Al Jazeera, ARIJ, B'Tselem, CS Monitor, Gisha, Palestinian CBS, World Bank and Ynet. Montage adapted from vector art by Natali Snajlcat and Alexzel/Shutterstock.
Gaza population http://bit.ly/pcbs-pop2014 | **Unemployment** http://bit.ly/wb-employment (p10) | **3-6nm Sea blockade** http://bit.ly/gisha-blockade | **Seaport** http://bit.ly/aje-seaport |
Airport http://bit.ly/ocha-airport (p3) | **$4bn Gas reserves** http://bit.ly/fmep-gas | **$92m Electricity** http://bit.ly/arij-cost | **Fish shoals** http://bit.ly/csm-fish |
Fishermen attacks http://bit.ly/ocha-fishermen | **$375m Imports** http://bit.ly/ynet-imports | **Restricted land** http://bit.ly/btselem-nogo

THE FIVE STAGE[S]

THE PEOPLE OF NEW YORK CITY HAVE PASSED THROUGH[...]
WHILE THE PEOPLE OF GAZA ARE TRA[PPED]

DENIAL 1

VICTIMS' FRIENDS AND FAMILIES POST AROUND 90,000 FLIERS OF THEIR MISSING LOVED ONES AROUND NYC.

2,823 CIVILIANS KILLED

ANGER 2

90% OF AMERICANS SUPPORT THE INVASION OF AFGHANISTAN AND 59% THE INVASION OF IRAQ.

BARGAINING 3

US GOVERNMENT PAYS AN AVERAGE OF $2.1 MILLION AS COMPENSATION TO EACH VICTIM'S FAMILY.

NYC

2001   2001 & 2003   2003

GAZA

2005 ISRAELI DISENGAGEMENT

DESPITE DISENGAGEMENT, ISRAEL CONTINUES TO CONTROL GAZA'S BORDERS, AIR SPACE AND COASTAL WATERS, **DENYING** PALESTINIANS THEIR RIGHTS TO FREE MOVEMENT AND TRADE.

2006 OPERATION SUMMER RAINS

ANGERED WITH THE CORRUPTION OF FATAH AND THE TIGHTENING OF ISRAELI RESTRICTIONS, PALESTINIANS IN GAZA AND THE WEST BANK ELECT A HAMAS GOVERNMENT.

2008–09 OPERATION CAST L[EAD]

VARIOUS ATTEMPTS SINCE 2006 TO **NEGOTIATE** A UNITY GOVERNMENT BETWEEN HAMAS AND FATAH ARE UNDERMINED BY ISRAELI AND INTERNATIONAL INTERFERENCE.

VISUALIZING**PALESTINE**

@visualizingpal
fb.com/visualizingpalestine

S OF GRIEF

E STAGES OF GRIEF TOWARDS HEALING,
O IN A CYCLE OF VIOLENCE.

DEPRESSION

MANY OF THE
0,000 PEOPLE
WHO SUFFERED
POST-TRAUMATIC
STRESS HAVE
NOT RECOVERED
A DECADE LATER.

ACCEPTANCE

PRESIDENT OBAMA
DEDICATES 9/11
MEMORIAL AND
MUSEUM AS
**"A SACRED PLACE
OF HEALING
AND HOPE."**

011   2014

2012 OPERATION PILLAR OF CLOUD   2014 OPERATION PROTECTIVE EDGE

WITH 40% OF
CHILDREN SUFFERING
DEPRESSION AND
59% SYMPTOMS OF
POST-TRAUMATIC STRESS,
A NEW GENERATION IS
GROWING WITH
PSYCHOLOGICAL
TRAUMA.

PALESTINIANS ARE
STUCK IN A
REPEATING CYCLE
THEY CANNOT HEAL,
NOR CAN THEY
ACCEPT THE
CONTINUATION OF
ISRAELI VIOLENCE
AND BLOCKADE.

2,847+
CIVILIANS
KILLED
INCLUDING
1,242+
CHILDREN

WWW.VISUALIZINGPALESTINE.ORG. JULY 2014.

SOURCES
Data aggregated from B'tselem, Bronson, Gallup, The Guardian, New York Times, OCHA, Open Democracy,
Palestinian Medical Relief Society, PCHR, White House. Estimates of Gaza civilian deaths up to 25 July 2014.
NYC deaths http://bit.ly/guardian-911 | **NYC facts** http://bit.ly/bronson-911 | http://bit.ly/gallup-afghanistan |
http://bit.ly/gallup-iraqinvasion http://bit.ly/nyt-post-911 | http://bit.ly/whitehouse-911 |
Gaza deaths http://bit.ly/btselem-killedgaza | http://bit.ly/ocha-killedgaza | http://bit.ly/pchr-gaza
Gaza facts http://bit.ly/btselem-restrictions | http://bit.ly/guardian-fatah | http://bit.ly/od-fatah-hamas | http://bit.ly/pmrs-depression

GAZA'S UNTOLD STORY

FROM DISPLACEMENT TO DEATH

An estimated 2,219 Palestinians were killed during the Israeli offensive against the Gaza Strip in the summer of 2014, yet an important part of this story is missing.

56% REFUGEES

More than half of Palestinians killed were refugees displaced since the Nakba in 1948.

MEDITERRANEAN SEA

TULKAREM

YAFA
SALAMA
AL-'ABASSIYYA

SARAFAND AL-'AMAR
RUBIN
AL-LYDD
RAMLA

YIBNA
AQER
BASHIT

ISDUD

BEIT DARAS

JERUSALEM

HAMAMA
AL-JORA
AL-MAJDAL
BARBARA
HARBIA
AL-FALUJA

SIMSIM
DAMRA
BURAYER
BEIT HANOUN

HEBRON

GAZA STRIP

AL-MUHRAQA

10km   25km   50km

KHUZA'A SHARQIYA

BEER AL-SABE'

LEGEND

Home town

1+ 10+ 25+ 80+

Death toll

REV 01

SOURCES bit.ly/vp-gazadeaths • **SEP** 2015

f fb.me/visualizingpalestine • 🐦 @visualizingpal

VP **DATA** SKETCH

SHORT WALK HOME
LONG WALK TO FREEDOM

Of Gaza's 1.9 million inhabitants, almost 70% are refugees whose families were expelled in 1948 from territory that became Israel.

In March 2018, Palestinians initiated the Great Return March, a recurring demonstration at the barrier between Gaza and Israel, demanding their right to return to their home villages and an end to the devastating Israeli-led blockade on Gaza.

Israeli forces have responded by opening fire, killing at least 95* unarmed protesters and injuring thousands. This map highlights the villages of origin of the refugees killed.

6 YAFA
1 SALAMA
2 SARAFAND AL-AMAR
ZARNUQA
3 YIBNA **1** **1** **1** NA'ANI
AQIR
1 YASUR
AL-JURA **1**
ISDUD **3**
2 AL-SAWAFIR
HAMAMA **6**
1 JULIS
1 AL-MAJDAL
NI'LIYA **2**
1 BAYT TIMA
BEIT JIRJA **3** **1** HULAYQAT
SIMSIM **5** BURAYER
DIMRA **1** **1**
1 BEIT HANOUN
2 HOJ

TAMMUN (1)

95* PALESTINIANS KILLED IN GAZA

30 NON-REFUGEES

17 BEER AL-SABE'

MEDITERRANEAN SEA

0km 10km 25km 50km

*Data includes only those killed while participating in demonstrations
Data from Al Mezan Center, **26 May 2018.**
SOURCES bit.ly/vp-returnmarch
WWW.VISUALIZINGPALESTINE.ORG

@visualizingpalestine
@visualizingpal
@visualizing_palestine

VISUALIZINGPALESTINE

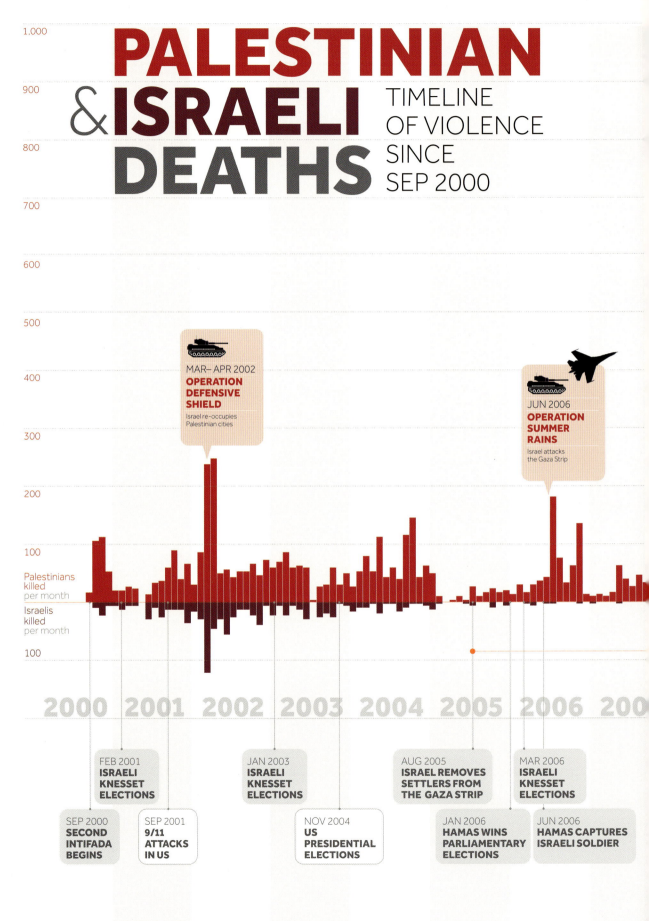

PALESTINIAN & ISRAELI DEATHS

TIMELINE OF VIOLENCE SINCE SEP 2000

MAR– APR 2002
OPERATION DEFENSIVE SHIELD
Israel re-occupies Palestinian cities

JUN 2006
OPERATION SUMMER RAINS
Israel attacks the Gaza Strip

Palestinians killed per month

Israelis killed per month

2000 2001 2002 2003 2004 2005 2006 200

FEB 2001
ISRAELI KNESSET ELECTIONS

JAN 2003
ISRAELI KNESSET ELECTIONS

AUG 2005
ISRAEL REMOVES SETTLERS FROM THE GAZA STRIP

MAR 2006
ISRAELI KNESSET ELECTIONS

SEP 2000
SECOND INTIFADA BEGINS

SEP 2001
9/11 ATTACKS IN US

NOV 2004
US PRESIDENTIAL ELECTIONS

JAN 2006
HAMAS WINS PARLIAMENTARY ELECTIONS

JUN 2006
HAMAS CAPTURES ISRAELI SOLDIER

VISUALIZING**PALESTINE** WWW.VISUALIZINGPALESTINE.ORG. NOVEMBER 2012.
SHARE AND DISTRIBUTE FREELY. CREATIVE COMMONS BY-NC-ND 3.0 LICENSE.

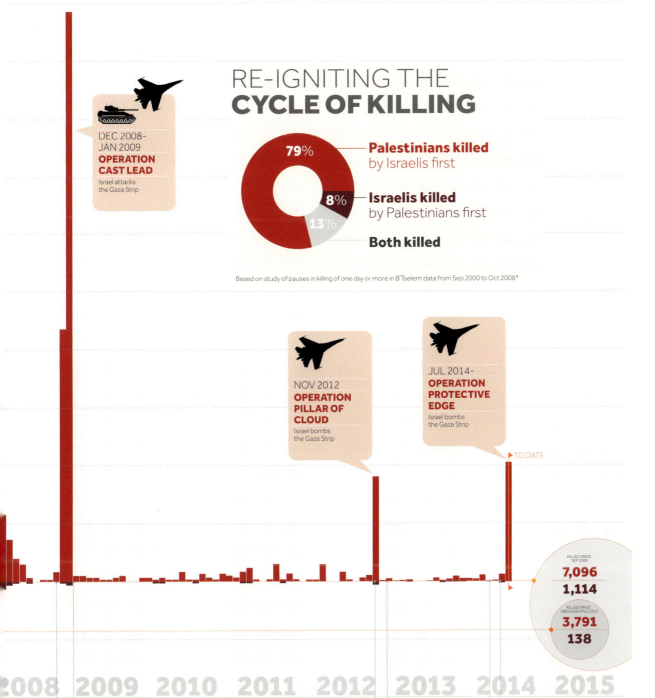

RE-IGNITING THE
CYCLE OF KILLING

79% Palestinians killed by Israelis first

8% Israelis killed by Palestinians first

13% Both killed

Based on study of pauses in killing of one day or more in B'Tselem data from Sep 2000 to Oct 2008*

DEC 2008–JAN 2009
OPERATION CAST LEAD
Israel attacks the Gaza Strip

NOV 2012
OPERATION PILLAR OF CLOUD
Israel bombs the Gaza Strip

JUL 2014–
OPERATION PROTECTIVE EDGE
Israel bombs the Gaza Strip

▶TO DATE

KILLED SINCE SEP 2000
7,096
1,114

KILLED SINCE 2005 GAZA PULLOUT
3,791
138

2008 2009 2010 2011 2012 2013 2014 2015

FEB 2009
ISRAELI KNESSET ELECTIONS

JAN 2013
ISRAELI KNESSET ELECTIONS

JUN 2014
3 ISRAELIS KIDNAPPED AND KILLED

NOV 2008
US PRESIDENTIAL ELECTIONS

NOV 2012
US PRESIDENTIAL ELECTIONS

APR 2014
BREAKDOWN OF PEACE TALKS

SOURCES

B'Tselem Statistics on Fatalities, http://www.btselem.org/statistics. Data presented from B'Tselem includes all Palestinians killed by Israeli military or civilians, and all Israelis killed by Palestinians. It does not include data on foreign nationals or 'friendly fire' deaths. Data for June and July 2014 fatalities collated from Palestinian Ministry of Health.

*Nancy Kanwisher et al, 2009, Reigniting Violence: How Do Ceasefires End? http://www.huffingtonpost.com/nancy-kanwisher/reigniting-violence-how-d_b_155611.html .

REVISION 01
16 JUL 2014

@visualizingpal
fb.com/visualizingpalestine

ISRAELI IMPUNITY FOR ATTACK ON GAZA
JUSTICE DENIED

500 COMPLAINTS
FILED WITH ISRAELI MILITARY

360 INCIDENTS IDENTIFIED

31 CRIMINAL INVESTIGATIONS

3 CONVICTED
FOR MINOR OFFENSES

> " The commission is concerned that impunity prevails across the board for violations of international humanitarian law and international human rights law allegedly committed by Israeli forces.
>
> —UN Human Rights Council independent commission

ONLY 3 FROM 500 CASES RECEIVE CONVICTIONS
Israel's 2014 bombardment of Gaza killed 1,545 Palestinian civilians, including 556 children, and made 11,166 families homeless. Their only legal recourse is through Israel's own military justice system.

مركز الميزان لحقوق الإنسان
AL Mezan Center for Human Rights

VISUALIZING**PALESTINE**

PHOTO Eman Mohammed
JUL 2017 **SOURCES** bit.ly/vp-gaza
WWW.VISUALIZINGPALESTINE.ORG

f @visualizingpalestine
@visualizingpal
@visualizing_palestine

ACCORDING TO ISRAEL, PALESTINIANS NEED 43% LESS DAIRY THAN ISRAELIS.

The Red Lines Policy

The Red Lines Policy: Israel controls all food that enters the Gaza Strip. In 2007, Israeli authorities mandated that Palestinians in Gaza should receive only the minimum of food to avoid malnutrition, featuring 43% less dairy than the average Israeli. Though Israel claims to have ended this policy, as of 2017, 40% of Gaza's households suffered from severe food insecurity, largely as a result of Israel's blockade.

VISUALIZINGPALESTINE

SOURCES COGAT, Gisha, bit.ly/vp-gazafood
WWW.**VISUALIZINGPALESTINE**.ORG

@visualizingpal
/visualizing_palestine
fb.me/visualizingpalestine

SEP 2018

ACCORDING TO ISRAEL, PALESTINIANS NEED 19% LESS MEAT THAN ISRAELIS.

The Red Lines Policy

Israel controls all food that enters the Gaza Strip. In 2007, Israeli authorities mandated that Palestinians in Gaza should receive only the minimum of food to avoid malnutrition, featuring 19% less meat than the average Israeli. Though Israel claims to have ended this policy, as of 2017, 40% of Gaza's households suffered from severe food insecurity, largely as a result of Israel's blockade.

VISUALIZING**PALESTINE**

SOURCES COGAT,
Gisha, bit.ly/vp-gazafood
WWW.**VISUALIZINGPALESTINE**.ORG

@visualizingpal
/visualizing_palestine
fb.me/visualizingpalestine

SEP 2018

ACCORDING TO ISRAEL, PALESTINIANS NEED 37% FEWER FRUITS AND VEGGIES THAN ISRAELIS.

The Red Lines Policy

Israel controls all food that enters the Gaza Strip. In 2007, Israeli authorities mandated that Palestinians in Gaza should receive only the minimum of food to avoid malnutrition, featuring 37% fewer fruits and veggies than the average Israeli. Though Israel claims to have ended this policy, as of 2017, 40% of Gaza's households suffered from severe food insecurity, largely as a result of Israel's blockade.

VISUALIZING**PALESTINE**

SOURCES COGAT, Gisha, bit.ly/vp-gazafood
WWW.**VISUALIZINGPALESTINE**.ORG

@visualizingpal
/visualizing_palestine
fb.me/visualizingpalestine

SEP 2018

THE INTERNET PIGEON NETWORK

Helga Tawil-Souri

how many times can you put my soul's addresses
in the beaks of these pigeons?
and vanish like the distance on the slopes
so that I may realize that you are Babylon, Egypt, and Syria
—"Homing Pigeons," Mahmoud Darwish[1]

It is for man to adapt to his own ends, to utilize for his own human purposes,
the extraordinary tenacity with which the domestic homing pigeon seeks
to regain his loft.
—Captain H. T. W. Allatt[2]

1. Mahmoud Darwish, "Homing Pigeons," trans. Lena Jayyusi and W. S. Merwin, in *Anthology of Modern Palestinian Literature*, ed. Salma Khadra Jayyusi (New York: Columbia University Press, 1995), 152–55.

2. Captain H. T. W. Allatt, "The Uses of Pigeons as Messengers in War and the Military Pigeon Systems of Europe," *Royal United Services Institution Journal* 30, no. 133 (1886): 107–48.

PIGEONS MIGHT FLY

A homing pigeon Internet network can provide Gaza with a self-reliant, Israel-free means of being plugged into the global network for sending and receiving data. It will not require an exorbitant amount of capital investment or upkeep, nor depend on Israel's doling out bandwidth spectrum or its permission to import equipment. It will be resilient and reliable, and able to overcome Gaza's geographic and maritime containment, as it is mostly impervious to infiltration and surveillance and not even in need of electricity!

Instead of wishing to be an "equal" player in the high-tech network—assuming that more wires, cables, routers, software, and thus more foreign expertise, capital, and debt are needed—what if Gaza embraced its low technologization? The homing pigeon Internet network—IPN—may at first strike the reader as technological satire and a geopolitical dream. While this is the case to a certain extent, in what follows, I hope to demonstrate its feasibility and benefits.

A network is a distributive system of interconnection and exchange between different nodes.[3] Being part of a network can be beneficial because it provides the ability to rapidly exchange information across space. However, a network node cannot be autonomous or self-sufficient, nor can it be free of the network's standards, need for upgrades, protocols, or policies—whether these are architectural and technological, or political and economic. For example, being plugged-in requires one to adopt increasingly complex architectures that drive up costs, as well as

points of failure, blockage, difficulty, and other unknown elements or outcomes. Being plugged-in also means being susceptible to controls, interception, or surveillance—whether by corporate entities (e.g., Google, Facebook), national or foreign governments, or supragovernmental organizations (e.g., Internet Corporation for Assigned Names and Numbers, or International Telecommunications Union). In other words, more "technologization" means more surveillance of users. Moreover, being part of the network today is to participate in and be dependent on a system largely ruled by profit, capital accumulation, enclosure, and corporate and governmental power. Given the constraints of being networked and the challenge posed in this volume of imagining and building a self-sustainable future for Gaza, we should start with what might seem a ridiculous question: Why does Gaza need to be part of the network? Can Gaza be free and autonomous on the level of telecommunications, while also being plugged-in?

Currently, there is no Internet and telephone access in the Gaza Strip that is not physically dependent on Israel.[4] Gaza's telecommunications connection to the world runs underground through the Karni Crossing and to points inside Israel. This sole fiber-optic connection is sometimes severed, and Israel keeps it under constant surveillance, controlling its bandwidth and speed. To say that for Gazans, Internet access and its technological development is fully dependent on and controlled by Israel is to state the obvious.[5] Israel forbids the import of many of the latest kinds of communication

3. When using the term "network," I generally refer to a communications and/or information-technology network.

4. Helga Tawil-Souri, "Digital Occupation: Gaza's High-Tech Enclosure," *Journal of Palestine Studies* 41, no. 2 (2012): 27–43; Helga Tawil-Souri, "The Technological End between the 'Inside' of Gaza and the 'Outside' of Gaza," *7iber*, September 2014.

5. Not only the fiber-optic but the electromagnetic spectrum is limited as well, impacting both landlines necessary for Internet access and cellular signals for mobile phones, Wi-Fi access to the Internet, even walkie-talkies. By limiting spectrum allocation, Israel has prevented Palestinian providers and users from having any cellular technology newer than 2G, thus precluding GPS and mobile access or services such as direct online payments.

technologies to both Gaza and the West Bank, stultifying Palestinian technological development. Given the gamut of restrictions imposed by Israel, is it possible to imagine a telecommunications network connected to the outside world that would circumvent these draconian limitations?

Many systems are technically feasible, but run into political or economic limitations. Fiber-optic cable landing points, which would provide Gaza with a direct connection to the maritime global network through a consortium or private network to one of the regional landing points, would amount to upwards of fifty million dollars in start-up costs alone, and would require permission from Israel, which controls the maritime boundary around Gaza.[6] Floating modem balloons could wirelessly connect to underwater fiber-optic cables jacked with waterproof routers and modems, and beam wireless signals to Gaza. Gazans could commandeer satellite signals.[7] Or "piggyback" on nearby Israeli and Egyptian towns by intentionally accessing open Wi-Fi networks, or seek out "Super Wi-Fi" access (lower-frequency white spaces between television channel frequencies).

The outrageousness is not these systems per se, but that *any* solution must work around nightmarish and absurd (non-technical) constraints. One cannot assume reliable electric power, an increase in spectrum allocation, nor a fiber-optic connection that runs through Israel that will be free of Israeli-imposed controls; one cannot assume that importing necessary equipment will be permitted, nor that whatever infrastructure is built will not be purposefully destroyed by Israel. Finally, all of this will have to be done while recognizing that the high capital costs of building, maintaining, and insuring this infrastructure would either have to be swallowed by a generous benefactor or otherwise passed on to the users, the majority of whom live under the poverty line. Is a self-reliant Internet connection for Gaza, without Israeli oversight of any kind, perhaps just a pipe dream?

HOMING PIGEONS: A BRIEF HISTORY ACROSS THE REGION

The homing, or carrier, pigeon has been used for millennia as a means of long-distance communication by a variety of actors, rich and poor, and of various political inclinations. If we define a network as fundamentally distributive, and distribution as fundamentally about control over speed and territorial reach, the homing pigeon certainly serves as an early historical model of communication networking. The homing pigeon is cost-effective and a relatively easy way to communicate across expansive territories, impervious to eavesdropping and surveillance technologies.

The pigeon post remained the world's fastest communication system until the invention of the telegraph and radio in the mid-1800s. Although largely displaced by newer technologies, homing pigeons' ease of access to different geographies, astounding reliability, and ability to carry small items means that they are still used in many ways: to carry blood samples from remote regions, smuggle drugs, race in competitions, and to function as collectors' items, in live sport-shooting and as food. In

6. A closeup map of undersea cables in the Mediterranean is available here: https://thefunambulist.net/app/uploads/2015/03/middle-east-telecom-map-2015-x.png.

7 . Pierluigi Paganini, "Hack Satellite Connection and Surf Anonymously with High-Speed Internet," *Security Affairs*, August 13, 2015.

Figure 1. Homing pigeon Internet, 2018.

short, the pigeon's "primitiveness" is neither irrelevant, nor should be made extinct.

The art of pigeon rearing and training is first noted in the Sumerian Epic of Gilgamesh, and also figures in Mesopotamian tablets and Egyptian hieroglyphics, suggesting that pigeons were domesticated as early as 3000 BCE. It was developed to perfection by the Arabs during the Middle Ages. A regular pigeon courier service was, presumably, first set up under Fatimid rule (969–1099 CE) and later perfected by the Mamluks (1250–1517 CE), lasting in the region for centuries. European historians note, for example, that during the siege of Acre/Acca (1189–1191 CE) by Richard the Lionheart and the Crusaders, the inhabitants of the besieged city kept a regular correspondence with Sultan Saladdin's forces by way of carrier pigeon. It was likely Lionheart and his men brought pigeons to Europe from the Middle East.[8]

Gaza constituted an important node in pigeon courier networks. The mid-twelfth-century Sultan of Baghdad, Noureddin, for example, developed a system of pigeon communication between Baghdad and towns in Syria.[9] This network was later extended to Egypt. The central station was established in Cairo around 1173, with stations placed at fifty-mile intervals. Captain Allatt noted that: "From that point [Cairo] radiated lines of pigeon stations towards Alexandria, towards Damietta, and towards Gaza. This last town communicated with Jerusalem, Damascus, Bagdad [sic], and Aleppo."[10] Whether as a middle point between the highly used Alexandria–Aleppo route, or as a stopping point on the way to/from other parts of the Levant and North Africa, Gaza remained a critical node along the pigeon route well into the eighteenth century.

Palestinian pigeon trainers dwindled with the advent of modern technologies, but were still prevalent at the time of the colonization of Palestine. The use of pigeons by Zionist forces—the Palmach and Haganah groups—shared more similarity to their Western uses in modern warfare.[11] As one Israeli journalist writes: "Pigeon trainers [...] are some of those who laid down the [Israeli] infrastructure, and they are a part of the strong foundation on which our present capabilities were built."[12] Among Palestinian communities, however, carrier

8. Friedrich von Raumer, *Geschichte der Hohenstaufen* (Lepizig: F.A. Brokhaus, 1823).

9. Allatt, "Uses of Pigeons," 111.

10. Ibid.

11. See Lieutenant J. A. C. Nicol, "The Homing Ability of the Carrier Pigeon and Its Value in Warfare," *The Auk: Ornithological Advances* 62, no. 2 (April 1945): 286–98.

12. Noah Kosharek, "IDF Corps Honors Pre-State Palmach and Haganah Carrier Pigeon Trainers," *Haaretz*, February 23, 2009.

pigeons were more often used for communication outside of combat.

The tradition continues, albeit on a less popular scale, today. For example, in the Southern Lebanese city of Tyre (Sour), Deeb Zebid—locally known as *rajoul al-zajel* (carrier pigeon man)—maintains what he calls one of the busiest "pigeon airports." Driven by necessity and a belief that pigeons "are more reliable than the Lebanese post," many Palestinians have turned to pigeons. Another Palestinian refugee from the Al-Bas camp near Tyre explains: "The electricity, the water, the phones, everything is so unreliable here, so I just rely on my pigeons for communication and entertainment."[13]

IPN: INTERNET PIGEON NETWORK

An Internet Pigeon Network (IPN) will rely on homing pigeons to carry and deliver saved data to and from various nodes within flying distance from Gaza, located in Jordan and Egypt. Situated at the nexus of three continents, and with a climatic diversity that ranges from arid desert in the south to a cooler mountainous region in the north, Palestine/Israel already draws an astounding five hundred million birds annually, with Gaza being its only coastal wetland.[14] Based on the country being part of a migratory superhighway, a number of projects have imagined using bird migration to challenge territorial borders. For example, one researcher proposes a bird migration watching station, positing: "What if a bird park, functioning as an ecological buffer, were to replace the existing separation structure?"[15] The Decolonizing Architecture project has also proposed converting abandoned Israeli military spaces in the West

Bank into bird watching zones.[16] Certainly, the IPN builds on these, and draws on the metaphor of bird migration and flight as symbols of freedom and the absence of borders. However, it goes a few steps further in positing a technically viable, reliable, affordable, environmentally friendly, robust, and scalable solution to a modern-day problem.

In order to ensure delivery and secure against loss or interference, the same data will be sent to and come from at least two different nodes in the network. At first, the network can be set up to send/receive messages only once or twice a day at predetermined times. The development of the system will be driven by Gaza's own capabilities and needs, rather than by external corporations, funders, or foreign governments. The infrastructure will be built by establishing local solutions supporting local practices, subsequently linking them together, rather than by defining universal (and often corporate) standards. This will create a largely autonomous and decentralized system high in safety, reliability, and availability, and one that provides an opportunity for Gazans to build, control, and own. As such, it will exist not simply to facilitate communication, but also to reduce the costs of transacting communication, and reduce control, profit motives, surveillance, and interception by others. The system will be cost-effective and require relatively low capital investment, and the sending and receiving of data would require no electric or fuel power. This architecture would need zero reliance on the Israeli network and will be more difficult to slow down, intercept, or surveil than

13. Rym Ghazal, "In e-mail age some still swear by pigeons," *Daily Star*, February 27, 2007:

14. For a month-by-month breakdown of migrating birds passing through the area, see the Israel Birding Portal: https://www.birds.org.il/en/index.aspx. See also, Abdel Fattah N. Abd Rabou et al., "The Avifauna of Wadi Gaza Nature Reserve, Gaza Strip—Palestine," *The Islamic University Journal (Series of Natural Studies and Engineering)* 15, no. 1 (2007): 39–85.

15. Shuangshuang Wu, "Peace/Time Landscape Proposals for the Israeli and Palestinian Border," (MA Thesis, University of Illinois at Urbana-Champaign, 2011), 34.

16. "Project: Return to Nature," Decolonizing Architecture Art Residency, http://www.decolonizing.ps/site/texts.

virtually any high-tech architecture.

The network will be delay-tolerant and asynchronous. Data will be saved to be sent out of and received in Gaza—whether email messages, video and audio files, or otherwise. With enough planning and knowledge of local needs, popular websites—such as those for news—can be mirrored and saved, and copied onto local servers in Gaza, providing users with the ability to browse them, with delay, without relying on the Israeli backbone. Data such as movies, videos, music, and even entire copies of newspapers or magazines can also be saved, sent to Gaza via pigeon, and accessed asynchronously.

A few propositions and experiments exist that have shown the feasibility of such a setup. In April 1990, a scientist published a paper describing "an experimental method for the encapsulation of IP datagrams in avian carriers," whereby an Internet Protocol diagram was printed on a small scroll of paper and wrapped around a pigeon's leg.[17] This may well have been the first imagined "Internet pigeon network." Two very different examples come closest to the IPN described below. First, there was an experiment-*cum*-critique of South Africa's telecommunications speeds. USB sticks were carried by pigeons and were proven to be substantially faster than the connection available via the telcommunications company's DSL connection: in the time that it took the messengers to copy data onto a USB stick, attach it to a pigeon, have the pigeon fly, and have someone on the other side copy the data off the USB stick, the DSL connection was only able to download 4 percent of the

total data.[18] Second, a more serious scheme proposed a "CoLi-DTN" (*Columba Livia*-based Delay Tolerant Network) to provide Internet access in developing countries, places, and situations where other types of connectivity are not options.[19] As the two researchers state: "It is quite conceivable that CoLi-DTNs will in fact be competitive against DSL, ISDN, and point-to-point WiFi connections in many settings."[20] However, the CoLi-DTN was mostly imagined as supplemental to existing telecom services, or only necessary for hard-to-reach, less developed areas in poorer countries. It also problematically positions "lower" technologies as good enough for the Global South, rather than judging each technology—high or low—by its feasibility, efficiency, and scalability.

Other experiments and real-life uses of pigeons comparable to the IPN are those that have used pigeons (or cows, mules, deer, and a variety of either domesticated or wild animals) in telemedicine or environmental programs, whereby an animal transports medicine or blood samples to far-flung scientific outposts, is outfitted with a camera or GPS device to send information back to scientists conducting research, or outfitted with a sensor or device for wildlife habitat monitoring and management.[21]

BUILDING THE IPN

This section is an initial blueprint for what is possible, leaving room for local decisions on how best to pursue network control, maintenance, growth, cost, and security. While details are technically accurate, prices are provided as guidelines and calculated based on the cost of materials in the US.

17. David Waitzman, *RFC 1149* (request for comments, IETF, April 1, 1990).

18. "Pigeon transfer data faster than South Africa's Telekom," *Reuters*, September 9, 2009.

19. Other low-tech means of bringing internet connectivity to far-flung places have included, for example, a DTN network supported by boats for the Amazon.

20. Jeremiah Scholl and Anders Lindgren, "Considering Pigeons for Carrying Delay Tolerant Networking Based Internet Traffic in Developing Countries," *Electronic Journal on Information Systems in Developing Countries* 54, no. 4 (2012): 14.

21. Jacob Shell, *Transportation and Revolt: Pigeons, Mules, Canals, and the Vanishing Geographies of Subversive Mobility* (Cambridge, MA: MIT Press, 2015).

Figure 2. USB Pigeons, or high tech meets low tech, 2018.

1. The Carriers

A. Breeding, Housing, Training
At least two breeding pairs of pigeons (to fly to two separate nodes) will be purchased, trained, and used to breed future carriers. Pigeons breed "enthusiastically in captivity" and, in safe conditions, can live over twenty years.[22] A pigeon can be bred all year long, is naturally docile, and easy to train. A breeding pair will begin producing between twelve and eighteen young annually by the time they are six months old, will keep procreating until at least seven years old, and can do so up to six times per year if overfed. Selective breeding has transformed the pigeon into a "super-homing pigeon with a particularly aerodynamic and muscular body and enhanced homing ability."[23] Homing pigeons can now easily fly distances of five to eight hundred miles at speeds greater than sixty miles per hour, with gender having little bearing on performance.[24] While specially bred racing pigeons are available, the training of any breed of homing pigeon can produce extraordinary results.

At present, there are already pigeon breeders and enthusiasts in Gaza who trade (and smuggle) pigeons into Gaza from Israel, the West Bank, Jordan, and Egypt, and as far afield as Europe and North Africa. These enthusiasts can be integrated into this new network by becoming the chief suppliers, breeders, and trainers of the "data carriers," building the network's infrastructure from the ground up. Traders in Jerusalem often serve as middlemen between Israeli handlers, importing certain breeds from Europe (namely English Carrier pigeons, Damascene pigeons, and homing pigeons) and the West Bank, who bring in these birds in small boxes through the Erez checkpoint.[25] Smuggling is more common because of the siege imposed on Gaza, and because between 2011 and 2015, Israel's Agriculture Ministry imposed a ban on trade with Gaza, the West Bank, and Jordan as a measure against the spread of bird flu. In short, the trade of pigeons in Gaza—whether smuggled or not—is well established.

Training can begin when the bird is five weeks old. The first step is to release and call the bird into its loft by rattling a feeding can or blowing a whistle. Once it passes through the door it is given its food allowance. Lofts can be moved as much as fifty kilometers every three to seven days,

22. Andrew Blechman, *Pigeons: The Fascinating Saga of the World's Most Revered and Reviled Bird* (New York: Grove Press 2006), 8.

23. Blechman, *Pigeons*, 185.

24. Ibid.

25. Moath al-Amoudi, "Pigeon Lovers Flock to Gaza Expo," *Al-Monitor*, May 6, 2016; Roy Arad, "Enthusiasts Flock to this Israeli Pigeon Market, a Rare Nest of Dovish Coexistence," *Haaretz*, August 26, 2016.

and at each location the birds are given a toss in a direction set as the axis of advance. During this training phase, pigeons will be smuggled out of Gaza, until the pigeon has learned the required route. A conservative calculation, estimating that a pigeon will need a week to learn its way home through six separate intervals, translates into a six-week period for getting a communication route up and running.

Lofts have a basic architecture and are easy and cheap to build. Essentially, the only materials needed are plywood and wire-mesh netting (or similar). A pigeon loft should have two rooms: one for mature birds and one for the young. Mature birds have nest boxes (about eight-by-eight-by-eight inches), and the young ones have small perches. There are endless specs for a loft, and improvements that one can make, such as installing a grated floor to facilitate cleaning and allow for more ventilation, or outfitting the floor with cat litter, shavings, straw, or sand. However, as long as fundamental needs are met, lofts can be modest. A loft simply needs ventilation, cleanliness, dryness, and sunlight, and to provide the pigeons with enough space. Ideally, twelve to fifteen pigeons can inhabit a five-by-five foot loft section. Trapdoors can be built from a range of materials, such as plastic or meshing, and simple automation can be built in to provide flexibility to the handlers, with bells or signals made to ring when a pigeon reenters its loft.

B. Flight Patterns, Speeds, and Nodes
Trained pigeons can fly phenomenal distances, and do so at amazing speeds. They average between 80 and 100 kilometers an hour, with frequent spurts of 140 kilometers an hour. The record flight for a US Army Signal Corps pigeon was a whopping 3,700 kilometers (2,300 miles), with routine flights of 1,600 kilometers (1,000 miles). With special training, champion-racing pigeons can fly between 1,000 and 1,100 kilometers in a single day. A more modest training regimen is sufficient for Gaza, as the distances range from 80 kilometers to reach the West Bank, and between 200 and 450 km to reach points in Jordan and Egypt. Not only are they fast, they can also handle extreme temperatures (from well below zero to above sixty degrees Celsius) and are incredibly reliable.

The success rate for pigeons flying 150 kilometers nears 100 percent. Adding more kilometers to a bird's path introduces more variables—weather, predators, accidents, mistakes in navigation, etc.—but even at 300 kilometers, the return rate of pigeons is more than 98 percent. By 650 kilometers, it is still an amazing 90–95 percent, and even in the conditions of enemy fire and mortal injuries that pigeons faced in World War II, they achieved a 98-percent success rate.[26]

Pigeons can handle a load that is about ten percent of their weight without interrupting their capability and speed. Weighing between 300 and 500 grams each, they can easily carry 30–50 grams (1.5–1.8 ounces). With training, they can carry up to 75 grams (2.5 ounces), either with pouches strapped to their bellies or sewn on the feathers of their back without harming them.

Pigeons do not migrate, but adapt to their chosen (or imposed) location year-round. They do not fly a particular route, and can therefore be transported to wherever they are needed, to be released, and expected to fly home.

26. Blechman, *Pigeons*. Shell, *Transportation and Revolt*.

While homing pigeons have largely been used in one-way patterns, it is possible to train them to reliably cover round-trip flights of up to 200 kilometers by placing their food in one location and their home in another, or breeding them in another location. Some trainers are attempting to make flight paths more flexible, by having pigeons fly to three different stations: one for morning feeding, a second for evening feeding, and a third for resting (where their nest is).

The Gaza network will consist of a number of nodes: central hubs containing pigeon coops that connect to smaller nodes, which only have feeding stations. Locations in the network that do not need to handle pigeons in order to receive or send messages will largely be in-between points, such as Al-Arish, Hasna, and Nekhel in the Sinai. Different network configurations can be modeled to calculate the desired potential bandwidth: extra pigeons can be used to increase capacity and/or reduce delays, thus allowing the link to provide predictable and reliable performance and generally reduce the network's latency (its "downtime"). Just as importantly, a network must have built-in redundancy: if one node fails, the data still needs to get through. In the IPN network, this will be done by setting up at least two stations outside of Gaza that will serve to duplicate all incoming and outgoing data. As the network grows, more redundancies can be built in.

Pigeons prefer to fly inland or along a coast, and generally have an aversion to large bodies of water. Considering the location of Gaza, the best routes are southwest towards Suez; southwest along the coast to Arish, Port Said, and Alexandria; southeast towards Aqaba; as well as northbound towards the West Bank and the inland cities in Jordan. Of these possibilities, the most technologically useful are routes to Alexandria, Suez, and Zaafarna in Egypt and Aqaba in Jordan, based on the fact that these are critical landing points in the existing fiber-optic global infrastructure, and thus decrease the distance to the fastest "entry" points in the global network.

C. Costs

Keeping pigeons healthy is easy and inexpensive with sufficient drinking water, a well-balanced diet, and regular cleaning of their coop being the most important factors. Pigeons naturally eat a variety of grains, seeds, greens, berries, and fruits, and will occasionally eat insects, snails, and earthworms. An adult-size pigeon will eat between twenty and fifty grams of food a day, needing a balanced diet that should include about 50 percent grains and 10 percent oil seed such as sunflower, along with the occasional vegetable. The cost of feeding adds up to less than five cents per day per pigeon. Pigeons will need some preventative care against parasites and canker to strengthen them and prolong their lives, and can be given vitamin supplements if necessary. These are relatively low costs as well, and homemade remedies work with equal results.

The subtotal costs of the carrier part of the network, functioning on a minimum of two pairs of breeding pigeons, is $1,840, broken down into:
- $20 x 4 pigeons
- $50 x 4 feeding supplies
- $40 x 4 vitamins and medicine
- $50 x 4 other costs per pigeon
- $100 x 2 lofts

Table 1. Data Load Details and Start-Up Costs.

Brand	Capacity in Gigabytes (GB)	Size in Millimeters (mm)	Weight in Grams (g)	Individual Cost in Dollars	Weight of 1 TB (terabyte) of data	Cost of 1 TB of data*
USB stick (SanDisk Cruzer Blade)	64 GB	60.2 x 20.8 x 11.2 mm	4 g	$20	64g	$640
MicroSD (SanDisk Extreme Pro microSDHC/ microSDXC UHS-I memory card)	64 GB	15 x 11 x 1.0 mm	0.25g	$30	4g	$960

Costs are calculated twice because of redundancy; e.g. (16x$20) x 2 in the example of the USB stick.

- $1,000 smuggling, fuel, and transportation costs during the training period[27]

2. The Load

Any kind of data, in a variety of formats, and across various platforms, can be stored and sent or received. Data will be saved and/or retrieved on a local computer, tablet, or other device when those devices are powered (whether by electricity, a battery, or otherwise); the same will be true of saving in order to upload. All data will be saved onto USB and/or micro drives, which can be password-protected if desired. These are the most affordable, robust, and efficient storage devices that can handle a variety of data, are easy to use, and both light and small enough for pigeons to carry.

There are many different kinds of USB and micro drives that would serve the purpose of this network. As long as the storage capacity, size, weight, cost, and reliability of the drives are taken into consideration, any brand will work. In the arrangement in Table 1, I am calculating conservatively: 1) I am choosing expensive top brand name devices with only 64 GB capacity; 2) costs are based on US consumer prices for units sold individually. Table 1 breaks down the costs and weight of two different drives, providing the start-up cost only, since a drive can be used multiple times.

As technological developments advance, memory sticks will get smaller, lighter, cheaper, and sturdier, and will have a larger storage capacity. A likely development in the near future is a memory stick that allows for automated download once the pigeon lands—through wireless transfer for example. Moreover, the continuing miniaturization of hardware might make it possible to develop wearable microcomputers, or implanted microchips, enabled with network routing and local wireless connectivity.

3. The Network

The network would operate as a store-and-forward system, also called a "delay-tolerant" network. This type of network is common when there is a lack of supportive infrastructure or when the electricity or connection is down. However, given Gaza's power shortages, the delayed arrival of messages may very well occur before the electricity comes back on. Multiple nodes will ensure redundancy, with many located near maritime fiber-optic cable landing points, including those in Egypt and Jordan. This is based on the assumption that being as "near" as possible to one of these can insure speedier and more immediate further transportation of data to sites across the global network. These pigeon landing points are only the "final" stop for the pigeon-reliant

27. Blechman, *Pigeons*. Shell, *Transportation and Revolt*.

Figure 3. Possible network nodes, 2018.

part of the network, where data will be offloaded or uploaded. They are themselves nodes connecting to the larger global infrastructure.

Within Gaza, at least three sites can be set up for relaying data—minimizing reliance on the Israeli backbone. Three sites can be established in the northern, central, and southern parts of the Strip, near water resources:

- Beit Lahiya, Gaza Strip N 31.55, E 34.51
- Deir el Balah, Gaza Strip N 31.40, E 34.31
- Rafah, Gaza Strip N 31.30, E 34.24

At least one node could be established in the West Bank, in close proximity to the Palestinian telecommunications company's main routers:[28]

- Ramallah, West Bank N 31.91, E 35.22

One node could be established in Jordan, preferably near a cable landing point:

- Aqaba, Jordan N 29.51, E 35.00

Four possible nodes exist in Egypt, each with a cable landing point:

- Alexandria, Egypt N 31.21, E 29.92
- El Agamy, Egypt N 31.11, E 29.76
- Suez, Egypt N 29.95, E 32.54
- Zaafarana, Egypt N 29.11, E 32.65

Future nodes could be placed in Beirut, Lebanon (N 33.90, E 35.54), or farther afield.

The speed of the network will be higher than currently available speeds in the Gaza Strip. It will take a pigeon about three hours to get from Gaza to Suez or Aqaba, and another three hours to return. Nonetheless, as an effective transfer rate, the IPN proves to be quick, reliable, and affordable. For a 64 GB drive flown from Gaza to Suez at a rate of one hundred kilometers an hour, the resulting speed is an effective 69 Mbps (megabits per second), not accounting for the time it takes to copy the data, attach the drive to a pigeon, detach it, and download the data.[29] For a pigeon carrying three

28. The West Bank's telecommunications infrastructure shares a dependency on the Israeli backbone similar to Gaza's. If part of the objective of the IPN is minimize and eventually stop reliance on the Israeli backbone, then a node in the West Bank does not make sense; one could be set-up in Amman, Jordan instead, for example.

29. The speed of the transfer of messages is calculated as follows: (Memory size in bytes x 8 bits) / (60 seconds x 60 minutes x distance / speed per hour); in the first example, this is translated as: (64 x 8,000) / (3,600 x 205 km / 100km/h) = 69Mbps.

Table 2. Data Load Details and Start-Up Costs.

Departure-Destination	Distance (in km)	Time of One-Way Flight, Based on One Pigeon at 100 Km/H (in Minutes)	Time of Round-Trip Flight, Based on One Pigeon at 100 Km/H (in Minutes)	Mbps Based on One Pigeon's One-Way Flight at 100 Km/H Carrying One 64 Gb Card (in Mbps)	Mbps Based on One Pigeon's One-Way Flight at 100 Km/H Carrying Three 64 Gb Cards (in Mbps)
Beit Lahiya — Deir el Balah	25	15	30	569	1707
Deir el Balah – Rafah	22	13	26	646	1939
Beit Lahiya – Rafah	47	28	56	303	908
Gaza City — Ramallah	83	50	100	171	514
Gaza City — Aqaba	225	135	270	63	190
Gaza City — Arish	75	45	90	190	569
Gaza City — Suez	205	123	246	69	208
Gaza City — Port Said	207	124	248	69	206
Gaza City – Zaafarana	317	190	380	45	135
Gaza City — Alexandria	433	260	520	33	99
Gaza City — El Agamy	448	269	538	32	95

* Distances to points outside of Gaza are calculated from Gaza City as an average.

30. As points of reference, DSL speeds can vary between 128 Kbps and 3 Mbps, and often provide lower upload speeds than download speeds, denoted as 3 Mbps/128 Kbps, for example—where the first is the maximum bandwidth available for downloads, and the latter the maximum bandwidth available for uploads. But speed is also dependent on the technologies used (or permitted), as well as overall bandwidth capacity. Given the constraints listed above, speeds in Gaza tend to always hover on the lower scale of the spectrum. Wi-Fi speeds vary greatly, depending on a variety of factors, and especially different Wi-Fi standards (802.11b, 802.11a, etc.). Wi-Fi speeds are also listed according to a maximum bandwidth that is seldom approached in practice; instead 50 percent of that speed is much more frequent. In this case, a user on a 802.11b–Wi-Fi network that can offer up to 11 Mbps is probably not surfing faster than 5 or 6 Mbps.

31. Rasha Abou Jalal, "To Beat Unemployment, Young Gazans Turn to Birds," *Al-Monitor*, December 26, 2014.

sticks, the rate will be three times as fast (207 Mbps); a pigeon carrying five smaller drives increases the transfer rate to 345 Mbps. These calculations also assume only one data set at a time being sent out (two pigeons to two different nodes, but with the same data load). Even with these relatively conservative calculations, this is faster than any Internet speed—whether through Wi-Fi, cable, or DSL connections—currently available in Gaza, or many parts of the world for that matter.[30] Moreover, unlike regular Internet connections, the upload (flying out of Gaza) and download (flying into Gaza) speeds will be equivalent.

The IPN network is certainly not foolproof. Israel has banned the import of birds in Gaza, and could easily introduce hawks and/or drones to divert or stop pigeons. But with the heavy traffic of birds crossing Israel, the hope is that the pigeons will often be "camouflaged." Birdcages have already been destroyed by Israeli warplanes in previous wars on Gaza: for example, Mohammed Abu Ghalyoun lost his entire collection of pigeons and lofts, sustaining a financial loss estimated at $10,000.[31] There is no method to structure a network that will be completely impervious to Israeli violence, profit (for Israeli telecommunication firms), direct control, or surveillance (through whatever data still reliant on the Israeli backbone). But losing $10,000 worth of pigeons and lofts, and even another $10,000 in technological costs (such as drives), is substantially easier to overcome than the loss of other network architecture alternatives.

BENEFITS OF IPN

The immediate benefits of the IPN respond to the original challenge of designing a network that is as self-sustaining as possible, with minimum Israeli interference, control, and profit. The IPN establishes a system that is a great deal cheaper than other alternatives, channels a large chunk of data transfer away from the Israeli backbone, and is more impervious to interception and surveillance than many other (newer) technologies. The IPN provides upload and download speeds at substantially faster rates than what is currently available. It also helps decrease dependence on and lower the cost of newer (and foreign corporate) technologies, expertise, as well as contingent infrastructure such as routers, modems, and electricity. There are obviously trade-offs, but what is relinquished in immediacy, synchronicity, and newness is gained in economic and operational sustainability.

One important contribution of the IPN is the reliance on and employment of local labor, and the creation of new employment opportunities. The labor involved in establishing and maintaining the network will not require the high cost of foreign training or foreign expertise, nor need continued support from corporate entities or foreign governments (whether for software or hardware training, certificates, or the like). It will plug in to the robust landing points that already exist in locations such as Jordan and Egypt, where local nodes will be established. The network can also spur the development of local data centers, a local Internet exchange, and the creation of local software based on open-source programs, driven by Gazan labor.

The Gaza Internet Sky Geeks, to name only one existing high-tech group, could undertake a lot of this development, eventually creating its own search engines, software, and a local private network, requiring no costs or upkeep by external entities. Similarly, local pigeon breeders and trainers, as well as existing groups of pigeon enthusiasts in Gaza, will become part of this network.[32]

Various offshoot industries can further extend from the IPN: open-source software coders, veterinarians, loft-architects, and designers, among others. Lofts can double as public art installations; pigeon feathers could be used in arts, crafts, and toys; pigeon excrement can function as robust and free fertilizer (thanks to its high nitrogen content); older pigeons can eventually be consumed as a tasty protein-rich meal. Pigeons also eat different types of insects and worms and thereby keep the environment safe. And contrary to popular belief, pigeons are resistant or minimally susceptible to avian flu.[33] The IPN can also foster eco-conservation groups or research programs into the wide array of birds (and flora and fauna) that exists in Gaza.

By reclaiming control and agency over its own infrastructure, based on mostly local resources, Gaza would gain symbolically as well. Taking one's infrastructure into one's own hands is a sign of progress and autonomy. By embracing its "low-technologization," Gaza would balk against the rhetoric and representation of it lagging behind, and demonstrate its ability to creatively build and maintain efficient and affordable solutions. Self-subsistence and creativity, the reliance on local labor, and the

32. As a symbol of the possibility of overlapping multiple technologies, many pigeon growers, trainers, and fans in Palestine already keep in touch over Facebook and transact deals over WhatsApp, with a range of private and public Facebook groups available. See for example the Facebook group *Pigeons in Palestine*, whose tag line reads: "Our hobby is a message of peace to the world."

33. Blechman, *Pigeons*, 133.

creation of offshoot industries and creative outputs would further bring an element of pride. The IPN is a way for Gaza to contribute to the global network too, by identifying a material-biological-technical architecture that has concrete benefits in terms of sovereignty, security, intelligence, energy, and public access to resources. As such, the benefits extend much further than Gaza.

Setting up an autonomous and decentralized system, within which each subsystem or node independently controls its own area of responsibility and coordinates its individual objectives, speaks to trends (certainly in the Global North) concerned with reliable and equitable systems of distribution and access. Making infrastructure more "intelligible" helps maximize efficiencies in processing and transmission by *decreasing* the network's dependence and complexity. The simplicity of the IPN's architecture maximizes efficiencies in processing and transmission, and does not interfere with the nature of applications or processes. The IPN is also a means to take back control, and uncover and reclaim the unseen operations that shape the political and economic systems underlying our technologies. The IPN allows us to de-fetishize infrastructure (or the network) while also, in this case, simultaneously making it illegible to surveillance cameras and drones. The IPN is a model of a more flexible production, organization, and control of networks, evoking what Manuel Castells once called "grassrooting the space of flows."[34]

The IPN provides an environmentally friendly architecture because it requires less power and machinery, but also because it relies on and can propagate natural "resources"—for example, in the case of the first, the pigeons themselves; in the case of the second, turning "waste" into fertilizer. The IPN is a "green" network that contributes to biodiversity, or at least does not harm it. It would help redefine what an "intelligent network" or "smart city" can be: not marked by an overabundant plethora of expensive machinery, but a low-tech mechanism that has proved effective, reliable, and cheap for millennia. Moreover, it puts the "intelligence" back into the human and animal component of a network. It thus also takes seriously the idea that a technological system is an organism with a life of its own—thus challenging what actor network theory might mean.[35] The IPN is in many ways a biosystem—a model of sustainable animal–human–machine relations[36]—that can grow and adapt.

By (re)introducing the carrier pigeon to Gaza, both the pigeon's history as a reliable and speedy means of information sharing and Gaza's history as an important node in a broader network are (re)invigorated. Finally, given the history of Palestinian dispossession, there is a symbolic pleasure gained by the homing pigeon's innate ability to return to a place called "home."

34. Manuel Castells, "Grassrooting the Space of Flows," *Urban Geography* 20, no. 4 (1999): 294–302.

35. Michel Callon, "Techno-Economic Networks and Irreversibility," in *A Sociology of Monsters: Essays on Power, Technology, and Domination*, ed. J. Law (New York: Routledge, 1991), 132–61; Bruno Latour, "Technology is Society Made Durable," in *A Sociology of Monsters: Essays on Power, Technology, and Domination*, ed. J. Law (New York: Routledge, 1991) 103–31.

36. The metaphor can be pushed even further in positing future developments such as electronic pigeons or drone-pigeon hybrids. On animal–human–technological systems, see Clara Mancini, "Animal–Computer Interaction (ACI: A manifesto," *Interactions* 18, no. 4 (2011): 69–73; and Donna Haraway, *Simians, Cyborgs, and Women* (New York: Free Association Books, 1996).

WORKS CITED

Abd Rabou, Abdel Fattah, Al Agha, R. Mohammad, Maged M. Yassin, Abdel Karim S. Ali, Dawi M. Hamad. "The Avifauna of Wadi Gaza Nature Reserve, Gaza Strip—Palestine." *The Islamic University Journal (Series of Natural Studies and Engineering)* 15, no. 1 (2007): 39-85.

Abou Jalal, Rasha. "To Beat Unemployment, Young Gazans Turn to Birds." *Al-Monitor*, December 26, 2014,

al-Amoudi, Moath. "Pigeon Lovers Flock to Gaza Expo." *Al-Monitor*, May 6, 2016.

Allat, Captain H. T. W. "The Uses of Pigeons as Messengers in War and the Military Pigeon Systems of Europe." *Royal United Services Institution Journal* 30, no. 133 (1886): 107-48.

Arad, Roy. "Enthusiasts Flock to this Israeli Pigeon Market, a Rare Nest of Dovish Coexistence." *Haaretz*, August 26, 2016

Birds. "Israel Birding Portal." Accessed January 30, 2019. https://www.birds.org.il/en/index.aspx.

Blechman, Andrew. *Pigeons: The Fascinating Saga of the World's Most Revered and Reviled Bird*. New York: Grove Press 2006.

Callon, Michel. "Techno-Economic Networks and Irreversibility." In *A Sociology of Monsters: Essays on Power, Technology, and Domination*, edited by J. Law. New York: Routledge, 1991.

Castells, Manuel. "Grassrooting the Space of Flows." *Urban Geography* 20, no. 4 (1999): 294-302.

Darwish, Mahmoud. "Homing Pigeons." Translated by Lena Jayyusi and W. S. Merwin. In *Anthology of Modern Palestinian Literature*, edited by Salma Khadra Jayyusi, 152-55. New York: Columbia University Press, 1995.

Decolonizing Architecture Art Residency. "Project: Return to Nature." Accessed January 30, 2019. http://www.decolonizing.ps/site/texts.

Ghazal, Rym. "In e-mail age some still swear by pigeons." *Daily Star*, February 27, 2007.

Govendor, Peroshni. "Pigeon transfer data faster than South Africa's Telekom." *Reuters*, September 9, 2009.

Haraway, Donna. *Simians, Cyborgs, and Women*. New York: Free Association Books, 1996.

Kosharek, Noah. "IDF Corps Honors Pre-State Palmach and Haganah Carrier Pigeon Trainers." *Haaretz*, February 23, 2009.

Latour, Bruno. "Technology is Society Made Durable." In *A Sociology of Monsters: Essays on Power, Technology, and Domination*, edited by J. Law, 103-31. New York: Routledge, 1991.

Mancini, Clara. "Animal-Computer Interaction (ACI: A manifesto." *Interactions* 18, no. 4 (2011): 69-73.

Nicol, Lieutenant J. A. C. Nicol. "The Homing Ability of the Carrier Pigeon and Its Value in Warfare." *The Auk: Ornithological Advances* 62, no. 2 (April 1945): 286-98.

Paganini, Pierluigi. "Hack Satellite Connection and Surf Anonymously with High-Speed Internet." *Security Affairs*, August 13, 2015.

Scholl, Jeremiah, and Anders Lindgren. "Considering Pigeons for Carrying Delay Tolerant Networking Based Internet Traffic in Developing Countries." *Electronic Journal on Information Systems in Developing Countries* 54, no. 4 (2012).

Shell, Jacob. *Transportation and Revolt: Pigeons, Mules, Canals, and the Vanishing Geographies of Subversive Mobility*. Cambridge, MA: MIT Press, 2015.

Tawil-Souri, Helga. "Digital Occupation: Gaza's High-Tech Enclosure." *Journal of Palestine Studies* 41, no. 2 (2012): 27-43.

———. "The Technological End between the 'Inside' of Gaza and the 'Outside' of Gaza." *7iber*, September 2014.

von Raumer, Friedrich. *Geschichte der Hohenstaufen*. Lepizig: F.A. Brokhaus, 1823.

Waitzman, David. *RFC 1149*. Request for comments, IETF, April 1, 1990.

Wu, Shuangshuang. "Peace/Time Landscape Proposals for the Israeli and Palestinian Border." Master's Thesis, University of Illinois at Urbana-Champaign, 2011.

COLLECTIVE EQUIPMENT

Royal College of Art,
School of Architecture
MA Architecture, ADS7

Tatiane Britto
Rickesh Chandi
Joseph Dalgleish
Caroline Fok
Jieqi Ge
Ines Gulbenkian
Alberte Lauridsen
Lachlan McTaggart
Alice Meyer
Saijel Taank

Supervised by
David Burns
Platon Issaias
Godofredo Pereira
Francesco Sebregondi
and in collaboration with
B'Tselem
GISHA
OCHA OPT
Centre for Research Architecture
Forensic Architecture

All images by ADS7,
Royal College of Art unless
otherwise noted.

Regular military conflicts between Hamas and the IDF both exacerbate and obfuscate the violent consequences of the blockade.[1] Israel has increasingly restricted the conditions under which people and basic goods are allowed into Gaza. This has resulted in the majority of Gazans being reliant on humanitarian aid for their basic needs, of which reconstruction is one of the most pressing issues. The damage caused to buildings during military conflicts is severe and widespread (see figure 1). Unable to domestically produce the materials necessary to rebuild, Gazans are forced to apply for construction materials using the costly, inefficient, and restrictive Gaza Reconstruction Mechanism (GRM). This process is managed by several partners, including the United Nations and the Government of Palestine. However, it is ultimately controlled by Israel. The latter, citing security concerns, restricts the flow of even the most basic construction materials. Since the formalization of this process, just 10 percent of materials needed for Gaza's reconstruction have been allowed to cross the border.[2] At the same time, in its report, *Gaza: Two Years After,* the United Nations identifies "spatial and urban planning" as a key component lacking in the reconstruction of Gaza.[3]

Following detailed research into the conditions and processes in Gaza, ADS7 at the Royal College of Art—in collaboration with the Centre for Research Architecture and Forensic Architecture at Goldsmiths College—views the GRM and its mode of operation as one of the main obstacles to the reconstruction process. We propose three lines of intervention to ensure

that the reconstruction can proceed: (1) to make the process of filing planning applications to municipal authorities more accessible and streamlined; (2) to develop a tool for the quantification of materials, labor, time, and costs associated with a proposed project to allow for effective design; and (3) to provide a cost-effective, efficient, and easily understood series of construction techniques that can provide a level of design autonomy from the strict material limits and algorithmic space quantification of the application process. Making optimal use of the materials provided under the hard limits of the GRM allows for an efficient and iterative design process following the application.

Collective equipment has a long history in architecture, traditionally understood as instruments of religious and military powers, as tools deployed by the modern nation–state or, increasingly, by private entities. However, ADS7 argues that they are also part of an important tradition of emancipatory and transformative politics. Collective equipment is not just buildings that host public programs. Water distribution systems, land-use regulations, or transport infrastructures are equally capable of constituting a social collective around them. The focus here is not on the relation between infrastructure and a social group, or between a particular space and its "users," but on the ways in which these are one and the same. The protocols designed by Israel in support of its blockade of Gaza deny Palestinians agency over the reconstruction of their built environment. Efforts to intervene in this reconstruction should look to disrupt these protocols such that

1. While conflict is continual, fighting intensifies intermittently, such as during the IDF offensives of 2008 and 2014 known as Operation Cast Lead and Operation Protective Edge, respectively.

2. *Ten Years Later* (Tel Aviv–Jaffa: GISHA, 2015).

3. *Gaza: Two Years After* (Jerusalem: OCHA oPT, 2016).

**Figure 1: Damage to buildings during
Operation Protective Edge in 2014.
Source: UNOSAT Satellite Derived
Geospatial Analysis, September 30, 2014.**

Mediterranean Sea

Erez
Open for aid
workers and
humanitarian
cases, six days
a week

Beit Lahiya

Beit Hanoun

Jabalia

Gaza City

Nahal Oz fuel pipeline
Closed

Karni
Closed

Israel

Deir al Balah

High density urban areas

Refugee camps

Roads

Border

Border crossings

Khan Yunis

Egypt

Rafah

Sufa
Closed

Rafah
Controlled by Egypt,
closed apart from
limited authorized
people in exceptional
cases

Kerem Shalom
Controlled by Israel,
open for authorized
goods five days a week

**Figure 2: Israeli control of Gaza's
borders. Map data copyright
OpenStreetMap contributors
and available from http://www.
openstreetmap.org under an Open
Database License, accessed 2019.**

Gazans can affirm their existence as political and spatial actors through architecture.

THE GAZA RECONSTRUCTION MECHANISM (GRM)

The Gaza Reconstruction Mechanism (GRM) is a temporary agreement between the Government of Palestine (GoP) and the Government of Israel (GoI), brokered by the United Nations in 2014 following the war in Gaza. The United Nations Development Programme (UNDP) carried out and published a damage assessment alongside the development of the GRM in order to quantify the damage to Gaza and reinforce the urgent need for construction materials in the Strip.

The GRM was set up to facilitate and monitor the flow of dual-use materials coming into Gaza. Israel's complete control of Gaza's borders give it absolute control of these material flows. The dual-use list identifies materials that could potentially be used for military purposes. The GRM's stated aim is to balance Israel's security concerns and Gaza's economic needs.[4] To gain access to dual-use materials, individual beneficiaries must apply through the GRM, request specified quantities of materials in order to receive a permit, and subsequently purchase materials from the ninety-seven participating vendors.

The GRM is an independent mechanism within the construction process and does not assist in obtaining planning permission in Gaza, nor does it provide any financial aid to applicants. Its stated objective is to serve as a monitoring system for dual-use materials coming into Gaza.[5] Since 2014, a total of 1,139 large-scale projects have been registered in the GRM, with 468 projects currently active.[6]

STREAMS

The GRM is organized into three streams. Each application is processed through one of these streams depending on the nature of the construction project. As detailed in figure 4, each stream has distinct procedures and involves various parties.

The Shelter Stream is designed to help restore and rebuild homes that were damaged but not destroyed in the 2014 war. Damage assessments of shelters are carried out by the United Nations Relief and Works Agency for Palestinian Refugees in the Near East (UNRWA) and UNDP to help determine the amount of aggregate, steel rebar, and concrete (ABC materials) required to rehabilitate the shelters. After being processed through the GRM, the assessments enable homeowners to access the required materials from approved vendors.[7]

The Residential Stream facilitates the construction of new housing in Gaza. Calculations of the required amounts of dual-use materials required for the property are submitted to the GRM. Once processed, the materials can be purchased, by either the beneficiary or a contractor working on behalf of the beneficiary.[8]

The Project Stream is for large-scale projects. These include schools, hospitals, and other collective equipment, as well as large-scale residential schemes. The United Nations Office for Project Services (UNOPS) also includes any individual building over four stories in the project stream of the GRM. A detailed

4. "Dual Use Lists," Office of the Quartet, 2016.

5. "About: Gaza Reconstruction Mechanism," GRM Report, 2016.

6. Ibid.

7. Ibid.

8. Ibid.

Appropriate Government Ministries

- Director General of the Ministry of Defence
- Head of Defence Ministry's Expert Supervision Department
- Coordinator of Government Activities in the Territories (COGAT)
- Officers of the Civil Administration

GRM Material Flow

- Application for Permission
- Ministry of Economy Gaza
- Palestinian Coordination Commitee for the Entry of Goods
- Israel's Army Gaza DCO
- Appropriate Officer
- Approval
- Finalize transaction with Israeli vendor/broker
- Kerem Shalom crossing
- Gaza

Figure 3: Responsible bodies and processes for material flows through the GRM.
Sources: Gaza Reconstruction Mechanism, www.grm.org; Shelter Cluster Palestine, Gaza Reconstruction Mechanism—Engage?, July 31, 2015.

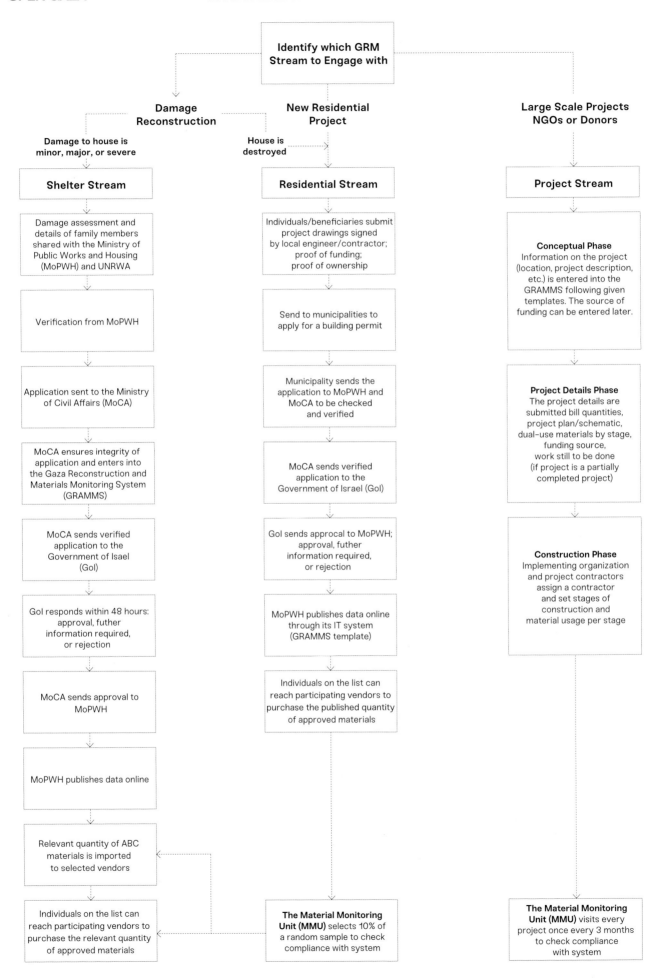

Identify which GRM Stream to Engage with

Damage Reconstruction

Damage to house is minor, major, or severe

Shelter Stream

Damage assessment and details of family members shared with the Ministry of Public Works and Housing (MoPWH) and UNRWA

Verification from MoPWH

Application sent to the Ministry of Civil Affairs (MoCA)

MoCA ensures integrity of application and enters into the Gaza Reconstruction and Materials Monitoring System (GRAMMS)

MoCA sends verified application to the Government of Isael (GoI)

GoI responds within 48 hours: approval, futher information required, or rejection

MoCA sends approval to MoPWH

MoPWH publishes data online

Relevant quantity of ABC materials is imported to selected vendors

Individuals on the list can reach participating vendors to purchase the relevant quantity of approved materials

New Residential Project

House is destroyed

Residential Stream

Individuals/beneficiaries submit project drawings signed by local engineer/contractor; proof of funding; proof of ownership

Send to municipalities to apply for a building permit

Municipality sends the application to MoPWH and MoCA to be checked and verified

MoCA sends verified application to the Government of Israel (GoI)

GoI sends approcal to MoPWH; approval, futher information required, or rejection

MoPWH publishes data online through its IT system (GRAMMS template)

Individuals on the list can reach participating vendors to purchase the published quantity of approved materials

The Material Monitoring Unit (MMU) selects 10% of a random sample to check compliance with system

Large Scale Projects NGOs or Donors

Project Stream

Conceptual Phase
Information on the project (location, project description, etc.) is entered into the GRAMMS following given templates. The source of funding can be entered later.

Project Details Phase
The project details are submitted bill quantities, project plan/schematic, dual-use materials by stage, funding source, work still to be done (if project is a partially completed project)

Construction Phase
Implementing organization and project contractors assign a contractor and set stages of construction and material usage per stage

The Material Monitoring Unit (MMU) visits every project once every 3 months to check compliance with system

Figure 4: The process for procuring construction materials through the GRM, split into shelter, residential, and project streams. Sources: Gaza Reconstruction Mechanism, www.grm.org; Shelter Cluster Palestine, Gaza Reconstruction Mechanism—How to Engage?, July 31, 2015.

bill of quantity must be submitted to the GRM. Once this bill is processed, the contractors implementing the project can procure materials either from participating GRM vendors or independently.[9]

Figure 5 shows the convoluted application process for individual beneficiaries constructing new residential properties as detailed by UNOPS and UNRWA. The diagram includes the initial planning process that the applicant must implement before applying to the GRM and procuring materials in order to obtain a building permit.

In the first instance, the beneficiary must submit full planning documentation to the local municipality. This includes plans, sections, elevations, and electrical and mechanical service drawings. These drawings must be signed off by local architects and engineers before being submitted to the municipality. The beneficiary must also include proof of ownership of the site and proof of funding for the project.

Once processed, the drawings are sent to the Ministry of Public Works and Housing (MoPWH) and the Ministry of Civil Affairs, to be verified. The project is then assigned a name, identification number, GPS location, and floor area totals in square meters.

The drawings are then sent to the GoI to be checked and approved. Around 10 percent of applications sent to the GoI are rejected due to one of three reasons: the Israeli government believes the applicant is deceased, under eighteen years of age when the application is made, or a security risk.[10]

If the application is approved, it is sent back to the MoPWH and the material data and quantities are uploaded to an online information

management system (GRAMMS). The beneficiary is then able to procure the registered materials from one of the participating suppliers.

DUAL-USE LIST
The dual-use list was created as part of the GRM to collate all materials that can be used for military as well as civilian purposes. The list, and the procedures in place to satisfy its requirements as shown in figure 5, create numerous complications that delay import times and raise costs for Palestinian importers.

Since the 2014 ceasefire and the introduction of the GRM, material flows across Gaza's borders have steadily increased (see figure 6).[11] Israel is now allowing a controlled flow of construction materials for private use and reconstruction into Gaza within the GRM framework. However, the flow is still slow and delivers an insufficient supply compared to demand. This severely compromises the construction process and time scale of reconstruction. There is continuous pressure from the GoP, humanitarian organizations, and NGOs to allow the free movement of construction materials into Gaza.

PLANNING CONTEXT
For most of Gaza's history, urban planning has been controlled by external actors rather than internal ones, consequently urban planning institutions are weak.[12] Land laws were imposed under the Ottomans (1850–1917), the British Mandate (1917–48), the Egyptian administration (1948–1967), and most recently under Israeli occupation, leaving Gaza with multiple planning orders (see figure 7).[13]

9. Ibid.

10. Rafiq Abed, Chief of Infrastructure and Camp Improvement Project, UNRWA, Skype interview, November 29, 2016.

11. "Entrance of Construction Materials," GISHA, accessed December 9, 2016.

12. Ali Abdelhamid, "Urban Development and Planning in the Occupied Territories: Impacts on Urban Form" (paper presented at Nordic and International Urban Morphology: Distinctive and Common Themes, Stockholm, Sweden, 2006).

13. Sara Roy, The Gaza Strip: The Political Economy of De-Development (Washington, DC: Institute for Palestine Studies, 2015).

Figure 5: Process for submitting a planning application, applying for materials through the GRM, and the procurement process. Sources: Gaza Reconstruction Mechanism, www.grm.org; Shelter Cluster Palestine, Gaza Reconstruction Mechanism—How to Engage?, July 31, 2015.

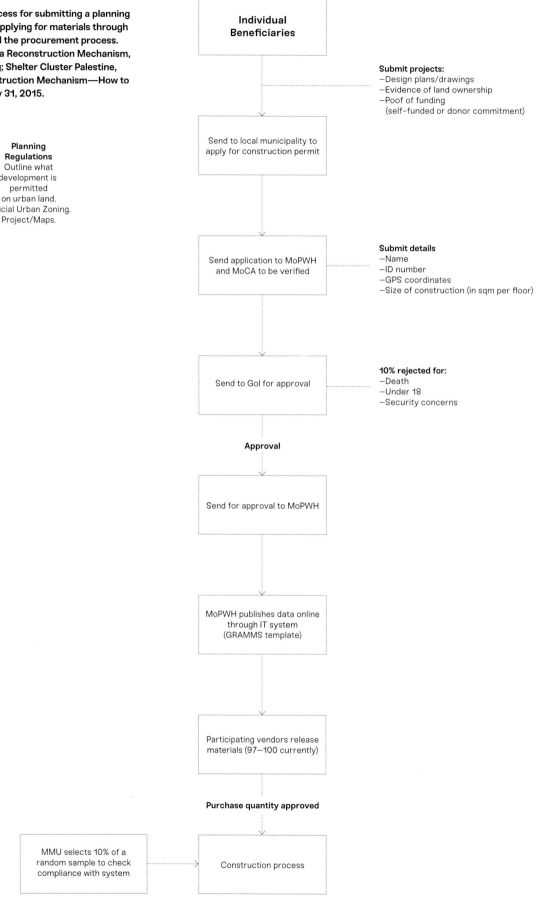

Planning Regulations
Outline what development is permitted on urban land. Official Urban Zoning. Project/Maps.

Individual Beneficiaries

Submit projects:
—Design plans/drawings
—Evidence of land ownership
—Poof of funding
  (self–funded or donor commitment)

Send to local municipality to apply for construction permit

Send application to MoPWH and MoCA to be verified

Submit details
—Name
—ID number
—GPS coordinates
—Size of construction (in sqm per floor)

Send to GoI for approval

10% rejected for:
—Death
—Under 18
—Security concerns

Approval

Send for approval to MoPWH

MoPWH publishes data online through IT system (GRAMMS template)

Participating vendors release materials (97–100 currently)

Purchase quantity approved

MMU selects 10% of a random sample to check compliance with system

Construction process

Figure 6: Cement, steel, and gravel entering into Gaza (2010–2016).
Source: "Entrance of Construction Materials," GISHA, accessed December 9, 2016.

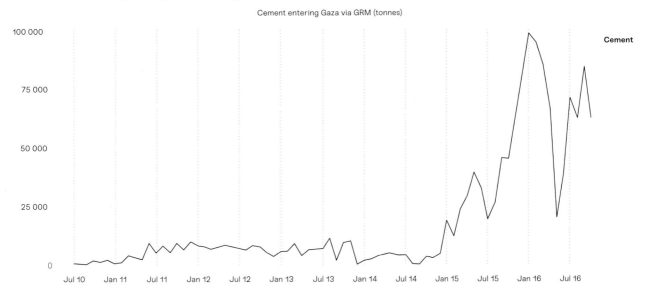

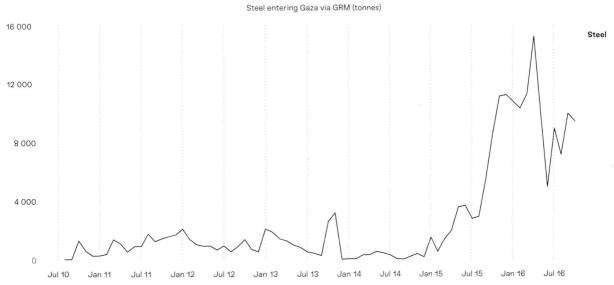

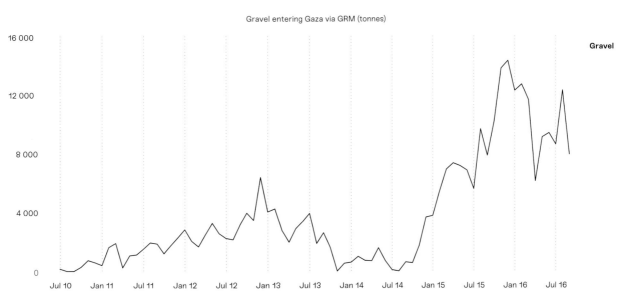

Under the Israeli occupation, urban growth was managed by the military to maximize Israeli control of the Gaza Strip and support Israeli settlements, rather than to promote sustainable urban growth. Infrastructure that was not related to the settlements was neglected. In the Hamas administration, there is currently no central agency responsible for the planning and financing of development in the Gaza Strip.

After the Oslo agreement, there were three main levels of government in Palestine: the central, the regional or governorates (*mohafaza*), and the municipal. At the central level, the Ministry of Local Government (MLG) was established in 1994, intended to provide local government with legal supervision.

The governorates (*mohafaza*) represent the regional level. They are administered by the Ministry of the Interior and are led by directors selected by the President of the Palestinian Authority. They are responsible for coordinating some state services (health, education, transportation, etc.) at the regional level. There are fourteen governorates: nine in the West Bank and five in the Gaza Strip (North Gaza, Gaza City, Deir el-Balah, Khan Yunis, and Rafah).

Municipalities and village councils are the third level of government and work at the local level and are controlled by the MLG. In 1994, there were thirty-one municipalities (twenty-six in the West Bank and five in the Gaza Strip), eighty-six village councils, and 225 localities without legal status. Currently there are 121 municipalities (96 in the West Bank and 25 in the Gaza Strip) and 355 village councils.

The 1997 local government law manages the system of local government. It aims to define the legal framework for local government, mentioning 27 fields of activity under municipal responsibility. The most important tasks include issuing building permits, regulating commerce and industry, promoting urban development, and approving budgets. Municipalities are accredited to issue orders or decisions that administer their service activities and specify, for example, the opening hours of the municipal market.

Palestinian legislation also differentiates between different types of localities, such as municipalities and village councils, according to demographic weight. Municipalities are local governments with autonomy in decision making, budgets, and personnel management, and members elected by the population. The village councils are administrative structures that depend on a directorial ministry and whose purpose is to represent the central power in detached remote areas. Their directors are nominated.

INTERNATIONAL FUNDING

The Palestinian Authority was set up in 1994 following the Oslo agreement and is seen internationally as the only legitimate authority in Palestine. However, Hamas has controlled the Gaza Strip since 2007, an entity that is classified internationally as a terrorist organization and therefore not seen as a legitimate power by international parties including the United States and the European Union. International donors share these concerns—Hamas rearming and rebuilding defenses on the ground—and are at the same time

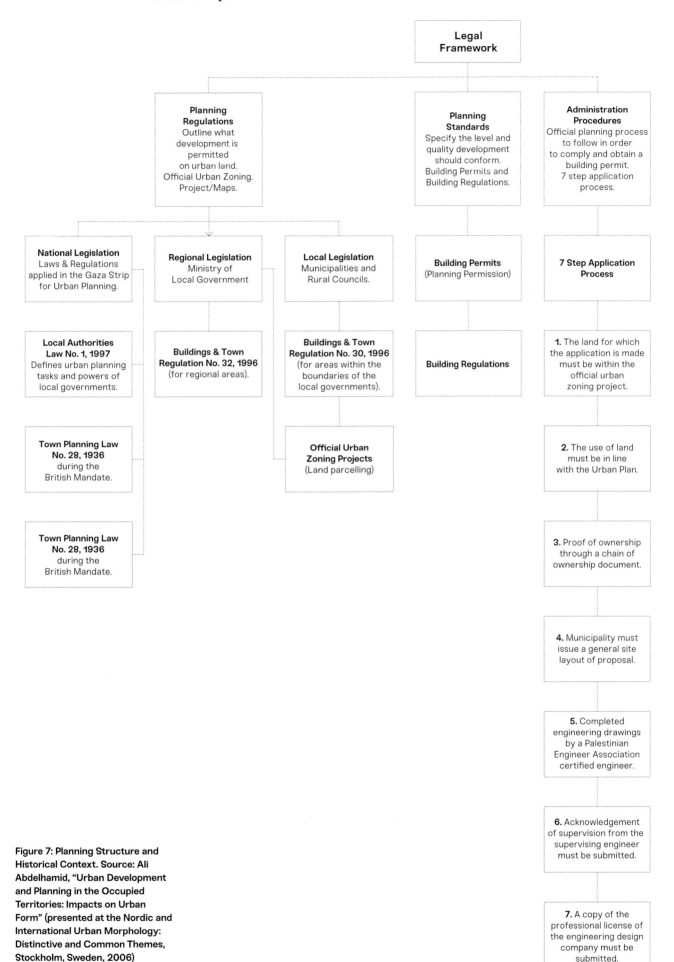

Figure 7: Planning Structure and Historical Context. Source: Ali Abdelhamid, "Urban Development and Planning in the Occupied Territories: Impacts on Urban Form" (presented at the Nordic and International Urban Morphology: Distinctive and Common Themes, Stockholm, Sweden, 2006)

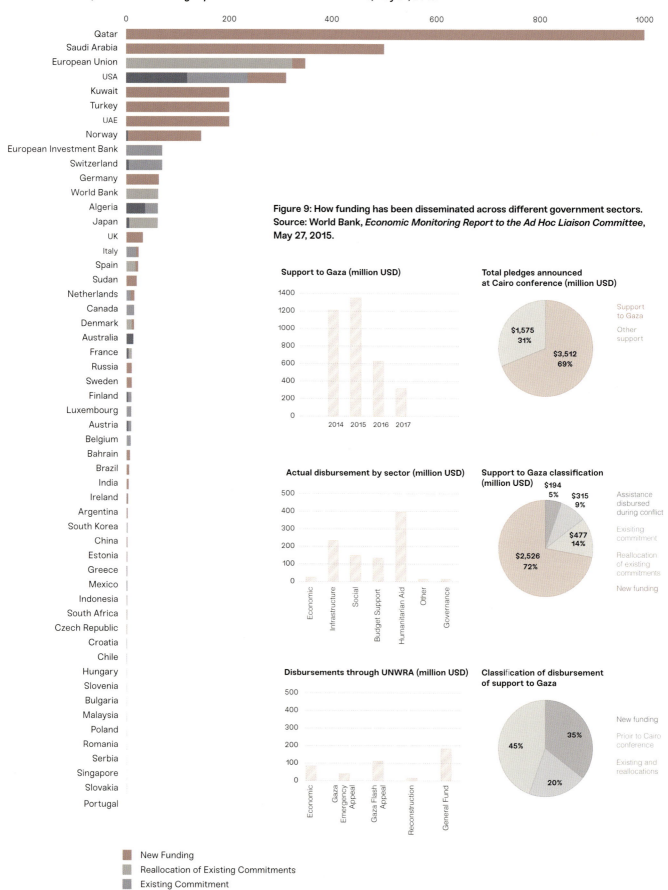

Figure 8: International funding, both pledged and received, to Gaza since Operation Cast Lead in 2014.
Source: World Bank, *Economic Monitoring Report to the Ad Hoc Liaison Committee*, May 27, 2015.

Figure 9: How funding has been disseminated across different government sectors.
Source: World Bank, *Economic Monitoring Report to the Ad Hoc Liaison Committee*, May 27, 2015.

Support to Gaza (million USD)

Total pledges announced at Cairo conference (million USD)
$1,575 31%
$3,512 69%
Support to Gaza
Other support

Actual disbursement by sector (million USD)

Support to Gaza classification (million USD)
$194 5%
$315 9%
$477 14%
$2,526 72%
Assistance disbursed during conflict
Exisiting commitment
Reallocation of existing commitments
New funding

Disbursements through UNWRA (million USD)

Classification of disbursement of support to Gaza
35%
45%
20%
New funding
Prior to Cairo conference
Existing and reallocations

New Funding
Reallocation of Existing Commitments
Existing Commitment
Assistance Disbursed During Conflict

afraid that Israel will permanently sever Gaza from the West Bank.[14] Israel largely controls access to and resources in Gaza and remains the occupying power in the Gaza Strip under international law. The delays inherent in this convoluted system have led those awaiting construction to work outside it, with many families selling the reconstruction materials received from the UN to fix their homes out of a need for cash.[15]

International funding is key to the reconstruction of Gaza. Figure 8 outlines the international funding that was received by or pledged to Gaza since the 2014 conflict, both through private investment and humanitarian organizations. The data in figure 9 details how funding has been disseminated across different government sectors. It goes on to highlight how funding from UNRWA has been dispersed, before finally showing how the projected flow of international investment is expected to dramatically fall over the next few years.[16]

CONSTRUCTION TECHNIQUES

The restriction of material flows into Gaza necessarily affects the nature of construction in the Strip. Concrete construction is a recent addition to its urban fabric. In recent years, it has overtaken mud construction as the dominant architectural technique. Concrete construction offers several advantages over mud construction, but the Israeli blockade of Gaza makes the technique, which relies on imported building materials, costly and inaccessible to the majority of Gazans.

In general, concrete structures perform better than mud structures in relation to several key indicators. Concrete construction techniques are versatile, cost effective, and structurally sound. They allow for flexibility in typology and extension following completion of the initial project. The structural strength of the material can allow for an efficient use of space through reduction of structural members in comparison to mud-brick techniques.[17]

However, these advantages are largely negated by the conditions in Gaza created by the blockade. Gaza has no domestic capacity to produce concrete.[18] Israel allows very little cement to enter the region. The material that does enter is largely earmarked for large, international projects with financial backing.[19] Consequently, the price of concrete fluctuates daily, but is often more than three times as high as the price in an open market.[20]

14. Sultan Barakat and Omar Shaban, *Back to Gaza: A New Approach to Reconstruction* (Doha: Foreign Policy at Brookings, 2015).

15. Ibid.

16. *Economic Monitoring Report to the Ad Hoc Liaison Committee* (Washington, DC: World Bank, 2015).

17. Eman Y. Ismail, "Evaluation and Development Study of Housing Types Used in the Gaza Strip to Rebuild the Place Identity" (paper presented at the 4th International Engineering Conference–Towards Engineering of 21st Century, Islamic University of Gaza, October 15, 2012).

18. Ibid.

19. "Control Means Responsibility: Israel is Obliged to Allow Construction Supplies into Gaza," B'Tselem, January 14, 2014.

20. *Shelter Advocacy Fact Sheet 2* (Global Shelter Cluster, June 2010).

MUD-BRICK CONSTRUCTION

Due to the difficulty in obtaining materials for concrete construction, mud and adobe are more common in Gaza. Prior to 2009, when many projects began to be implemented with UNRWA's backing, mud construction techniques were the most prevalent form of construction in the region. Prevailing attitudes in Gaza are that mud construction interiors provide for a more comfortable building environment than newer concrete construction.

In many ways, mud construction techniques are advantageous. Little or no specialist labor is required when constructing with mud brick or block. Material costs are low, as materials are readily available and can often be found on-site. This also lowers transportation costs and material lead times. Only simple tools are required for mud construction. Furthermore, these techniques inherently have good fire-resistant properties, and sound and thermal insulation. Mud-brick construction techniques can also create significant economic benefits. The unskilled labor creates employment opportunities. Using locally sourced building materials generates income for the local economy.

However, mud-brick construction has several constraints that limit its viability. Importantly, it tends to be very labor-intensive. The structural limitations of the material restrict the building typologies it can be used for. These limitations have significant implications in earthquake-prone regions like Gaza.

Two main types of mud construction are widely used in Gaza. The first is traditional adobe or mud-brick construction. Soil or subsoil is mixed with water, chopped straw, and clay. This mixture is then put into a mold and left to dry in the sun. After the drying process is complete, the bricks are laid and joined with mortar to create walls. These are then often rendered with a mud mixture.

The second commonly used technique is compressed earth block (CEB) or compressed stabilized earth block (CSEB). These blocks use soil or subsoil mixed with small amounts of lime or cement. The blocks are then mechanically compressed. CSEBs perform significantly better than traditional mud-brick or adobe construction, and remedy many of their problems. Specifically, CSEBs are much more durable, less susceptible to water damage, and require far less maintenance than sun-dried mud bricks. This construction technique is a relatively recent arrival in Gaza and prior to, it was rarely used. Only since UNRWA—in collaboration with the International Labour Organization (ILO)—began backing projects that utilized CSEBs did the process become widely used. This technique requires access to skilled labor, as well as specialized machinery and concrete both of which are on the dual use list, making them difficult to obtain.

These mud-brick construction techniques can be coupled with structural systems such as domes and arches to increase their versatility and structural strength (see figure 12). However, this requires specialist labor and formwork, which can be difficult to source.

Using the research discussed in the previous section, we can identify a series of key issues. The first stems from the GRM and the convoluted planning process. Protocols set out in these processes are incredibly

Figure 10:
Case Study: UN Residential Project

Projects sponsored by the UN have the benefit of having ready access to funding and materials. The size and political influence of the stakeholders generally mean that these projects can effectively engage with the application process and the GRM. This section presents a case study of a UN-sponsored project for a 100-unit housing complex.[21]

The project is funded by a donation of the Custodian of the Two Holy Mosques Campaign for the Relief of the Palestinian People, a committee based in Saudi Arabia. The funding and project management is coordinated by the UNDP and the Program of Assistance to the Palestinian People. In this case, the donor has pledged $6.7 million. The project is a complex made up of sixteen, four-story buildings that house eight apartments each, to be completed in phases. In addition to these housing units, the complex will also contain a mosque, a school, and extensive physical infrastructure.

Reverse engineered from UN construction documentation by ADS7, this figure shows concrete domino construction techniques are employed, which are ubiquitous around the world. With fewer material restrictions, these projects are able to employ foundations that are suitable for use in sandy, earthquake-prone soil. A combination of isolated and combined footings are used, with retaining shear walls dug into the basement. Typical wall details are blockwork and cavity blockwork. It is important to note that the majority of the building materials listed in the schedule of quantities and specifications appear on the dual-use list. Only the political influence of the stakeholders makes it possible to obtain them.

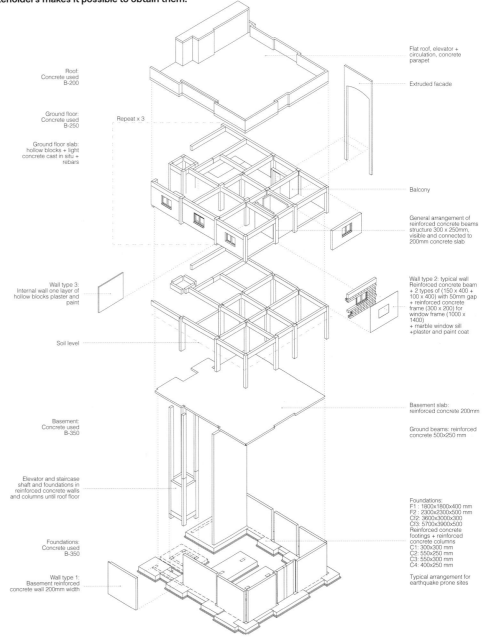

Roof:
Concrete used
B-200

Ground floor:
Concrete used
B-250

Repeat x 3

Ground floor slab:
hollow blocks + light
concrete cast in situ +
rebars

Wall type 3:
Internal wall one layer of
hollow blocks plaster and
paint

Soil level

Basement:
Concrete used
B-350

Elevator and staircase
shaft and foundations in
reinforced concrete walls
and columns until roof floor

Foundations:
Concrete used
B-350

Wall type 1:
Basement reinforced
concrete wall 200mm width

Flat roof, elevator +
circulation, concrete
parapet

Extruded facade

Balcony

General arrangement of
reinforced concrete beams
structure 300 x 250mm,
visible and connected to
200mm concrete slab

Wall type 2: typical wall
Reinforced concrete beam
+ 2 types of (150 x 400 +
100 x 400) with 50mm gap
+ reinforced concrete
frame (300 x 200) for
window frame (1000 x
1400)
+ marble window sill
+plaster and paint coat

Basement slab:
reinforced concrete 200mm

Ground beams: reinforced
concrete 500x250 mm

Foundations:
F1 : 1800x1800x400 mm
F2 : 2300x2300x500 mm
Cf2 3600x3000x300
Cf3: 5700x3900x500
Reinforced concrete
footings + reinforced
concrete columns
C1: 300x300 mm
C2: 550x250 mm
C3: 550x300 mm
C4: 400x250 mm

Typical arrangement for
earthquake prone sites

21. Documentation and information for this project is available through the United Nations Development Program.

Figure 11:
Case Study: Informal Residential Project

In stark contrast to the previous project, many housing projects in Gaza are completed informally on a small-scale as family units. The rapid increase in population, shortage of suitable housing stock, and unclear or inaccessible planning policy result in unplanned, illegal structures with little coordination.[22] Since these developers are unable to apply through legitimate planning processes, building materials are unavailable. Hence, materials must either be purchased illegally on the black market or recycled.

The drawings and structural details shown here for these buildings are reverse engineered by ADS7 through reviewing photographs and videos. This analysis reveals that, generally, structural elements in these informal dwellings are less suitable for sandy soils in earthquake-prone regions. The individual footings are generally less for seismic regions, as they do not provide the necessary rigidity and allowance for deformity. This is especially true in areas with soft soil. Under these conditions, it is typically best practice to provide continuous footings under all walls. Furthermore, there appear to be no shear walls, and very little cross bracing. Without these structural elements, the building is vulnerable to damage or collapse during an earthquake. In the absence of a collar beam around the head of the wall to support the roof, there is a tendency for the roof to act as a disc.

Given the financial restrictions of private projects of this kind, the materials must be cheaper than those used in more formal construction methods. Estimated costs of the typical structure examined stand at $8,078. The average monthly salary in Gaza is $174.[23]

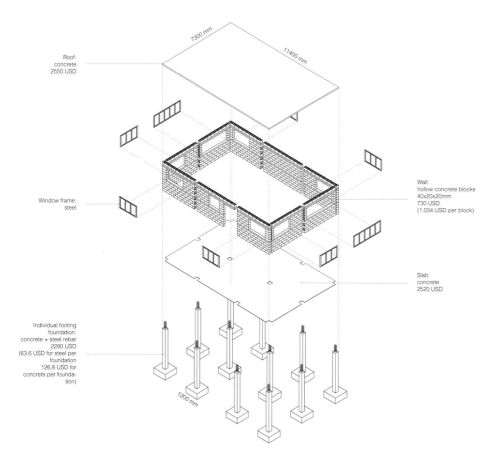

Roof:
concrete
2550 USD

7300 mm

11400 mm

Window frame:
steel

Wall:
hollow concrete blocks
40x20x20mm
730 USD
(1.034 USD per block)

Slab:
concrete
2520 USD

Individual footing
foundation:
concrete + steel rebar
2280 USD
(63.6 USD for steel per
foundation
126.8 USD for
concrete per founda-
tion)

1200 mm

22. Musallam F. Abu Helu, "Urban Sprawl in Palestinian Occupied Territories: Causes, Consequences and Future," *Environment and Urbanization ASIA* 3, no. 1 (March 2012): 121–41.

23. *Economic Monitoring Report* (World Bank).

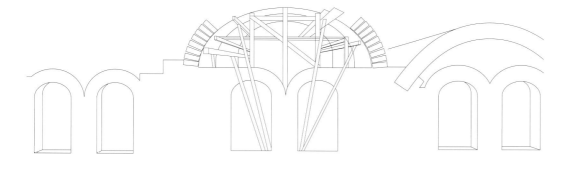

Figure 12: Mud Brick Arch

onerous and restrictive. Completing a full planning application with a complete drawing package, technical specification, and other required documents is cost and time prohibitive, given the poor economic outlook and knowledge gaps. Even when planning applications can be successfully lodged, the GRM is inefficient and ineffective. This results in severe shortages of construction materials, particularly for small-scale, private self-build projects. These actors lack the financial resources and political influence to effectively engage with the processes in place.

The second key barrier to reconstruction is the dual-use materials list. While the IDF cites security concerns and maintain that these materials serve both a military and a civilian purpose, this comprehensive list contains the majority of building materials and tools required for even the most basic structures. It imposes strict requirements on the quantity of building materials, limiting their availability and suitability for use in construction. As a result, construction techniques that are fit for purpose are largely impossible. Techniques that can be readily implemented are structurally unfit and have limitations, typological and otherwise, that make them inappropriate to the pressing need for reconstruction.

Figure 13:

Case Study: UNRWA-Sponsored Residence

The following project is an UNRWA-sponsored house, in collaboration with the ILO, which typifies small-scale housing projects utilizing CSEBs. It forms part of a complex of twenty identical housing units, intended to house internally displaced refugees. All details and specifications in figure 13 are reconstructed from the UNRWA-project data sheet unless otherwise specified.

The total floor area of the unit is 60 square meters and is intended to house families with fewer than eight members. Despite this, the plan allows for only two bedrooms. The project specifications indicate that the construction process was due to take 16 weeks, but it is unclear whether this target was met. The average cost of a unit is estimated at $18,000.

The project uses CSEBs stabilized with cement. The material makeup of the CSEB is gravel (15 percent), sand (47 percent), clay (20 percent), silt (15 percent), and cement (3—8 percent). This mixture results in a cost per brick of 0.15 Israeli New Shekels (USD $0.04). These bricks are laid into a wall with 10 mm mortar joints. These walls are load bearing, with no support from structural columns or cross bracing. While CSEBs are more structurally sound than traditional adobe construction, they still represent a risk in terms of structural stability in a seismic event. The walls benefit from a collar beam at the head of the wall, which also serves to support the domed roofs. This structural member should aid with structural stability to some extent. The foundations are continuous and support each wall, which is in line with best practice for structure in soft soil (sand) regions that are prone to earthquakes.

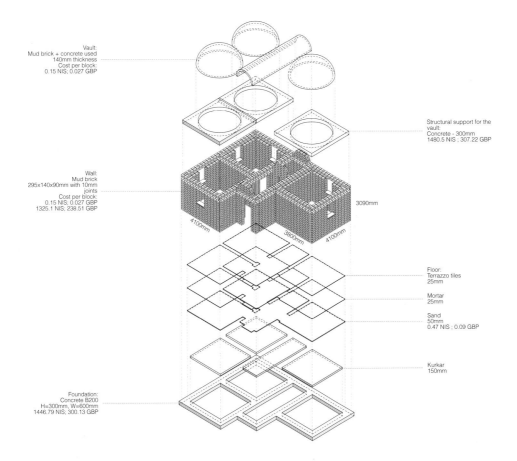

Vault:
Mud brick + concrete used
140mm thickness
Cost per block:
0.15 NIS; 0.027 GBP

Structural support for the vault:
Concrete - 300mm
1480.5 NIS ; 307.22 GBP

Wall:
Mud brick
295x140x90mm with 10mm joints
Cost per block:
0.15 NIS; 0.027 GBP
1325.1 NIS; 238.51 GBP

3090mm

4100mm

3800mm

4100mm

Floor:
Terrazzo tiles
25mm

Mortar
25mm

Sand
50mm
0.47 NIS ; 0.09 GBP

Kurkar
150mm

Foundation:
Concrete B200
H=300mm, W=600mm
1446.79 NIS; 300.13 GBP

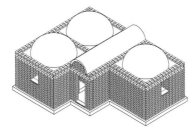

Figure 14:

Informal Residential Project

The axonometric (figure 14) depicts a common mud–brick house construction adopted in Gaza. The building consists of three rooms: a kitchen, a bathroom, and one bedroom. These houses provide a temporary solution to those that have lost their homes due to conflicts. The dried bricks are held together with wet mud, due to the restrictions on cement imposed by Israel. Mud–brick construction does not rely on imported construction materials, making it freely accessible to Gazans and minimizing construction time.

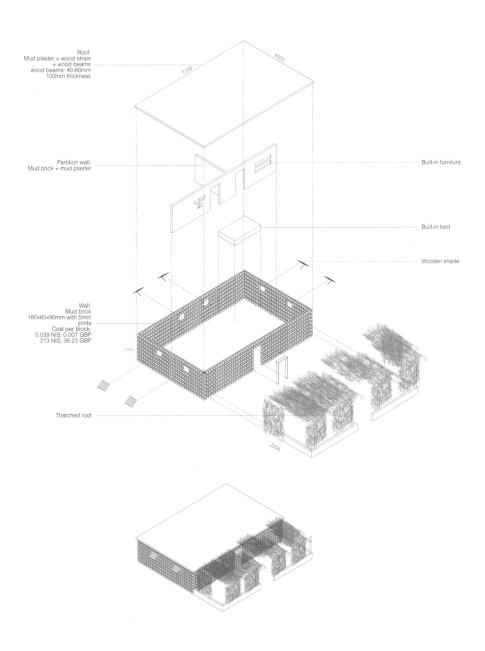

INTERVENTION

The research team proposes to intervene in the reconstruction process in three distinct ways:

1. Make the process of submitting planning applications to municipal authorities more accessible and streamlined. The first step of any scheme is submitting a planning application. The major barriers for small–scale actors are cost and knowledge deficits that make producing this package difficult. A system of drawing tools to quickly and accurately satisfy the requirements of the application process will enable small–scale builders to engage with this system easily, without significant cost outlays, and with minimal specialized knowledge.

2. Facilitate the quantification of materials, labor, time, and costs associated with a proposed project to allow for effective design. Detailed quantification of the required materials is a necessary part, both of the formal application and of designing spaces that are achievable under the strict material limits imposed by the GRM.

3. Provide a cost–effective, efficient, and easily understood series of construction techniques that can make builders more independent from the material limits of the application process. As part of the assessment of an application, the Israeli government and the MoPWH in Gaza have agreed upon a flat rate for calculating material requirements per square meter of floor area, using an algorithm. Introducing a set of construction techniques that use materials more efficiently can allow for iterative and flexible design. These techniques incorporate concrete, mud–brick, and hybrid construction techniques aimed at minimizing material costs and procurement time.

WORKS CITED

Abdelhamid, Ali. "Urban Development and Planning in the Occupied Territories: Impacts on Urban Form." Paper presented at Nordic and International Urban Morphology: Distinctive and Common Themes, Stockholm, Sweden, 2006.

Abu Helu, Musallam F. "Urban Sprawl in Palestinian Occupied Territories: Causes, Consequences and Future." *Environment and Urbanization ASIA* 3, no. 1 (March 2012): 121–41.

Barakat, Sultan, and Omar Shaban. *Back to Gaza: A New Approach to Reconstruction*. Doha: Foreign Policy at Brookings, 2015.

"Construction Techniques; Survey in Palestinian Territories." Ministry of Local Government, Palestine, August 2012.

"Control Means Responsibility: Israel is Obliged to Allow Construction Supplies into Gaza." B'Tselem, January 14, 2014.

"Dual Use Lists." Office of the Quartet, 2016.

Economic Monitoring Report to the Ad Hoc Liaison Committee. Washington, DC: World Bank, 2015.

"Entrance of Construction Materials." GISHA, accessed December 9, 2016.

Gaza: Two Years After. Jerusalem: OCHA oPT, 2016.

GRM Report, "About Gaza Reconstruction Mechanism," GRM Report, 2016.

Ismail, Eman Y. "Evaluation and Development Study of Housing Types Used in the Gaza Strip to Rebuild the Place Identity." Paper presented at the 4th International Engineering Conference—Towards Engineering of 21st Century, Islamic University of Gaza, October 15, 2012.

Muhaisen, Ahmed, and Johan Ahlback. "Towards Sustainable Construction and Green Jobs in the Gaza Strip." International Labour Organization, June 15, 2012.

Roy, Sara. *The Gaza Strip: The Political Economy of De-Development*. Washington, DC: Institute for Palestine Studies, 2015.

Shelter Advocacy Fact Sheet 2. Global Shelter Cluster, June 2010.

Ten Years Later. Tel Aviv-Jaffa: GISHA, 2015.

Zami, Mohammad Sharif, and Angela Lee. "Economic Benefits of Contemporary Earth Construction in Low-Cost Urban Housing—State-of-the-Art Review." *Journal of Building Appraisal* 5, no. 3 (2010): 259–71.

FRONTIER URBANIZATION

Francesco Sebregondi

The reconstruction of Gaza is among the largest urban development projects in the world today. Over 170,000 housing units require rebuilding or repair, estimated to cost $4 billion.[1] Despite its enormous scale, stretching across the entire Palestinian enclave, so far this building site has not drawn much attention from urban scholars and practitioners. The exceptional status of Gaza prevents it from qualifying as a relevant case study of our global and ever-expanding urban condition.

The context of Gaza is, of course, unique—even more so today. The current wave of building activity across the Strip is a response to the unprecedented level of destruction that the 2014 Israeli military operation brought about. Nearly five years after the ceasefire, the reconstruction job is far from done. Only half the amount of cement required has been allowed into the enclave, and about thirty thousand people remain displaced as a result of the war.[2] Based on the most up-to-date rate of progress, the reconstruction is officially forecast to end in 2020— the year the UN predicted Gaza would become "unliveable."[3] This excruciating slowness has a clear cause: in spite of the critical need for reconstruction in the aftermath of the war, the blockade of Gaza has remained in force: 1.8 million people are denied entry to the outside world, and the import of building materials is restricted.

War, the primary cause of urban destruction in Gaza, is intrinsically *abnormal*; as such, it tends to exceed the conventional realm of urban thought and practice. As a corollary to this distinction, the reconstruction of Gaza is primarily framed as a *humanitarian* project; it thus appears through a different lens, and is approached with different standards, than a development of the same scale in the United States, Europe, or China. In spite of its de facto permanence, the state of emergency in force in Gaza largely suspends the rules and principles that would normally apply to city building. Given that the current round of postwar reconstruction is the third since 2009, it can be safely assumed that its overall aim is less the construction of an environment that the community can live and thrive in durably, but rather, to build a place where it can survive for a little longer.

A common trait of humanitarian operations is to override qualitative questions with purely quantitative assessments undertaken in the name of pragmatic efficiency.[4] The reconstruction of Gaza is no exception to this logic, where figures and calculations reign supreme. Scattered across numerous reports, the "plan" for the rebuilding of the Strip shows few signs of considering the quality of the environment to be built, beyond quantifiable measures.[5] It is no wonder then that most urbanists and architects lack interest in the rudimentary and stripped-down version of the modern city that is ostensibly being erected in Gaza. A well-intentioned minority of them may praise it as an example of architecture for a good cause, or perhaps good enough for refugees.[6] Regardless, at first sight it would seem foolish to search for any remarkable architectural innovation or cutting-edge urban design in, of all places, Gaza.

1. Ministerial Committee for the Reconstruction of Gaza, *Detailed Needs Assessment (DNA) and Recovery Framework for Gaza Reconstruction* (State of Palestine, 2015). This "DNA" serves as the main reference document for all actors involved in the reconstruction.

2. Global Shelter Cluster, "Palestine: Shelter Cluster FactSheet" June, 2017.

3. See date updated in real-time at "About," GRM Report, 2017; See also United Nations Country Team in the occupied Palestinian territory, "Gaza in 2020: A liveable place?" (Jerusalem: Office of the United Nations Special Coordinator for the Middle East Peace Process [UNSCO], 2012).

4. Eyal Weizman, *The Least of All Possible Evils: Humanitarian Violence from Arendt to Gaza* (London: Verso, 2011), 1–24.

5. Ministerial Committee for the Reconstruction of Gaza, Detailed Needs Assessment (DNA); *State of Palestine, Gaza Strip: A Reconstruction and Development Plan* (Jerusalem: Palestinian Economic Council for Development and Reconstruction [PECDAR], September 2014).

6. The Good Cause: Architecture of Peace, exhibition at the Canadian Centre for Architecture (June–September 2011); See connected publications: Arjen Oosterman, ed., "Architecture of Peace," special issue, *Archis* 26 (December 2010); Arjen Oosterman, ed., "Architecture of Peace Reloaded," special issue, *Archis* 40 (July 2014).

But what if the disastrous situation in Gaza today, together with the mode of response to such a permanent and engineered disaster, provided a glimpse of the endgame of contemporary urbanization processes? To what degree does Gaza capture, in an extreme form, some of the critical trends of urbanization? In other words, what happens if we cease to frame Gaza as an exception, and instead approach it as a radical example of a new normal? Could such a reframing bring about a shift in the way the Gaza crisis is commonly approached—from an unfortunate yet isolated glitch, to a testing ground for a soon-to-be widespread urban future?

1. FRONTIER AND SECURITY

The frontier is an essentially dynamic site. Always on the move, at times expanding and at others contracting, it is produced through conflict and confrontation. The frontier does not exist prior to a meeting of opposite forces; it moves and takes shape through their clash, at the same time as it mediates their encounter.

The Gaza Strip emerged as a frontier from the very beginning of its brief history. An accidental territorial entity sprung from the ruins of Mandatory Palestine, Gaza's geographical contours correspond to an entrenchment of the frontline of the Arab-Israeli war at the time of the 1949 cease-fire.[7] This linear demarcation, also known as the Green Line, has not moved since it was first established, contrary to the frontier of the State of Israel, which has gradually thickened outwards to the point of covering the entirety of the occupied Palestinian Territories.

To this day, the fragmented geography of Palestine continues to bear the mark of its colonial origin. It is no longer necessary to argue that, far from ending the occupation of Gaza, the Israeli disengagement of 2005 inaugurated an occupation of a new kind. Recognizing the disengagement as a mere reconfiguration of the colonial regime in place, the legal scholar Darryl Li described the Gaza Strip as a "laboratory" where "Israel fine-tunes a dubious balance of maximum control and minimum responsibility."[8] Partly due to its strong evocative power, the image of the laboratory returned in other writings about Gaza, as it enabled authors to draw links between observable conditions in the Palestinian enclave and emerging trends beyond its sealed borders.[9]

While powerful, the frame of the laboratory carries some limitations. Palestinians in Gaza and the West Bank are anything but "guinea pigs," as the media theorist Ariella Azoulay and the philosopher Adi Ophir remind us.[10] Both pictures imply the "passivity of the forsaken Palestinian," while the deployment of ever more advanced technologies of security in the Territories is better understood as "a response to active, persistent, and often painful Palestinian resistance."[11] It follows from this that neither the State of Israel nor any of the enterprises that would compose a posited "military-security-industrial complex"[12] are likely to fit the role of the scientist conducting experiments in a "Gaza lab" under conditions of quasi-total control. Arguably, the notion of frontier better captures the contingent character of the technology of power deployed over

7. Jean-Pierre Filiu, *Gaza: A History* (New York: Oxford University Press, 2014).

8. Darryl Li, "The Gaza Strip as Laboratory: Notes in the Wake of Disengagement," *Journal of Palestine Studies* 35, no. 2 (2006): 38.

9. Naomi Klein, "Laboratory for a Fortressed World," *The Nation*, June 14, 2007; Stephen Graham, "Laboratories of War: United States-Israeli Collaboration in Urban War and Securitization," *The Brown Journal of World Affairs* 17, no. 1 (2010): 35–51; Eyal Weizman, *Hollow Land: Israel's Architecture of Occupation*, (London: Verso Books, 2012): 1–22.

10. Ariella Azoulay and Adi Ophir, "Abandoning Gaza," in *Agamben and Colonialism*, ed. Marcelo Svirsky and Simone Bignall (Edinburgh: Edinburgh University Press, 2012): 178–203.

11. Azoulay and Ophir, "Abandoning Gaza," 184.

12. Stephen Graham, *Cities Under Siege: The New Military Urbanism* (London: Verso, 2014), xxiii.

Gaza, understood as a permanently contested territory. Conversely, contested territories such as Gaza reveal the crucial entanglement of the territorial and technological senses of the frontier.

If primarily focused on the American case, the study of the "ecology of powers" in the context of the global War on Terror proposed by the philosopher Brian Massumi insists on the crucial role of contingency and unpredictability in shaping contemporary security practices.[13] Rather than an obstacle to be overcome, uncertainty has come to be accepted as a permanent and irreducible condition. In Gaza, as elsewhere, the uncertain nature of the perceived *threat* gives technologies of security their essentially protean character. One consequence of this new logic of security's particular relation to uncertainty—which Massumi characterizes as "preemptive"—is its agents' obsession with the collection and processing of ever-larger amounts of data from their field of operation. But rather than reacting to threats that have been identified as such, the driving principle of preemption is to act on mere signals before a threat has emerged. Within this logic, it is essentially the response that produces the threat, retroactively.

If we are to consider the configuration of power deployed in Gaza as one instance of the logic of security that characterizes our present epoch, the 2005 disengagement may initially appear as a false move. As a result Israeli security forces can no longer count on any personnel on the ground to gather intelligence on potential threats. In

reality, Israel has bet on its highly advanced surveillance technology to make up for any loss in monitoring capacity. The very enforcement of the blockade effectively consists in a vast monitoring operation, with the gaze of the Israeli state projected inwards from the land and sea borders that it keeps closed, looking into Gaza as deeply as possible.

Increasingly "smart," the fence itself is regularly upgraded with passive and active sensors that scan the Gazan territory ever more thoroughly. Far from being confined to a mere linear feature, the border of Gaza operates as a thick apparatus of surveillance and firepower. From the new subterranean barrier allegedly under construction, to the swarm of armed and unarmed drones permanently circling over the Strip, through the specifically tasked Electronic Observation Unit that was recently appointed by the Israeli Defense Forces (IDF), Gaza's "high-tech enclosure" consists of a stack of constantly updated components.[14] Their joint task: to gather ever-larger amounts of actionable information, produce a real-time, high-definition image of the neighboring "hostile entity" of Gaza, and enable Israeli security forces to act on any dissonant signal before it challenges the status quo of the blockade.[15]

Developed and field-tested throughout the occupied Palestinian Territories, Israel's pioneering security technology is considered by many to be the best in the field. Over the past decade, it has attracted an increasing number of buyers from all over the world: its products can now be found from Glasgow to Rio de Janeiro, Baltimore, or Chongqing.[16] Borrowing Aimé

13. Brian Massumi, *Ontopower* (Durham: Duke University Press, 2015).

14. Helga Tawil-Souri, "Digital Occupation: Gaza's High-Tech Enclosure," *Journal of Palestine Studies* 41, no. 2 (Winter 2012): 27–43; Gili Cohen, "Israeli Army Reveals Massive Barrier Being Built to Stop Hamas' Gaza Terror Tunnels," *Ha'aretz*, August 10, 2017; Anna Ahronheim, "Israel's Eye On Gaza: The IDF's Electronic Observation Unit," *The Jerusalem Post*, February 16, 2017.

15. Israel Ministry of Foreign Affairs, "Security Cabinet declares Gaza hostile territory," September 19, 2007.

16. NICE Systems, "NICE Safe City Solutions Deployed in Glasgow to Bolster Security, Safety, and Operations Management," press release, 2014; Viva Sarah Press, "Israelis Manage Olympic Security Budget of $2.2 billion. Rio de Janeiro Games to serve as real-time platform for Israeli security innovations and defense capabilities," *Israel21c*, August 2, 2016; Stephen Babcock, "Israel-Based Cyberbit Makes Another Move in Maryland," *Technical.ly Baltimore*, July 18, 2017; NICE Systems, "China's Chongqing Metro Monorail Selects NICE's Digital Video Security Solution to Protect Passengers and Assets Against Crime and Potential Terror Threats," press release, 2009.

Césaire's notion of the "boomerang effect of colonisation,"[17] Michel Foucault famously noted how colonial frontiers fueled a dynamic process of experimentation with practices and technologies of power, the most successful of which tended to be brought back to metropolitan areas.[18] The enduring reality of this loop is a telling confirmation of the persistence of our "colonial present," although the increasingly insidious form that such technologies take today render them all the more invisible.[19] Wherever *security* becomes a watchword of society, one can witness a blurring of the distinction between the military and civilian domains—a trend that is, once again, pushed to the limit in Gaza. And thus, the same security concerns were invoked by the Israeli state to justify, on the one hand, the thorough destruction of Gaza's built environment, and on the other, the establishment of a reconstruction mechanism that enabled it to vastly upgrade its monitoring of Gaza.

2. THE SMART CITY

In September 2014, the UN Office of the Special Coordinator for the Middle East Peace Process (UNSCO) brokered a temporary tripartite agreement between Israel, the Palestinian Authority (PA), and the United Nations–sponsored Gaza Reconstruction Mechanism (GRM), which was presented as a means to lift some of the restrictions on the entry of construction materials into the enclave. In practice, the GRM functions through a purpose-built online database system of unprecedented size and granularity, named GRAMMS (Gaza Reconstruction And Materials

Monitoring System). For each construction project—from single housing unit repairs to a piece of municipal infrastructure—an application must be submitted electronically that includes the details of the applicant, the exact location of the building, the purpose of the construction, and the amount of materials requested. Assembled and maintained by the UN, with the distant involvement of the PA, the database is regularly reviewed by Israeli authorities. They approve or reject projects, determining which packets of materials will be allowed into the enclave and which ones will be refused.[20] Overall, the GRM introduces a centralized database system that gathers micro-data coming from every corner of Gaza and enables a modulated response in real time. After it was leveled by smart bombs, Gaza is arguably being turned into a smart city.

Officially presented as a mere technical solution to the problem of coordinating the trade of materials across the Gaza border, the implementation of the GRM has far-reaching political and urbanistic consequences. As soon as it was announced, the mechanism was strongly criticized by a number of observers who saw it as a move towards an institutionalization of the blockade, which remains illegal by all international standards.[21] Legal experts have argued that, by playing an active part in establishing and maintaining this ad hoc mechanism, the UN was in violation of international law and its own mandate.[22] Furthermore, over the course of nearly three years of activity, the GRM has plainly demonstrated itself to be

17. Aimé Césaire, *Discourse on Colonialism* (New York: Monthly Review Press, 2000), 41.

18. Michel Foucault, *Society Must be Defended: Lectures at the Collège de France, 1975–6* (London: Allen Tate, 2003), 103.

19. Derek Gregory, *The Colonial Present: Afghanistan, Palestine, Iraq* (Malden, MA: Blackwell, 2004).

20. Only a short fact-sheet regarding the Gaza Reconstruction Mechanism was released publicly by the UN Office of the Special Coordinator for the Middle East Peace Process. The full text of the agreement was meant to remain secret, but ended up online following a leak in January 2016. Much of the analysis developed in this essay relies on a close reading of the procedures and regulations described in this document.

21. Nuriya Oswald, "Gaza Reconstruction Mechanism: Profiting Israel, Entrenching the Blockade," *Jadaliyya*, July 7, 2015.

22. Nigel White, "Expert Opinion on the Legality of the Gaza Reconstruction Mechanism (GRM)," confidential expert opinion, January 26, 2015, leaked full text in Ali Abunimah, "UN database for Gaza aid may give Israel targets to attack—secret memo," *The Electronic Intifada*, January 13, 2016.

unfit for its official task—a point of criticism which is regularly voiced by humanitarian actors on the ground.[23] As a circulatory machine, not only is its overall flow rate insufficient to meet the material needs of Gaza's people, but the irregular and intermittent character of its output also keeps choking off the construction industry it is supposed to support.[24] This marks a further step toward normalizing the blockade in the international discourse, and entrenches the material power relations that the blockade established. As a result, the people of Gaza find themselves even more vulnerable to minute reductions or interruptions of the inflow of their most basic needs—from electricity to water, fuel, calories, and now cement.

As revealed by the now infamous "red lines" document, cutting down the already minimal flow of supplies that are allowed into Gaza has long been the Israeli state's policy of choice for putting pressure on the Hamas-controlled enclave.[25] While the GRM supports the continuation of this broad policy, it also marks a significant shift in the technology of power deployed in Gaza. In order to measure this shift, it is useful to consider the impact of the GRM on the urban form of the Palestinian enclave, and to examine the particular kind of urbanism that is ingrained in the mechanism itself.

In Gaza, the built environment tends to be measured in weight: millions of tons of rubble had to be cleared before further millions of tons of cement could be allocated to reconstruction.[26] As a consequence of its cyclical unmaking and remaking, architecture is caught in a discourse that reduces it to an uncountable substance; broken down into mere quantities of its elementary components, it becomes prey to a vast apparatus of calculation. This is most obvious in the public façade of the GRM.[27] On this dedicated website full of bold figures and interactive data charts, one can track how much "ABC material"—A for aggregate, B for reinforced steel bars, C for cement—enters Gaza each month; how many tons of each are allocated to the "shelter," "residential," "finishing," or "infrastructure" project streams; and how many applications for such projects were received by the GRM administration, broken down according to their present status. All the while, a real-time data feed provides updates about the latest transactions on the GRM market: "3 hours ago, [anonymous] beneficiary purchased 20 bags of [generic] cement."

As any database management system, GRAMMS requires structured data. This is what enables it to compute aggregate figures or issue statistical assessments. The benefits of coordination among the disparate actors involved in the reconstruction are evident: the system provides everyone with a common template that can be used to apply for, review, monitor, approve, or reject building activities. The data template captures a multiplicity of diverse objects—in this case, architectural and urban projects—in the regular nets of a database. Yet because it was established as the only route by which any building can be materialized, the GRM actually converts its own tabular logic into a virtual urban grid, which it projects onto the entire territory of Gaza. As it delineates the parameters of

23. "'Palestinians stuck in a permanent cycle of humanitarian relief'—UN Humanitarian Chief," OCHA, November 23, 2016.

24. The option of blocking the mechanism is always available to Israeli authorities, as demonstrated in April 2016 when the Coordination of Government Activities in the Territories (COGAT) suddenly imposed a complete ban on private imports of cement, following allegations that cement was being diverted from its intended beneficiaries toward Hamas. The ban was lifted only forty-five days later.

25. GISHA, "Reader: 'Food Consumption in the Gaza Strip—Red Lines'" (Tel Aviv: October 2012).

26. "War Left Four Million Tons of Rubble in Gaza, Says Environmental Group," Haaretz, September 16, 2014.

27. See GRM website for updates in real time.

the possible—i.e., every project must fit within one of the four project streams recognized by the mechanism, have a circumscribed location, and be built in ABC material—the GRM can only be described as the new matrix of Gaza's urban fabric, which is realized one bag of cement at a time.

Furthermore, the GRM replaces the administrative division of Gaza's territory with its own fine-grained grid. Designed to bypass the Hamas-led administration of the enclave, the mechanism requires that individual applications for construction materials be entered into the system by the PA, via its Ministry of Civil Affairs. In the same way as civil society was left out of any discussion about its establishment, the architecture of the GRM prevents the essential question of reconstruction from being addressed at any collective level— be it that of a district, municipality, or neighborhood—and instead imposes the separate treatment of each individual plot of land. As such, it largely hinders, if not completely rules out, the possibility of *composing* spaces together, beyond the scale of each separate building project. The lines of its tables isolate plots just like they separate cells, and as it feeds on disaggregated data, the GRM regurgitates a disaggregated urbanism.

This *a priori* fragmentation of a shared spatial condition goes hand in hand with a splintering of time into an array of distinct temporalities. The GRM regulations require that each application be divided into four distinct phases, each of which must be submitted and approved separately. Each project is thereby

assigned its own parallel timeline, along which progress is contingent on intermediate checks by the Materials Monitoring Unit—a UN body policing the enclave in armored vehicles to "monitor contract compliance and report via the central IT database."[28] Broken down into so many conditional and at all times interruptible timelines, it is impossible to assess the progress of the overall reconstruction.

What is more, at the core of the GRM lies a logic of control over the import of so-called dual-use items into Gaza, namely items that are "liable to be used, side by side with their civilian purposes, for the development, production, installation or enhancement of military capabilities and terrorist capacities."[29] This "dual-use" regime helps shed light on a key aspect of the terror/security dialectic that has been so central to the post-9/11 governmentality. *Both* terrorism *and* the counter-terror security practices implemented in response consist in a weaponization of the everyday, and if the former manifests itself through isolated blasts, the latter spreads through all aspects of everyday life, pervading its very fabric. Following this logic, even the most basic building materials such as cement and rebar are treated as potential weapons by Israeli authorities, because they could be used to build "terror tunnels."

It is by invoking this threat, and its own sovereign right to preempt it, that through the GRM the State of Israel obtained the power to oversee every step of the circulation of cement in Gaza. While ABC materials certainly do not constitute the only items considered "dual-use,"

28. Oswald, "Gaza Reconstruction Mechanism," 6; Sultan Barakat, "The Situation in Gaza Requires Immediate Action," *Al-Jazeera*, May 11, 2016.

29. Israel Ministry of Foreign Affairs, "Gaza: Lists of Controlled Entry Items," announcement, July 4, 2010.

the Coordinator of Government Activities in the Territories (COGAT) has been wary of publishing a list of those items, and instead reserves the right to review and decide on a project-by-project basis.[30]

Instead, a list of submitted requests is published on the GRM website, comprising more than ten thousand distinct construction items and including statistics about the actual approval rate of each.[31] While this list is meant to help "contractors and project managers operating under the GRM to anticipate the materials that will generally be available," what it actually brings to light is the depth of control exercised by the State of Israel over the urban form that is to emerge in Gaza, down to the most minute architectural detail. From the approval of building phases to that of dual-use items, the process holds GRM applicants in Gaza hostage to external sovereign decisions that determine what they can build, how, where, and when. Yet even more than the right to decide, the State of Israel has the right to indefinitely suspend its decision, which best captures the power it exercises over the reconstruction of Gaza—and over the people that depend on it.

The establishment of the GRM constitutes an extension of what Stephen Graham has called Israel's "military urbanism," the ultimate objective of which is to make the built environment entirely *transparent* to the authorities in charge of monitoring it.[32] After the targeted destruction of alleged tunnel networks, including everything covering them above ground, or the deployment of a horde of autonomous "eyes in the sky"

continuously patrolling over Gaza, the GRM represents a significant upgrade of Israel's surveillance capability: it constructs a nearly one-to-one map of the urban and social fabric of Gaza, updated in real time by the very users it is forced upon. Anticipating a chilling feedback loop of the mechanism, some have pointed to "the potential misuse of the database by the Government of Israel for the identification of targets" in the next war.[33]

3. FROM LOGOS TO LOGISTICS

Israeli authorities have long used planning in Palestine as "a tool in the scramble for control over space."[34] As Christine Boyer's essay in this volume illuminates, the murky and opaque system of planning laws in place throughout the West Bank and Gaza is, to a large extent, the result of policy rather than poor administration. The designed deficiencies of the legal framework surrounding land use and planning can be understood as the specifically urbanistic dimension of the overall suspension of the law that, according to Giorgio Agamben, characterizes the "state of exception."[35] In the theoretical model that Agamben proposes, the state of exception brings about a kind of crude and stripped-down form of power: no longer encumbered by law, power would attain directly to life, "without any mediation."[36] The popularity of this model in critical writings about Palestine is not surprising. Given the level of violence that Palestinians in Gaza and the West bank must endure on a daily basis, the degree of violation of their human and citizen rights, and the widespread impunity enjoyed by the perpetrators of such

30. Following a long legal battle, GISHA recently obtained COGAT's list of dual-use items, but the list includes uses terms defined so broadly—such as "vehicles" or "communication equipment"—that it is, in practice, useless. See also their publication on the subject: "The dual use list finally gets published, but it's the opposite of useful," GISHA (blog), April 20, 2017.

31. "Dual-use Requests," GRM Report, 2017, https://grm.report/#/DualUse/List.

32. Graham, *Cities under Siege*.

33. White, "Expert Opinion," 11.

34. Meron Benvenisti, quoted in Rami S. Abdulhadi, "Land Use Planning in the Occupied Palestinian Territories," *Institute for Palestine Studies* 19, no. 4 (1989–90): 51.

35. Giorgio Agamben, *State of Exception* (Chicago: University of Chicago Press, 2005).

36. Ibid.

violence, the occupied Palestinian Territories (OPT) may appear as a kind of wild frontier where the rule of law has given way to the rule of the strongest.

Nonetheless, this diagnosis may be misleading. The focus on what is *missing* from a postulated normative picture prevents one from seeing and describing what has actually emerged within the juridical void created by the state of exception: what other, and comparably complex, technologies of government have been deployed instead of a "juridico-discursive" model of power.[37]

The case of Palestine vividly demonstrates how the diminishing role of the law as an ordering principle is accompanied by the growth of a different operative logic, primarily concerned with the technical management of material flows across a territory—what could be called a shift from the *logos* of the law to the *logistics* of flow. Interestingly, this logistical order takes on a different form in each of the two entities that constitute the Palestinian Territories: an extensive model in the West Bank, and an intensive one in Gaza.

From hilltops to wells and arable land, the relentless expansion of Israeli settlements over the past fifty years has slowly eaten away at the West Bank's most valuable sites, all the while breaking up its territorial integrity. Yet, as Eyal Weizman has argued insightfully, this dotting and speckling of the territory is but one component of the West Bank's occupation; the other, which activates it as an operative process, is the crisscrossing of the territory by an infrastructure of segregated circulation.[38] Through the network of checkpoints operated by its security forces, Israel achieves a distributed and dynamic control of the entire West Bank. Its physical presence at every strategic crossroad enables it to sift and filter all traffic across the territory it occupies, hindering the movement of Palestinians *and* fast-tracking that of settlers. This is where the dialectical dimension of Israel's logistics of power plays out: the slowing down of one type of flow goes hand in hand with the acceleration of another. For instance, the pristine network of settlers-only roads—locally called the "apartheid roads"—enables Israeli settlers and security forces to move about swiftly, at the same time as their material construction on top of old Palestinian roads entails the obstruction or closure of the latter.[39] Similarly, the West Bank separation wall is only disguised as a static divider between two orders of territorial sovereignty; it rather works as a membrane within an apparatus of segregated traffic control that emanates from Israel's mainland and extends over the entire West Bank.

In Gaza, on the other hand, the exercise of logistical power follows a different model. The combined effects of the disengagement and the blockade established a clear-cut separation between the occupying force and the occupied territory, which materializes in a barrier much more hermetic than the one in the West Bank. Rather than distributed across a physically occupied territory in the form of a multitude of checkpoints, the nodes of traffic control are concentrated in just a couple of strategic points along the Gaza barrier. By managing the terminals of Erez (for people)

37. Michel Foucault, *The History of Sexuality, Vol. 1: An Introduction*, trans. Robert Hurley (London: Penguin, 1980), 82.

38. Weizman, *Hollow Land*, 139–60.

39. Ramzi Jaber et al., "Segregated Road Systems in the West Bank," Visualizing Palestine, infographic, 2012.

and Kerem Shalom (for goods)—the only two crossings that are not permanently closed today—Israel is able to control and obstruct the flow of everything coming in or out of the Palestinian enclave.[40] Regardless of how such flows are routed and distributed inside Gaza—a task that Israel has gladly delegated to the international humanitarian complex on-site[41]—the control of a few centralized gateways is enough to guarantee Israel's capacity to monitor the full spectrum of Gaza's logistics. The model of occupation enacted by the blockade therefore shifts the focus from an extensive control of the territory to an intensive control of its border. Accordingly, the declared objective of the 2014 Israeli military operation, aptly code-named "Protective Edge," was the destruction of Gaza's tunnels that—by opening up channels of unmonitored communication across the border—posed a fundamental, *topological* threat to Israel's current structure of power over Gaza.[42]

While the West Bank and Gaza are each subjected to a different model of traffic control, namely fully-distributed versus fully-concentrated, together they attest to the rise of a logistical form of governance that has substituted itself for the discourse of law as the main ordering principle of the occupied territory. In fact, the distinction between these two models may be starting to fade away in practice. A closer look at the latest conditions on the ground in Palestine reveals signs of a hybridization of the two models.

When describing it as "laboratory," Darryl Li was accurately pointing to Gaza as a potential blueprint for future developments in the West Bank, which he feared could soon turn into "an archipelago of isolated 'Gaza Strips.'"[43] The sections of the separation wall that were erected over the past decade have, with their tortuous path, indeed considerably hardened the isolation of Palestinian villages and communities, creating a multitude of micro-enclaves in the "seam zone" between the Green Line and the effective route of the wall.[44] In addition to such permanent enclosures, Israeli security forces maintain a widespread policy of imposing curfews on neighborhoods, villages, or entire towns across the West Bank—both as a punitive measure and, increasingly, as a preemptive one.[45]

Implemented by lethal force, those temporary closures effectively constitute a small-scale, mobile version of a blockade. The West Bank's distributed closures can therefore be approached as a projection of Gaza's carceral conditions onto the wider Occupied Territories. Far from a compromise between the two models, the occupation of the West Bank remains one of extensive and minute control over the territory, to which, inspired by Gaza, an additional layer of security is added by sealing off entire Palestinian communities. This picture should be complemented with the sharp increase in the targeted destruction of Palestinian homes in the West Bank.[46] Demolishing the family homes of alleged "terrorists" has recently become a routine policy, resonating with the main "strategy" that underpinned Operation Protective Edge: to bomb the houses of all individuals suspected of links with Hamas, even if their entire

40. "Gaza Strip Access and Movements," OCHA Occupied Palestinian Territory, August 2016.

41. Weizman, *Least of All Possible Evils*, 81-96.

42. Israeli Ministry of Foreign Affairs, "Objectives and Phases of the 2014 Gaza Conflict" (executive summary, Jerusalem, June 14, 2015).

43. Li, "Gaza Strip as Laboratory," 39.

44. Quoting from a recent UN report: "Some 11,000 individuals live in 12 Palestinian communities between the Barrier and the Green Line, inside the area Israel declared as the 'Seam Zone.' According to various estimates, when the Barrier is completed, 25,000 more Palestinians will be living in similar enclaves." United Nations Country Team in the Occupied Palestinian Territory, "Leave No One Behind: A Perspective on Vulnerability and Structural Disadvantage in Palestine," United Nations, November 25, 2016.

45. "General Closure to be Imposed on West Bank Starting Rosh Hashana Eve," *The Jerusalem Post*, October 2, 2016; Anna Ahronheim, "IDF to Impose Week-Long Closure of West Bank, Gaza ahead of Passover Holiday," *The Jerusalem Post*, April 9, 2017.

46. "Sharp Increase in West Bank Demolitions," OCHA Occupied Palestinian Territory, March 2016; Ruth Eglash, "Israel Steps Up Home Demolitions to Punish Palestinian Attackers," *The Washington Post*, January 17, 2016.

family is inside.[47] From Gaza to the West Bank, the Palestinian domestic environment is weaponized by being assimilated in bulk to a terrorist infrastructure—a process which then turns it into a legitimate target of destruction.

Conversely, the establishment of the GRM in Gaza, discussed in the previous section, can be seen as a reintroduction of the West Bank's extensive model of logistical governance. As we saw, one of the consequences of the GRM is to place the entire (re)constructible land of Gaza under the detailed supervision of Israeli authorities, who can monitor the distribution of construction materials down to the scale of individual home repairs. The management of circulatory flows remains the crux of the exercise of power here: in Gaza, it is no longer achieved through the physical presence of Israeli security forces at strategic points along a road network, but rather mediated by a new digital infrastructure of data collection and processing.

The GRM is, in fact, a network of checkpoints passing through every plot of land, whereby every Palestinian in Gaza has to interface with the State of Israel to access the cement they need to build their home. It does not take much to imagine a near-future situation in which such a digital access portal could mediate Gaza residents' access to all other resources, from electricity to water or food. And when it comes to the problem of acquiring "ground truths" to match the data available in the system, Israel can count on the UN as a particularly collaborative partner. After the United Nations Office for Project Services (UNOPS) built the database system, UNSCO took up the role of policing building sites and warehouses in Gaza on behalf of Israeli authorities, essentially acting as their proxy. To a certain extent, the "civilian occupation" of the West Bank, whereby outwardly neutral actors such as architects and planners are enrolled in the scramble for territorial control, finds its counterpart in Gaza, where the UN and the broader NGO complex end up playing an active role in maintaining the regime of the blockade.[48]

Rather than a hybridization, what we are witnessing between Gaza and the West Bank is an *integration* of the two models of logistical order into a third one, which is *both* intensive *and* extensive. Regardless of their respective legal status or declared sovereignty regime, it is important to acknowledge that Gaza and the West Bank are essentially governed by a common operative logic. The feedback loops between these two frontiers with similar technologies of government that enable them to constantly reconfigure, and to advance in the shadow of the law— as the GRM case illustrates vividly.

The oblique way the GRM penetrates the domain of planning, urbanism, and architecture in Gaza is not by placing the State of Israel on top of a pyramid of authorities organized according to scales of collectivity—from the territorial to the architectural—as planning would traditionally proceed. Rather, the GRM establishes itself *beside* this nested structure of decision-making, beside the legal framework of planning; by creating an additional, direct interface between every

47. Amnesty International and Forensic Architecture, *Black Friday: Carnage in Rafah During 2014 Israel/Gaza Conflict* (New York: Amnesty International, July 2015).

48. Rafi Segal and Eyal Weizman, eds., *A Civilian Occupation. The Politics of Israeli Architecture* (London: Verso, 2003).

construction project and the State of Israel, it undercuts the entire structure of planning, causing its collapse.

In the process, what the GRM sets in motion is nothing less than a novel form of urbanism: one that no longer operates through *plans*—through the design of a coherent image of a projected spatial ensemble—but rather, through the real-time modulation of a built environment at an ever-increasing spatial resolution. By reintroducing an extensive network of distribution and communication under the control of Israeli authorities in Gaza, the GRM solves, for the occupying force, the problem of *addressability* of the Gaza territory. This problem arose since Israel's withdrawal to the border, and refers to the problem of the resolution at which the occupier can channel its orders and responses.[49] Subdivided into as many territorial cells as the GRM can store in its database, the built environment of Gaza is deprived of its capacity to reflect, or sustain, the social relations of the community that inhabits it. Instead, it turns into the equivalent of a pixel grid of territorial dimensions, which Israel can monitor and modify at a very high definition. This constitutes a logistical upgrade with far-reaching consequences: while it was only able to strike them beforehand, Israel can now *govern* each pixel of Gaza's built environment independently.

4. GOING GLOBAL

Returning to the problem posed in the introduction, what parallels can be drawn between Gaza and some of the global trends of contemporary urbanism? Two parallels can be

drawn. The first one concerns what could be termed a subtractive form of urbanism.[50]

In Gaza as elsewhere, urban environments are undergoing ever-faster cycles of destruction and reconstruction. Those cycles, in turn, are best understood as updates—the means by which the urban fabric is regularly conformed to the requirements of the political economy that it mediates. The perspective of urban subtraction questions any conceptual framing of urban and architectural practices as proceeding along a linear trajectory, whether historical or progressive. It challenges the common assumption that architecture and urbanism only operate through the positive process of adding new built forms on top of earlier ones. When reckoning with additive and subtractive spatial practices on the same theoretical plane, the urban fabric appears as a field in constant flux: a medium of circulation, continuously optimized through the creation of new channels *as well as* the removal of old obstacles. Vast clearings of urban terrains are as much part of urban design as large building operations.[51]

The other analogy relates to the multiplication of fences across the global urban landscape; the prominent role of enclosure in defining the contemporary urban condition. With nearly two million inmates, the open-air prison of Gaza is one of a kind, both in terms of its dimensions and of the intensity of its isolation. Yet it is also one instance of the proliferating typology of enclosed spaces that seems to characterize the urban world today.[52] Camps and ghettos on one side of the spectrum, condos and exclusive zones on the

49. For a thorough discussion of the problem of addressability in relation to sovereignty, infrastructure, and technology, see Benjamin H. Bratton, *The Stack: On Software and Sovereignty* (Cambridge, MA: MIT Press, 2016).

50. Keller Easterling, *Subtraction*, Critical Spatial Practice no. 4, Nikolaus Hirsch and Markus Miessen, eds. (Berlin: Sternberg Press, 2014).

51. Gregory Clancey, "Vast Clearings: Emergency, Technology, and American De-Urbanization, 1930–1945," *Cultural Politics* 2, no. 1 (2006), 49–76.

52. Giorgio Agamben famously proposed to consider the "camp" as "the nomos of the modern." See Giorgio Agamben. *Homo Sacer: Sovereign Power and Bare Life*, trans. Daniel Heller-Roazen (Stanford, CA: Stanford University Press, 1998), 166–80; See also Keller Easterling, *Extrastatecraft, The Power of Infrastructure Space* (London: Verso, 2014), 25–69. On the reversibility of camps and enclaves, see Bratton, *The Stack*, 21.

other; the same architectural profile is universally reused, for seemingly opposite functions. However, approaching the urban fabric as a medium of circulation helps identify the relationship between these two functions, just as it clarifies how contemporary fences and walls act as membranes, rather than mere isolating machines. Their relative closure and/or openness play an essential regulatory role within a generalized economy of circulation, where access is currency. Like the rise of a subtractive form of urbanism, the multiplication of fences across an urban network on a planetary scale should be considered from the perspective of the constant optimization of the urban fabric's capacity to channel and filter circulatory flows. Rather than thinking of the fence as halting circulation, it is perhaps more useful to approach it as a device enabling the particular kind of *differential* circulation that characterizes our globalized urban condition.[53]

Gaza, like the whole of the occupied Palestinian Territories, constitutes an extreme case of an urbanism of subtraction and enclosure. These key dynamics of urbanization appear most vividly in the starkly contrasted picture they form. Accordingly, Palestine may also be approached as a theoretical frontier, where the conceptual and practical tools can be developed to confront the violent dialectics of the contemporary urban condition—not only *there*, but elsewhere too. Moving further into this frontier and going beyond the relatively well-known urban dynamics mentioned so far, what is to be learned from Gaza specifically? To what extent can

the analysis of the GRM inform our understanding of the smart city?

In his contribution to a much-needed critical theory of these new urban formations, Antoine Picon argues that the ongoing emergence of the smart city as a global urban model may signal a significant historical shift: from an "urbanism of flows" to one of "occurrences."[54] Gaza's new apparatus of urban development not only matches this proposal distinctly, but also helps elucidate it conceptually.

The optimization of the urban medium of circulation involves the reduction of the latency with which it can react and adjust to new conditions. The smart city—the thorough entanglement of physical and digital networks of circulation—marks a considerable upgrade of the urban capacity to respond to shifting circumstances and to reconfigure itself in approximate real time. If modern urbanism emerged out of an engineering effort to channel relatively constant and predictable hydraulic flows across the city, contemporary urban networks are expected to perform much better, by adjusting to the minute variations, over time and in space, of all circulatory flows.[55] This demands an acceleration of their response time to varying conditions—from a wave of regeneration to a wave of panic or, as the effects of climate change become increasingly tangible, to an actual wave—as well as much more localized adjustments to such phenomena and conditions, via responses that are targeted to specific locations and to mobile users. By channeling swarms of signals and responses, digital technology supports a process of

53. "The globe shrinks for those who own it; for the displaced or the dispossessed, the migrant or refugee, no distance is more awesome than the few feet across borders or frontiers." Homi Bhabha, "Double visions," *Artforum* 30, no. 5 (1992): 88.

54. Antoine Picon, *Smart Cities: A Spatialised Intelligence* (Chichester: Wiley, 2015), 16, 119.

55. Matthew Gandy, *The Fabric of Space: Water, Modernity, and the Urban Imagination* (Cambridge, MA: MIT Press, 2014).

specification of how each user can circulate within the urban network, at any time. Increasingly, the problem of circulation is no longer addressed by aggregating figures and defining a single integrated response to accommodate a large population of users, but rather by processing disaggregated real-time data and formulating as many custom responses as computationally possible. As software takes over regulatory functions that were formerly only performed by physical infrastructure, the most thorough transformations of urban networks may no longer be registered at the macroscale of their material configuration, but rather at the microscale of the multitude of circulations that they mediate. From Rio to London, via Gaza: the data dashboard is replacing the master plan as the primary instrument of contemporary urbanism.

Accordingly, the model of urbanism ingrained in the GRM is no longer one of flows. By breaking down the material circulation of cement into infinitesimal allocations moving through a highly ramified distribution network, it turned such flows into "occurrences": material arrangements that are specific and conditional to the present moment. There is no assured continuity between those occurrences, no causal nor dynamic link: for a GRM user in Gaza, access to a given allocation of cement does not guarantee its renewal at the following building phase, nor comparable access for its neighbor with the exact same needs. In that sense, those occurrences are actual *events*, which the GRM, via a combination of physical and digital

infrastructure, channels to each user while monitoring the status of the entire network. The disaggregation of both supply and demand enables a modulated response that can produce macro-effects while only acting on micro-inputs. As a result, whatever entity can access and act upon the full set of data collected by the system in real time finds itself in a position of exceptional power over each and every user.

Of course, Gaza's "smart city" technology is relatively rudimentary, and its present domain of application only concerns the circulation of the materials required for its own reconstruction. Yet if it lags behind in terms of digital infrastructure, it knows no competition when it comes to demonstrating the potential of the smart city as a technology of power. While the smart-city model is rolled out lightheartedly across the urban landscape of the global north, key questions of urban politics remain largely unaddressed: Who manages the smart city? Who controls its data? Who has oversight of the protocols of circulation, exchanges, and responses at work in a smarter urban environment? If such problems still seem too abstract when the smart city is approached through the lens of its current sleek and green prototypes around the world, Gaza presents a compelling example of what can truly go wrong with it. Pondering the extreme vulnerability that residents of Gaza are exposed to via the GRM, a glimpse can be caught of the dark side of the urban future that awaits if the new infrastructural networks currently being deployed in urban environments remain designed as an opaque architecture of highly centralized control.

Sold as a means to optimize the circulation of the privileged users of the global urban network, the current, deeply asymmetrical model of smart-city infrastructure can and most likely will simultaneously be used to further hinder the mobility of all its unworthy users. Wherever a dialectic of fast lanes and enclosures is at play, this infrastructure will dramatically reinforce its effects. And as we come to terms with the displacement of power's center of gravity from a discursive realm to a logistical one— not only on the Gaza frontier, but everywhere across our increasingly urban planet—the design of alternative infrastructures and protocols of urban exchange may emerge as an increasingly urgent political problem.

WORKS CITED

"About." GRM Report. 2017. https://grm.report/.

Abunimah, Ali. "UN database for Gaza aid may give Israel targets to attack – secret memo." *The Electronic Intifada*. January 13, 2016.

Agamben, Giorgio. *Homo Sacer: Sovereign Power and Bare Life*. Translated Daniel Heller-Roazen. Stanford, CA: Stanford University Press, 1998.

———. *State of Exception*. Chicago: University of Chicago Press, 2005.

Ahronheim, Anna. "IDF to Impose Week-Long Closure of West Bank, Gaza ahead of Passover Holiday." *The Jerusalem Post*. April 9, 2017

———. "Israel's Eye On Gaza: The IDF's Electronic Observation Unit." *The Jerusalem Post*. February 16, 2017.

Amnesty International and Forensic Architecture. *Black Friday: Carnage in Rafah during 2014 Israel/Gaza conflict*. New York: July 2015.

Azoulay, Ariella, and Adi Ophir. "Abandoning Gaza." In *Agamben and Colonialism*, edited by Marcelo Svirsky and Simone Bignall. Edinburgh: Edinburgh University Press, 2012.

Babcock, Stephen. "Israel-Based Cyberbit Makes Another Move in Maryland." *Technically Baltimore*. July 18, 2017.

Barakat, Sultan. "The Situation in Gaza Requires Immediate Action." *Al-Jazeera*. May 11, 2016,

Benvenisti, Meron. Quoted by Rami S. Abdulhadi. "Land Use Planning in the Occupied Palestinian Territories." *Institute for Palestine Studies* 19, no. 4 (1989-90): 46-63.

Bhabha, Homi. "Double visions." *Artforum* 30, no. 5 (1992).

Bratton, Benjamin H. *The Stack: On Software and Sovereignty*. Cambridge. MA: MIT Press, 2016.

Césaire, Aimé. *Discourse on Colonialism*. New York: Monthly Review Press, 2000.

Clancey, Gregory. "Vast Clearings: Emergency, Technology, and American De-Urbanization, 1930–1945." *Cultural Politics* 2, no. 1 (2006): 49–76.

Cohen, Gili. "Israeli Army Reveals Massive Barrier Being Built to Stop Hamas' Gaza Terror Tunnels." *Haaretz*. August 10, 2017.

"Dual-use Requests." GRM Report. 2017. https://grm.report/#/DualUse/List.

Easterling, Keller. *Extrastatecraft: The Power of Infrastructure Space*. London: Verso, 2014.

———. *Subtraction*. Critical Spatial Practice no. 4, edited by Nikolaus Hirsch and Markus Miessen. Berlin: Sternberg Press, 2014.

Eglash, Ruth. "Israel Steps Up Home Demolitions to Punish Palestinian Attackers." *The Washington Post*. January 17, 2016.

Filiu, Jean-Pierre. *Gaza: A History*. New York: Oxford University Press, 2014.

Foucault, Michel. *Society Must be Defended: Lectures at the Collège de France, 1975-6*. London: Allen Tate, 2003.

———. *The History of Sexuality, Vol. 1: An Introduction*. Translated by Robert Hurley. London: Penguin, 1980.

Gandy, Matthew. *The Fabric of Space: Water, Modernity, and the Urban Imagination*. Cambridge, MA: MIT Press, 2014.

"General Closure to be Imposed on West Bank Starting Rosh Hashana Eve." *The Jerusalem Post*. October 2, 2016.

Gisha. "Reader: 'Food Consumption in the Gaza Strip—Red Lines.'" Tel Aviv: October 2012.

Graham, Stephen. *Cities under Siege: The New Military Urbanism*. London: Verso, 2014.

———. "Laboratories of War: United States–Israeli Collaboration in Urban War and Securitization." *The Brown Journal of World Affairs* 17, no. 1 (2010): 35–51.

Gregory, Derek. *The Colonial Present: Afghanistan, Palestine, Iraq*. Malden, MA: Blackwell, 2004.

Israeli Ministry of Foreign Affairs. "Objectives and Phases of the 2014 Gaza Conflict." Executive summary. Jerusalem, June 14, 2015.

———. "Security Cabinet declares Gaza hostile territory," September 19, 2007.

Jaber, Ramzi, Joumana al Jabri, Ahmad Barclay, Hani Asfour, and Joe Sahyouni. "Segregated Road Systems in the West Bank." Visualizing Palestine. Infographic. 2012.

Klein, Naomi. "Laboratory for a Fortressed World." *The Nation*. June 14, 2007.

Massumi, Brian. *Ontopower*. Durham: Duke University Press, 2015.

Ministerial Committee for the Reconstruction of Gaza. *Detailed Needs Assessment (DNA) and Recovery Framework for Gaza Reconstruction*. State of Palestine: 2015.

NICE Systems. "China's Chongqing Metro Monorail Selects NICE's Digital Video Security Solution to Protect Passengers and Assets Against Crime and Potential Terror Threats." Press release. 2009.

NICE Systems. "NICE Safe City Solutions Deployed in Glasgow to Bolster Security, Safety, and Operations Management." Press release. 2014.

OCHA Occupied Palestinian Territory. "Gaza Strip Access and Movements." August 2016.

———. "'Palestinians stuck in a permanent cycle of humanitarian relief' — UN Humanitarian Chief." OCHA. November 23, 2016.

Oosterman, Arjen, ed. "Architecture of Peace." Special issue. *Archis* 26 (December 2010).

———, ed. "Architecture of Peace Reloaded." Special issue. *Archis* 40 (July 2014).

"Palestine: Shelter Cluster FactSheet, June 2017." Shelter Cluster. 2017.

Picon, Antoine. *Smart Cities: A Spatialised Intelligence*. Chichester: Wiley, 2015.

Press, Viva Sarah. "Israelis Manage Olympic Security Budget of $2.2 billion. Rio de Janeiro Games to serve as real-time platform for Israeli security innovations and defense capabilities." *Israel21c*. August 2, 2016.

Segal, Rafi, and Eyal Weizman, eds. *A Civilian Occupation. The Politics of Israeli Architecture*. London: Verso, 2003.

"Sharp Increase in West Bank Demolitions." OCHA Occupied Palestinian Territory. March 2016.

State of Palestine, Gaza Strip: A Reconstruction and Development Plan. Jerusalem: Palestinian Economic Council for Development and Reconstruction (PECDAR), September 2014.

Tawil-Souri, Helga. "Digital Occupation: Gaza's High-Tech Enclosure." *Journal of Palestine Studies* 41, no. 2 (Winter 2012): 27–43.

The Good Cause: Architecture of Peace. Exhibition. Canadian Centre for Architecture, Montreal. June–September 2011.

United Nations Country Team in the Occupied Palestinian Territory. "Gaza in 2020: A liveable place?" Jerusalem: Office of the United Nations Special Coordinator for the Middle East Peace Process [UNSCO], 2012.

United Nations Country Team in the Occupied Palestinian Territory. "Leave No One Behind: A Perspective on Vulnerability and Structural Disadvantage in Palestine." United Nations. November 25, 2016.

"War Left Four Million Tons of Rubble in Gaza, Says Environmental Group." *Haaretz*. September 16, 2014.

Weizman, Eyal. *Hollow Land: Israel's Architecture of Occupation*. London: Verso Books, 2012.

———. *The Least of All Possible Evils: Humanitarian Violence from Arendt to Gaza*. London: Verso, 2011.

White, Nigel. "Expert Opinion on the Legality of the Gaza Reconstruction Mechanism (GRM)." Confidential expert opinion. January 26, 2015.

NORMALIZING THE SIEGE: THE GAZA RECON-STRUCTION MECHANISM (GRM)

Pietro Stefanini

A portion of this paper was previously published in the contribution: Pietro Stefanini, "Normalizing the Siege: The 'Gaza Reconstruction Mechanism' and the Contradictions of Humanitarianism and Reconstruction," *The Politics of Post-Conflict Reconstruction*, POMEPS Studies 30 (2018).

1. INTRODUCTION

In Gaza, the politics of postwar reconstruction are situated at the intersection between humanitarianism and settler colonialism. This essay analyzes the politics of the Gaza Reconstruction Mechanism (GRM), which was set up in 2014 as a temporary tripartite agreement between the Palestinian Authority (PA), the Israeli government, and the United Nations (UN). I argue that the GRM has normalized the Israeli blockade, instead of advancing the reconstruction. Rather than empowering Palestinians to rebuild their homes, the GRM's operational approach is driven by Israel's "security concerns." This has been a key obstacle to the success of the mechanism. As well as legitimizing Israel's hegemonic narrative, it severely limits the entrance of "dual-use" materials and turned the reconstruction process into another technique of domination.

Prior to June 2007, construction materials were treated as ordinary civilian materials. Their entry into Gaza depended on Israel's opening and administration of the commercial crossings. Until mid-2013, tunnels on the Gaza–Egypt border fulfilled most of the demand for building materials. The destruction of these tunnels following the military coup in Egypt, along with other restrictions, including Israel's treatment of building materials as "dual use" (i.e., they could be used for military purposes), posed a serious challenge to the reconstruction effort in postwar Gaza. In response to this situation, international governments and the UN invested in the creation of the GRM. The two UN agencies mandated to oversee the implementation of the GRM are the United Nations Special Coordinator for the Middle East Peace Process (UNSCO) and United Nations Office for Project Services (UNOPS). Drafted between Israel, the UN, and the PA, the GRM's official mandate is to:

> enable the parties to: provide security assurances to the GoI [Government of Israel]; work at the scale required in the Gaza Strip; enable the PA [Palestinian Authority] to play the lead role in the reconstruction effort of the Gaza Strip and assure donors that any investments will be implemented without delay.[1]

Following Eyal Weizman, I argue that the "disengagement" from and the subsequent siege of Gaza constituted a shift in Israeli techniques of power and control, from direct physical occupation and settlement to withdrawal in 2005 and "humanitarian management" thereafter. I explore the notion that the Israeli settler-colonial logic of control and domination converged with the UN's "neutral" humanitarian approach, which led to the GRM entrenching the siege on Gaza. The failures of this UN-brokered deal raises questions on the role of international actors in postwar reconstruction, specifically in Palestine-Israel. They urge us to interrogate the consequences of humanitarianism, and its relationship with structures of domination, such as settler colonialism. Scholarship on the history of humanitarian intervention in the lives of Palestinians underscores a paradox of

1. Sara Roy, *The Gaza Strip: The Political Economy of De-Development*, 3rd ed. (Washington, DC: Institute for Palestine Studies, 2016), 431.

humanitarianism: the possibility that assistance did not bring them any closer to their main aspiration, namely to return to their homes.[2]

This chapter situates the processes unfolding in the GRM within the prolonged Zionist settler-colonial project. The analysis draws on Linda Tabar's intuition that humanitarianism "can actually extend the logics of settler colonialism and further its imperatives."[3] Israel's settler-colonial structure in Gaza is able to exploit humanitarian interventions such as the GRM, which do not challenge the dominant configuration and reproduce the settler administration's "security" interests. Humanitarian ideology and practice, embodied in the GRM, has seemingly colluded with Israel's colonial siege, producing a reconstruction system that entrenches the domination of Palestinians. The underlying assumption of the GRM is that without humanitarian assistance, a new round of violence will emerge. However, it keeps intact the siege, a primary source of settler-colonial violence, absolving the power systems that produced the suffering that the GRM seeks to alleviate. This arrangement fits into a wider trend in which the international community, instead of opposing Israel's settler colonialism, responds with humanitarian aid. Indeed, reports suggest that by 2008 "Palestinians were the world's largest per capita recipients of humanitarian aid," and yet, conditions on the ground appear to deteriorate at an increasing rate.[4]

Can humanitarianism provide mechanisms through which settler-colonial logics are normalized and hidden? A closer analysis of the relationship between settler colonialism and humanitarianism will provide a better understanding of the politics of postwar reconstruction in the Gaza Strip. Zionist settler colonialism in Palestine has subjected Palestinians to "ongoing structural and violent forms of dispossession, land appropriation, expulsion and displacement."[5] Attentive to critical scholarship on the role of humanitarianism in international relations, and in particular its connection with structures of domination, I challenge the mainstream humanitarian ethics paradigm. This paradigm portrays humanitarianism as merely a justified imperative to "save lives" and "alleviate suffering," in other words to "do good." Contrary to this view, when we look at the colonial origins of humanitarianism, its role in furthering imperialism and settler colonialism is revealed. For instance, in the nineteenth century, humanitarianism was embedded in the colonial civilizing mission. Throughout the efforts of humanitarians to make the injustices of empire and settler colonialism somewhat more bearable, an important feature of humanitarianism (during the European settlement of Australia) was the extent to which it corresponded to the settlers' concerns, rather than challenging them in any way.[6]

The current "international humanitarian order," as Mahmood Mamdani describes it, draws on the history of modern Western colonialism.[7] In the post–World War II international system, humanitarian agencies and interventions are effectively mobilized as an "auxiliary

2. Ilana Feldman, "Gaza's Humanitarianism Problem," *Journal of Palestine Studies* 38, no. 3 (2009): 22–37.

3. Linda Tabar, "Disrupting Development, Reclaiming Solidarity: The Anti-Politics of Humanitarianism," *Journal of Palestine Studies* 45, no. 4 (Summer 2016): 21.

4. Ibid, 16.

5. Linda Meari, "Colonial Dispossession, Developmental Discourses, and Humanitarian Solidarity in 'Area C': The Case of the Palestinian Yanun Village," *Community Development Journal* 52, no. 3 (2017): 511.

6. Robert Van Krieken, "Celebrity, Humanitarianism and Settler-Colonialism: G.A. Robinson and the Aborigines of Van Diemen's Land," in *Celebrity Humanitarianism and North-South Relations: Politics, Place and Power*, ed. Lisa Richey (London: Routledge, 2015), 13.

7. Mahmood Mamdani, "The New Humanitarian Order," *The Nation*, September 10, 2008.

system of governance alongside imperialist wars and predatory capitalism profiting from disasters."[8] Instead of becoming a tool of resisting injustice and apparatuses of violence, humanitarian principles have made humanitarianism "an accomplice and instrument of power."[9] I do not deny that humanitarian interventions by certain international actors in Palestine-Israel are driven by well-intentioned concerns to alleviate suffering. However, it is important to note the unintended consequences that humanitarian relief can have on the oppressed people it seeks to assist. In particular, we must confront the paternalistic humanitarian gaze that targets Palestinians as abject victims, denying them agency over the political processes affecting their lives, and restricting their capabilities for emancipation.

2. HUMANITARIANISM AND SETTLER COLONIALISM IN PALESTINE-ISRAEL

The particular aspects of the humanitarianism/settler colonialism nexus that I wish to investigate are best illustrated by the juxtaposition of international actors' humanitarian logic and Zionists' use of humani-tarianism in Palestine. Zionist settlement in Palestine was justified using, among other pretexts, the reasoning that it was a humanitarian project. Inherent in the 1917 Balfour Declaration, a founding document of British colonialism in Palestine (and a core rationalization for the creation of the Israeli state), is the assumption of a humanitarian gesture towards a persecuted Jewish population in need of assistance. More to the point, as Fayez Sayegh states, in the early 1900s:

Zionists were coming in relatively small numbers and emphasizing the religious or humanitarian motives of their enterprise, while concealing the political, ideological, and colonial-racist character of their movement[10]

It is politically strategic for settlers to employ humanitarian language to characterize their relations with indigenous people. Humanitarianism is a flexible political language that can be harnessed for various ends.[11] Israel initially characterized its 1967 invasion of Palestinian territories as an "enlightened occupation";[12] this stance was based on the contradictory position that Israel did not have any legal obligations towards Palestinians under international law, while affirming that it would "respect its 'humanitarian provisions.'"[13]

Since the 2000s, Israel's military rule in the Occupied Palestinian Territories (OPT) increasingly shifted from colonization of the natives to a separation process between the colonizer and the colonized.[14] The settler-colonial nature of Palestinian space is characterized by the formation of enclaves and segregation between settlers and natives. Indirect forms of governance, including through humanitarian aid, serve the settler-colonial logic of maintaining a subjugated and separate indigenous population. Leila Farsakh suggests that the Oslo process institutionalized a "contradictory process of societal separation and territorial integration," paving the way for a South African-style "Bantustanization" of the West Bank and the Gaza Strip.[15]

In a seminal piece, anthropologist Patrick Wolfe stated that "[s]ettler

8. Tabar, "Disrupting Development," 17.

9. Ibid.

10. Fayez Sayegh, "Zionist Colonialism in Palestine (1965)," *Settler Colonial Studies* 2, no. 1 (2012): 221.

11. Kenton Storey, *Settler Anxiety at the Outpost of Empire: Colonial Relations, Humanitarian Discourses and the Imperial Press* (Vancouver: UBC Press, 2016), 3–24.

12. Tom Segev, *1967: Israel, The War, and the Year That Transformed the Middle East* (New York: Metropolitan Books, 2007).

13. Lisa Hajjar, *Courting Conflict: The Israeli Court System in the West Bank and Gaza* (Berkeley: University of California Press, 2005), 54.

14. Neve Gordon, "From Colonization to Separation: Exploring the Structure of Israel's Occupation," *Third World Quarterly* 29, no. 1 (2007): 25–44.

15. Leila Farsakh, "Independence, Cantons, or Bantustans: Whither the Palestinian State?" *Middle East Journal* 59, no. 2 (2005): 239.

colonizers come to stay: invasion is a structure not an event."[16] While settlers in the Gaza Strip have left, the colonial structure has remained in place, albeit in a different form. Drawing on Eyal Weizman, I suggest that the Israeli "disengagement" from Gaza points to a shift in techniques of domination, from physical occupation to a humanitarian government of the indigenous population largely imposed through management of the blockade.[17] "Disengagement" without decolonization of the Israeli–Palestinian relationship has produced a siege that functions as a settler–colonial modality of domination, segregation, and control through ostensibly humanitarian means.[18] Israel's siege, enforced with Egypt's support, aims to discipline the local population (and Hamas) into submission while retaining a minimum humanitarian concern to protect civilians' lives. The siege further allows for the geographical separation of Palestinian territory, where the natives are given some form of limited autonomy, but not independence. It also prevents the return of Palestinian refugees who were displaced from their homes and lands in what is now Israel. While the movement of goods and people in the West Bank is controlled through checkpoints, the Gaza Strip is regulated through what the Israeli military calls "humanitarian corridors."[19]

Israel's incorporation of humanitarianism into its military strategy in Gaza is increasingly evident. Following the 2005 "disengagement plan," Israel declared that the new regime "will be applied following a legal examination, taking into account the humanitarian situation and with the intention of preventing a humanitarian crisis."[20]

In 2007, after Hamas took control of the Strip, Israel outlined its policy to the High Court of Justice, stating that the law of belligerent occupation no longer applies in Gaza (although it already claimed it did not apply back in 1967) and, therefore, Israel bears only humanitarian duties toward its population.[21] In order to prevent a complete collapse of the situation, Israeli officials also calculated a "humanitarian minimum" required to sustain the population.[22] Following a legal battle, the Israeli government was forced to release the "red lines" document. This document outlined the minimum number of calories necessary to sustain the people of Gaza, estimated by Israel's Health Ministry based on humanitarian standards, without falling below the level of the UN definition of hunger. For the reconstruction mechanism, instead of the "red lines" formula, a security rationale has been articulated to prevent construction materials from being used for purportedly military purposes. Israeli academic Adi Ophir argues that the logic underpinning humanitarian assistance to Gaza serves to "suspend the catastrophe," which allows Israeli authorities to avoid the creation of chronic disaster.[23] The overarching strategy for Gaza, as one Israeli official put it, was, "No prosperity, no development, no humanitarian crisis."[24] Humanitarianism was, thus, not a challenge, but part of the functioning mechanism of Israel's colonial siege.[25]

This builds on what political economist Sara Roy coined "de-development," a process that she argues has been completed with the 2005 Israeli "disengagement" and the subsequent denial of a

16. Patrick Wolfe, "Settler Colonialism and the Elimination of the Native," *Journal of Genocide Research* 8, no. 4 (2006): 387–409.

17. Eyal Weizman, *The Least of All Possible Evils: Humanitarian Violence from Arendt to Gaza* (London: Verso, 2012), 81.

18. Lorenzo Veracini, *Israel and Settler Society* (London: Pluto Press, 2006), 5.

19. Israeli Government. "The Gaza Strip: The humanitarian lifeline," Consulate General of Israel in New York, 2010.

20. Ayel Gross, *The Writing on the Wall: Rethinking the International Law of Occupation* (Cambridge: Cambridge University Press, 2017), 232.

21. Gross, *The Writing on the Wall*.

22. Amira Hass, "2,279 Calories per Person: How Israel Made Sure Gaza Didn't Starve," *Haaretz*, October, 17, 2012.

23. Adi Ophir, "The Politics of Catastrophization: Emergency and Exception," in *Contemporary States of Emergency: The Politics of Military and Humanitarian Interventions*, eds. Didier Fassin and Mariella Pandolfi (New York: Zone Books, 2010), 77.

24. Gisha, "Not your average trip to the mall," *Gaza Gateway* (blog), July 29, 2010.

25. Yves Winter, "The Siege of Gaza: Spatial Violence, Humanitarian Strategies, and the Biopolitics of Punishment." *Constellations* 23, no. 2 (2015), 308–19.

viable economy.[26] In fact, due to Israeli policies, over 60 percent of Palestinians in Gaza survive through foreign humanitarian aid.[27] Roy argues that the GRM's ultimate aim was not the reconstruction of Gaza, but its ongoing de-development. As early as 2009, Israeli authorities were planning for the reconstruction process in Gaza to become another element in Israel's politics of siege. "We are studying it," Isaac Herzog, former Israeli minister of welfare and social affairs, said in a telephone interview with the *New York Times*, "The exact mechanism hasn't been devised yet." He added: "Israel helps fully on the humanitarian issue. Thereafter it's a red line."[28]

3. RECONSTRUCTION AS A WEAPON

In addition to a policy of siege, Palestinians have faced multiple, major military operations in the last decade. Laleh Khalili explains that Israel's 2014 assault on Gaza was "yet another repetition of Israeli settler-colonial apparatus' habit of destruction."[29] She frames Israel's actions not as "an episodic 'cycle of violence' but in the very ideology and practice of the settler-colonial movement."[30] Wolfe states that "[s]ettler colonialism destroys to replace."[31] As further evidence for this logic, he draws on Theodor Herzl, founding father of Zionism, in his assertion, "If I wish to substitute a new building for an old one, I must demolish before I construct."[32] This continues to be true in areas where Israel's demolition of homes and infrastructure paves the way for settlement expansion, whereby the settler replaces the native. However, in Palestinian space such as the Gaza Strip, where the settler-

colonial movement has abandoned its quest for land largely due to native resistance, a different logic might be in place. To rephrase Wolfe's statement, in the Gaza Strip, "settler colonialism destroys and *repairs*." In the arsenal of weapons used against the natives, the reconstruction process is cast as a form of violence and control. The infrastructural violence that occurred during the 2014 attacks did not end the moment buildings were destroyed and damaged. It rather continues, as the regulated and hindered reconstruction prolongs the violence inflicted on the displaced and brings new techniques to oppress the colonized.

Accompanying the processes of Bantustanization of Palestinian space and "disengagement" from Gaza, another important arrangement formed the basis for Israel's policy vis-à-vis Palestinians. This arrangement consisted of outsourcing elements of colonial rule to other actors and mechanisms. In this regard, the rationale behind the GRM is not new and is similar to the US-brokered Agreement on Movement and Access (AMA) signed by Israel and the PA in 2005. The AMA reduced closure, mobility restrictions, and their associated infrastructure to a "technical and nonpolitical question."[33] According to Salamanca, the AMA "placed Israel's 'security' conditions before Palestinian freedom of movement, let alone other fundamental rights."[34] Both points are relevant to the GRM. First, the highly political issue—a colonial siege and the reconstruction of infrastructure destroyed during Israel's aerial attacks—was turned into a merely technocratic exercise that consisted of providing

26. Roy, *The Gaza Strip*.

27. World Bank, "Gaza Economy on the Verge of Collapse, Youth Unemployment Highest in the Region at 60 Percent," press release, 2015.

28. Sabrina Tavernise, "In Gaza, the Wait to Rebuild Lingers," *New York Times*, January 26, 2009.

29. Laleh Khalili, "A Habit of Destruction," *Society & Space*, August 25, 2014.

30. Ibid.

31. Wolfe, "Settler Colonialism," 388.

32. Theodor Herzl, *Old—New Land*, trans. Lotta Levensohn (New York: M. Wiener, 1941), 38.

33. Omar Jabary Salamanca, "Assembling the Fabric of Life: When Settler Colonialism Becomes Development," *Journal of Palestine Studies* 45, no. 4 (Summer 2016): 64—80.

34. Salamanca, "Assembling the Fabric of Life."

humanitarian assistance. Second, the GRM reproduces the logic that uses Israel's "security" concerns to justify the normalization and maintenance of settler colonialism.

Rhetoric based on the core humanitarian principle of neutrality is exposed in the GRM as a way in which the UN allows Israel to impose its "security" imperatives. The reconstruction mechanism was proposed to reassure Israel through instituting a "neutral" apparatus that would inspect all materials entering the territory.[35] The operational approach of this apparatus is detailed in the Materials Monitoring Unit (MMU) Project Initiation Document, agreed between the two UN agencies UNSCO and UNOPS.[36] The logic of humanitarian concern reproduced in the GRM agreement is exemplified in the "Option Justification" provided in the MMU document.[37] The "do nothing" option has been discounted because of the prediction that if selected, "the humanitarian crisis will persist, economic recovery will be severely limited and the drivers causing conflict will worsen."[38] Instead of "do nothing," the document states that the option chosen is the only one that:

> will reduce the GoI security concerns of items being used for the 'enhancement of military capabilities and terrorist capacities' sufficiently enough to permit import approval of significant quantities of construction materials into Gaza.[39]

We can see how an economy of the lesser evil emerges, with the UN assessing Palestinian needs merely in humanitarian terms, and presenting the framework selected as the only alternative to "doing nothing." The preemptive logic of the humanitarian "lesser evil" is invoked to justify the use of a lesser violence (siege) to prevent a supposedly greater, projected violence (renewed conflict).[40] This agreement leads to the UN institutionalizing the Israeli siege in order to guarantee access of humanitarian aid. According to a Gaza-based analyst, under this mechanism the UN "was transformed into a contractor and a guarding company."[41] In this process, the UN continues to render Palestinians "bare lives,"[42] falling into the trap of Israeli sovereign power that has disqualified the life of this population from having political meaning.[43] This approach does not pose the question of whether Palestinians, too, have legitimate "security concerns" in regards to Israel's occupation, siege, and colonization of their lands.

The key operational approach driving the GRM is framed as "a mechanism to allow the entry into Gaza of large amounts of materials considered 'dual-use' for the purposes of reconstruction following the conflict in 2014."[44] The implication behind the term "dual-use" is that items that are primarily civilian in nature could also have military uses (for example, in building tunnels and rockets). Interestingly, as the GRM sought to limit the entrance of "dual-use" materials, supposedly to hinder the construction of tunnels and advance the rebuilding of Gaza, a 2012 study by Nicholas Pelham found that the tunnel expansion and its impact on the reconstruction process and local economy "precipitated a recovery that rapidly reversed

35. Sultan Barakat and Firas Masri, *Still in Ruins: Reviving the Stalled Reconstruction of Gaza* (Washington, DC and Doha, Quatar: Brookings Institute and Brookings Doha Center Publications, 2017).

36. Roy, *The Gaza Strip*, 440.

37. Ibid., 452.

38. Ibid., 431.

39. Ibid.

40. Eyal Weizman, "665: The Least of All Possible Evils," *e-flux Journal* 38 (October 2012).

41. Omar Shaban, "UN Gaza Reconstruction Mechanism (GRM) Must Come To An End; not to Be Reviewed," *Palthink For Strategic Studies*, 2018.

42. Giorgio Agamben, *Homo Sacer: Sovereign Power and Bare Life* (Stanford: Stanford University Press, 1998).

43. Sari Hanafi, "Anti-Humanitarianism," Refugee heritage conversations, e-flux Conversations, 2017.

44. "About," GRM Report, 2017.

much of Gaza's earlier decline."[45] The closure of numerous tunnels also led to a spike in unemployment to 45 percent in mid-2014, compared with 28 percent in the previous year.[46] Only in April 2017, after a prolonged legal battle, did the Coordinator of Government Activities in the Territories (COGAT) publish a list of what may be considered "dual-use" materials. According to Israeli NGO Gisha, the published list includes broad definitions of "categories" and not "items," which provide COGAT with virtually total control over the materials permitted to enter.[47] This has led to a widespread refusal of materials, with over two thousand different types of "dual-use" items "rejected on every occasion they have been requested permission" through the GRM.[48] These "dual-use" items include aggregate, steel bars, and cement (ABC)—effectively all essential construction materials necessary to rebuild infrastructure.[49]

Crucially, the GRM provides veto power to the Israeli government over the materials permitted, based on what is described as "legitimate security concerns." The UN and the PA have capitulated to Israel's hegemonic security narrative, effectively legitimizing the domination of the oppressed by the oppressor.[50] While the PA certainly has agency, as it has become Israel's occupation subcontractor in many respects, it should be pointed out that it is seemingly presented as an equal player. In reality, it is hardly possible to expect the PA to manage the reconstruction process by remote control from Ramallah, or by guarding the Gaza crossing points, shielded from Israel's ultimate authority. Attempts to

draw the PA into the reconstruction process perhaps reflect the ongoing Palestinian geopolitical split following Hamas' electoral victory in the legislative council elections in 2006, and the subsequent "no-contact" policy by the international community. Yet, scholars have urged us to recognize that Zionist settler colonialism in Palestine remains dependent "on willing (or unwilling) native collaboration regarding security arrangements, all with the continued support and backing of imperial powers."[51] In fact, the logic behind the GRM is not novel, and is similar to that of previous and ongoing deals between Israel and the PA. A more recent development is the UN complicity with the GRM, which lends it greater legitimacy.

The GRM has been criticized for being a "labyrinth of bureaucracy" with regard to project selection and implementation.[52] Palestinian families must go through a multi-step process of applications to the PA and the UN, and at the end of the "labyrinth" looms COGAT's veto power over all project approvals. For instance, according to a Shelter Cluster update from November 2017, "500 households with available funding whose names were submitted in September 2017 are still awaiting approval in the GRM after three months."[53] Overall, UNSCO suggests that there has been some relative progress in terms of actual homes rebuilt. From the 171,000 affected homes, about 61,086 need repairs or require new construction.[54] As of May 2017, of the 17,800 homes that were totally destroyed or severely damaged, 57 percent have been rebuilt and 38 percent of the cement for the 2014 housing

45. Nicholas Pelham, "Gaza's Tunnel Phenomenon: The Unintended Dynamics of Israel's Siege," *Journal of Palestine Studies* 41, no. 4 (2012): 16.

46. Sari Bashi, "Justifying Restrictions on Reconstructing Gaza: Military Necessity and Humanitarian Assistance," *Israel Law Review* 49, no. 2 (2016): 160.

47. Gisha, "Dual use list published by COGAT," *Gisha Gateway* (blog), April 20, 2017.

48. GRM. "Dual-use Requests," GRM Report, 2017.

49. Oxfam International, *Treading Water: The Worsening Water Crisis and the Gaza Reconstruction Mechanism* (Oxford: Oxfam GB, March 2017).

50. Bezen Coskun, "Hegemonic Securitisations of Terrorism and the Legitimacy of Palestinian Government," *Political Perspectives* 1, no. 1 (2007): 1–26.

51. Omar Jabary Salamanca et al., "Past is Present: Settler Colonialism in Palestine," *Settler Colonial Studies* 2, no. 1 (2012): 2.

52. Barakat and Masri, *Still in Ruins."*

53. "Shelter Cluster Palestine," Sheltercluster.org, 2017, accessed December 20, 2017, https://www.sheltercluster. org/sites/default/files/ docs/one_page_factsheet_ november_2017.pdf.

54. Barakat and Masri, *Still in Ruins.*

reconstruction caseload is still required.[55] Meanwhile, as of August 2017, 29,000 (over 5,500 families) of the 100,000 people displaced at the end of the conflict were still displaced.[56] In an update from June 2018, nearly four years since the conflict, "over a third of the homes that sustained some type of damage (some 59,000 out 171,000) are yet to be repaired."[57] The estimated date for the earliest reconstruction completion varies, depending on available funds, although no official end date has been given. Also notably absent from the mechanism is any mention of addressing the pre-2014 housing crisis.

The UN moreover claims that the slow pace of reconstruction is due to donors not fulfilling pledges made at the Cairo Conference in October 2014.[58] As of July 31, 2017, 1.851 billion dollars of the support for Gaza announced at the Cairo Conference was disbursed, which puts the disbursement ratio at 53 percent.[59] Various factors account for the unfulfilled pledges. Some donors certainly share the view of former spokesperson for Israel's prime minister, Mark Regev: "We want to make sure that the rehabilitation of Gaza doesn't turn into the rehabilitation of Hamas."[60] At the same time, the slow reconstruction process, along with the possibility that investments may be destroyed (once again) in another war, has discouraged Western donors.[61] Moreover, Middle Eastern states' donations have reflected the changing geopolitical situation: Qatar and Turkey have delivered the largest aid packages and are considered closer to Hamas than other states in the region.[62]

However, as long as foreign donors continue to bear these costs, Israel faces no financial penalty for its repetitive destruction.[63] Rather, ongoing foreign funding incentivizes Israel's development of techniques of domination[64] and treatment of the Gaza Strip as a laboratory.[65] One apt example is Israeli cement company Nesher reaping massive profits from the reconstruction process,[66] turning Gaza's destruction into a fertile ground for "disaster capitalism."[67] The ongoing process of "destroy and repair" feeds a variety of sectors and actors that are invested in the "rehabilitation" of postwar Gaza, who Jasbir K. Puar suggests are "embedded in corporate economies of humanitarianism."[68] This state of affairs seems likely to continue, since in 2018 the Israeli government proposed a Gaza reconstruction plan of one billion dollars to international donors.[69]

Reconstruction could potentially have been an opportunity for the affected population to take control and shape new political, economic, and social structures for their society. However, Gaza's de-facto government and civil society have been excluded from taking part in the creation and implementation of the GRM. The mechanism's main function is seemingly to allow the access of material needed for the reconstruction. However, other objectives are being pursued by the Israeli military in the process of approving or rejecting requests. An additional criterion for allowing the entrance of materials has been the location of the planned school, hospital, or other building. According to a study by Sari Bashi, departments within the Israeli government and

55. UNSCO, *Report to the Ad Hoc Liaison Committee* (New York: 2017).

56. OCHA Occupied Palestinian Territories, "Three years on from the 2014 conflict, 29,000 people remain displaced," September 11, 2017.

57. "Humanitarian Bulletin Occupied Palestinian Territory—June 2018," ReliefWeb, 2018.

58. Nora Murad, "The Gaza Reconstruction Mechanism: Smoke and Mirrors?" *Journal of Palestinian Refugee Studies* 5, no. 2 (2015): 59—66.

59. World Bank, "Reconstructing Gaza—Donor Pledges," 2017.

60. Joshua Mitnick, "Newest Gaza Fight: Who Controls Reconstruction Aid?" *Christian Science Monitor*, January 23, 2009.

61. Barakat and Masri, *Still in Ruins*.

62. Ibid.

63. Louisa Emslie, "Aid Watch Palestine Raises Awareness of Failed Reconstruction Efforts in Gaza," Alternativenews.org, 2017.

64. Jeff Halper, *War Against the People* (London: Pluto Press, 2015).

65. Darryl Li, "The Gaza Strip as Laboratory: Notes in the Wake of Disengagement," *Journal of Palestine Studies* 35 no. 2, (2006): 38–55.

66. Who Profits. "Reconstruction of Gaza: Zero Buildings, Massive Profit," *Who Profits* (blog), 2016.

67. Naomi Klein, *The Shock Doctrine: The Rise of Disaster Capitalism* (New York: Metropolitan Books/Henry Holt, 2007).

68. Jasbir K. Puar, "The 'Right' to Maim: Disablement and Inhumanist Biopolitics in Palestine," *Borderlands E-Journal* 14, no. 1 (2015).

69. Noa Landau, "Israel Presents $1 Billion Rehabilitation Plan for Gaza, but Demands Palestinian Authority Take Over," *Haaretz*, 2018.

army must approve the location of internationally funded projects in order to evaluate whether "it would get in the way of future combat plans."[70] According to Bashi, in certain instances the Israeli government refused the entry of construction materials for projects, "the location of which was seen to interfere with such plans."[71]

Furthermore, Palestinians have to submit to GPS tracking systems, video cameras, as well as a centralized database (GRAMMS)[72] of private information in order to receive materials, contributing to Israel's control over Gaza's inhabitants.[73] In certain instances, beneficiaries of construction material refused the aid due to fears arising from their personal information being shared with the Israeli military. It has also been reported that a black market has emerged, where people eligible for materials decide to sell them.[74] The Israeli military has admitted that tunnels are being built with materials obtained on the black market, thus defeating the main purpose of the creation of the GRM: improving Israel's security.[75] Some of these issues have led to Palestinian and Israeli civil society groups calling on policy makers to pressure the UN to end the GRM, and for donors to stop their funding.[76] According to a UN staffer involved in the GRM, Israeli authorities are "happy" with the functioning of the mechanism.[77] Failing to take into consideration the main concerns of Palestinians, the UN announced in February 2018 that the system will continue and that, along with the PA and Israel, they are reviewing the GRM to improve "its functionality, transparency and predictability."[78]

CONCLUSIONS

Israel's contemporary settler colonialism in the Gaza Strip "destroys and repairs," mobilizing humanitarianism, native collaborators, and international actors to advance its "security" logics through the reconstruction process. It remains a serious possibility that the short-term gains in the form of the construction of homes will normalize the existence of a siege that holds almost two million Palestinians in carceral conditions. What was conceived as a temporary mechanism bears the risk of becoming a permanent arrangement, as has historically been the case with humanitarian intervention in the lives of Palestinians. As the reconstruction process shows, humanitarian intervention under settler colonialism does not significantly challenge the dominant structure and can serve the political aims of the settler rather than assist the indigenous people. Recognizing the collusion of humanitarianism with settler-colonial logics should warn of strategies that do not oppose the system of domination, which is the root cause of the injustices affecting oppressed people.

To conclude, reconstruction is, at its core, a political rather than purely technical process. The reconstruction of Palestinians' homes and infrastructure is not just about materials and buildings, but should be part of a wider political framework that seeks to decolonize Israel's settler-colonial project in Palestine. It should be emphasized that the normalization of the siege stems from a longer process, perhaps dating back to the Oslo agreement , in

70. Bashi, "Justifying Restriction," 161.

71. Ibid.

72. UNOPS, "Gaza Reconstruction and Materials Monitoring System," The Materials Monitoring Unit—Gaza Reconstruction Mechanism, 2015.

73. Ibrahim Shikaki and Joanna Springer, *Building a Failed State: Palestine's Governance and Economy Denied* (Al-Shabaka: The Palestinian Policy Network, policy brief, 2015).

74. Nuriya Oswald, "Gaza Reconstruction Mechanism: Profiting Israel, Entrenching the Blockade," *Jadaliyya*, July 7, 2015.

75. Gisha, "Where's the Housing Boom?" August 17, 2015.

76. Aid Watch."Questions and Answers about the Gaza Reconstruction Mechanism (GRM)," Aid Watch Palestine, 2015.

77. United Nations staffer involved in the GRM who wishes to remain anonymous, personal interview, 2017.

78. UNSCO. "Statement by UN Special Coordinator Mladenov Following His Joint Meeting Yesterday with PM Hamdallah and Head of COGAT General Mordechai," UNSCO, 2018.

which international actors deal with Palestine-Israel as a "post-conflict" situation rather than considering it a settler colony, which should be framed as an "in-conflict" setting.[79]

If a radical change to the status quo does not occur, reconstruction will remain part of a settler-colonial "humanitarian attack" on the people of Gaza.[80]

79. Jamil Hilal, "Rethinking Palestine: Settler-Colonialism, Neo-Liberalism and Individualism in the West Bank and Gaza Strip," *Contemporary Arab Affairs* 8, no. 3 (2018): 351–62.

80. Weizman, *The Least of All Possible Evils*, 90.

WORKS CITED

Agamben, Giorgio. *Homo Sacer: Sovereign Power and Bare Life*. Stanford: Stanford University Press, 1998.

Aid Watch Palestine. "Questions and Answers about the Gaza Reconstruction Mechanism (GRM)." Aid Watch Palestine, 2015.

Barakat, Sultan, and Firas Masri. *Still in Ruins: Reviving the Stalled Reconstruction of Gaza*. Washington, DC and Doha, Qatar: Brookings Institute and Brookings Doha Center Publications, 2017.

Bashi, Sari. "Justifying Restrictions on Reconstructing Gaza: Military Necessity and Humanitarian Assistance." *Israel Law Review* 49, no. 2 (2016): 149–68.

Coskun, Bezen. "Hegemonic Securitisations of Terrorism and the Legitimacy of Palestinian Government." *Political Perspectives* 1, no. 1 (2007): 1–26.

"Dual-use Requests." GRM Report. 2017. https://grm.report/#/DualUse/List.

Emslie, Louisa. "Aid Watch Palestine Raises Awareness of Failed Reconstruction Efforts in Gaza." *Alternativenews.org*. 2017.

Farsakh, Leila. "Independence, Cantons, or Bantustans: Whither the Palestinian State?" *Middle East Journal* 59, no. 2 (2005): 230–45.

Feldman, Ilana. "Gaza's Humanitarianism Problem." *Journal of Palestine Studies* 38, no. 3 (2009): 22–37.

Gisha. "Dual use list published by COGAT." Gisha Gateway (blog). April 20, 2017.

———. "Not your average trip to the mall." *Gaza Gateway* (blog), July 29, 2010.

———. "Where's the Housing Boom?" August 17, 2015.

http://features.gisha.org/wheres-the-housing-boom/.

Gordon, Neve. "From Colonization to Separation: Exploring the Structure of Israel's Occupation." *Third World Quarterly* 29, no. 1 (2007): 25–44.

GRM. "About." GRM Report. 2017. https://grm.report/.

Gross, Ayel. *The Writing on the Wall: Rethinking the International Law of Occupation*. Cambridge: Cambridge University Press, 2017.

Hajjar, Lisa. *Courting Conflict: The Israeli Court System in the West Bank and Gaza*. Berkeley: University of California Press, 2005.

Halper, Jeff. *War Against the People*. London: Pluto Press, 2015.

Hanafi, Sari. "Anti-Humanitarianism." Refugee heritage conversations. e-flux Conversations. 2017.

Hass, Amira. "2,279 Calories per Person: How Israel Made Sure Gaza Didn't Starve." *Haaretz*. October 17, 2012.

Herzl, Theodor. *Old–New Land*. Translated by Lotta Levensohn. New York: M. Wiener, 1941.

Hilal, Jamil. "Rethinking Palestine: Settler-Colonialism, Neo-Liberalism and Individualism in the West Bank and Gaza Strip." *Contemporary Arab Affairs* 8, no. 3 (2015): 351–62.

Israeli Government. "The Gaza Gaza Strip: The humanitarian lifeline." Consulate General of Israel in New York. 2010. https://embassies.gov.il/new-york/AboutIsrael/Pages/Gaza-Strip-humanitarian-lifeline.aspx.

Khalili, Laleh. "A Habit of Destruction." *Society & Space*. August 25, 2014.

Klein, Naomi. *The Shock Doctrine: The Rise of Disaster Capitalism*. New York: Metropolitan Books/Henry Holt, 2007.

Landau, Noa. "Israel Presents $1 Billion Rehabilitation Plan for Gaza, but Demands Palestinian Authority Take Over." *Haaretz*. 2018.

Li, Darryl. "The Gaza Strip as Laboratory: Notes in the Wake of Disengagement." *Journal of Palestine Studies* 35 no. 2, (2006): 38–55.

Mamdani, Mahmood. "The New Humanitarian Order." *The Nation*. September 10, 2008.

Meari, Linda. "Colonial Dispossession, Developmental Discourses, and Humanitarian Solidarity in 'Area C': The Case of the Palestinian Yanun Village." *Community Development Journal* 52, no. 3 (2017): 506–23.

Mitnick, Joshua. "Newest Gaza Fight: Who Controls Reconstruction Aid?" *Christian Science Monitor*. January 23, 2009,

Murad, Nora. "The Gaza Reconstruction Mechanism: Smoke and Mirrors?" *Journal of Palestinian Refugee Studies* 5, no. 2 (2015): 59–66.

OCHA Occupied Palestinian Territories. "Three years on from the 2014 conflict, 29,000 people remain displaced." September 11, 2017.

Ophir, Adi. "The Politics of Catastrophization: Emergency and Exception." In *Contemporary States of Emergency: The Politics of Military and Humanitarian Interventions*, edited by Didier Fassin and Mariella Pandolfi. New York: Zone Books, 2010.

Oswald, Nuriya. "Gaza Reconstruction Mechanism: Profiting Israel, Entrenching the Blockade." *Jadaliyya*. July 7, 2015.

Oxfam International. *Treading Water: The Worsening Water Crisis and the Gaza Reconstruction Mechanism*. Oxford: Oxfam GB, March 2017.

Pelham, Nicholas. "Gaza's Tunnel Phenomenon: The Unintended Dynamics of Israel's Siege." *Journal of Palestine Studies* 41, no. 4 (2012): 6–31.

Puar, Jasbir K. "The 'Right' to Maim: Disablement and Inhumanist Biopolitics in Palestine." *Borderlands E-Journal* 14, no. 1 (2015).

ReliefWeb. "Humanitarian Bulletin Occupied Palestinian Territory—June 2018." ReliefWeb. 2018.

Roy, Sarah. *The Gaza Strip: The Political Economy of De-Development*, 3rd ed. Washington, DC: Institute for Palestine Studies, 2016.

Salamanca, Omar Jabary. "Assembling the Fabric of Life: When Settler Colonialism Becomes Development." *Journal of Palestine Studies* 45, no. 4 (Summer 2016): 64–80.

Salamanca, Omar Jabary, Mezna Qato, Kareem Rabie, and Sobhi Samour. "Past is Present: Settler Colonialism in Palestine." *Settler Colonial Studies* 2, no. 1 (2012): 1–8.

Sayegh, Fayez. "Zionist Colonialism in Palestine (1965)." *Settler Colonial Studies* 2, no. 1 (2012): 206–25.

Segev, Tom. *1967: Israel, The War, and the Year That Transformed the Middle East*. New York: Metropolitan Books, 2007.

Shaban, Omar. "UN Gaza Reconstruction Mechanism (GRM) Must Come To An End; not to Be Reviewed." Palthink For Strategic Studies. 2018.

Shelter Cluster. "Shelter Cluster Palestine." Sheltercluster.org. 2017.

Shikaki, Ibrahim, and Joanna Springer. *Building a Failed State: Palestine's Governance and Economy Denied*. Al-Shabaka: The Palestinian Policy Network, policy brief, 2015.

Storey, Kenton. *Settler Anxiety at the Outpost of Empire: Colonial Relations, Humanitarian Discourses and the Imperial Press*. Vancouver: UBC Press, 2016.

Tabar, Linda. "Disrupting Development, Reclaiming Solidarity: The Anti-Politics of Humanitarianism." *Journal of Palestine Studies* 45, no. 4 (Summer 2016): 16–31.

Tavernise, Sabrina. "In Gaza, the Wait to Rebuild Lingers." *The New York Times*. January 26, 2009.

UNOPS. "Gaza Reconstruction and Materials Monitoring System." The Materials Monitoring Unit—Gaza Reconstruction Mechanism. 2015.

UNSCO. Report to the Ad Hoc Liaison Committee. New York: 2017.

———. "Statement by UN Special Coordinator Mladenov Following His Joint Meeting Yesterday with PM Hamdallah and Head of COGAT General Mordechai." UNSCO. 2018.

Van Krieken, Robert. "Celebrity, Humanitarianism and Settler-Colonialism: G.A. Robinson and the Aborigines of Van Diemen's Land." In *Celebrity Humanitarianism and North-South Relations: Politics, Place and Power*, edited by Lisa Richey. London: Routledge, 2015.

Veracini, Lorenzo. *Israel and Settler Society*. London: Pluto Press, 2006.

Weizman, Eyal. "665: The Least of All Possible Evils." *e-flux Journal* 38 (October 2012).

———. *The Least of All Possible Evils: Humanitarian Violence from Arendt to Gaza*. London: Verso, 2012.

Who Profits. "Reconstruction of Gaza: Zero Buildings, Massive Profit." *Who Profits* (blog). 2016.

Winter, Yves. "The Siege of Gaza: Spatial Violence, Humanitarian Strategies, and the Biopolitics of Punishment." *Constellations* 23, no. 2 (2015): 308–19.

Wolfe, Patrick. "Settler Colonialism and the Elimination of the Native." *Journal of Genocide Research* 8, no. 4 (2006): 387–409.

World Bank. "Gaza Economy on the Verge of Collapse, Youth Unemployment Highest in the Region at 60 Percent." Press release. 2015.

———. "Reconstructing Gaza—Donor Pledges." 2017.

CITY OF CRYSTAL

Craig Konyk

Figure 1: Hiroshima Peace Memorial. Courtesy of WikiCommons, 2005.

Figure 2: Hiroshima Peace Memorial, detail. Courtesy of WikiCommons, 2005.

Throughout history, the destruction of cities perpetrated through warfare has occurred with catastrophic regularity. As enlightened as we may wish our current moment to be, the ongoing civil war in Syria, the continued suicide bombings inflicted on civilian population centers in Iraq, and the cyclical missile attacks by militants in Gaza followed by the asymmetrical bombing of civilian targets by Israeli jet fighters betray the falsity of that "enlightenment." Warfare is not a historical fact, but rather an ongoing and present reality.

Cities are the physical bodies that register the scars of war. Violence can obliterate them in their entirety, but more often than not the destruction is targeted and distributed unevenly throughout an urban area. Cities bear physical witness to the terrible acts of violence that have been committed against their populations. Inevitably, they are rebuilt in a process that often does not acknowledge the horrors that came before. A collective amnesia over past events seems to pervade reconstruction plans; it is as if the entire population has a deep psychological need to forget. Like a traumatized body in shock, the city as a whole attempts a form of self-preservation through denial, to return to a time from before the destruction.

There are instances when the severity and circumstances of the destruction lead to the conscious decision not to rebuild. A prime example is the Hiroshima Dome (see figures 1 and 2). Given the extreme and unprecedented use

Figure 3: Wall Street Bombing, September 16, 1920. Courtesy of WikiCommons.

Figure 4: Pockmarked Granite, 23 Wall Street, 2016. Courtesy of WikiCommons.

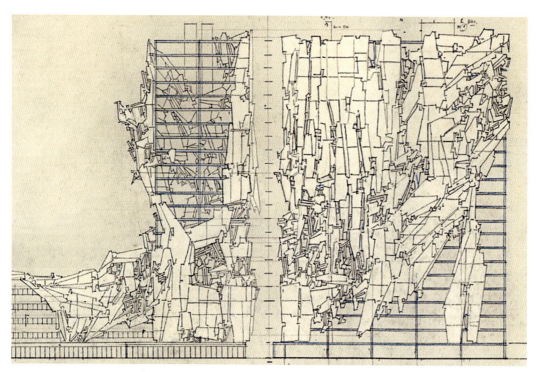

Figure 5: Lebbeus Woods, *Pamphlet Architecture 15: War and Architecture*, Copyright © 1993 Princeton Architectural Press.

of an atomic weapon on a civilian population, this vigilant reminder of the total destruction wreaked on the city in a few seconds starkly warns future generations of the risk of complete annihilation. There are also other reasons to leave the traces of destructive urban violence intact. J. P. Morgan, in a defiant act of "still here," ordered that no repairs be made to the pockmarked and gouged granite cladding of his headquarters, located at 23 Wall Street, after the anarchist flower-cart bombing of September 16, 1920, which killed thirty-eight people. The evidence of that fatal act remains

visible to this day (see figures 3 and 4).

The late Lebbeus Woods, in his powerful architectural imagery for *Pamphlet Architecture 15: War and Architecture* (1993), describes another kind of reconstruction: one that acknowledges the genocidal destruction of Sarajevo within its rebuilt fabric. Resembling scar tissue, his urban interventions are "wounds that refuse to heal," maintaining the presence of past atrocities' intensity even as the residents of Sarajevo move forward into a challenging and forever changed future (see figures 5 and 6). These responses to war

Figure 6: Lebbeus Woods, *Pamphlet Architecture 15: War and Architecture*, Copyright © 1993 Princeton Architectural Press.

Figure 7: Fused, slumped, laminated glass. Courtesy of WikiCommons.

Figure 8: Cast wire glass. Courtesy of WikiCommons.

and its destruction are not traditional memorials, because they are not celebratory. They are memorials only in that they evoke memory. They are more in alignment with the response to war as represented by the Vietnam War Memorial, seeking not to validate or celebrate war, but rather to acknowledge its deep loss and horror. They strive to convey war's harsh emotional toll, the intensity of physical destruction of known landmarks and civic symbols, and the erasure of religious symbols of ethnic distinction. These issues are difficult to express in architectural terms. Woods was one of the first to architecturally convey these physical nightmares of our hatred and contempt for one another. He was the first to make architecture confront atrocities, to confront yet another version of ethnic cleansing on European soil.

The level of mistrust and animosity and the cyclical nature of the conflict, coupled with Israel's economic blockade of Gaza, have created a recurring pattern of Gazan provocation followed by the asymmetrical destruction of targets by Israel, leading to a chronic condition of devastation that seems never-ending. Thinking about how to respond architecturally to the ongoing warfare in Gaza and its brutal aftereffects presents us with an inherent paradox: should we rebuild Gaza as it was before? Or should we allow the destruction to bear witness to the horrors of war?

Gaza City is, like many Arab cities, built of pale sandstone and dolomitic limestone. High temperature fuses sand into a form of cast glass. (see figures 7 and 8). This fused crystalline sand-cast glass possibly constitutes the ideal reconstruction material for Gaza: inherently fragile, yet made of common materials found on its beaches. Sites of destruction can be preserved, providing evidence of the violent acts of war, and rebuilt in a sand-cast glass cocoon so their use can continue as before, although they are now physically altered by war.

This is an accumulative strategy. If the destruction persists, Gaza itself will soon be transformed into a massive crystalline urban structure. And if the new cast-glass structures are destroyed again, more can quickly be sand-cast and deployed to "tent" the new damage, creating a subsequent layer of false resilience-preserved evidence. This is also an interim strategy; selective sites would be preserved in their damaged state for future generations as deemed appropriate once Gaza is made whole again.

Gaza is a fragile reality. The destructive transformations recorded in its fabric will only highlight this truth until the day that real stability, in political, economic, and physical terms, is established.

Aerial view of Gaza City
with proposed "crystal
tented" sites that
were either damaged
or destroyed by the
attacks, 2019.

CITY OF CRYSTAL

A rebuilding strategy for Gaza City is proposed where glass is the material choice that allows the destruction to remain visible. Each is a public site damaged or destroyed by attacks. By rebuilding this way, the damage wrought is demonstrable and yet the incorporation of the modern material of glass simultaneously speaks to a more open and progressive future.

Residential apartment
buildings in glass overlay,
2019.

Mosque with rebuilt
minaret. The original
toppled minaret
is reinforced and
preserved as a reminder
of how religious sites
were targeted, 2019.

Office tower
cocooned in cast
glass, 2019.

Glass and metal pyramid
over the Engineering
Building at Al–Azhar
University, 2019.

Mosque preserved in
its damaged state, 2019.

Family homes in the
state of repair, glass
panel as windows,
2019.

NATURAL GAZA

Romi Khosla

Figure 1: Reconstructing
the Sense of the
Possible, 2019.

Having lived in the southern Levant during its varied seasons and wandered about its deserts and cities, I am still unsure whether I feel damned, entranced, or bewitched by the place. Jerusalem is, in every sense, a magical place, where thoughts race to catch up with possibilities. Despite its modernity, the place feels deeply ancient as one brushes past its limestone fabric, under arches and doorways, and into dark passageways. The entire square mile within the old city's walls inhabits one's consciousness; the most ancient parts are sewn into its contemporary

life. I had dreams about Jerusalem long after returning home, dreams that panned a vaguely biblical past.

Once you have been there, the place never leaves you. Over fifteen years ago, I drafted a proposal called *New Canaan*, and presented it at a seminar on Jerusalem, organized by Michael Sorkin in Bellagio, Italy, in 2000. Now I present it again, focused on Gaza, arguing as I did then, that the conflict can be resolved by reducing the cleavage between the dependent economies of Israel and Palestine that are ultimately inter- dependent. In this project, which has developed into *Natural Gaza*, there is potential for a merger into a shared, autarkic, sustainable system to end the divisions and distortions. One instrument of change is a railway-cum-irrigation channel that links Haifa and Tiberias to Gaza and Beersheba as it passes through the West Bank. Others address the potentials of autarky. Natural Gaza is a fractal of Natural Canaan.

GEOGRAPHICAL AND SOCIAL TIME
In 1948, Israel's history was transposed onto the much-contested region. Israel has countered Palestine's rejection of this history with imprisoning boundaries that affect the ecology and human relationships of the entire region and continue to destroy far too many lives. The people of the southern Levant have lost their memories of living and surviving within a natural geographical landscape. Their memories of a shared culture have been replaced by political nightmares and the abuse of geography, with an uneven distribution of the region's common resources.

Resurrecting that larger geographical connection is vital for the proposals made here, and so we begin with a discourse on justice. The starting point of our proposal is an acceptance of the differences that exist between the two communities. From this follows a discussion of new responsibilities and reciprocities. In the second part of the proposal, we retrieve the common geography of this region, which forms the context for a just, equitable, and sustainable direction for the future.

There are historical obstructions that are both physical and mental that lie in the way of sharing geography between the two communities. These obstructions have deep historical roots and could be removed if discussions can be facilitated. By identifying and agreeing to remove obstructions through discussions in the Corbusian "Pit of Contemplation" and then unifying the natural geographical resources of the region, a new relationship between human and natural environments becomes

Figure 2: Left map: Palestinian territories in 1947.

Right map: Palestinian territories today, 2019.

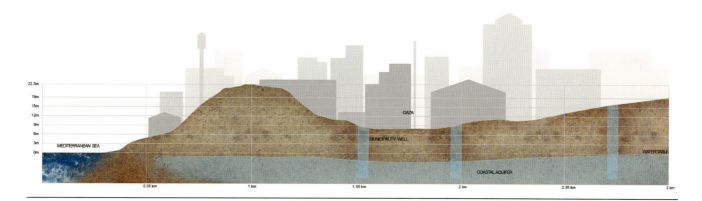

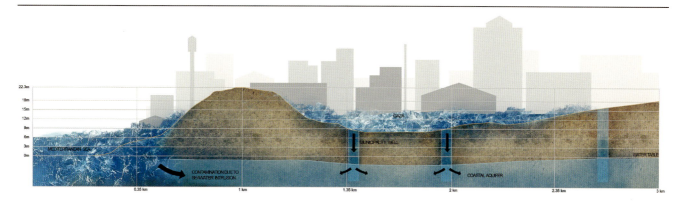

Figure 3: Sections across Gaza city showing the present day (above) and a speculative image of how sea levels will rise with the effects of global warming (below), 2019.

possible. The Pit of Contemplation is a physical space for precipitating discussion. Conflicting communities need to agree to descend into it to initiate and explore discussions.

In a sense, the Pit of Contemplation is a bowl in which it is possible to mix attitudes and views to receive unexpected outcomes. Such discussions will foster common ground and allow the region to collectively face the threat of global warming. Idiographic or qualitative geography is a design tool for crafting survival solutions in a region threatened by the geomorphological dimensions of global warming, which will alter the surface of the earth and the relationship between human settlements. In the geography of the Levant, the scale of this geomorphological threat outweighs the daily threats that combatants hurl at each other across the barbed wires and walls that demarcate territories and jurisdictions.

The gradual rise in sea levels resulting from global warming will transform settlement patterns in coastal Gaza, Israel, and the West Bank. An estimated three million Israelis will be uprooted, and Gaza will lose its freshwater aquifers. A disaster of such magnitude will shift the geography and history of the region onto a new path. Our proposal argues that survival in the Levant relies on a reintegration of geography into the lives of its people, enabling them to survive in a composite economy.

To build autarky or economic self-sufficiency in any of Canaan's cities, connections to long duration geographical-temporal flows must be explored. The name Canaan is an ancient name and suggests a common origin. The connecting events outlined here begin as short historic events, like ripples on the surface of contemporary history initially in Gaza. These short-term events begin with multilateral discussions about reconciliation based on the Difference Principle within the ambit of justice. Reconciliation would be followed by new habitats designed to reallocate resources but not redistribute them. The distinction between the two is important.

Reallocation refers, in this context, to the ways of sharing of resources and identifying particularly those resources that influence the pattern of production. Redistribution, here, refers principally to changing the financial balance between the communities. Conventionally redistribution is done by fiscal methods that focus on taxation and subsidies and primarily influence the pattern of purchasing capacities or expenditure. In other words, the design initiative begins as a short event on the surface of the contemporary, as ripples stirred in the Pit of Contemplation.

This is the first healing event. It could be regarded as an event occurring in the shortest duration of historical time, an event that relates to individual action against the occurrences and influences of historical rhythms of a longer duration. The longer rhythms are for later phases; they are like currents with deeper influences. Making such distinctions for the varying durations of historical time has reference to Fernand Braudel's conceptions of historical and social time.[1] We have devised a tool for historical analysis and cognition of the Levant by precipitating a short duration term event in time, the Pit discussion. This event fits into the larger understanding of the structure of the shared history of the Levant. The discussion in the Contemplation Pit is

an event of short duration that would lead to a bi-communal consensus for changes in their conceptions of the intermediate or conjunctural duration of social time. The three durations of time used as a tool for cognition are integrated into the movements of historical changes for the Levant.

Historical Levantine time is the long duration, the conjunctural or intermediate duration and the shortest of these which is the event. Taken together they dovetail into the longer period of Levantine time. The proposed train and water channel are the currents of social changes in the conjunctural, or intermediate, duration that take the influence of the event that the discussions begin to a deeper level, under the short ripples of events—of discussion and individual action—to become ultimately immersed into the duration of Levantine time in which the train and water are shared. Such currents or slower changes of the intermediate duration can eventually link to forgotten, slower joint cycles of shared social time for the Levant by beginning with Gaza.

The train and water channel would be constructed alongside building activities, forming what we call a naturally sustainable architecture. Eventually, our design connects time in the future with the geographical tempos of the past, the permanence of autarky stitching the long, slow currents of geography and environment into the Levant's future history. Thus, the Natural Canaan design solutions connect across three simultaneous temporal rhythms of history—individual, social, and geographic. The design interventions are considered in greater detail below.

1. .See Fernand Braudel, *Memory and the Mediterranean* (New York: Random House Vintage, 2002).

Figure 4: Imaged Gaza after a storm in a context of rising sea levels from global warming, 2019.

Figure 5: The top left image of present day Gaza before sea level rises and the top right is an imagined image after sea levels have risen. The bottom left image shows present day Haifa and the bottom right is imagined image after sea levels have risen, 2019.

Figure 6: An imagined train and the water channel cross the landscape of Canaan sewing together the Southern Levant, 2019.

JUSTICE AND THE PIT OF CONTEMPLATION

During the many months I spent in conflict areas in Palestine and the Balkans,[2] I noticed among freshly arrived "consultants" from the European Union an unwillingness to engage with questions of justice. Walking through streets smoked out by burning tires, over fields and the remains of a highway bridge blasted by missiles, or across borders with a gun pressed into my back, I realized that the consultants' mission was always to make communities comply with treaties and directives. For the governors and managers from the World Bank, the United Nations, European Union, or the United States, any reference to the principles of justice was difficult to

defend. Community engagements, I was assured, simply end up being emotionally charged, holding up compliance and discipline. Money talks, they said, and pressed the lever of deprivation to ensure compliance in Gaza.

We consider the principles of justice the basic element for gestating a longer time cycle of peace that is fair on both sides. Engaging with justice involves listing mutual agreements and joint oversight. Listing the conditions of justice is not about compiling a roster of suffering, but about relating to geography, ecology, autarky, and the lives of both communities. Such a list enumerates the inequalities and asymmetries that both sides would like to address. The resources listed—such as solar

2. In Kosovo, Montenegro, Cyprus, Bulgaria, and Romania. See Romi Khosla, *The Loneliness of the Long Distant Future* (New Delhi: Tulika Press, 2007).

Figure 7: Sketch of LeCorbusier's *Hand of Justice and Pit of Contemplation in Chandigarh*, designed to help participants see that there are two sides to every question, 2019.

power and water supply—would be reallocated to incubate new opportunities that promote autarky and social justice.

The Pit of Contemplation in Gaza explores new possibilities and accepts John Rawls's "Difference Principle" as a guide for the negotiations.[3] By adopting the Difference Principle, both communities agree to regulate existing inequalities rather than magically abolish them. Both communities would agree on what constitutes shared basic liberties and accept that the inequalities that exist between them do not inhibit the free use of all spaces, in media and on land, by both communities.

These negotiations are conducted in a specially designed place in Gaza that is a replica of the Hand of Justice pit designed by Le Corbusier in Chandigarh, in north India. It consists of a sunken pit where each community sits on seats placed at right angles to each other, facing a lectern. Participants are thus positioned to agree with Le Corbusier's contention that "there are always two sides to every question." The pit will be located within a new memorial to those who have fallen since the *Nakba*, or exodus of Palestinians following the 1948 war. The entire memorial is modeled on the Holocaust monument in Berlin, in honor of those victims.

The new memorial in Gaza prepares the ground for dialogue. It replicates the memorial in Berlin and elevates an architectural statement to a symbolical level that is accessible to both communities. Both have suffered enormous losses, inflicted deliberately without remorse. The replication of the monument is important because it enables the losses to be remembered in a shared way. The Holocaust and other genocides have characterized the nineteenth and twentieth centuries and their terrible consequences were shared and felt by many communities across the Americas, Europe, and the Middle East. We erect this monument in memorial as a replica of one that already exists in Berlin and suggest that, formally, its "transportation" is intended as an act of sharing the monument with other communities. This is a space for reflection, for regretting the Holocaust and the *Nakba*, but also a space for thinking about how to move beyond the horrors of all genocides across the world. The opportunity for contemplation about the past and the future therefore becomes central to the architectural conception of the monument.

ENABLING THE PURSUIT OF JUSTICE

In the sunken Pit of Contemplation, with people sitting at right angles to each other after the antagonisms of both sides have abated, it will be possible to have a philosophical discourse on social justice. The abstraction of a philosophical discourse will come down to the practicalities of social justice in the listing and reallocation of resources

3. John Rawls's "Difference Principle" permits a divergence from strict equality as long as the inequalities in question make the least advantaged in society materially better off than they would be under strict equality. See John Rawls, *A Theory of Justice* (New York: Belknap, 1971).

and the hammering out of an agreement in which neither side is worse off.

New directions for reaching such an agreement have been suggested in the work of Nobel Prize—winning economist Amartya Sen. He connects the search for the abstract goal of justice to the pursuit of freedom through its five instruments—political freedom, transparency of exchange, open economic opportunities, safety nets, and unhindered social opportunities. In his *Idea of Justice* (2009), Sen distinguishes between the need for justice in the day-to-day life of a community and the justice that would define a just society. The balance between these two aspects of justice provides a society with moral and ethical stability, Sen explains. Because we are optimists, we assume that deep down, neither the Israelis nor the Palestinians are driven solely by self-interest, that they do want to stop paying the price of perpetual conflict, and are ready to be rational and reasonable about both aspects of justice. The discussion in the Pit would provide the framework for both communities to cooperate in a shared society, despite each of them subscribing to deeply opposed, though reasonable, doctrines. The discussion would also establish the limits of fairness and define equality of opportunity.

Figure 8: Representation of the new Nakba Memorial (imagined) located in the heart of Gaza, against the backdrop of its conflicted present. The Pit of Contemplation is placed here to initiate the first healing touch and first dialogues for conflict resolution, 2019.

Naturally Sustainable Architecture

In traversing the geography of the region, we limited ourselves to engagement with autarky and naturally sustainable habitats. The principles for governance and economic systems are excluded here.[4] For the design of the new urban landscape of the region, man-made habitats and the agricultural practices of Gaza are regarded as fractals or autarky systems for 100 percent renewability at all levels—habitat, neighborhood, community, city, region, and nation. Renewability extends to energy, land wastage, agriculture, food processing, water resources, and waste management.

The Permanence of Autarky

Autarky engages with influences that emanate from the deep, slow currents of the past and continue into the future. The proposed design makes the urban layout of Gaza porous, with an idiographic checkerboard of urban agricultural cultivation. A typical location could be on high ground, with a spring or harvested water sourced from a branch of the main north-south water channel.

In the template illustrated here, a typical habitat block occupies an area of one square kilometer, divided into four quadrants with 175 households each. There are seven hundred homes (in the template) living amid their urban agricultural lots, using solar power and relying on significant self-employment. Surrounding the urbanized blocks are the commons—collectively owned community resources shared between the inhabitants of Natural Gaza. The commons include energy and all other natural resources, which cannot be appropriated by any individual or group. The commons of Gaza are derived from the notion of village ownership of lands used for food, grazing, fishing, or irrigation.

The commons also include properties used for cultural activities such as music festivals, carnivals, and farmer's fairs; heritage properties, religious structures, and in some cases agricultural fields, as well as daily infrastructure such as electricity or water distribution systems.

Some of the finest work on the frameworks of the commons has been done by Nobel laureate Elinor Ostrom. She explained the eight principles of sustainable governance of common pool resources (CPR).[5] These principles laid out by Ostrom will be included in the charter for the governance of Gaza that states:

1. Clearly defined boundaries that exclude unentitled parties;
2. Rules for the use of common property resources and provisions to adapt their use to local conditions;
3. Collective choice arrangements that allow resource appropriators to participate in decision making;
4. Effective monitoring;
5. Sanctions for violations;
6. Affordable and easily accessible mechanisms for conflict resolution;
7. Recognition by higher-level authorities of the right of local communities to self-determination;
8. Layered governance mechanisms for larger common pool resources.

4. For their exploration see Romi Khosla, "Natural Cities: Strategy for Future Cities in Asia," *Future Cities*, accessed February 19, 2019.

5. Elinor Ostrom, *Governing the Commons: The Evolution of Institutions for Collective Action* (Cambridge: Cambridge University Press, 1990).

Figure 9: The urban texture of Natural Gaza settlements is interspersed with agricultural and horticultural possibilities. The dark dashes on rooftops represent solar panels, 2019.

Figure 10: Diagrammatic representation of a reconstructed urbanism, 2019.

Restored habitats like Natural Gaza would be surrounded by date palm groves of varying size and density. The urban agricultural spaces are irrigated by offshoots of the main canal that brings water from the north along the rail link.

Natural Gaza is largely self-sustaining in terms of water, energy, food, and governance. For instance, one of the ways to design for self-sufficient energy is to reduce the ambient temperature of the city environment by natural convection from currents of air passing over the agricultural lots. Each potential site for a restored habitat, whether an existing town or a greenfield site, requires designers and evaluators to propose the levels of sustainability. The inhabitants of Natural Gaza would be able to choose between "alternative types of economic progress . . . to respond to diverse concepts of human progress in different communities with diverse histories, entitlements, aspirations, potentials, capabilities and capacities for happiness."[6]

Unsustainable living—like mercantilism and laissez-faire capitalism—has no limits. Sustainable living constantly reminds one of limits. To consider these limits, Natural Gaza pays particular attention to Ostrom's fourth and fifth principles of effective monitoring and sanctions for violations. Monitoring is designed to bridge the gap between the limits of personal ideals and the limits of sustainability set by global and ecological imperatives, which are applicable in the fractal structure of new cities at the individual, local, metropolitan, and national levels. Monitoring programs can identify, by enumeration, the multiple ways in which individuals and the community can realize an ideal. They also serve as a bridge between the macro—universal concerns of the ecological health of the planet—and the micro—personal ways of thinking. The criteria for monitoring programs are scientific and measurable, with socially determined indices and trends that would guide the individual as well as the community to reconcile human and governance values.

To enhance the proportion of locally available food in Gaza, the masterplan is designed for porosity, introducing cultivated plots for urban agriculture. These plots are primarily for seasonal and perennial vegetables, and distinct from crop supplies from the hinterland of the city, which are computed separately. For each area occupied by a block of built-up space, an equivalent area has been set aside as an agricultural space for food production. These areas can be distributed unevenly across the cityscape.

Energy Requirements

Gaza City avoids fossil fuels, and nuclear reactors. Micro-hydroelectric sources can be used if they are non-invasive. The likely power requirements in our current model can be gauged at a level between Israel which uses 7,500 kilowatt hours per head, per year and the European Union which uses 5,400 kilowatt hours per head, per year for the residential needs of the city. Additional capacity would be required for industrial needs. Given existing technologies, solar energy parks and wind generation would feed energy into neighborhood, regional, and national grids.

6. Romi Khosla, "India's Urban Landscape: Black Towns of the 21st Century," *Economic and Political Weekly* 52, no. 1 (2017).

Water Requirements

The next component of the certification program in Gaza is to balance water consumption with availability. Water is a finite resource, unlike power; it cannot be generated except by desalination. Gaza would harvest seasonal water, tap water stored below the surface of floodplains, use desalinated water, and recycle all water in use. It needs to meet most of its non-agricultural water requirements from within the ecological footprint of each city, since the availability of water determines a city's population size. A water channel—supported closed-loop water system would be required for domestic, commercial, and agricultural use. Each inhabitant requires 150–200 liters a day, while agricultural and industrial demand will vary from region to region and city to city. It is likely that agriculture will constitute 80 percent of the demand for water, which will have to be supplemented by the north–south water channel.

Waste Management

A zero-waste policy in Gaza would significantly reduce waste output at all points—household, commercial, and industrial. While segregation of waste is commonly in place at the household level, each city will recycle its entire waste into either biodegradable manure or recycled materials. This would influence production processes, packaging, and the retailing of goods.

Unsustainability can be analyzed as an interconnected cluster of obstructions that cause malfunctions in the relationship between human and natural environments. Energy, food, water resources, and the natural environment need to be tackled at the level of governance. While individuals and civil society organizations can handle some malfunctions, at the level of social engagement, governance is the instrument of change.

Scaling the Engagement

This preliminary description of Gaza is a skeletal blueprint. It lacks the institutional structures, real-time opportunities, finance, and technological and operational commitments to enable coordination with the global discourse on new urban ecosystems. However, all the nuts and bolts required to convert the idea into new national solutions for a post-industrialized urbanization are potentially available. There are ample skills within the disciplines of science, evaluation, and information technology to enable government and non-government groups to begin the development of Canaan's new natural cities.

Gaza's new cities would be designed and built in phases, absorbing the fresh migration that would otherwise focus on the metropolitan areas. The new cities are designed to provide alternative employment to young agents of change living in existing metropolitan cities, drawing them into a much more sophisticated and sustainable living environment. As the number of Canaan cities increases, the mega-cities would be depopulated to sustainable levels.

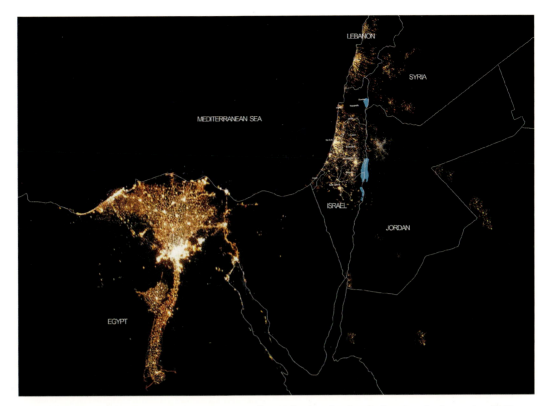

Figure 12: Current regional settlement pattern in Israel and Palestine, showing the location of urban nodes, 2019.

Figure 13: Imagined greening of Canaan, 2019.

CONCLUSION

Any city, particularly a natural one, is a complex organism derived from the obsolete remnants of nineteenth century cities, irretrievably unsustainable and continuing to be governed by outmoded economic and planning models centered on the accumulation of wealth and indifference to poverty. The declining allure of the old standards can help to inspire the adoption of new development models for prosperous but natural ways of urban living.

Gaza's new cities can become part of a regional web that promises balanced and sustainable living environments. Such new cities would probably be established as a leap of faith by pioneers who believe in sustainability, rather than by conventional investors. However, one can be sure that these new cities will inherit all the hidden values, cultural practices, and assets of the outmoded mega-city. They will have their own share of entertainment, recreation, joy and sadness, creative communities, brokers and hustlers, criminals and charities, honest campaigners, corrupt politicians, commission agents, bureaucrats, and policemen, all of which are components of any human settlement.

Natural Gaza is a metaphor, a guide for a different human experience that transcends a utilitarian life fixated on laissez-faire avarice and material accumulation. Our plan is to transform Canaan into a place where people live naturally and where renewability, regeneration, and sustainability are the guides for a way of life that places utilitarianism within the wider pursuit of being part of the natural world.

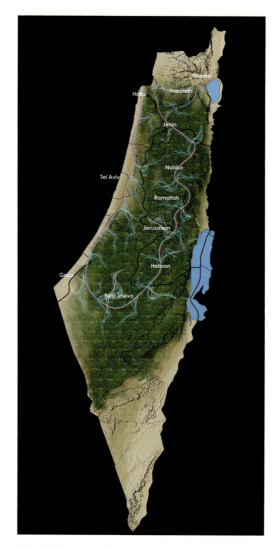

Fiure 14: The sense of the possible: overview of Natural Canaan after reconstructing its natural potential, 2019.

WORKS CITED

Braudel, Fernand. *Memory and the Mediterranean*. New York: Random House Vintage, 2002.

Khosla, Romi. "India's Urban Landscape: Black Towns of the 21st Century." *Economic and Political Weekly* 52, no. 1 (2017).

———. "Natural Cities: Strategy for Future Cities in Asia." *Future Cities*, accessed February 19, 2019.

———. *The Loneliness of the Long Distant Future*. New Delhi: Tulika Press, 2007.

McLennan, J. F. *The Philosophy of Sustainable Design*. Kansas City, KS: Ecotone LLC, 2004.

Ostrom, Elinor. *Governing the Commons: The Evolution of Institutions for Collective Action*. Cambridge: Cambridge University Press, 1990.

Rawls, John. *A Theory of Justice*. New York: Belknap, 1971.

ZOO, OR THE LETTER Z, JUST AFTER ZIONISM

Malkit Shoshan

A portion of this essay first
appeared in the catalog of
the exhibition *ZOO, or the
letter Z, Just after Zionism*.

All drawings and images by
Malkit Shoshan with Laura
van Santen.

The book *Atlas of the Conflict, Israel-Palestine* maps the territorial transitions that took place in Israel and Palestine over the past century.[1] It visualizes major processes and mechanisms that led to the emergence of Israel and the disappearance of Palestine. It examines issues such as border fluctuations, settlement distributions and typologies, land ownership, cultural heritage sites, demography, water, and landscaping. I started this mapping project in 2001 as an architecture student in Israel. Since 2001, I have continued collecting, drawing, adding, and editing maps and assembling a lexicon with terms that are directly or indirectly linked to the illustrations. The work was published in 2010. I was then approached to exhibit the work in an architecture gallery in Maastricht. Having spent about ten years drawing maps, I decided to use a new medium, the gallery, to engage the public and raise awareness of daily life in a state of perpetual conflict in an unexpected way. I went through the book and ended up spending one year on the last page of the lexicon, remapping, spatializing, and reconstructing a new narrative in order to address the ongoing crisis in the Gaza Strip.

Under the letter "Z," there are only two, seemingly disconnected entries: "Zionism" and "zoo." Yet the two concepts are linked, both having arisen out of the passion for classification that came into being during the age of reason, and they each represent ideas fundamental to the nature of the conflict in Israel-Palestine. Perhaps, after all, these final entries are where it all began.

In this essay, I have tried to extrapolate and superpose multiple narratives and trace some of the events that led to the current state of the Strip.

Nimrod was searching for a quarry.[2] He went to the forest, looking for tracks, broken branches and droppings, trying to locate the hart, which he would ideally manage to glimpse before the chase . . . Later, when the quarry could no longer run, it would turn and try to defend itself.[3]

THE AGE OF ENLIGHTENMENT

The origins of both Zionism and zoos can be traced back to two revolutionary developments that emerged in the Age of Enlightenment: the classification of nature and the classification of nations.[4] A new, obsessive, interest in classifying, archiving, grouping, and gathering lay behind both tendencies.

Zionism, the ideology that calls for the establishment of a homeland for the Jewish people, emerged in Europe during the nineteenth century, a time dominated by revolutionary movements. A series of national uprisings inspired by the French Revolution led to the formation of modern Europe, with new borders delineating new nation-states.[5]

The Jews were excluded from this new reality of classified territory, with its divisions determined according to race or national origin. Without a place of their own in newly remodeled Europe, they aspired to a Jewish homeland, a nation-state, where they could feel safe and free.

To the living, the Jew is a corpse, to the native a foreigner, to the homesteader a vagrant, to the proprietary a beggar, to the poor

1. Malkit Shoshan, *Atlas of the Conflict, Israel-Palestine* (Rotterdam: nai010, 2010).

2. Nimrod, according to the Books of Genesis and Chronicles, was the son of Cush, great-grandson of Noah and king of Shinar. He is depicted in the Tanakh as a man of power and a mighty hunter.

3. Gaston Phoebus. *The Book of Hunting, 1387–89*. https://www.wdl.org/en/item/14787.

4. Between the fifteenth and eighteenth centuries, members of "exotic" ethnic groups arrived in Europe. By the early nineteenth century, ethnic shows were a feature of theater cafés. Between 1870 and World War II, many venues started specializing in ethnic performances, including the Crystal Palace, Barnum and Bailey in Madison Square, the Folies Bergères, and the famous Panoptikum in Berlin. It was a time of professionalization, and exotic performances morphed into mass entertainment. Reconstructed ethnic villages, zoos, colonial and international fairs, science, and spectacle merged in multiple places. "Exotic" individuals and physical difference were brought together on stage as representations of the realm of abnormality.

5. Tony Judt, *Postwar: A History of Europe Since 1945* (London: Heinemann, 2005).

*an exploiter and a millionaire,
to the patriot a man without a
country, for all a hated rival.*[6]

Around the time that Zionism was gathering strength, another, seemingly unrelated development took place: the emergence of the urban zoo. At that time, the beauty of the system was as important as nationality: science was preoccupied with classification and comparison, according to foundations laid by Linnaeus and Darwin. The first zoos, in big cities like London and Berlin, sorted animals into their families: houses of birds, reptiles, apes, and so on. The cages were highly ornamented, but still resembled prison cells, and buildings, scattered pavilion-like in a garden setting, were isolated from each other. Animals were scientifically classified objects, ornaments, or both.

The Quest

Before the hunt could start, an expert huntsman, accompanied by a lymer, a scent hound, would seek out the quarry. Following the clues left by tracks, broken branches and droppings he would try to locate the hart as accurately as possible. Ideally, the huntsman would see it to determine its worthiness as a quarry.[7]

As Jewish activist groups searched for a potential homeland, they considered various alternatives: Uganda, Madagascar, Brazil, and even Siberia. Young Jewish people started exploring these ideas. Pioneering groups went out into the wild to locate a setting that might furnish the raw material for the desired nation-state.
    Almost like a divine intervention,

Mark Twain published *The Innocents Abroad* in 1867, his account of traveling in Lebanon, Syria, and Palestine. In it, he described Palestine as if it were empty:

> *For about four hours we travelled down hill constantly. We followed a narrow bridle-path which traversed the beds of the mountain gorges, and when we could we got out of the way of the long trains of laden camels and asses, and when we could not we suffered the misery of being mashed up against perpendicular walls of rock and having our legs bruised by the passing freight ... However, this was as good a road as we had found in Palestine, and possibly even the best, and so there was not much grumbling.*[8]

The young pioneers followed Mark Twain as if he were the expert huntsman. They sought to practice their national identity and redeem their fathers' lands; they were anxious to create a new reputation for themselves and rise above their oppressors. A heroic move, leading to the start of a new life, seemed to be the answer. Romantically, they looked toward Palestine as the most enticing idea, as it linked the idea of a Jewish nation with its biblical saga.

The Assembly

Early on the day of the hunt, the hunting party would meet, examine the huntsman's information and the deer's droppings, and agree on how best to conduct the hunt. This would be a social gathering too, and breakfast would be served.[9]

6. Leon Pinsker, "Auto Emancipation: An Appeal to His People by a Russian Jew," trans. Dr. D. S. Blondheim, Federation of American Zionists. Jewish Virtual Library. Pinsker was a Zionist pioneer.

7. Gaston, *The Book of Hunting.*

8. "Sometimes, in the glens, we came upon luxuriant orchards of figs, apricots, pomegranates, and such things, but oftener the scenery was rugged, mountainous, verdureless and forbidding. Here and there, towers were perched high up on acclivities which seemed almost inaccessible. This fashion is as old as Palestine itself and was adopted in ancient times for security against enemies. We crossed the brook which furnished David the stone that killed Goliath, and no doubt we looked upon the very ground whereon that noted battle was fought." Mark Twain, *The Innocents Abroad* (San Francisco: Bancroft, 1869).

9. Gaston, *The Book of Hunting.*

Young Jewish people started arriving in Palestine, measuring, mapping, and photographing the land. They created a strategy for future expansion. They believed they were redeeming a wilderness, connecting with their ancestors, and proving their courage and strength—and, above all, their emancipation—to those who had denied them homes in Europe.

Although they were not necessarily religious, their religion became their new national ethos. The young pioneers built new settlements and invented some new habitation typologies like "wall and tower," "kibbutz," and "moshav." They had ideas about how the perfect society should be organized. They settled in collective groups. There was a period when they all wanted to look alike, so they dressed in khaki uniforms. Redefining their lifestyle and their environment, they planted gardens and forests, transforming the landscape to resemble their old European homes and to camouflage the existence of Palestine.

Institutions like the Jewish National Fund were established to support their operation, collecting funds from Jewish communities all over the world to buy land in Palestine and to spread the story of a new home for the Jewish people in Palestine. They bought so much land that their settlements were no longer scattered, but formed a geographically continuous presence, delineating the desired borders of their developing nation-state. The Zionist ideology became a movement, and the land of Palestine was continuously settled and transformed, as an abstract idea became reality.

Baying
When the hart could run no longer, it would turn and try to defend itself. It was said to be "at bay." The hounds would now be kept from attacking, and the quarry would be killed or caged.[10]

THE MODERNIST ZOO
The zoo as a phenomenon continued to evolve in the twentieth century. Its development can be read retrospectively as a reflective, measurable typology of the progression of society in terms of values, applied sciences, and aesthetics.

Between and after the World Wars, the study of nature and its classification became less important. Most of the natural world was already classified, and whatever was not was considered problematic, even to the point of requiring extermination. During this period, science was predominantly about problem solving. Vaccination became prevalent, and the idea of killing germs to increase health and extend life expectancy became widespread.

The physical typology of the zoo evolved as well. It came to resemble an art gallery: the animals were treated almost as works of art. There were some attempts to illustrate a habitat background and occasionally to transform this into three dimensions. Carl Hagenbeck created the first cage without bars. This was the time of the rise of modernism, of form following function, and there was an obsessive desire to sterilize the zoo and ensure that the exhibits were cleaned regularly. Concrete was widely used.

As environmental awareness and human rights grew in importance from the mid-twentieth century

10. Ibid.

Figure 1: Inhabitants of the Gaza Zoo.

Animal	Amount	Source	Cage in relation to animal	Status
Monkey	[1, 2, 3, 4]	Tunnels		mostly died, war 1 alive
Dog	[2, 3]	Domestic		alive
Zebra	[1, 2]	(If) smuggled from Egypt[2] $40,000		died, lack of nutrition
Donkey	[1, 2]	Domestic		1 died, paint poison
Camel	[1]	Domestic		1 died, war 1 alive
Rabbits	[1]	Domestic		died, war
Tiger	[1]	Tunnels		died, war
Ostrich	[2]	Domestic		died, war
Peafowl	[2]	Domestic		died, war
Wolf	[3]	Local Wild		died, war
Goat-Antelopes	[3]	Domestic		died, war
Hawk	[3]	Local Wild		died, war
Gazelle	[3]	Local Wild		alive
White Stork	[3]	Local Wild		alive
Cat	[3]	Domestic		alive
Fox	[4]	Local Wild		alive
Tiny Fox	[3, 4]	?		died, war
Owl	[5]	?		1 died, 1 alive
Lion	[5]	Smuggled,[5] Selling For $700		alive [5, 6]
Fish	[6]	?		alive

1. AP : Gaza Zoo Paints Donkeys to look like Zebras
2. CNN : Gaza's confused Donkey
3. Al Jazeera: Gaza's only zoo is up for sale
4. Al Jazeera: In Gaza, The Zoo After the War
5. http://www.slate.com/id/2222991/
6. http://www.independent.ie/world-news/middle-east/for-sale-gaza-zoo-where-the-zebras-were-not-all-they-seemed-2053258.html

Figure 2: Rats by FAST.

Figure 3: Pigeon by FAST.

onwards, the concept of animal rights began to gain more attention. In the 1950s, psychiatrist Humphrey Osmond developed the concept of socio-architectural hospital design, first used at Weyburn Mental Hospital in 1951 and partly based on Heini Hediger's species-habitat work. With advances in healthcare, animals in captivity were treated for physical and mental conditions. Zoo design began to simulate the original habitat of the wild animal.[11]

Birth of a State

In 1948, the United Nations declared Palestine to be Israel, a homeland for the Jewish people. In a sense, the victory of Zionism is related to the increasing global awareness of the importance of human rights. Zionism was associated with justice (the Jewish people deserve a safe home) and the establishment of Israel was seen as an accomplishment of the international community, which had learned from the tragedies of the past.

Yet the triumph of one nation (Israel) was a disaster for another (Palestine). Over five hundred Palestinian villages were destroyed and about one million Palestinians became refugees.[12] The Israeli enterprise was superimposed on another people's present, history, culture, and landscape. Israel was built on top of Palestine.

The Israeli-Palestinian conflict is a conflict between two nations that have been suppressed by other peoples throughout history. While the Palestinians were oppressed at home by Ottoman emperors and other colonial powers, the Jews were driven from theirs and forced to search for an alternative.

After decades of war and violence over the ownership of the land, it seems that Israel and Palestine completely overlap, yet are separated by language, culture, nature, walls, observation towers, and military patrols. The overlapping nations are fragmented and isolated in enclaves. While one nation, Israel, enjoys freedom of movement and the full rights of citizenship, the Palestinians are captive. For them, every aspect of life, however ordinary, requires a permit—including mobility, agriculture, access to education and medical care, and even home ownership.

UNMAKING (ZEBRA AND DONKEY)

The donkey was painted in a careful, ritualistic manner. Transformed into a zebra, it was put in a cage.

The "unmaking" of an animal is an important part of the hunting ritual; you transform the animal into something else and then you share it with your partners.

Captive in Gaza

Two white donkeys dyed with black stripes at a small Gaza zoo delighted Palestinian kids who had never seen a zebra in the flesh.[13]

Marah Land is an improvised private zoo near Gaza City. Opened by a local family endeavoring to live in normality, it is a symbol of ordinary urban reality, a place of leisure in the Gaza Strip. A zoo under siege, like an exotic alien, needs to reinvent itself and its resources.

About 250,000 Palestinian refugees ended up in the Gaza Strip during the 1948 war. In the early 1950s, they were placed in camps organized by the international community through UNRWA. These

11. Heini Hediger described a number of standard interaction distances used in one form or another among animals. Two of these are flight distance and critical distance, used when animals of different species meet, whereas others are personal distance and social distance, observed during interactions between members of the same species. Hediger's biological social distance theories were used as a basis for Edward T. Hall's 1966 anthropological social distance theories.

12. In total, 678 Palestinian localities were destroyed by Israel during the 1948 war; see Eitan Bronstein Aparicio, "Mapping the Destruction: Launching the First Nakba Map in Hebrew—at Zochrot and on Tel Aviv Streets," Zochrot, last modified March 2013. According to UNRWA, approximately 711,000 Palestinians met the UN criteria of Palestinian refugees in 1950; see United Nations Conciliation Committee for Palestine, "Supplement 18, General Progress Report and Supplementary Report, A/1367/Rev.1" (October 23, 1950).

13. Douglas Hamilton, "Donkeys Get Dye-Job, Take On Zebra Role," *Reuters*, October 8, 2009.

camps were first composed of canvas tents, then of mud hovels, and finally of small shelters measuring five by six meters. Today, there are about 1.1 million registered Palestinian refugees living in UN-built refugee camps in the Gaza Strip.

After the establishment of Israel, Gaza was annexed by Egypt, with its population and refugees. In 1967, during the Six-Day War, it was claimed by Israel, together with the Sinai Peninsula. The Strip and its population have been under Israeli occupation ever since. Following Israel's evacuation of its settlements in 2005 and Hamas's rise to power in 2007, the Gaza Strip has found itself in a state of almost hermetic closure.

The Strip is very dense; about 360 square kilometers (140 square miles) of walled territory is home to about 1.8 million people.[14] In addition to it being sealed-off, Gaza is in a constant state of violence and war. It is appalling to see the scale of Israel's destruction of Palestinian private property, mainly homes, which now appear as a sea of ruins: demolished houses, semi-collapsed structures, perforated homes and walls breached by F16 bombs, shells, and detonators. Human Rights Watch documented the complete destruction of 189 buildings, including eleven factories, eight warehouses, and 170 residential buildings, leaving at least 971 people homeless during the operation, which began in December 2008.[15]

The siege of the Strip and the ongoing state of war make it difficult and, in fact, often impossible to access basic necessities such as food, medical equipment, medicine, and building materials—let alone to have wild animals to reside in the cages of the zoo.

Cure'e[16]

The monkeys and lions were drugged, tossed into cloth sacks and pulled through smuggling tunnels under the border between Egypt and the besieged Gaza Strip before ending up in their new homes in a dusty Gaza

14. In the early 1960s, the National Institute of Mental Health acquired property in a rural area outside Poolesville, Maryland. The facility held the American ethologist and behaviroal researcher John Calhoun's most famous experiment, the rat4 universe. In July 1968, four pairs of rats were introduced into the Utopian universe. The universe was a 2.7 m2 metal pen with 1.4 m sides. Each side had four groups of vertical, wire-mesh "tunnels." The "tunnels" gave access to nesting boxes, food hoppers, and water dispensers. There was no shortage of food or water or nesting material. There were no predators. The only adversity was the limited space. The population peaked at eighty rats, which then exhibited a variety of abnormal, often destructive behaviors; his conclusion was that space itself is a necessity.

15. Human Rights Watch, "Rain of Fire: Israel's Unlawful Use of White Phosphorus in Gaza," (Human Rights Watch, 2009).

16. The "Cure'e" is part of the hunt, as described by Phoebus in *The Book of Hunting*. It means a quarry—when the animal is offered to the pack to be devoured.

Figure 4: Zonkey by FAST.

zoo. But to draw the crowds, what zoo manager Shadi Fayiz really wants to bring through the underground passages is an elephant. The Zoo, stocked almost entirely with smuggled animals, is a sign of Gaza's ever-expanding tunnel industry . . . allowing the flow of products like cigarettes, weapons, and lion cubs to continue unhindered.[17]

Gaza's population is enclosed within a wall, fenced in by barbed wire, and monitored by observation towers and military patrols by sea, air, and land. Its people rarely have contact with the outside world, which has effectively become a phantom to Gazans because Israeli technology has substituted automated instruments and robots for human contact, which facilitate the exchange of goods without any physical encounter.

When on-the-ground passages, networks, and power institutes are blocked or closed, people resort to the underground and to mastering obscurity in transactions, rather than clarity and transparency. The Hamas government has consolidated a network of illegal means to help improve daily life in the Gaza Strip. Underground tunnels cross borders unseen, while the black market replaces the banking system and legal trade. In captivity, people's creativity is challenged to the extreme.

In the kind of reality where daily groceries must be smuggled from Egypt through illegal underground tunnels, a lion, a monkey, or a tiger can be smuggled too. For the family running the zoo in Gaza as a small business, smuggling exotic animals

soon became prohibitively expensive. Imagine the zoo owners calculating the cost of importing a zebra ($25,000) while looking at a white donkey or two, leading naturally to the thought: why smuggle when you can DIY and dye?

Marah Land Zoo is a flashback to the Enlightenment, when cages were almost the same size as the animal and the landscape was a two-dimensional drawing in the background. In an overcrowded environment under siege, the exotic is defined by mental creativity and physically shaped by the imagination. Marah Land's walls are painted with Disney figures copied from smuggled, pirated, made-in-China DVDs and with nationalist motifs that are completely decontextualized: a golden dome resembles Temple Mount, but is placed in the desert like an oasis and decorated with palm trees and donkeys.

Gaza, an oasis, used to be the place were troops and traders could easily access water before a long march into the desert. It was also a place of learning, scholarship, and international trade. Nowadays, Gaza is under siege and enclosed within walls, just like a forgotten paradise.[18] Its biblical beauty and its history are like a mirage that bears no relation to its current distorted mode of existence. The current reality makes its history completely unrecognizable.

Zoo, or the letter Z, just after Zionism, offers, from afar, a rare glimpse of Gaza—a view almost as exotic as the zoo animals, or the concept of a zoo itself. A glimpse of territories, people, animals under siege.

Zoos and Zionism are two

17. The Jerusalem Post, "Lions, Monkeys Take Underground Route to Gaza Zoo," *The Jerusalem Post*, August 8, 2008.

18. There is a strong association between the concept of Islamic gardens and paradise. The Persian word, *pairidaeeza*, is a combination of two words that mean "surrounding wall"; thus, the concept of paradise is of a garden surrounded by a wall, isolating those within and enabling them to enjoy the features established within the wall. The concept of paradise as a garden predates Islam, Christianity, and Judaism by thousands of years. Originating with the Sumerians, paradise gardens were also a feature the Babylonians reserved for their gods, introducing two of what were to become basic elements of an Islamic garden: trees and water. With its adoption by the Greeks, paradise became associated with heaven in the Abrahamic religions.

phenomena that emerged out of the age of reason as an attempt to introduce a space for a new order for the world of things, life, and culture. Sorting into groups linked what was similar and separated what was different. This separation was not only an abstract concept; one of the consequences of this new order was the reorganization of space. New borders were drawn to divide nations and new cages were designed to divide animals and species from one another. A side effect of grouping the similar was the exclusion of difference.

The caged donkey and the Gaza Strip represent possible consequences of classification gone wrong. The study of the boundaries that divide the world, whether between nations or species, professions or programs, touch on a topic crucial to understanding our living environment: boundaries and border conditions.

WORKS CITED

Aparlcio, Eltan Bronstein. "Mapping the Destruction: Launching the First Nakba Map in Hebrew—at Zochrot and on Tel Aviv Streets." *Zochrot.*

Hamilton, Douglas. "Donkeys Get Dye-Job, Take on Zebra Role." *Reuters*, October 8, 2009.

Human Rights Watch. "Rain of Fire: Israel's Unlawful Use of White Phosphorus in Gaza." *Human Rights Watch*, 2009.

Judt, Tony. *Postwar: A History of Europe Since 1945*. London: Heinemann, 2005.

Phoebus, Gaston. *The Book of Hunting, 1387–89*. https://www.wdl.org/en/item/14787.

Pinsker, Leon. "Auto Emancipation: An Appeal to His People by a Russian Jew." Trans. Dr. D. S. Blondheim, Federation of American Zionists. Jewish Virtual Library.

Shoshan, Malkit. *Atlas of the Conflict, Israel–Palestine*. Rotterdam: nal010, 2010.

The Jerusalem Post. "Lions, Monkeys take Underground route to Gaza." *The Jerusalem Post*, August 8, 2008.

Twain, Mark. *The Innocents Abroad* (San Francisco: Bancroft, 1869).

United Nations Conciliation Committee for Palestine. "Supplement 18, General Progress Report and Supplementary Report, A/1367/Rev.1." October 23, 1950.

SOLAR DOME

Chris Mackey and Rafi Segal

Even the most ambitious projections for the application of photovoltaics show solar producing less than 5 percent of the world's energy supply by the year 2050.[1] Although Chinese industry has mass-produced panels cheaper than the labor needed to install them, the simple fact is that solar energy, while plentiful, is too diffuse to be useful for most of the needs of the developed world. It is less concentrated and thus less practical than other forms of renewable energy like wind, hydro, and geo-thermal. For this reason, many experts now agree that direct solar is neither the most effective way to combat global climate change, nor is it the energy source likely to satisfy most of the world's growing power demand in the coming decades.[2]

However, there is a very good reason for why experts have come to this conclusion, and it does not hold universally across the planet. The reasoning is perhaps best summarized by comparing the energy-use intensity of average lifestyles in different nations. Consuming an incredible 301 GJ (Gigajoules) of energy annually, the lifestyle of the typical US resident is among the highest energy-consuming per individual in the world. In comparison, the average resident of the European Union consumes roughly half of what a US resident consumes.[3]

Figure 1. Lifestyle Energy Intensity
Energy-Consumption Comparison Between US, European, and Gazan resident (today and projected for 2030). Yearly average in GJ.

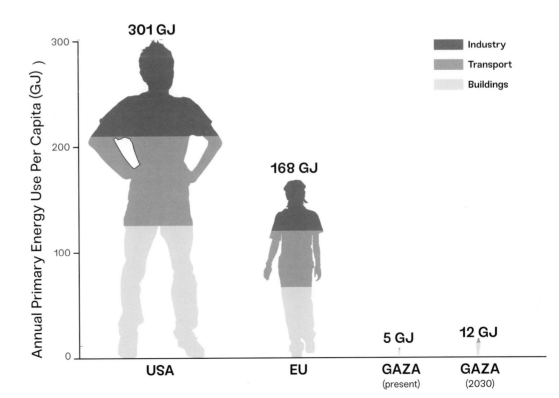

1. "World Energy Outlook" (Paris: International Energy Agency, 2016).

2. Ibid.

3. "Key World Energy Statistics" (Paris: International Energy Agency, 2016).

Figure 2: Land Area Needed to Sustain Gaza's Population with Different Lifestyles*

*Assuming 10% of available solar energy can be converted into useful primary energy.

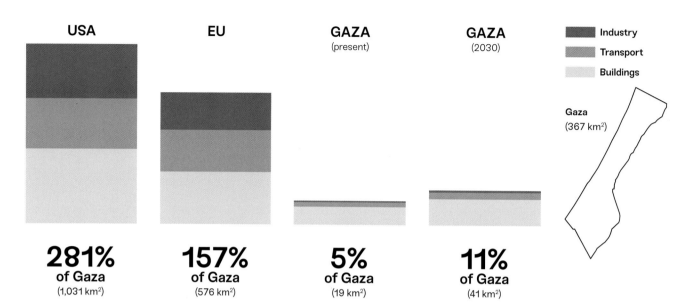

USA	EU	GAZA (present)	GAZA (2030)
281% of Gaza (1,031 km²)	**157%** of Gaza (576 km²)	**5%** of Gaza (19 km²)	**11%** of Gaza (41 km²)

Industry
Transport
Buildings

Gaza (367 km²)

While this difference is significant, and one can endlessly argue about why the United States should learn from Europe and invest in a low energy-use lifestyle, it overlooks a broader issue, namely that the average resident of Gaza presently consumes just 5 GJ of primary energy annually, which is less than 2 percent of that consumed by the average US citizen.[4]

While this figure is the result of a great amount of resourcefulness in the Gazan lifestyle, it is also an indication of Gaza's present lack of basic resources. Such low quantities of energy consumption are not enough to support the critical infrastructure that most would argue should be accessible to all: working sewage systems, clean drinking water, a reliable power grid, and food security. For all these reasons, Gaza's per-capita energy use is projected to more than double between now and 2030, assuming that the average Gazan citizen receives these essential services.[5]

While this doubling of energy use

signifies an enormous improvement in the Gazan lifestyle, it is important to emphasize that all this change is happening on a much smaller scale than that of the US lifestyle. The doubling of Gaza's per-capita energy usage still results in only 4 percent of the average US resident's energy expenditure. For this reason, Gaza has opportunities for powering itself that are simply not available to those in the developed world.

By observing the minimum quantity of land that must be covered in solar panels to fulfill the energy needs of Gaza's population, one quickly realizes that it would be absurd to power Gaza's 1.8 million residents assuming a US lifestyle. Even if a European lifestyle were followed, the amount of land needed would still be more than 1.5 times what Gaza has available. However, Gaza's projected energy use in 2030 would only require 11 percent of its total land area, meaning that there is space for a complete solar power regime within its borders.

There is still a multitude of cost barriers, logistic issues, and laws

4. Daniela Gressani et al., "Report No. 39695–GZ: West Bank and Gaza Energy Sector Review" (Washington, DC: Sustainable Development Department [MNSSD], Middle East and North Africa Region, 2007).

5. Mohamed Ouda, "Analysis and Prediction of Household Energy Consumption in West Bank and Gaza Strip" (Gaza City, Palestine: Islamic University of Palestine, Electrical Engineering Department, 2008).

Figure 3. Energy Diagram Matching Gaza's Building Energy Demand with Supply from Different Solar Resources.

Solar resources are mapped onto the land area of Gaza illustrating the amount of land needed to harvest them.

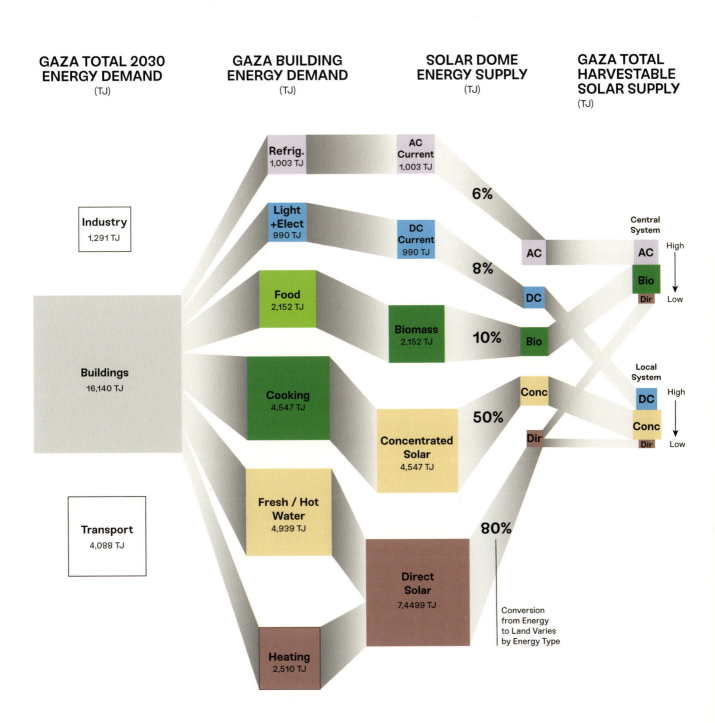

GAZA TOTAL 2030 ENERGY DEMAND (TJ)

Industry 1,291 TJ

Buildings 16,140 TJ

Transport 4,088 TJ

GAZA BUILDING ENERGY DEMAND (TJ)

Refrig. 1,003 TJ

Light +Elect 990 TJ

Food 2,152 TJ

Cooking 4,547 TJ

Fresh / Hot Water 4,939 TJ

Heating 2,510 TJ

SOLAR DOME ENERGY SUPPLY (TJ)

AC Current 1,003 TJ

DC Current 990 TJ

Biomass 2,152 TJ

Concentrated Solar 4,547 TJ

Direct Solar 7,4499 TJ

6%
8%
10%
50%
80%

Conversion from Energy to Land Varies by Energy Type

GAZA TOTAL HARVESTABLE SOLAR SUPPLY (TJ)

AC
DC
Bio
Conc
Dir

Central System
High
Low
AC
Bio
Dir

Local System
High
Low
DC
Conc
Dir

of physics that would have to be confronted if a solar-sustained Gaza were to be a reality. However, the Strip's unique situation presents opportunities to address nearly all of these challenges.

The biggest cost barrier to the application of photovoltaics in the developed world is labor, which is in extraordinarily high supply in Gaza, with its dense population of 1.8 million. If the cost of labor is removed, solar energy's cost would currently only be slightly larger than that of conventional energy sources, and it would be at least as competitive as other renewable alternatives. Furthermore, there are a number of clear political arguments for a strategy of energy independence within Gaza's borders, because it might be less expensive than importing energy from outside. If Gaza's neighbors are intent on charging high rates for electricity, an investment in solar power and energy storage could pay itself back within a few years.

Gaza has another advantage in comparison with other places that seek to operate on solar power: it has a reliable solar pattern, with very few cloudy days in the year. These climate facts reduce the need for costly systems that store solar energy reserves for use when sunlight is not available. Energy storage is a major hurdle to the widespread application of solar power and sometimes constitutes half of its total cost.

Gaza's final major advantage as a prime target for solar is the fact that the majority of its energy use occurs within buildings. Compared to Europe and the United States, which use approximately 40 percent of their primary energy in buildings, Gaza consumes 75 percent of its total energy within buildings.[6] Any architect who has worked on a net-zero building would probably agree that solar energy is typically the best way to offset a building's energy use on-site. The reasons for this are manifold.

Buildings are particularly suited to being powered with diffuse energy sources such as solar, because most of their processes do not require high energy densities to run. Energy density is defined as the amount of usable energy in a fuel (or energy storage) system, divided by its mass. Sectors such as transportation necessitate a low fuel weight, so that the vehicle is light and efficient. This is why the majority of our vehicles today use one of the highest energy-density sources: petroleum. This is also why transportation sectors such as air travel have all but given up on transitioning to renewables other than biofuel, or have resorted to buying carbon offsets to address our warming planet. Similarly, many industrial processes use very high temperatures to induce changes within materials, and these require high energy densities to initiate. The melting of glass and metals, the manufacturing of concrete, and the electrocution of aluminum ore are all examples of industrial processes that require high concentrations of energy in order to run. While it is possible to concentrate large amounts of sunlight to produce these conditions, it is far more cost-effective to simply use sunlight "as is," and this is where buildings excel.

A building's space heating, hot water, and lighting demands are prime examples of energy needs that can be

6. Ibid.

directly fulfilled by solar energy. With a relatively small concentration of solar power, one can also meet most of the other demands of a building, such as cooking, and the charging of electronics. Notably, most of our electronics—such as computers, televisions, and LED light bulbs—are meant to use direct current.

This is precisely what photovoltaic solar panels produce and what most batteries discharge. Only a select few of a building's energy demands require highly concentrated energy sources, including alternating electrical current, and these are typically limited to refrigeration and space cooling.

Figure 4: Two systems of solar energy combined: local system scattered across building rooftops, and a central system along Gaza's borders.

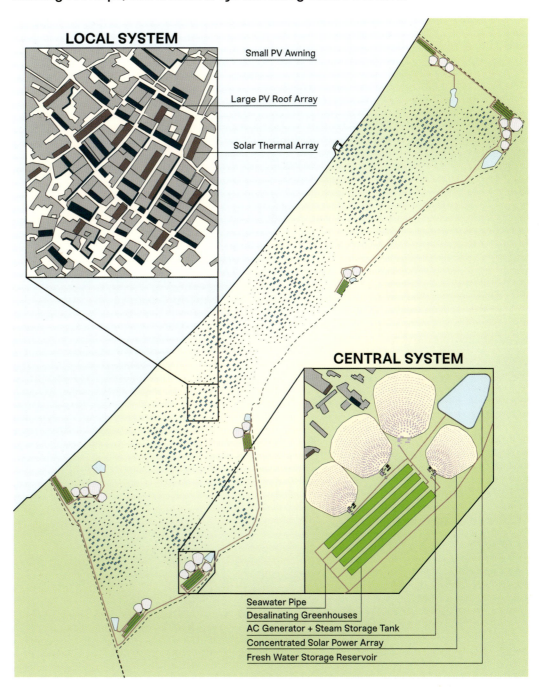

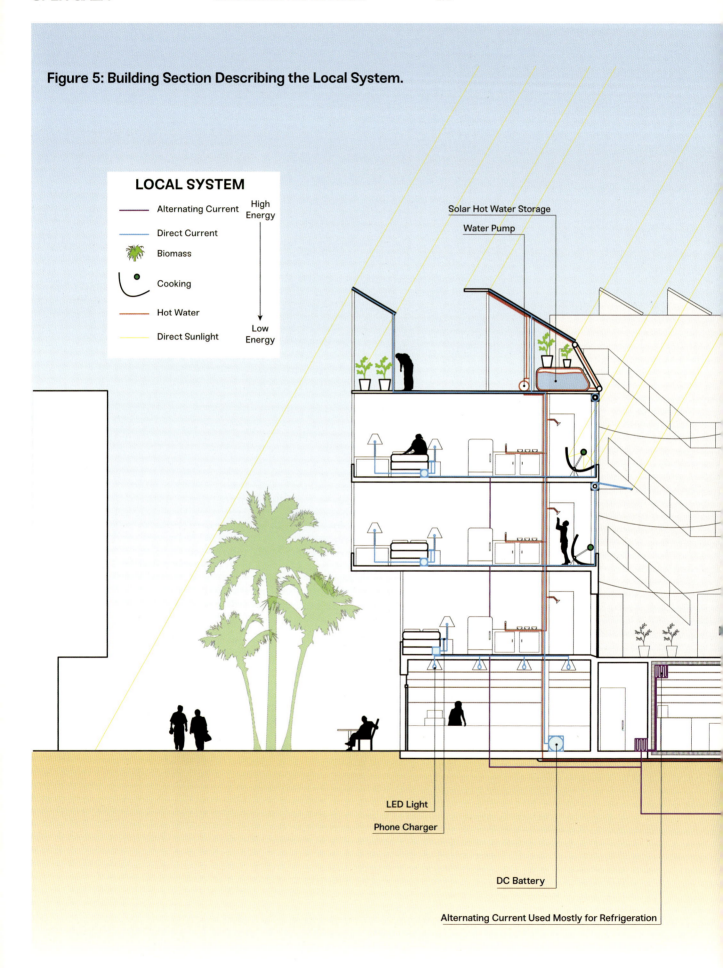

Figure 5: Building Section Describing the Local System.

LOCAL SYSTEM

—— Alternating Current

—— Direct Current

Biomass

Cooking

—— Hot Water

—— Direct Sunlight

High Energy

Low Energy

Solar Hot Water Storage

Water Pump

LED Light

Phone Charger

DC Battery

Alternating Current Used Mostly for Refrigeration

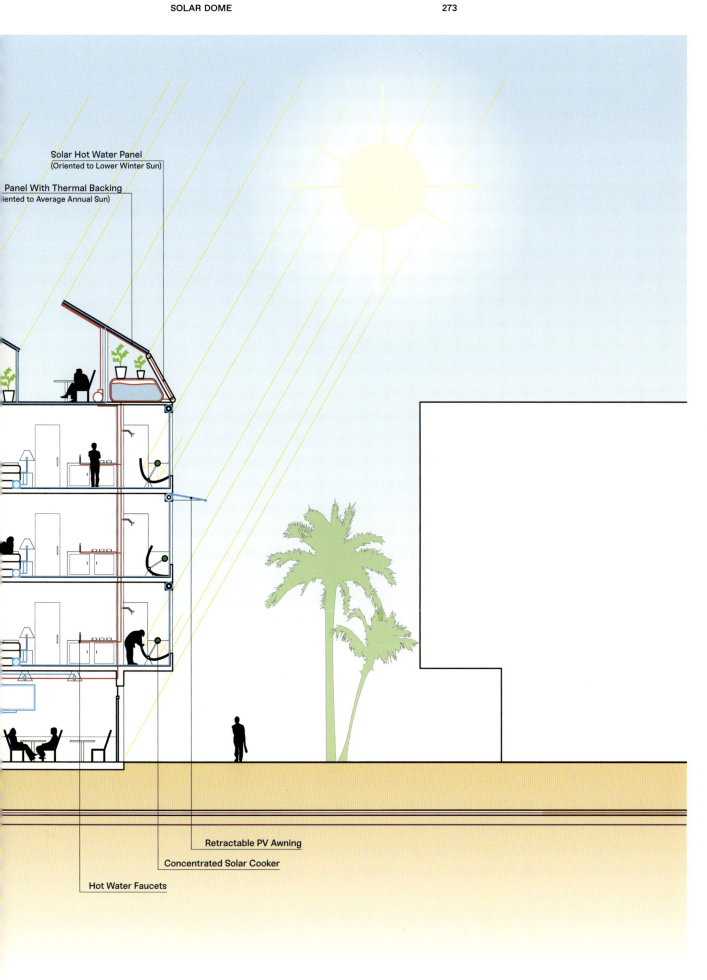

Solar Hot Water Panel
(Oriented to Lower Winter Sun)

Panel With Thermal Backing
(Oriented to Average Annual Sun)

Retractable PV Awning

Concentrated Solar Cooker

Hot Water Faucets

Figure 6: Section Describing the Central System.

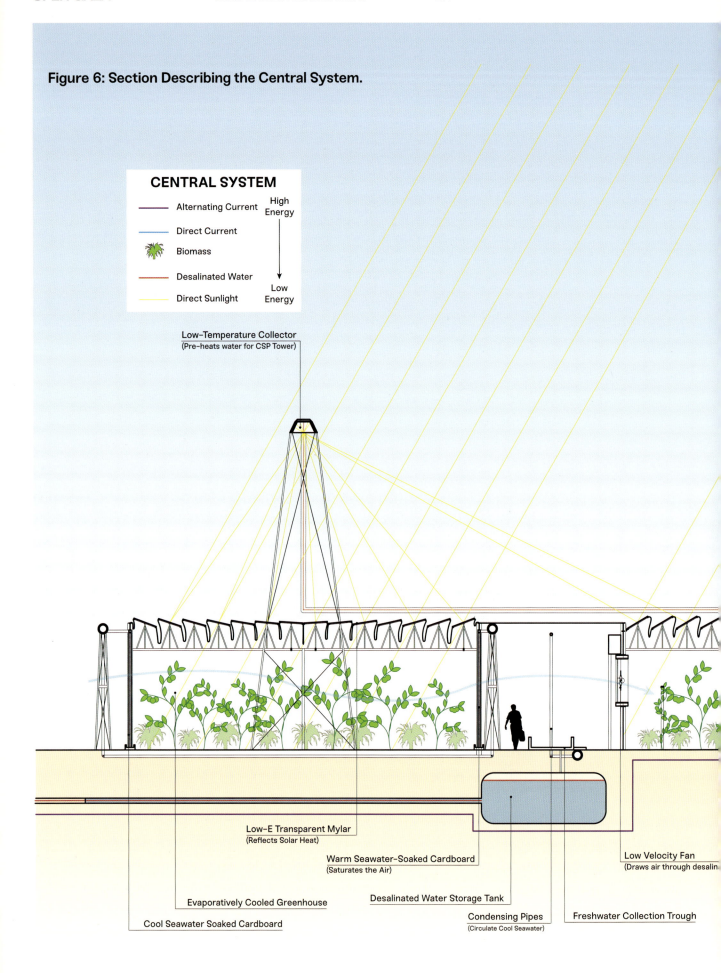

CENTRAL SYSTEM

High Energy
↓
Low Energy

— Alternating Current
— Direct Current
🌿 Biomass
— Desalinated Water
— Direct Sunlight

Low-Temperature Collector
(Pre-heats water for CSP Tower)

Low-E Transparent Mylar
(Reflects Solar Heat)

Warm Seawater-Soaked Cardboard
(Saturates the Air)

Desalinated Water Storage Tank

Low Velocity Fan
(Draws air through desalin

Evaporatively Cooled Greenhouse

Cool Seawater Soaked Cardboard

Condensing Pipes
(Circulate Cool Seawater)

Freshwater Collection Trough

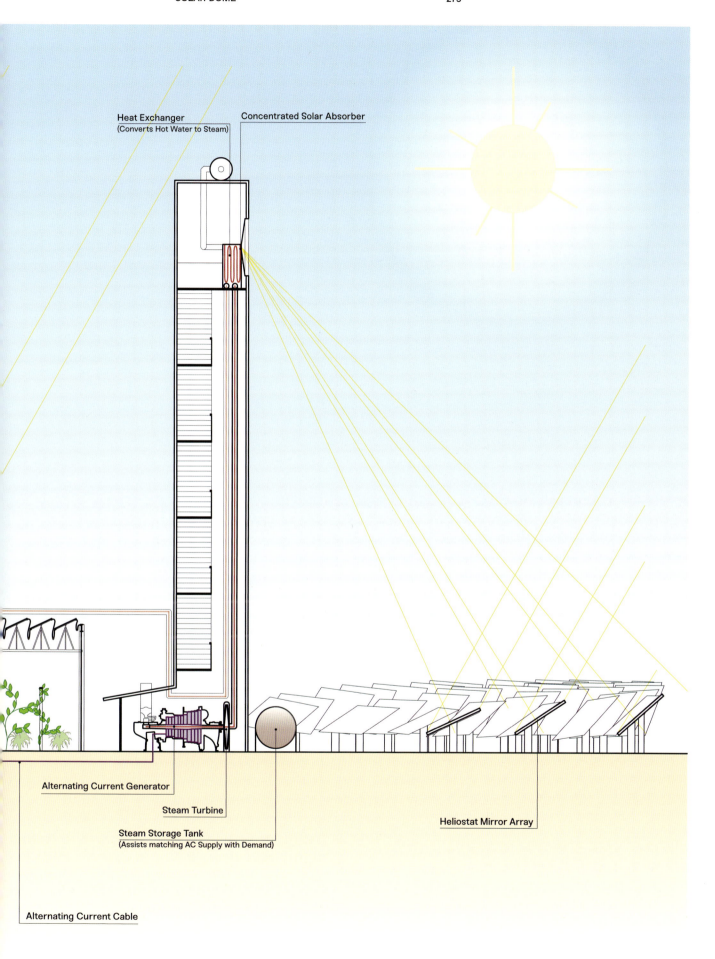

Heat Exchanger
(Converts Hot Water to Steam)

Concentrated Solar Absorber

Alternating Current Generator

Steam Turbine

Steam Storage Tank
(Assists matching AC Supply with Demand)

Heliostat Mirror Array

Alternating Current Cable

Our buildings' energy-density hierarchies (from high to low concentration) provide us with a roadmap for planning a solar-powered Gaza. Breaking down its buildings' energy consumption into these different demands, we can fit all of it into two major "energy flows," from concentrated to diffuse.

One system could exist entirely within Gaza's current buildings, concentrating sun into direct current electricity with photovoltaics, and directing it into higher-temperature cooking chambers with solar ovens. The lower-temperature excess heat from these processes can then be harvested for applications like space heating and hot water for showers/faucets. Together, all this could constitute a "local system" that might be deployed incrementally through a series of kits that individual Gazans install. The production of such kits could be funded by outside sources, and could include elements such as retractable solar awnings, rooftop photovoltaic canopies, rooftop railings of evacuated tube thermal collectors, insulated hot-water storage tanks, and batteries for storing energy to power LED bulbs or phones after sunset.

While such an incrementally built system could address a large fraction of Gaza's building energy demands, several needs cannot easily be satisfied with this approach. Most notably, the provision of a stable food source, a clean drinking water supply, and alternating current for refrigeration and food storage could all be addressed more efficiently on a larger infrastructural scale. However, solar power could still play a major role in satisfying these demands, particularly because Gaza is surrounded by large swaths of unoccupied land on its border. These large areas could support the concentration of sun at far higher levels than that of buildings, making use of the most cost-effective form of solar power discovered to date: concentrated solar towers. By focusing the solar power of one square kilometer of land onto a single point at the top of a tower, arrays of synchronized moving mirrors (or heliostats) can produce temperatures as high as 500 degrees Celsius. This is comparable to conditions found in modern coal-fired power plants and enables the production of alternating-current electricity. It also provides a highly concentrated means of storing solar energy for a few hours at a time, by simply keeping solar-generated steam in insulated tanks.

As in the local system, this process of concentration and electricity production will result in a lot of "waste" heat that can be reused for other applications. Most notably, desalinating greenhouses are capable of producing both fresh water and food, with an input of seawater at a relatively low desalination temperature of 40 degrees Celsius.[7] By drawing air across cardboard panels saturated with warm seawater, such greenhouses can create suitably humid conditions for the plants inside them, while also condensing the humid air to produce distilled drinking water. In the past, researchers have identified the potential for synergy between concentrated solar power's waste heat and the warm seawater found in desalinating greenhouses, and a few experimental examples are currently under construction.[8] As a result, a combination of concentrated solar towers and desalinating greenhouses could

7. S. S. Sablani et al., "Simulation of Fresh Water Production Using a Humidification–Dehumidification Seawater Greenhouse," *Desalination* 159, no. 3 (2003): 283–88.

8. Franz Trieb et al., "Combined Solar Power and Desalination Plants for the Mediterranean Region—Sustainable Energy Supply Using Large-Scale Solar Thermal Power Plants," *Desalination* 153, nos. 1–3 (2003): 39–46.

constitute a "central system" that meets the remaining energy demands that Gaza's local system cannot fulfill.

With these two hierarchical systems in place, the amount of land needed to meet Gaza's energy demands could be reduced to an area much smaller than the forty-one square kilometers needed to meet the demand with a brute-force photovoltaic approach. These systems could be deeply integrated into Gaza's current infrastructure, making use of both its underutilized rooftops and the borderland between Gaza and Israel. Ultimately, this distributed system of energy infrastructure could constitute a protective solar dome, enabling Gaza to be energy-independent from its neighbors.

WORKS CITED

Gressani, Daniela, A. David Craig, Inger Andersen, Jonathan D. Walters, John Besant-Jones, and Somin Mukherji. "Report No. 39695-GZ: West Bank and Gaza Energy Sector Review." Washington, DC: World Bank, Sustainable Development Department (MNSSD), Middle East and North Africa Region, 2007.

International Energy Agency. "Key World Energy Statistics." Paris: International Energy Agency, 2014.

———. "World Energy Outlook," Paris: International Energy Agency, 2016.

Ouda, Mohamed. "Analysis and Prediction of Household Energy Consumption in West Bank and Gaza Strip." Gaza City, Palestine: Islamic University of Palestine, Electrical Engineering Department, 2008.

Paton, C., W. H. Shayya, and H. Al-Hinai. "Simulation of Fresh Water Production Using a Humidification-Dehumidification Seawater Greenhouse." *Desalination* 159, no. 3 (2003): 283–88.

Trieb, Franz, Joachim Nitsch, Stefan Kronshage, Christoph Schillings, Lars-Arvid Brischke, Gerhard Knies, and G. Czisch. "Combined Solar Power and Desalination Plants for the Mediterranean Region—Sustainable Energy Supply Using Large-Scale Solar Thermal Power Plants." *Desalination* 153, nos. 1–3 (2003): 39–46.

SOCIAL HYDROLOGY: A DESIGN RESISTANCE

Denise Hoffman Brandt

DESIGN RESISTANCE

Safe drinking water is essential for human health and well-being; an adequate supply of clean water is an internationally accepted human right (UN 2010). The World Health Organization (WHO 2013) calculates that the minimum water requirement to sustain life is 7.5 to 15 liters per capita per day exclusive of toilet flushing, laundry, bathing, hospitals, crop growing, gardens, or recreation. A health center requires an additional 5 L/person/day, while a hospital uses 40-60 L/inpatient/day. A maternity ward or operating theater requires 100 L/intervention/day and a fever isolation ward uses 300-400 L/patient/day. Schools need 3 L/pupil/day and a mosque is estimated to require 2 L/person/day. Livestock require between 10 and 30 L/head/day and a vegetable garden uses 3-6 L/square meter/day. The WHO's standard recommendation for a minimum of 100–120 L/person/day of safe water is the averaged out accumulation of quantities like these. The Coastal Aquifer, Gaza's traditional water supply, is too depleted to meet Gaza's long-term needs. Gazans consume 88.7 L/person/day—under the minimum WHO standard. As a reference, Israel's water company, Mekorot, supports an average per capita usage of 280 L/capita/day up to 369 L/capita/day for Jewish settlers in the West Bank.

In Gaza, 81 percent of water is untreated, sourced from municipal water wells. Gaza's water treatment system is barely operative, destroyed both by Israeli bombs and their blockade of supplies needed to repair and maintain it. Water necessary for survival needs to be free of contaminates including salts, industrial chemicals, and pathogenic microbes. High levels of salts inherent to local geology and from coastal saltwater intrusion due to overdrawing the aquifer have made Gaza's well water unfit even for agriculture use without desalination. Without treatment, agricultural and effluent nitrates, among other contaminants, are present in water at levels debilitating to public health. Limited

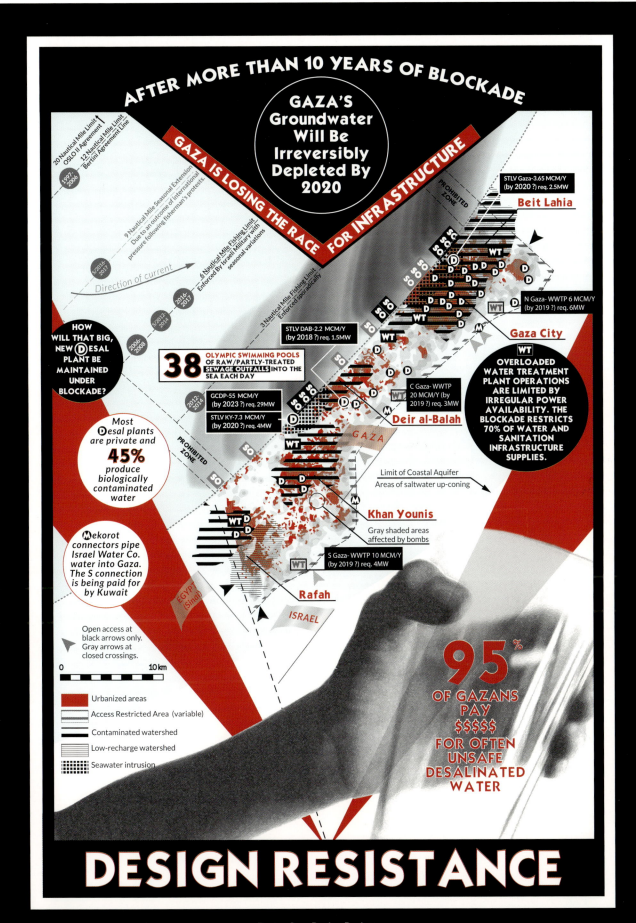

electricity diminshes the amount of time water treatment plants can operate. Bombed sewer pipes and water treatment plants have leaked E. coli and other pathogens into the groundwater and near shore seawater. The UN announced in 2015 that Gaza would be uninhabitable by 2020 because of this water crisis, yet EU and UN initiatives to quickly build new, more energy efficient desalination and water treatment plants continue to be stalled by the blockade.

Gaza's water kills by spreading infections and disease. An unnecessarily sickened populace is coping with the escalating degradation of its food system and economic infrastructure. The decline in local water quality has made Gaza increasingly reliant on potable water purchased from Israel. In 2013, less than 4 percent of domestic water was supplied by Mekorot, but by 2017, fully 11 percent of domestic water was sold to Gaza by Israel. The bombs and blockade have created a consumer market for water from Israel's desalination plants—constructed unimpeded by bombing or power cuts—or taken from the

Mountain Aquifer lying under West Bank Palestinian communities that are refused permits for well digging while new settlements expand Israel/Mekorot's reach into Occupied Territory. The World Bank has found Israel to be exceeding its water allocation agreed to in the Oslo Accord—an asymetric agreement brokered in its favor by powerful nations motivated by their own agendas, adversaries, and alliances.

Planning is impossible when urban systems are contingent on geopolitical brinksmanship, and Gaza's ecosystem has long been determined by forces outside its borders. Architecture, the construction of things, will not "fix" this scenario. Gaza cannot be reduced to a "problem" to be solved. What we can do is design a language and mechanisms for resistance and refuge. The following eight posters describe Gaza's complex socio-environmental hydrology and propose two tools that can work to reveal the scope of water-injustice and bind disrupted communities together by creating conditions of solace amid the turmoil.

The graphic style for the entire project was modeled on Russian propaganda posters, particularly the labor posters designed explicitly to convey information aimed to provoke united action.

Designers and planners often cloak the politic of design in a shroud of pragmatism. Claiming to solve a problem is an act of salesmanship promoting an aspirational invention. Using the graphic tactics of propaganda foregrounds the politcal bias inherent to any researched assertion. And in this case it syncs with the author's ambition to critique architectural rhetoric that assumes good intentions will result in favorable outcomes. Dynamic systems defy absolute accounting. Transformative practice is akin to R and D—research and development. And while admittedly the stakes are high, a pretense of surety does not influence actual performance. Truly aspirational practice does not seek to solve a problem, it works toward transforming the systems that created the destructive scenario. That, we can do.

NITRATES
Sources: **Agriculture, Sewage**

The WHO maximum of 50 mg/L Nitrate is based on evidence of **Blue Baby Syndrome** (methaemoglobinaemia). Met-Hb and water in infant formula were linked in Gaza (2013). (Data: PWA 2009)

Symptoms of methaemoglobinaemia include: **intellectual disability, developmental delay, failure to thrive, bluish skin, and seizures.**

96% of groundwater resources are unfit for consumption

- ☐ 0–50 mg/L SAFE
- 50–100 mg/L DANGER
- 100–150 mg/L DANGER
- 150–200 mg/L DANGER
- 200–250 mg/L DANGER
- Buffer Zone — NO ACCESS TO MOST OF THE SAFE-LEVEL H$_2$O

CHLORIDE
Sources: **Over-extraction of aquifer**

Chloride levels measure groundwater salinity. Salinity is attributable to seawater inrusion due to excessive withdrawals from the aquifer in the absence of other water resources and due to endemic geologic conditions. (Data: PWA 2015)

WHO: Chloride levels should be below 250 mg/L for human consumption.

Chloride over 350 mg/L: **reduces yield of irrigated agriculture.**

- ☐ 0–250 mg/L SAFE
- 250–600 mg/L DANGER
- 600–1000 mg/L DANGER/AG LOSSES
- 1000–2000 mg/L DANGER/AG LOSSES
- 2000+ mg/L DANGER/AG LOSSES
- Buffer Zone — NO ACCESS TO MOST OF THE SAFE-LEVEL H$_2$O

BOMBING
Sources: **Israel and the international community that refuses to stop it**

Bombing destroys piping, wells, and treatment plants. Water treatment ceases when Israel cuts off access to power. **Gaza is forced to purchase water from the destroyer of its water network.** Lack of access to rebuilding supplies prolongs costs and injuries of bombing.

WHO links Gaza's untreated water to: **sickness from diarrhea, dysentery, typhoid, hepatitis A, anaemia, infant mortality, kidney disease, and bluebaby syndrome.**

- ☐ No direct physical damage
- Low intensity damage (2009)
- Mid-high intensity damage (2009)
- Low intensity damage (2014)
- Mid-high intensity damage (2014)
- Buffer Zone (ALSO BOMBED)

GAZA'S H2O IS PRIME CAUSE OF CHILD-DEATH AND >25% OF ALL ILLNESS

"Fix-it" Architecture Can Not Do It!
Technological fixes and utopian imaginations do not effloresce into clean water and waste management infrastructure that can support millions of displaced Palestinians within the resource-limited confines of the Strip.

So you say you want to build a desalination plant...

You and what army?

The EU had to build a solar power network to fuel just one plant serving 75,000 people!

The other big plan: Gaza Sustainable Water Supply Project isn't even fully funded yet.

It will require 28,000 truckloads of supplies—potentially creating its own ecological fiasco—to cross any entry point that Israel controls. In July 2018, closure stopped most trucks. Even assuming supply trucks clear the blockade with no stoppages, the plant won't be done until 2022.

The UN has been saying GAZA WILL BE UNINHABITABLE BY 2020 since 2015

Poster Two: We Can Not Do It!

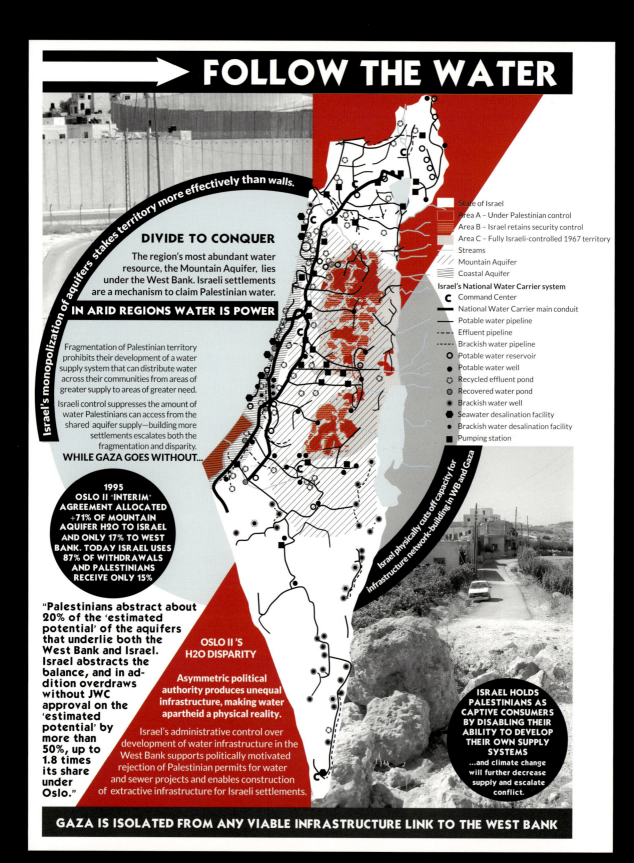

Poster Three: Follow the Water

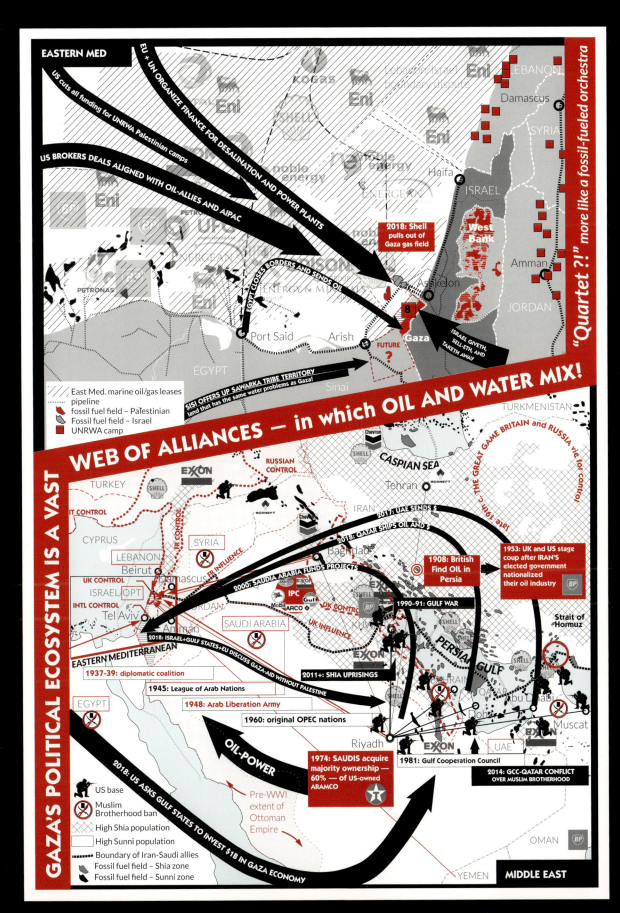

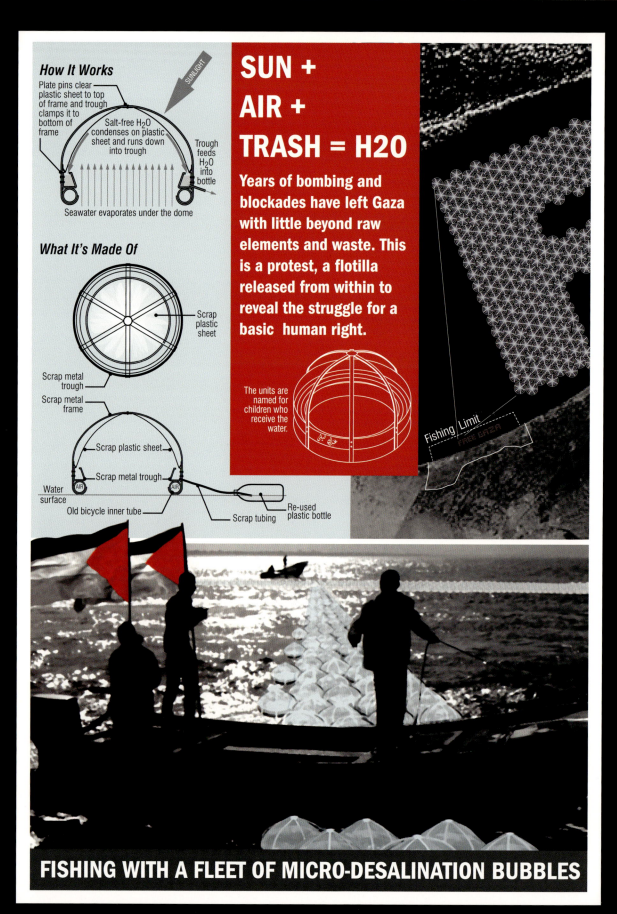

Poster Five: Micro–Desalination Bubbles

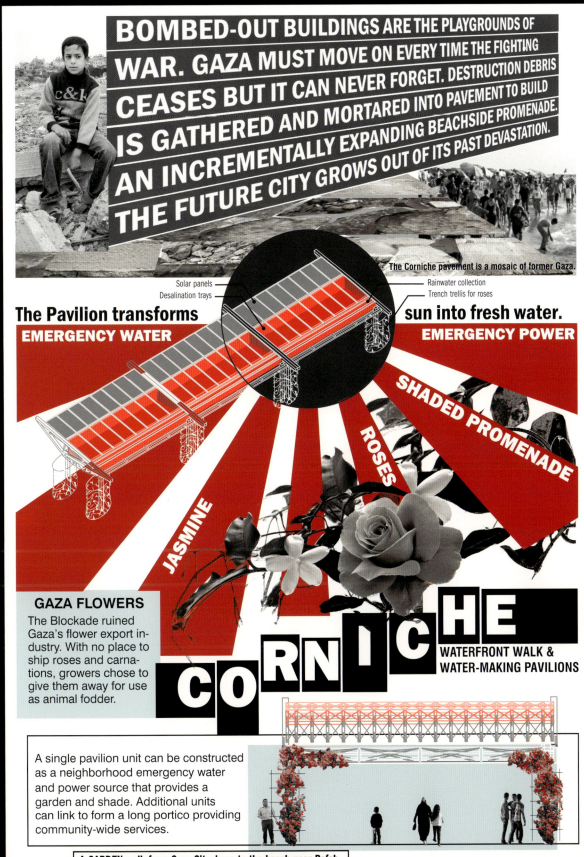

BOMBED-OUT BUILDINGS ARE THE PLAYGROUNDS OF WAR. GAZA MUST MOVE ON EVERY TIME THE FIGHTING CEASES BUT IT CAN NEVER FORGET. DESTRUCTION DEBRIS IS GATHERED AND MORTARED INTO PAVEMENT TO BUILD AN INCREMENTALLY EXPANDING BEACHSIDE PROMENADE. THE FUTURE CITY GROWS OUT OF ITS PAST DEVASTATION.

The Corniche pavement is a mosaic of former Gaza.

The Pavilion transforms ... **sun into fresh water.**

Solar panels
Desalination trays
Rainwater collection
Trench trellis for roses

EMERGENCY WATER
EMERGENCY POWER

SHADED PROMENADE

ROSES

JASMINE

GAZA FLOWERS
The Blockade ruined Gaza's flower export industry. With no place to ship roses and carnations, growers chose to give them away for use as animal fodder.

CORNICHE
WATERFRONT WALK & WATER-MAKING PAVILIONS

A single pavilion unit can be constructed as a neighborhood emergency water and power source that provides a garden and shade. Additional units can link to form a long portico providing community-wide services.

A GARDEN walk from Gaza City down to the beach near Rafah

Poster Six: Corniche

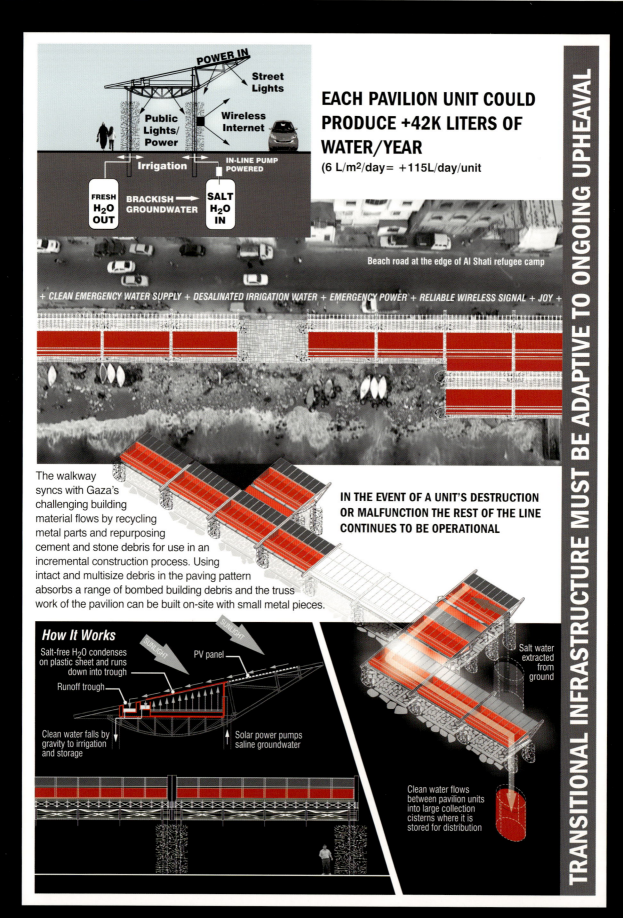

POWER IN

Street Lights

Public Lights/ Power

Wireless Internet

Irrigation

IN-LINE PUMP POWERED

FRESH H₂O OUT

BRACKISH GROUNDWATER →

SALT H₂O IN

EACH PAVILION UNIT COULD PRODUCE +42K LITERS OF WATER/YEAR
(6 L/m²/day= +115L/day/unit

Beach road at the edge of Al Shati refugee camp

+ CLEAN EMERGENCY WATER SUPPLY + DESALINATED IRRIGATION WATER + EMERGENCY POWER + RELIABLE WIRELESS SIGNAL + JOY +

The walkway syncs with Gaza's challenging building material flows by recycling metal parts and repurposing cement and stone debris for use in an incremental construction process. Using intact and multisize debris in the paving pattern absorbs a range of bombed building debris and the truss work of the pavilion can be built on-site with small metal pieces.

IN THE EVENT OF A UNIT'S DESTRUCTION OR MALFUNCTION THE REST OF THE LINE CONTINUES TO BE OPERATIONAL

How It Works

Salt-free H₂O condenses on plastic sheet and runs down into trough

PV panel

SUNLIGHT

SUNLIGHT

Runoff trough

Clean water falls by gravity to irrigation and storage

Solar power pumps saline groundwater

Salt water extracted from ground

Clean water flows between pavilion units into large collection cisterns where it is stored for distribution

TRANSITIONAL INFRASTRUCTURE MUST BE ADAPTIVE TO ONGOING UPHEAVAL

Poster Seven: Desalination Pavilion

Native rose species may have a degree of salt tolerance due to adaptation. An even more robust alternative: Earth-Kind® roses are tolerant of salt in sand and soil.

GAZANS CAN DRAW A LIVING LINE IN THE SAND

to commemorate and resist destructive forces.

Poster Eight: Roses

PROJECT 1:
DESIGNED RESEARCH

"To plan and to execute are two different things, and the proof is, that it is easy to dream but difficult to perform." from *Les Travailleurs de la Mer*, written by Victor Hugo in 1866 while in self-imposed exile protesting Napoleon's authoritarian regime.

Systems constantly in flux cannot be pinned down and determined with absolute precision. Research is design because through it we construct the contextual framework to ground a proposition. Posters are used to describe both the research and design proposals in order to assert the subjective and provocative nature of design practice. Maps and graphics compiled from many data sources build a complex picture of Gaza's hydrologic ecosystem.

Data has been sourced from international agencies and research groups that distance themselves from political rhetoric. Information common in the public realm is not referenced with a citation.

POSTER 1:
DESIGNED RESISTANCE
and Introductory images

Note: The entire map is within an area of excessive water extraction relative to groundwater resource capacity and severe desertification. Source: "Plan Bleu," http://planbleu.org/en/plan-bleu.

Photo and Quote Sources:
All photographs Creative Commons license unless noted.

J. Howard Miller, "We Can Do It!" Artist employed by Westinghouse, poster used by the War Production Coordinating Committee. From scan of copy belonging to the National Museum of American History, Smithsonian Institution. Retrieved from the website of the Virginia Historical Society. Image is in the Public Domain.

"Trud v Piatiletke (Labor in the Five Year Plan)." Woodburn Collection, National Library of Scotland. Creative Commons Attribution 4.0 International license.

"Technical Notes on Drinking-Water, Sanitation, and Hygiene in Emergencies," World Health Organization (WHO), 2013. Accessed January 10, 2019.

"Gaza Water Status Report 2017," Government of the State of Palestine (PLA), June 2018. Accessed January 10, 2019.

"The Economic Cost of the Israeli Occupation of the Occupied Palestinian Territories," The Applied Research Institute—Jerusalem (ARIJ), 2015. Accessed January 10, 2019.

Map Data
"Gaza Emergency Access Restrictions July 2014," UN Office for the Coordination of Humanitarian Affairs, 2014. Accessed September 21, 2016.

Bomb Damage: "Impact of the 2014 Conflict in the Gaza Strip UNOSAT Satellite Derived Geospatial Analysis," UN Institute of Training and Research, 2014. Accessed September 21, 2016.

Desalination Plants: Hossam Zaqoot, Adnan Aish, Samaher Abdeljawad, *Application of Artificial Neural Networks for Predicting Water Quality* (LAP Academic Publishing, 2017).

See also: "Water," Office of the Quartet. Accessed September 16, 2018.

Blockade: "Israel begins work on sea barrier to tighten Gaza Strip blockade," *Middle East Eye*, May 28, 2018. Accessed September 9, 2018.

M. H. Geriesh, A. E. El-Rayes, and K. Ghodeif, "Potential Sources of Groundwater Contamination in Rafah Environs, North Sinai, Egypt" (working paper, Geology Department, Faculty of Science, Suez Canal University, Ismailia, Egypt, Proc. 7th Conf. Geology of Sinai for Development Ismailia, 2004), 41–52.

Water Quality Data: "Seawater pollution raises concerns of waterborne diseases and environmental hazards in the Gaza Strip," United Nations Office for the Coordination of Humanitarian Affairs, August 9, 2018. Part of *The Monthly Humanitarian Bulletin*, July 2018.

Areas of Seawater Intrusion: Madhat Farouk Abu-alnaeema, Ismail Yusoff, Tham Fatt Ng, Yatimah Alias, May Raksmey, "Assessment of groundwater salinity and quality in Gaza coastal aquifer, Gaza Strip, Palestine: An integrated statistical, geostatistical and hydrogeochemical approaches study," *Science of the Total Environment* 29 (September 2017).

Low Recharge Watershed Data: T. Eshtawi, M. Evers, B. Tischbein, "Potential impacts of urban area expansion on groundwater level in the Gaza Strip: a spatial-temporal assessment," *Arabian Journal of Geosciences* 8, no. 12 (December 2015): 10565–10584.

Selected Supporting Information
"Israel Tightens Gaza Blockade, Civilians Bear the Brunt," Norwegian Refugee Council, July 2018. Accessed September 16, 2018.

On July 28 2010, through Resolution 64/292, the United Nations General Assembly explicitly recognized the human right to water and sanitation and acknowledged that clean drinking water and sanitation are essential to the realization of all human rights. The Resolution calls upon states and international organizations to provide financial resources, help capacity-building and technology transfer to help countries, in particular developing countries, to provide safe, clean, accessible and affordable drinking water and sanitation for all. UN General Assembly, Resolution 64/292, The human right to water and sanitation, A/RES/64/292 (August 3, 2010).

"Seawater pollution raises concerns of waterborne diseases and environmental hazards in the Gaza Strip," UN Office for the Coordination of Humanitarian Affairs, *The Monthly Humanitarian Bulletin*, July 2018. Accessed October 30, 2018.

"Assessment of Restrictions on Palestinian Water Sector Development," The World Bank, Report No. 47657-GZ, April 2009. Accessed September 27, 2016.

"Israeli-Imposed Power Shortages in Gaza Cut Water Access by One-Third," *Democracy Now*, August 23, 2017. Accessed September 11, 2018.

Geneva Convention IV (1949), Article 33, first paragraph, provides: "Collective penalties ... are prohibited." Quoted on the website of the International Committee of the Red Cross: "Practice Relating to Rule 103. Collective Punishments," International Committee of the Red Cross. Accessed November 10, 2015.

POSTER 2:
WE CAN NOT DO IT!
Photo and Quote Sources:
All photographs Creative Commons license unless noted.

Photo of "Gaza Children:" Jon Donnison for Amnesty International, 2014. Accessed October 2, 2015.

Map Data
Chloride Map Data: "Why is there a water crisis in Gaza? Chloride concentration in the Gaza Strip," Fanack Water of the Middle East and Africa, September 22, 2015. Accessed September 22, 2016.

Nitrate Map Data: "Nitrate Concentration Map 2010," Coastal Municipal Water Utility in Gaza, aquapedia.waterdiplomacy.org. Accessed December 21, 2014.

See also: World Health Organization publications on sanitation and water safety.

"Gaza Desalination Plant Delayed By Goods Blockade," Water Desalination+ Reuse, 2018. Accessed December 26, 2018.

Selected Supporting Information
"The human right to water is implicitly derived from the human right to an adequate standard of living." UN Committee on Economic, Social and Cultural Rights, General Comment No. 15, The right to water, E/C.12/2002/11, 2002. Para. 3. cited in: "Recognition of the human rights to water and sanitation by UN Member States at the international level. An overview of resolutions and declarations that recognise the human rights to water and sanitation," Amnesty International, Index no. IOR 40/1380/2015, 2, April 2015. Accessed September 11, 2018.

Nahed Al Laham, Mansour Elyazji, and Rohaifa Al-Haddad, "Prevalence of enteric pathogen-associated community gastro-enteritis among kindergarten children in Gaza," *Fouad Ridwan Journal of Biomed Research* 29, no. 1 (January 2015): 61–68.

"Nitrate and nitrite in drinking-water. Background document for development of WHO Guidelines for Drinking-water Quality," World Health Organization, WHO/SDE/WSH/07.01/16/Rev/1. Accessed March 4, 2016.

B. Shomar, S. Abu Fakir, and A. Yahya, "Assessment of Groundwater Quality in the Gaza Strip, Palestine Using GIS Mapping," *Journal of Water Resource and Protection* 2, no. 2 (2010).

"The Human Rights Council holds a Special Session to discuss the current situation in the Gaza Strip," United Nations Human Rights Office of the High Commissioner, July 23, 2014. Accessed September 27, 2016.

"A Systematic Literature Review and Recommendations on Water Usage in the Gaza Strip," Norwegian Institute of Public Health and The Palestinian National Institute of Public Health, September 2014. Accessed March 6, 2016.

Alexander Mcphail, "West Bank and Gaza — Gaza Sustainable Water Supply Program : P150494 — Implementation Status Results Report : Sequence 01," The World Bank, June 27, 2017, Accessed September 9, 2018.

"Water for Gaza: EU switches on the biggest solar energy field in the Gaza Strip to fuel projects providing drinking water to people in dire needs," The Office of the European Union Representative (West Bank and Gaza Strip, UNRWA, 2018). Accessed October 12, 2018.

"Gaza water project developments could generate costly traffic footprint," *Aquatech*, February 10, 2018. Accessed October 17, 2018.

POSTER 3:
FOLLOW THE WATER
Photo and Quote Sources:
All photographs Creative Commons license unless noted.

Photo of West Bank Wall: Léopold Lambert, "The Palestinian Archipelago: A Metaphorical Cartography of the Occupied Territories," *The Funambulist*, March 26, 2012. Accessed August 12, 2016.

Photo of West Bank earth mound blocking road from Wikimedia: "Earth Mound in Palestine," GNU Free Documentation License. Accessed August 12, 2016.

Quote: "West Bank and Gaza-Assessment of Restrictions on Palestinian Water Sector Development," The World Bank, Report No. 47657-GZ, April 2009. Accessed October 2, 2015.

Map Data
Israel Water Infrastructure: National Water Carrier of Israel (Hebrew: HaMovil HaArtzi), February 11, 2013, 21:32:34, NielsF, from https://en.wikipedia.org/wiki/Water_politics_in_the_Middle_East. Accessed August 12, 2016.

And: "Israeli National Water Grid," Itisapartheid.org. Accessed September 12, 2016.

And: "Water Infrastructure: Israel's national water infrastructure grid," *Fanack: Water of the Middle East and Africa*, October 19, 2015.

And: Dr. Dov Sitton, "The National Water Carrier System: Development of Limited Water Resources: Historical and Technological Aspects," Jewish Virtual Library. In Aubrey Wulfsohn, "What Retreat From the Territories Means For Israel's Water Supply," Think Israel. Accessed September 12, 2016.

And: "Israel National Water System," The Water Authority. Accessed September 12, 2016.

"Restricted Space in the West Bank, Area C.png," Wikimedia Commons. Accessed September 22, 2016.

Aquifer Data: "The Shared Waters of Israel, Palestine and Jordan," FoEME, 2010. In "Israel/Palestine/Jordan — EcoPeace/Friends of the Earth Middle East and the Good Water Neighbors Project," Eco Tipping Points, April 2014. Accessed September 21, 2014.

Selected Supporting Information
E. Weinthal, A. Vengosh, A. Marei, A. Gutierrez, and W. Kloppmann, "The Water Crisis in the Gaza Strip: Prospects for Resolution," *Ground Water* 43 no. 5, (Sept.–Oct. 2005): 653–60.

Report by the Director General of House of Water and Environment, Palestine to formulate a policy framework to support the establishment of mechanisms for inter-state cooperation on shared groundwater aquifers in the Mediterranean Region. A. Aliewi, "The Palestinian-Israeli Management of Shared Groundwater Aquifers: status, realities and lessons learned," (paper presentation, HWE Event, Beirut, April 24–25, 2006).

Amira Hass, "Israel Blocking Plan to Double Water Supply to West Bank," *Haaretz*, July 9, 2016. Accessed July 28, 2016.

"Troubled Waters — Palestinians Denied Fair Access To Water" Amnesty International, 2009. Accessed July 28, 2016.

"Israeli-Palestinian Interim Agreement on the West Bank and the Gaza Strip," UNSCO, Washington, DC, September 28, 1995. Accessed January 12, 2019.

POSTER 4:
GAZA'S ECOSYSTEM
Note: Gaza's hydrologic plight reveals the inextricable nature of environmental and social forces. These two maps are intentionally complicated, drawn as battle plans to reflect the chaos of past and current forces that have contributed to making Gaza's ground uninhabitable. Beyond the obvious, and previously described ravages of Israel's bombing and blockade, the US, Europe, and Russia are plotted as complicit through past aggressions and current policy. Latent intra-Arab conflicts: Sunni-Shia animus escalated by fossil-fuel monopolies; destabilized national and corporate alliances as natural gas extraction and a post-fossil economy emerge; and the Gulf States' suppression of the Muslim Brotherhood (the foundation on which Hamas arose), also sustain Gaza's water crisis. This is the currently intractable context in which I propose Design Resistance.

Map Data
Eastern Mediterranean Marine Oil and Gas Leases: "Concession map," Arab Republic of Egypt, Ministry of Petroleum. Accessed September 12, 2018.

And: "Opportunities and Risks in the E Med," *Natural Gas World Magazine*, October 12, 2018. Accessed September 12, 2018.

Gaza Gas Fields: "Israel's and Palestine's gas and oil too optimistic?" map, *The Economist*, January 23, 2014. Accessed September 9, 2018.

Egyptian Gas Fields: "Suez Canal, Sumed Pipeline are key parts of Egypt's role in international energy markets," map, US Energy Information Administration, August 2, 2013. Accessed September 12, 2018.

Eastern Mediterranean Energy Infrastructure: "Overview of oil and natural gas in the Eastern Mediterranean region," US Energy Information Administration, Report 15, August 2013. Accessed October 12, 2018.

Regional Fossil-Fuel Corporate Investment: corporate websites.

Sunni and Shia Populations: "A House Divided: Islam in Today's Middle East," NHPR, May 4, 2016. Accessed October 12, 2018.

UNRWA Camps: "Population of Jordan," *Fanack*, September 2009. Accessed January 12, 2019.

Historic boundaries and membership in international economic and military organizations were corroborated via a variety of public sources.

"Future?" Sinai Option: Ben Lynfield, "Gaza-Sinai' state idea a danger under Trump, warns Gaza analyst," *The Jerusalem Post*, February 21, 2017. Accessed December 26, 2018.

Water Quality in Al Arish, Egypt: Mohamed El Alfy* and Broder Merkel, "Integrated geostatistics and GIS techniques for assessing groundwater contamination in Al Arish area, Sinai, Egypt," *Arabian Journal of Geosciences* 5, no. 2 (March 2012): 197–215.

"Mohammad bin Salman to deal with the 'deal of the century,'" *Middle East Monitor*, March 8, 2018. Accessed September 13, 2018.

Jonathan Gorvett, "Risks Posed by Competing Claims to Eastern Mediterranean Oil and Gas Resources," *Washington Report on Middle East Affairs*, June–July 2018. Accessed September 12, 2018.

Selected Supporting Information:
"The Egyptian Military: Fighting Enemies Domestic, Not Foreign," The Stratfor Assessment, November 15, 2014. Accessed September 12, 2018.

"Mediterranean Information System on Environment and Development (SIMEDD)," Plan Bleu. Accessed September 12, 2018.

Lisa Watanabe, "Sinai Peninsula — from Buffer Zone to Battlefield," *CSS Analyses in Security Policy*, no. 168 (February 2015). Accessed September 13, 2018.

Michael Schwartz, "The Often Overlooked Role of Natural Gas in the Israel-Palestine Conflict," *Mother Jones*, March 27, 2015. Accessed September 12, 2018.

Amir Tibon and Amos Harel, "Trump Administration Will Ask Gulf States to Invest Up to $1 Billion in Gaza Economy," *Haaretz*, June 17, 2018. Accessed September 8, 2018.

Shoshanna Solomon, "Israel Nears Gas Sales to Egypt as Mideast Unrest Flares," *Bloomberg*, August 21, 2014. Accessed September 8, 2018.

**PROJECT 2:
DESIGNED RESISTANCE**
"To force an obstacle into service is a great stride towards triumph."
Les Travailleurs de la Mer, Victor Hugo.

Design research, design practice, and political action are not distinct practices. All of the design posters, like the research posters, can be read serially or independently. Each poster connects a specific agenda to the designed construction.

The two design proposals presented here in four posters are not predicated on a trajectory of construction based on a stable state. The attenuated process of implementing even small-scale desalination plants backed by global-scale powers is a clear warning against speculation on an optimized future with few constraints on building, no blockade on maintenance materials, and no threat of further bombing. Instead, I explored two possibilities for resistance and solace that could be constructed by communities out of common materials in Gaza such as scrap metal and plastic.

**POSTER 5:
MICRO-DESALINATION BUBBLES**
Photo and Quote Sources:
All photographs Creative Commons license unless noted.

Photo above: User gloucester2gaza, "Lunch in Gaza City," Flickr photo, March 10, 2009. Accessed November 25, 2016. Author's caption: "This is where we had a nice lunch spread out for us. It used to be one of Yasser Arafat's headquarters. Of course it's been bombed to hell. In fact after we left here, about 30 minutes later the Israelis bombed here killing 3 people. Most people who seem to have an opinion on this matter say that it was a message to the convoy — that they know we're here, and they're trying to push us along and out. I think this view is interesting because for me it reminds me that Gaza is actually a modern place. It's not third world. One and half million people live here."

Gaza is a modern place being technologically cast backward by successive waves of bombing that have destroyed its infrastructure. The destruction has also generated tons of building-material debris that needs to be cleared away and, ideally, reused. Community infrastructure is activism. The low-tech desalination apparatus uses waste metal to produce an emergency-scale potable water supply, but its greater strength is in image-making and community network-building. The personal or family scale micro-desal bubbles can be produced by individual metalworkers. Yet they aggregate to form an internally managed, bottom-up flotilla calling attention to water injustice and the return of basic human rights in the Strip.

The micro-desalination bubbles are targeted to recover day to day habits of occupation and meaning for Gaza's fisherman who have been severely constrained by the blockade. The units can be made by individuals or as small commercial ventures. Their technology is based on a product already on the market.

Photo of fishermen: "Palestinian fishermen and activists sail to protest Israel's siege of Gaza," photo, International Solidarity Movement, December 4, 2013. Accessed September 21, 2016.

Selected Supporting Information:
Desalination technology based on a number of open sources such as the plastic solar still shown at: "Saline Water Desalination," The USGS Water Science School. Accessed September 21, 2016.

POSTER 6: CORNICHE
Together, the following three posters present the design tactics and principles for building a promenade pavilion that brings beauty back to now-contaminated beaches as it desalinates groundwater for emergency use. Comprised of recycled building detritus (stone, concrete, and metal), the walkway is shaded by desalination basins and solar panels that provide electricity for groundwater pumping and supply a wireless communication hub. The pavilions are designed for incremental construction and to function independently of one another should ongoing bombing destroy one or more in the line.

The passive desalination requires no electricity, and they effectively remove salts as well as other contaminants from groundwater. The pavilion design accords with large format basins described in an array of open source research and technical publications. The blockade disrupted Gaza's export flower industry. Pavilion support posts are integrated with trellises for growing roses to commemorate that loss and encourage new modes of production.

It is important to note that the corniche pavilions are not intended to supplant the need for a viable water infrastructure

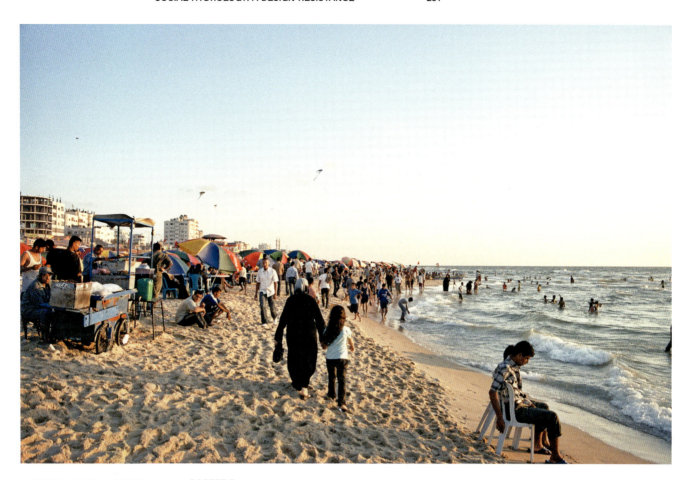

system to support a population of two million people. The project presents no fantasy of Gaza's community-scale resources having the capacity to support a closed and self-sustaining water system of that scale. The corniche is intended to recover joy without covering up loss. It is a tool for resistance, not a utopian solution to Gaza's hydrologic constraints. The pavilion marks a line in the sand for future water negotiations.

Photo and Quote Sources:
All photographs Creative Commons license unless noted.

Photo of child on rubble: User Andlun1, "UN Condemns War Crimes in Gaza," *Newsbarber*, photo in comment. Accessed September 27, 2016.

Gaza Beach: User: Gus, "Gaza Beach," Wikimedia, uploaded July 1, 2006. Accessed September 21, 2016.

POSTER 7:
DESALINATION PAVILION
Map Data
Aerial of beach and road from Google Maps.

Selected Supporting Information
Desalination basin technical sources: the version shown is most closely related to the technology described in: "Solar Distillation Technical Brief," Practical Action. Accessed October 2, 2015. Additional information (basis for calculations): G. Al-hassan and S. Algarni, "Exploring of Water Desalination by Single Solar Still Basins," *American Journal of Climate Change*, no. 2 (2013): 57–61.

POSTER 8: ROSES
Photo and Quote Sources:
All photographs Creative Commons license unless noted.

Selected Supporting Information:
Many roses have some degree of salt tolerance. *Rosa rugosa* is a species common in beach plant assemblages. Earth-Kind® roses were developed for heat tolerance and for use in situations with salt-spray and low quality irrigation water. "Earth-Kind Roses Analyzed for Salt Tolerance," *American Society for Horticultural Science Review*. Accessed September 27, 2016.

REDRAWING GAZA

Alberto Foyo and Postopia

Figure 1: Unruining Gaza—Architecture vis-à-vis conflict resolution.

In 1916, two military figures, one British and one French, sat down at a table, looked at a map, and drew the lines that would carve out the future of a sizable portion of the ancient Near East. The "line in the sand" drawn by Sykes, Picot, and the governments they embodied exemplifies in a very singular way the definition of politics as "the art of the possible."

Political illusion, in the hands of the architect, transcends this definition. Our Gaza project is a move that reacts to a stalemate situation in a chess game that was ill-conceived long ago. In trying to envision a strategy via design, we irremediably land in utopian territory; but this is how it is to try and find a way to reverse the stalemate, a move that does not exist in chess. Trying to understand a place as complex as Gaza, it did not take us long to realize that as architects, we can not position ourselves via intellectual analysis alone. Practically the entirety of Gaza's surface is choked with destroyed or semi-destroyed infrastructures, a ruined built fabric, fragile refugee camps, and pervasive soil and water pollution, to name just a few outstanding dilemmas. Its mental and social infrastructure is equally choked. While dealing with the practical and yet unreal forces that shape their daily lives, the inhabitants of Gaza seem to be condemned to an inhuman purgatory, one where reality and utopia have fused into one.

We resort to our empathy in tandem with our expertise to try to design an archetypal habitat—one that gravitates more toward Thomas More than George Orwell—and one that supports Gaza's *raison d'être* by proposing liberating, egalitarian, and ultimately self-sufficient modes of habitation, or so we hope.

Architects are obsessed with the act of drawing. There is something magical about what it embodies; more profound than what drawings represent. For us, to draw is a verb, not a noun, and drawing a line begins the embodiment of an idea, whether practical, utopian, useful, or useless. It constitutes above all the archetypal spirit and materiality of architecture. Inspired, paradoxically, by the line drawn by Sykes and Picot, we decided to push the possibilities of the internal logic of a line, of a drawing of architecture at its most primordial level. Whereas Sykes and Picot's line embodies the internal logic of politics, our line uses the internal logic of architecture. We are unapologetically trying an "other way," one that counterweights its naïveté with the undeterred use of architecture's pre-politicized logic, ethics, and aesthetics, a philosophical project. Inspired by Alvaro Siza's dictum, "Architects don't invent anything; they just transform reality."

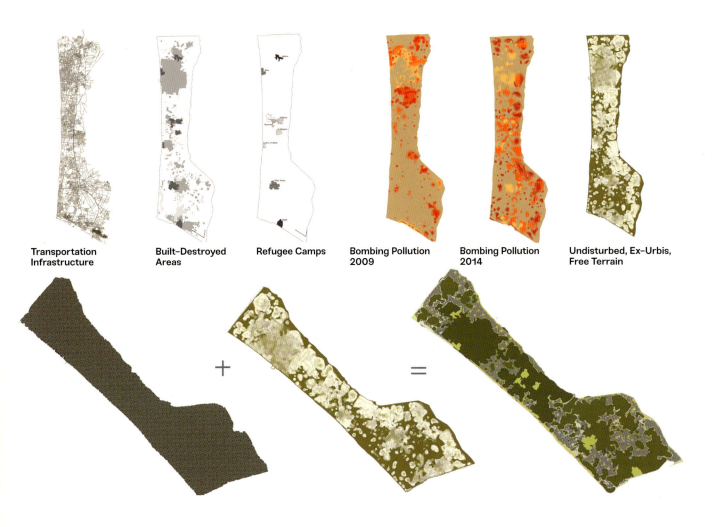

Transportation Infrastructure

Built-Destroyed Areas

Refugee Camps

Bombing Pollution 2009

Bombing Pollution 2014

Undisturbed, Ex-Urbis, Free Terrain

Figure 2: Architectural-agricultural character of the fertile fabric.

Figure 3: Overview of the architectural–agricultural character of the fertile fabric.

We develop the line into a fabric of architecture and agriculture, knitting these together to form a fertile fabric, one that can defiantly position itself as a reconceptualized utopia, a possible reality, the means for which are not yet available. We think of our project as a primordial architecture of emancipation. The *masharabiya*, a richly veiled negotiator between inside and outside, has inspired us to think about our fertile fabric in similar terms. Between the sides of the masharabiya-gone-horizontal, through primordial links between mass and void, darkness and light, past and future, tradition and modernity, rural and urban, roots and leaves. These dichotomies form a palimpsest that intertwines both the physical and the mental seeds required to grow the fertile fabric. We are not pursuing a local intervention under the existing constraints; we are experimenting with an unapologetic takeover of one landscape by another. From this collision, we hope a critical hybrid will emerge: one that is required to respect the cultural traces of the land, but equally obliged to assess what can remain and what must go.

Dwelling
Bayt

Area: 100m²
Dwellings: 1
Population: 6 people

Cluster
Jamah

Area: 1,000m²
Dwellings: 8
Population: One story =
48 people

Precinct
Mantaq

Area: 10,000m²
Dwellings: 64
Population: One story =
384 people

Quartier
Rubà

Area: 100,000m²
Dwellings: 512
Population: One story =
3,072 people

Neighborhood
Haay

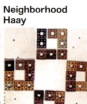

Area: 500,000m²
Dwellings: 2,048
Population: One story =
12,288 people

Settlement
Madinc

Area: 4km²
Dwellings: 10,240
Population: One story =
60,000 people

Habitat
Mohtin

Area: 365km²
Dwellings: 10,240
Population: 1.8 million

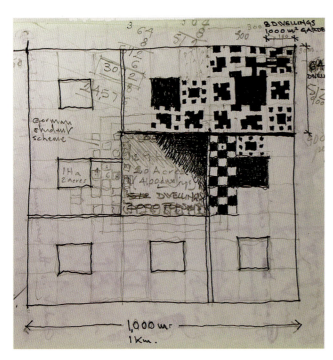

Figure 4: The reproductive system of the fertile fabric.

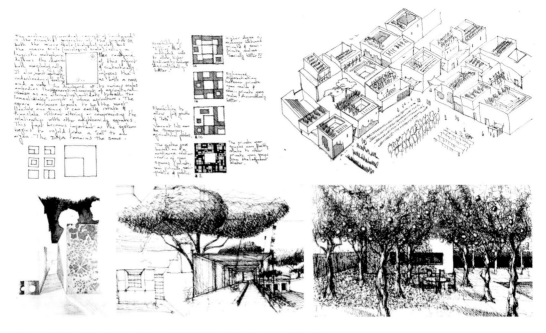

Figure 5: Morphological and Syntactical DNA of the Courtyard Typology.

Our project will not be an easy one to realize. In our postindustrial epoch, the cultural value of the productive rural farm has fallen into a limbo, as we as a society have become increasingly urbanized and have surrendered the rural world to the cult of agribusiness. The consequences of this syndrome include the steadfast disregard for the symbiotic relationship between architecture and agriculture. The synergistic fabric we propose synchronizes architectural and agricultural infrastructure with its objective, the elimination of anything superfluous or redundant. The austere economy of means that guides this inspires a "closed-loop" system, one that leaves behind the least possible amount of unaccounted waste. It is obvious to us that the just environment cannot be reduced to the idea of a just city, while dismissing the decay of the rural world as acceptable collateral damage. Not in Gaza, a place where people have been forcibly denied the means to grow their own sustenance.

Our work seeks to weld the urban and rural together, reinforcing the development of a production-distribution-consumption model harmonized with a decentralized, autonomous, and stable economy. We are trying to envision an environment where the "ethics of aesthetics" position agricultural systems in the foreground, human beings in the middle ground, and architecture systems in the background. We reject the urban design and rural design binary, combining them in the idea of civic design.

The task of designing a home for 1.7 million people, and a habitat that can sustain itself to the greatest extent possible, is surely daunting. In opposition to the monocropping developmental model, sustainable agricultural practices can constitute not only a nutritional lifeline, but also a fertile cultural backbone that fosters quality of life while dealing head-on with the agents of inequality who undermine it. By keeping this cultural sustainability in mind, we hope not fall into the trap of reactionary

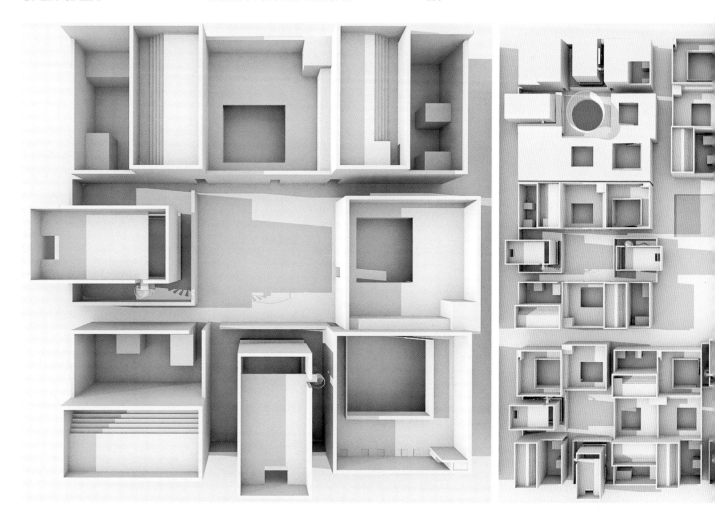

Figure 6: An accretion system that tries to balance private, semiprivate, and public space.

neocolonialist proposals that might further degrade Gaza's already fragile physical and cultural landscapes.

The Dutch architect Aldo Van Eyck used to say: "It is sadly true of architecture that it is not quality that counts but enough quantity of that quality." This project proposes a process in which the concept of quality is mediated by the reality of inequality, as an intentional provocation to steer architectural proposals toward an understanding of quality not as a luxury but as an antidote to inequality.

The "low-rise, low-density" model we've deployed is associated with the dilemmas of suburban sprawl with its mainly negative connotations. Frequently, we've tried to turn this perception around and define low-rise-low-density model as a new

model for urban innovation, the protective custodian of the land on which it sits. The model must change itself by itself to a new "low-rise-high-density" paradigm where low-rise is dictated by the need for natural light to nourish the plants, and density is determined by expected agricultural yield. While working on this project, it was interesting to test old and new developmental theories that argue for and against one side or the other of the agrarian-industrial dichotomy. This dichotomy has seldom led to an outcome that has not left behind either farming as a subsidized pariah, after it has paid the bill for forced industrialization, or industry as a cultural orphan of a disenchanted constituency that yearns for the reformulation of progress as a place of return.

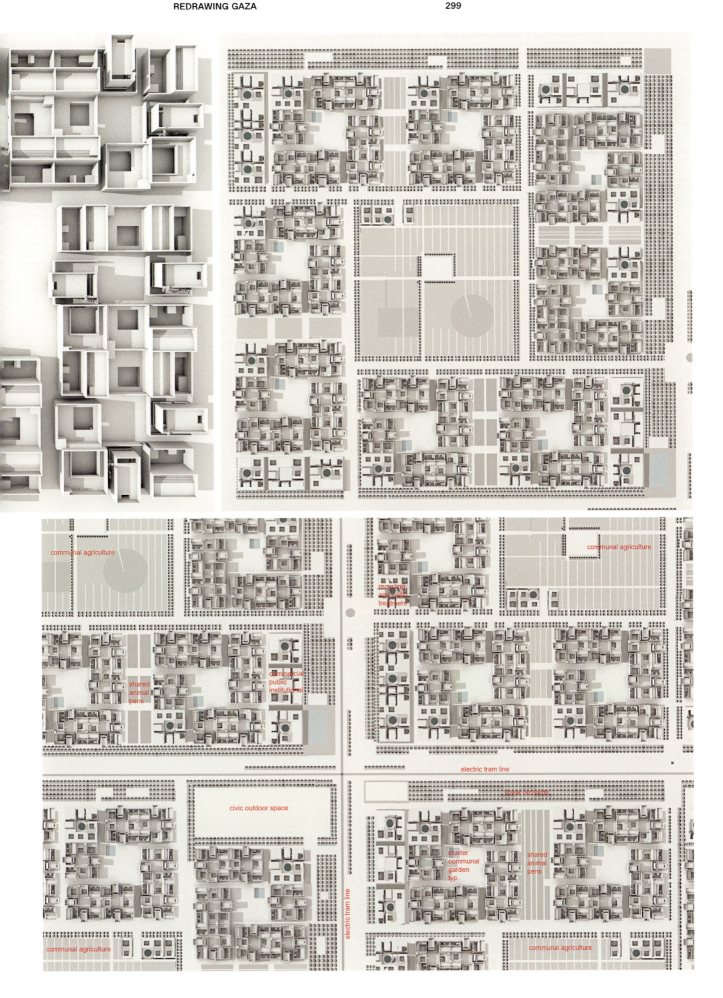

communal agriculture

communal agriculture

recycling
and waste
treatment

shared
animal
pens

commercial
public
institutional

electric tram line

civic outdoor space

linear program

electric tram line

cluster
communal
garden
typ

shared
animal
pens

communal agriculture

communal agriculture

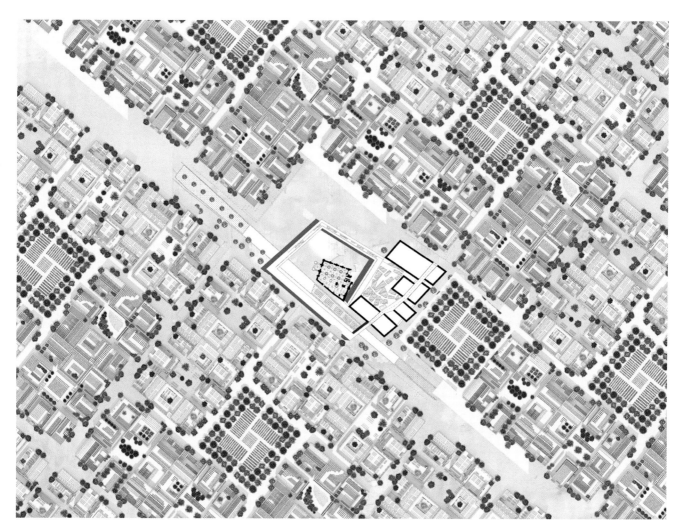

Figure 7: Fabric Meets Heritage.

POSTSCRIPT

In Gaza, it is too late for prevention. The Strip has already been denatured by extraction policies, wars, and the manipulation of its aquifers. Social context is, of course, critical: in Gaza, human relationships have evolved culturally over millennia through waves of migrations, forced displacement, forced placement, religious colonialism, military colonialism, and industrial colonialism.

Today's context is one in which cult and culture have become indistinguishable from one another. Society is undergoing a regression in which, to paraphrase Nietzsche, we cease to erect habitats that fit a particular culture, and we proceed to amass habitats that fit a particular cult. Are there any alternative, "non-romantic," courses of action left to us? Is there life beyond capitalism, beyond religion, beyond Monsanto, and beyond technocracy? Is it worthwhile trying to retrofit "progress" as a place of return, not playing into reactionary agendas, but into progressive ones?

INTER-DEPENDENCE AS A POLITICAL TOOL

Teddy Cruz and Fonna Forman

THE FACE OF A PLANET IN CRISIS

This project speculates about possible futures for Gaza. Drawing on our own research and practice at the US–Mexico border at San Diego/Tijuana, our contribution focuses on social and political imagination in sites of injustice and intractable conflict. Like our work at the US–Mexico border, our examination of Gaza inevitably begins with recognizing dramatic differentials in power, resources, and capacity. These manifest in their extreme form in Gaza, a site of political occupation. How can a community respond to political injustice when its collective capacity is splintered in myriad ways by exclusionary political and economic power? Can sites of injustice become sites of political and urban imagination for recuperating collective capacity and agency? How can we, in solidarity with Gaza, engage in such a speculative exercise without sounding naïve?

As we examine possible futures for Gaza, we want to explore the idea of "interdependence." Even if we risk seeming romantic or utopian, we want to work with the tool of mutual recognition among people on opposite sides of territorial struggle, despite asymmetries of power and often radically conflicting religious, cultural, and ideological commitments and agendas. In this essay, we advance the idea of mutual recognition not as a naïve call for peace and love, but as a valid, pragmatic political tool, that can be activated piecemeal and from the bottom up, in phases. We begin with the undeniable premise that the future of Israel depends on the future of Palestine. We assert that in border regions interdependence is often most acutely experienced in local contexts, where populations experience firsthand the consequences of arbitrarily fragmenting the environmental, economic, and social ecologies of a region. Regardless of the current polarization and antagonism at the border that cages Gaza, and beyond the emotional fury and ideological rhetoric of extreme views on both sides, it is an undeniable fact that the social and environmental destinies of Palestinians and Israelis are intertwined.

When evaluated more coolly from the perspective of mutual interest, border walls always constitute a double-edged sword. Only the most myopic or racist of politics will conclude that walling off the "other" will solve "our" problems. As a wall separates "us" from "them," satisfying protectionist urges for physical security and national self-determination, it simultaneously damages the resources of both sides. In other words, border walls, and border policies, are often self-inflicted wounds on the border-builders *themselves*, since they frequently interrupt the environmental, economic, and social flows that are essential to the health and sustainability of the larger region.

A key dimension of our work at the US–Mexico border has been to rethink citizenship in this contested region. We oppose conventional jurisdictional or identitarian definitions that divide communities and nation-states, proposing a focus on shared social norms and everyday practices, common interests, and aspirations for an intertwined future.

Over the last decades, we have been linking border regions across the world to investigate what these regions can learn from each other about civic, economic, and environmental interdependence. *The Political Equator* is an experimental visualization project that traces an imaginary line along the US-Mexico continental border and extends it directly across a world atlas, forming a corridor of global conflict between the thirtieth and thirty-eighth north parallels. Along this imaginary border lie some of the world's most contested thresholds, including: the US-Mexico border at San Diego/Tijuana, the most-trafficked international border checkpoint in the world and the main migration route from Latin America into the United States; the Strait of Gibraltar and the Mediterranean, the main funnel of migration from North African and the Levant (in particular Syria) into Europe; the Israeli-Palestinian border that divides the Middle East, emblematized by Israel's fifty-year military occupation of the West Bank and Gaza; the India/Pakistan border, a site of intense and ongoing territorial conflict since the British partition of India in 1947; and the border between North and South Korea, which represents decades of intractable conflict, carrying Cold War tensions forward to the present day.[1]

SPECULATIVE FUTURES FOR INTERDEPENDENCE: THREE BUILDING BLOCKS

We live and work at the US-Mexico border in the largest binational urban region in the world: the metropolis of San Diego/Tijuana. The current political climate in the US strikes an urgent chord in a region like ours—where Trump's prototypes for a new wall were built, and where public

debate over immigration and the fate of "Dreamers" gets very real.[2]

In this environment of escalating tension and increasing surveillance and militarization, we have been calling for transgressive experiments in "unwalling" that enable people to see each other anew and cultivate cross-border public commitments. We believe that border zones are laboratories for imagining new strategies for coexistence, and for provoking a more speculative imaginary of "cross-border citizenship."[3]

In this project for Gaza's reconstruction, we want to explore opportunities opened up by this essential fact of regional flows, convergences, and interdependencies. Our speculative proposal draws on case studies of coexistence in sites of seemingly intractable conflict and political violence. These are cases we are intimate with through research and engagement: the US-Mexico border where we live and work, and the Colombian cities of Bogotá and Medellín that have inspired our thinking about "citizenship culture" at the border, identifying interdependencies and activating new strategies of coexistence. What makes these Latin American cases distinctive is that their stand against inequality was activated through participatory democratic practices, often at the neighborhood scale. It is always difficult to compare sites of conflict, since the dynamics of any situation are unique and historically specific. But through these cases, we want to advance a generative framework for thinking about interdependence, a resource that has gained traction and opened productive opportunities

1. Of course, the actual political equator is not really a flat line, since border conditions are distributed across the globe in varied ways. Moreover, although we tend to think of border walls as physical fortresses against the encroaching global south, borders are reproduced in cities everywhere.

2. Dreamers are young immigrants who were brought into the United States by their parents as children, and granted special protected status under a deferred action program called DACA. For a discussion, see Fonna Forman and Teddy Cruz, "The Wall: The San Diego-Tijuana Border," *Artforum* (Summer 2016): 370–75; and Fonna Forman and Teddy Cruz, "Un-walling Citizenship," *Avery Review: Critical Essays on Architecture*, no. 21 (Winter 2017): 98–109.

3. Teddy Cruz and Fonna Forman, "The Cross-Border Public," in *Public Space? Lost and Found*, eds. Gediminas Urbonas, Ann Lui, and Lucas Freeman (Cambridge, MA: MIT Press, 2017), 172–95.

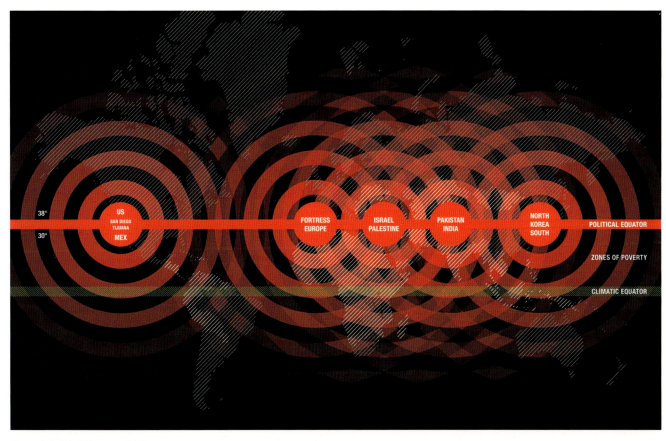

Figure 1: Political Equator, 2012.

Figure 2: Trump's Borderwall Prototypes, Otay Mesa, California, viewed over the existing wall from Tijuana, Mexico, 2018.
Several of the eight designs were inspired by Israel's wall. Image courtesy of Jona Maier.

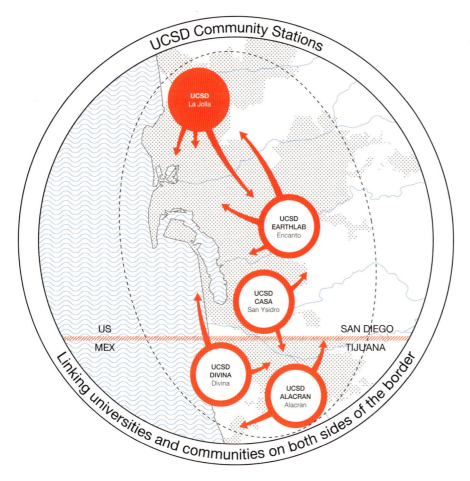

Figure 3: The UCSD *Cross–Border Community Stations* Network, 2018.

in other sites of severe inequality, violence, and political injustice.

Our essay will unfold as a set of three building blocks. The first explores the idea of citizenship as a transborder public process. Our work in the San Diego/Tijuana border region, divided by a wall, has helped us to rethink the constitution of citizenship. Building on this work, we propose a speculative exploration of a cross border "citizenship culture" for Gaza that aims toward identifying overlapping sensibilities, crosscutting resonances, and aspirations. The second building block spatializes the idea of transborder citizenship, with an emphasis on public space. We are imagining a more deliberate long-term infrastructure of public spaces for Gaza that spatializes partnerships and collaborative models between

Palestinians and Israelis. Finally, the third building block focuses on practical interventions. We argue that our cross-border environmental agenda, called MEXUS, in the US–Mexico bioregion contains important considerations for thinking about water and waste flows in and out of Gaza. Water, of course, knows no borders; and we see cause for hope in the transnational environmental commons that water creates.

1. CITIZENSHIP AS A TRANSBORDER PUBLIC PROCESS

In our work at the US–Mexico border, we have been seeking to reclaim the idea of citizenship for more inclusive cross-border agendas. In an increasingly walled world, and with the surge of reactionary nationalism everywhere, we challenge claims of

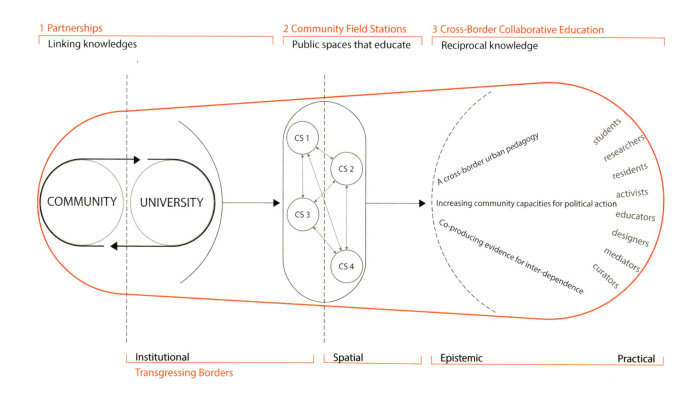

1 Partnerships
Linking knowledges

2 Community Field Stations
Public spaces that educate

3 Cross-Border Collaborative Education
Reciprocal knowledge

COMMUNITY UNIVERSITY

CS 1
CS 2
CS 3
CS 4

A cross-border urban pedagogy
Increasing community capacities for political action
Co-producing evidence for inter-dependence

students
researchers
residents
activists
educators
designers
mediators
curators

Institutional
Spatial
Epistemic
Practical

Transgressing Borders

Figure 4: UCSD Cross-Border Community Stations knowledge exchange platform, 2018.

post–citizenship or post–sovereignty on empirical grounds. Jurisdictional and identitarian ideas of citizenship are exclusionary, tethered to territory, and inherently closed to those beyond the gate. Cosmopolitan ideals of citizenship, on the other hand, are more intuitively appealing to an egalitarian sensibility, since belonging is expanded to the broadest reaches of humanity, evoking the ancient Stoic claim that the highest aspiration of ethics is to become a "citizen of the world." But for many, including us, the idea of a "cosmopolitan citizen" lacks visceral and practical content and avenues for meaningful political agency. We have been arguing instead for a sort of fusion of the local and the cosmopolitan: a grounded and pragmatic idea of citizenship that is nevertheless fluid and open, its

boundaries continually renegotiating themselves around the shifting challenges, opportunities, interests, and aspirations among diverse people who share contested space. Border regions become a natural laboratory for rethinking citizenship along these lines.[4]

It may seem starry-eyed or even insulting to some that we propose discussing citizenship in a context like Gaza, where "nationhood" has been denied through political violence and occupation. We have encountered similar resistance at the US–Mexico border, where citizenship is rigidly fixed to nation, formal documentation, and radical marginalization. But in both cases, we advocate turning the concept back on itself, recuperating the idea of citizenship not as a

4. The subject of our forthcoming monograph, *The Political Equator: Unwalling Citizenship* (London: Verso).

Figure 5: UCSD–Alacrán Community Station: Maquiladora–made frames for self–built immigrant housing, 2018.

jurisdictional or identitarian concept linked to nationhood, but instead as a cultural concept that emerges more inclusively from the bottom up, through mutual recognition. We propose rediscovering citizenship through intelligently curated agonistic "convergences," "meetings," and performative interventions in shared physical or virtual public spaces, through which mutual interests and common values across divided publics can be recognized and advanced. We believe that this approach, while appreciating that there are many current legal and cultural constraints on collaborative interaction between Gazans and Israeli activists and academics who self-identify as being in solidarity with Gaza is still valid and urgent.

Israeli law does not permit Israelis to enter Gaza, nor Gazans to leave it. Hamas does not tolerate interaction. In this speculative project, we propose an incremental approach to collaboration and recognition between Gazans and Israelis, which relies in its earliest stages on curated opportunities for virtual communication, scaling over time to more concrete physical manifestations in shared public spaces.

LEARNING FROM BOGOTA: BUILDING CITIZENSHIP CULTURE

In seeking strategies for more inclusive ideas of citizenship, we have found inspiration in Latin America—notably in the Colombian cities of Bogotá and Medellín. Sites of astonishing violence and poverty in the last decades of the twentieth century, these cities transformed themselves not only by reorienting municipal investment toward the poorest and most marginalized zones, but also by committing to working across sectors to cultivate a vibrant, participatory civic culture.[5] Drawing on a twentieth-century lineage of democratic experimentation and urban pedagogy across the continent, these cities transformed public culture from the bottom up, through new strategies of community engagement.

In the mid-1990s, Bogotá was often called the most dangerous city on the planet. *La Violencia* in Colombia was triggered in the early 1960s by the US-backed crackdown against "communist" rebels. In the years that followed, hundreds of thousands of Colombians lost their lives, on all sides, producing large-scale internal displacements, as well as one of the world's most intractable conflicts.

Today, Bogotá is recognized by urbanists and planners for the *Transmilenio* bus rapid transit (BRT) network of the late 1990s—at the time the most advanced multinodal transportation system in the world. Rarely do observers acknowledge, however, that these public works were immediately preceded by a set of cultural interventions that laid a social framework for urban change.

Antanas Mockus, a philosopher and former university rector, became mayor of Bogotá in 1995, as the city was unraveling from corruption, poverty, and severe infrastructural failure. He insisted that transforming the city must begin with repairing social fragmentation and transforming social behavior. Instead of guns, tanks, and "law and order," Mockus sought to change the hearts and minds of citizens. In other words, top-down investments in public infrastructure and social services were essential, but they were only half the story; he believed that a more foundational transformation of "citizenship culture" from the bottom up was the key to transforming Bogotá.

Mockus summoned artists and cultural producers to design a strategy of "urban pedagogy" to perform the norms of urban dignity: that human life is sacred, that radical inequality is unjust, that adequate education and health are human rights, that gender violence is intolerable, and so on. His use of street mimes, games, and theatrical public disruptions to cultivate a new citizenship culture has inspired generations of civic actors, urbanists, and artists across Latin America and the world to think more creatively about disrupting civic dysfunction and transforming urban norms and behavior.[6]

We have been inspired by several foundational commitments in Mockus's approach: that transforming the city begins with transforming social norms; that "law and order" does not produce new public values; and that art and culture are powerful engines of civic engagement. Bogotá fought violence with community processes, to reignite a bottom-up sense of civic commitment to overcome decades of violence and inequality, and to inspire a model of shared responsibility across sectors.

CROSS-BORDER CITIZENS?

After Mockus left office, he founded an organization called *Corpovisionarios,* to offer consultancy services to cities across Latin America. It uses a diagnostic

5. Fonna Forman and Teddy Cruz, "Latin America and a New Political Leadership: Experimental Acts of Co-Existence," in *Public Servants: Art and the Crisis of the Common Good*, eds. Johanna Burton, Shannon Jackson, and Dominic Wilsdon (Cambridge, MA: MIT Press, 2017), 71–90.

6. See *Cultural Agents Reloaded: The Legacy of Antanas Mockus*, ed. Carlo Tognato (Cambridge, MA: Harvard University Press, 2018).

instrument called the "Citizenship Culture Survey" to measure public trust in a city—vertical relations between publics and institutions and horizontal capacities for collective action within civil society. The survey has been in over fifty cities across Latin America, producing an impressive database of comparative urban knowledge. For each individual city, the survey becomes a mirror of civic self-knowledge, and a script for urban intervention.

In 2015, we brought Mockus to the San Diego/Tijuana border region to help us rethink citizenship in this region, which is divided by a wall.[7] We worked with the mayors' offices on both sides of the border and a cross-sector team of stakeholders to design the "Binational Citizenship-Culture Survey," a tool to help us identify a latent regional community that transgresses the line.[8] The results confirmed many of our intuitions: publics on both sides were open to collaborating on issues of mutual concern, ranging from border wait times and immigration to public health and environment— *even though they did not think their governments were ready.*

As a political and social context, Gaza is obviously very different from our own border region, as well as from Bogotá. The reality of occupation, political oppression, statelessness, and the impenetrability of the wall makes the discussion of "citizenship" there a daunting exploration. Moreover, the flat line of the US-Mexico border already suggests a less complex political envelope compared to the complexity of the Israeli–Palestinian border. In San Diego/Tijuana, there are skeptics who argued that a unified

jurisdiction like Bogotá has little to teach a jurisdictionally divided region like ours. But dramatic contextual differences should not invalidate speculative comparative exercises. Comparison can inspire, as long as it remains critical and conscious of its own biases and limitations.

By documenting invisible connections and flows across the wall, the Binational Citizenship Culture Survey became a mirror for our region, helping people on both sides to appreciate what they share and to realize that the two halves are intertwined. Insights like this—while intuitive for the activist—become powerful and more generative when they are cast as manifestations of collective sentiment and will. The survey becomes a powerful instigation for grassroots action and intervention.

We propose a speculative exploration of these values in the very different context of Gaza. We cannot know what will emerge. Although engaging the "other" in contexts of dramatic political violence is typically seen as compromise or futility, we have been committed to discovering convergent bottom-up energies as material for transborder civic imaginaries. The goal is to identify overlapping sensibilities, crosscutting resonances, and aspirations that might be emerging among jurisdictionally divided publics, hidden behind the shadows of walls. Perhaps there are opportunities to mobilize the pervasive mistrust of political leadership among the young, who may no longer connect with the dominant narratives of earlier generations. How can researchers, cultural producers, and agencies on the ground help grow these

7. For discussion, see Fonna Forman, "Social Norms and the Cross-Border Citizen: From Adam Smith to Antanas Mockus," in Tognato, ed., *Cultural Agents Reloaded*, 333–56.

8. For further discussion of the Binational Citizenship Culture survey, see Forman, "Social Norms." See also "Survey Says San Diegans, Tijuanans Want More Cross-Border Collaboration," *San Diego Union Tribune*, June 19, 2015, and "New San Diego-Tijuana Survey Holds Mirror Up to Border Cities," *Next City*, February 25, 2015.

convergences and mobilize them into productive forces, when the price of crossing lines is often so high? Outrage over policies of gratuitous hate—like family separation at the US-Mexico border, shooting unarmed protestors in Gaza, and now the Nation-State Bill—are opportunities to unite cross-border publics in solidarity. This kind of solidarity can be fleeting, but openings are essential when curating dialogue in contested places.

2. TRANSBORDER PUBLIC SPACES AS SITES FOR MUTUAL RECOGNITION

The second tool builds (literally) upon the first. This tool *spatializes* the idea of "cross-border citizenship," advancing the role of public space in mobilizing mutual recognition through cultural action. Can we envision a distributed platform of shared spaces straddling the wall, on both sides, designed for urban pedagogy, dialogue, and performance? Here, we propose transgressive experiments in "unwalling" for Gaza that would take place, virtually and eventually physically, in a transborder infrastructure of public spaces co-curated by grassroots organizations, university researchers, and cultural producers in Gaza and Israel to enable a circulation of knowledges.

Learning from Medellín: Public Spaces that Educate

The notorious cartel violence of Medellín was accompanied by severe poverty and urban decay. Twenty-some years later, Medellín has captured the attention of urbanists, architects, and planners across the world for its civic and spatial transformations in the city's most vulnerable zones.[9]

When mathematician Sergio Fajardo became mayor in 2003, he committed to a new era of "social urbanism," which involved massive cross-sector investments in infrastructure, public education, and social services in the poorest and most violent *comunas* in the city. Essential to this agenda was curating dignified spaces in these zones for civic participation and urban pedagogy.[10] Pursuing social urbanism meant choosing education over police repression as the best response to urban violence. Fajardo committed to transforming Medellín into "the most educated" city in Colombia.

Fajardo also understood that the municipal bureaucracy itself needed to change to steward the rapid interventions he envisioned. He transformed his mayoral office into an urban think tank to consolidate fragmented policies and agendas. He summoned the knowledges and resources of government, academia, community leadership, and the private sector. This opened an era of swift, intelligent public investment in space and infrastructure in Medellín's most vulnerable neighborhoods. The goal was to heal the wounds of history, to steward the young toward a new era of hope, and to mobilize a more cohesive civic identity through cultural action. It is symbolic that Medellín's physical transformations began in the neighborhood of Santo Domingo, which had been the stronghold of Pablo Escobar's Medellín Cartel, and the most violent and isolated neighborhood in the city.

9. Much of the discussion that follows is drawn from Fonna Forman and Teddy Cruz, "Global Justice at the Municipal Scale: The Case of Medellín, Colombia," in *Institutional Cosmopolitanism*, ed. Luis Cabrera (New York: Oxford University Press, 2018), 189–215; see also Fonna Forman and Teddy Cruz, "Changing Practice: Engaging Informal Public Demands," in *Informal Markets Worlds—Reader: The Architecture of Economic Pressure*, eds. Helge Mooshammer et al. (Rotterdam: nai010 Publishers, 2015), 203–23.

10. See Matthew Carmona et al., *From Public Places, Urban Spaces* (Oxford: Architectural Press, 2003), 22.

Figure 6: UCSD Cross–Border Community Stations knowledge exchange platform, 2018.

Figure 7: Alter Terra, Tijuana, B.C. Mexico.

CROSS-BORDER COMMUNITY STATIONS

Inspired by Medellín's commitment to mobilizing citizenship through cultural action in public space, we founded the "Cross-Border Community Stations at the University of California, San Diego." This constituted a network of field-hubs in underserved neighborhoods on both sides of the border, where research and urban pedagogy are curated *collaboratively* with community-based nonprofits. It advanced a new model of community-university partnership and cross-border cultural action.

While we recognize that universities and civil society, arts collectives, and NGOs in both Israel and Palestine are already doing collaborative research, cultural interventions, and planning exercises, what we are imagining for Gaza is a more deliberate, long-term infrastructure of public spaces that spatialize those partnerships and collaborative models. We have been dissatisfied in our own region by the recent uptick in ephemeral acts of resistance, and short term artistic and cultural interventions that dip in and out of the conflict, since the energy that produces them quickly dissipates. What happens the day after? We have been advocating a more rooted infrastructure of partnerships that are spatialized through a network of public spaces that educate, taking a longer view of resistance, strategic thinking, and anticipatory planning. We believe a similar agenda should be explored in both Israel and Palestine. And if a boycott exists, preventing Israeli universities from investing directly in Gaza, then the resources should be channeled to Palestinian universities, cultural institutions, nonprofits, or NGOs who can invest.

Our model, the UCSD Cross-Border Community Stations, is a platform for reciprocal knowledge production, linking the specialized knowledge of the research university with the community-based knowledges embedded in neighborhoods on both sides of the border. In the last few years, we have built strong relationships in two marginalized neighborhoods adjacent to the border wall and have cultivated long-term partnerships with the most rooted and active nonprofit organizations based there. The UCSD/Casa Community Station is located in the border neighborhood of San Ysidro, California, in partnership with the nonprofit Casa Familiar. San Ysidro is the first immigrant neighborhood in the United States, beyond the checkpoint. This station focuses on issues of immigration, affordable housing, public space, and equitable urban development. The UCSD Divina Community Station is located in the informal settlement of Laureles Canyon on the western periphery of Tijuana, in partnership with the nonprofit Los Colonos de Divina Providencia. The Laureles Canyon is the last slum of Latin America, literally crashing against the border wall and home to eighty-five thousand people. This station is focused on issues of environmental health, water and dust management, participatory climate action, and cross-border environmental and urban policy.

CULTURAL STRATEGIES
Cross–Border Tele-Learning

Physical sites for collaboration can only work if the border is porous enough for people to move back and forth without too much danger or difficulty. It is still fairly easy (though often time-consuming) for US citizens to cross into Tijuana and back into the United States. But the hardening of the border wall in recent years has made it increasingly difficult and dangerous for residents of Tijuana to cross into the United States. In addition to physical Community Station sites, therefore, we have also developed a telecommunications platform that enables virtual transgression. With large monitor consoles installed in our Community Station sites, programmed with cameras and conventional web-based technologies like Skype and Google Hangout, we are able to facilitate virtual cross-border dialogues, workshops, and performances with people who cannot or do not want to cross the border physically. We also retrofitted a movable trailer that enables nomadic access into otherwise inaccessible sites in the informal settlement in Tijuana. This remote capability also facilitates distance activities, such as telemedicine. Residents and community leaders connect periodically with doctors and researchers for health support and education.

COPRODUCTION OF EVIDENCE

Community activists, residents, and researchers have assembled bottom-up data and visualizations that are impossible to access through conventional top-down institutional research methods. These include the following "stories."

The Trash Sensors Story (Tijuana)

This was a project to measure the velocity of trash and sediment moving from an informal settlement in Tijuana into an environmentally protected estuary in San Diego, accelerated by the construction of a new border wall between them. Environmental activists, residents, and researchers equipped blue plastic bottles with sensors, and released them at strategic sites, accessible only to local communities, where trash is dumped illegally. The bottles flowed northbound towards the United States and appeared days later in the middle of the estuary. This information was visualized and became essential evidence for pressuring binational municipal and environmental agencies to recognize a problem that can only be tackled collaboratively. We proposed that the informal settlement, with a community-based participatory education initiative and the construction of public spaces doubling as water and waste management infrastructures, could protect the estuary, a binational and bioregional asset.

Bottom-Up Air Quality Story (San Diego)

Thousands of cars idle for hours while waiting to cross the border from Tijuana into San Diego. This has impacted the air quality of the community of San Ysidro and the health of many of its residents, east of the checkpoint, where our Community Station is located. San Ysidro's air pollution, and its public health impacts, have been virtually off the radar of local and state environmental agencies. The community did not even appear in CalEnviroScreen, the state's dashboard for environmental justice.

Figure 8: The Border
Lemons Story. Photo by
Andrew Sturm.

Figure 9: Density Game, San Ysidro, California.

Community activists, students, residents and researchers demanded recognition as an Environmental Justice (EJ) community, and raised small funds to deploy air quality monitors throughout the neighborhood, to produce evidence for state agencies. Community participation in the production of this data increased capacity for political action. San Ysidro now appears boldly in CalEnviroScreen, qualifying the neighborhood for resources that support climate mitigation and adaptation strategies.

The Border Lemons Story
Urban anecdotes can be important tools of social justice. The narrativization of urban crisis through everyday–life experiences can mobilize evidence to change hearts and minds in ways that hard data cannot. In San Ysidro, as part of the *Bottom–Up Air Quality* project, artist and MFA student Andrew Sturm worked with community residents to share their air quality stories. One resident showed him to his backyard, where he had planted a lemon grove. The fruits were covered in black silt, from months and months of air pollution. *The Border Lemons Story* became an important cultural strategy for mobilizing awareness of the air quality problem within the community and institutions more broadly.

**Radical Cartographies:
Geographies of Coexistence**
Youth on both sides of the border draw cognitive maps of the border region. Can a youth from Tijuana draw her city's main attributes, natural and artificial? Can she name and draw the shape and location of mountains, rivers, valleys, mesas, and shores? Can a youth from San Diego do the same for San Diego? Can each of them draw their immediate walled territory, and beyond the wall? How do we imagine the larger region, regardless of the political artifact that bisects those geographic features?

Figure 10: UCSD–CASA Community Station: Public space as seed for housing, 2018.

Figure 11: Border drain crossing, San Diego/Tijuana, 2011.

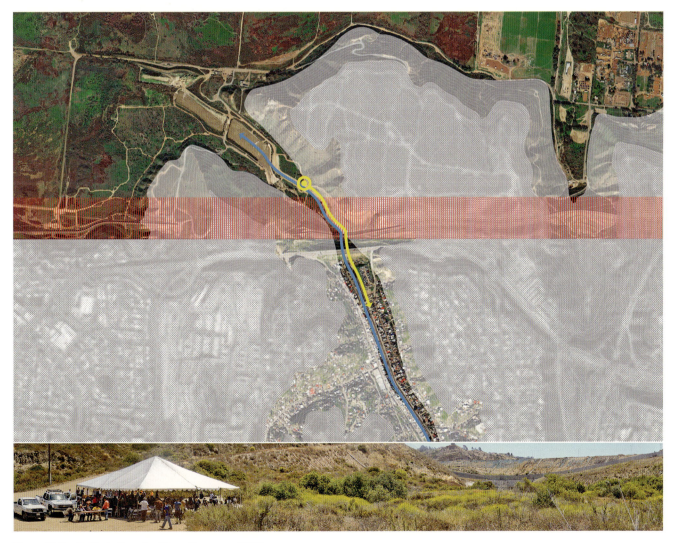

Figure 12: Border Drain Crossing Map + Panorama, 2018.

By drawing and performing the information they draw, they gain consciousness of the meaning and value of their environmental context. The visual cognition of the territory is a requisite for the urban curator.

Nomadic Planners: Itinerant Workshops

Another strategy involves the construction of urban pedagogical tools that mediate urban conversations and debates, in order to redraw the territory through narrative, anecdotal, and everyday practices. We are experimenting with the community-workshop format, designing games, objects, and images, and visualization tools to facilitate debates among community activists, neighborhood youth, and researchers about the complexity of urban processes and policy.

An example is the *Density Game*, a workshop we performed at the UCSD–CASA Community Station in the US border neighborhood of San Ysidro. This workshop did not deal with border conditions specifically, but the cultural strategies we developed can be adapted to any set of conditions. Here, we wanted to transcend generic advocacy–planning workshops that only focus on style

and identity as tools for consensus and private development. We wanted to help increase community capacity for political and urban action

We decided to orient the workshop around the question of urban density. The meeting with neighborhood activists and residents began with the provocation: What is density? We designed the *density game*: a board showing generic parcels representing an existing neighborhood block, accompanied by wood blocks representing housing units, trees, and cars. We set the game up at a community table, where residents participated in the conversation. The facilitator, a neighborhood youth mentored to lead the workshop, explained what the board and blocks represented. He announced to the group: "We are going to explore the idea of density. A developer usually says: let's build so many units on this block … but how many units can we really place in these parcels?"

Doña Maria, an elder community leader, made the first move: she placed one piece of wood in one parcel, another piece in another parcel, and so on. In effect, she reproduced the existing reality of her own block, one house per parcel. But

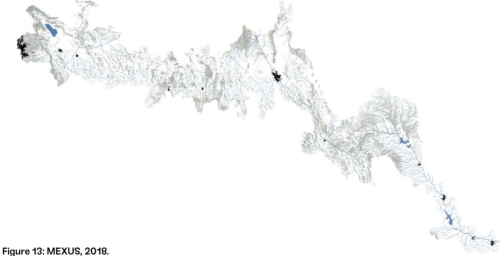

Figure 13: MEXUS, 2018.

then someone pushed two blocks against each other: "What if two owners collaborate and join their houses to generate extra space in the parcel, allowing for an extra unit? Or a shared space?" Very soon, everyone began to place a lot of wood on the block, and Doña Maria exclaimed: "Now I remember! When I was a young girl in Guadalajara, Mexico, I used to live in an older neighborhood, near downtown, and those (urban) blocks were not made of individual buildings on individual blocks, but they were a continuous building, with doors against the street: you would open a door and find patios inside." Another person asked: "Can density be about spaces rather than buildings?" Doña Maria punctuated the moment: "I cannot believe these houses are selfish!" Referring to her existing block: "Maybe density can be about neighborhood collaboration."

Codeveloping Housing and Public Space

Ultimately, the future of Gaza depends on the democratization of urban development, linking top-down resources and bottom-up agency and placing them in the hands of Gazans as urban curators. To curate is to accompany a process of urban transformation and to care for the larger territory through the development of mutual responsibility and empathy.

This last strategy democratizes urbanization itself. The Community Stations have demonstrated a new form of shared urban and economic development. A public university's economic and programmatic power can serve as leverage for community partners to develop their own public spaces and housing and to manage their own resources and modes of production.

The Community Station is the connective tissue between social housing and public space. We have committed to the idea that housing is not sustainable as units only, but needs to be supported by economic, cultural, and social programs. Public space is not an ambiguous and neutral place of beautification, but an incubator of cultural, social, political, and economic activity.

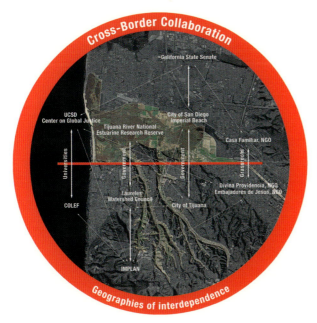

Figure 14: Cross Border Environmental Commons, linking a Tijuana slum with a San Diego estuary, 2018.

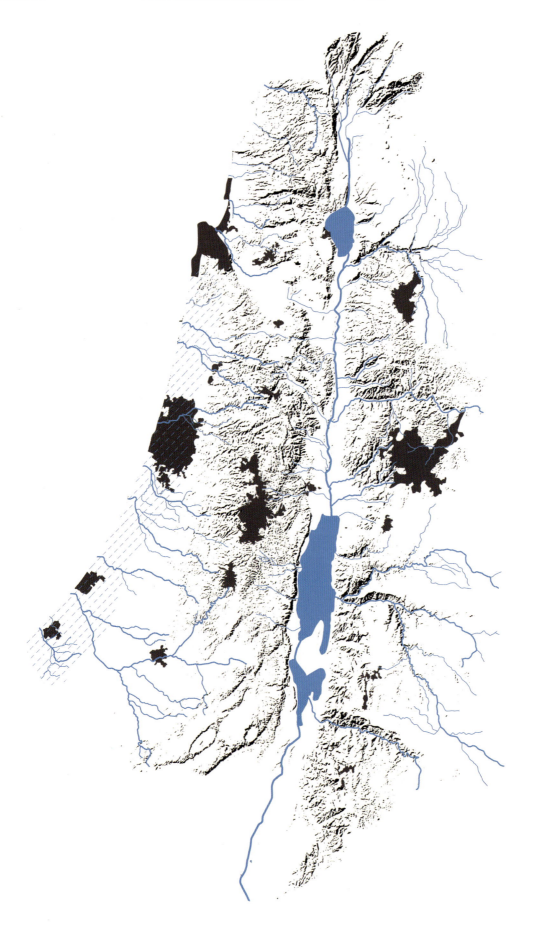

**Figure 15: A Cross–Border Water Commons, from the
Jordan River Valley to the Mediterranean Sea, 2018.**

Within informal environments, sweat equity can become leverage for a new economic pro-forma for social housing, since informal labor becomes collateral, leveraging other sources of investment and operationalizing the value of community participation to rethink affordability.

A public space that educates, the Community Station becomes a framework for housing. Units are embedded within an infrastructure of flexible social and pedagogical spaces, curated by cross-sector coalitions to inject funding, resources, and management to assure sustainable social and economic relations across time. In this context, social housing is always organized around an economic incubator managed by the local community partner. This pairing of social housing with a programmed public space becomes the urban infrastructure that can enable social exchange and small-scale local economy, decentralizing formal economic and political power.

Performative Tactics to Visualize Interdependence
Many of the cultural strategies, programs and activities of the Community Stations have been inspired by Brazilian pedagogue Paulo Freire, for whom knowledge is a social construct performed through everyday practices. The lineage of critical pedagogy he inspired sees teaching and learning as political processes, unfolding through a dialectical relationship between common-sense knowledge and methodical knowledge and with the negotiation between the visible and the invisible as its operative field.

Our activities emerge from concrete informal beliefs, bottom-up sensibilities, and narratives that are then incrementally shaped into knowledge through performance, practice, and critical dialogue. For Freire, in fact, democracy materializes through the habits of practice. The critical reflection that emerges through acts of doing makes education a political act, grounded in the existing reality.

Imagination is not an exercise for those detached from reality, those who live in the air. On the contrary, when we imagine something, we do it necessarily conditioned by a lack in our concrete reality. When children imagine free and happy schools, it is because their real schools deny them freedom and happiness.[11]

Our first major visualization project with our Community Stations partners in Tijuana took place in 2011, when we curated a cross-border public crossing through a sewage drain underneath a section of the border wall recently built by Homeland Security, located at the precise point where the Laureles Canyon settlement collides with the Estuary on the US side. We negotiated a permit with US Homeland Security to transform a drain under the wall into an official port of entry for twenty-four hours. They agreed, as long as Mexican immigration officials were waiting on the other side to stamp our passports. As three hundred participants moved southbound under the wall against the natural northbound flow of slum wastewater, we reached Mexican immigration officers, who had pitched a tent on the south side of the drain.

11. Paulo Freire, *Teachers As Cultural Workers: Letters to Those Who Dare Teach With New Commentary by Peter McLaren, Joe L. Kincheloe, and Shirley Steinberg Expanded Edition* (London: Routledge, 2005), 94.

3. VISUALIZING TRANSBORDER FUTURES

The third building block involves a practical intervention, as the meeting of knowledges in the community stations begins to coalesce around urgent issues of common concern. In recent years, we have been documenting the transborder ecologies that define the San Diego/Tijuana border region—the environmental, topographic, hydrologic, economic, and social flows that the wall cannot contain. These flows and circulations across the US-Mexico border wall are the armature of our region, but the invisibility of this information often prevents new transborder alliances from emerging. The visualization and mobilization of this transborder information has been essential for us and our community partners in the *Cross-Border Community Stations*, and has become the detonator of our cultural work together.

As we reflected on what a transborder environmental commons between Gaza and Israel might look like, we proceeded to develop a visual tool like we did for MEXUS: a map that visualizes the surface water networks and coastal aquifer, while erasing all jurisdictional lines. We recognized immediately what we already knew: that regional hydrologic systems transgress political lines across the entire territory.

In our exploration of cross-border interventions around water, we discovered many "bilateral and multilateral," "international and regional" agencies, organizations, initiatives, MOUs, workshops, studies, and interventions. Much of this information is invisible to the public, buried in academic research and NGO policy reports, and should be visualized and mobilized to provoke more aspirational regional thinking. One initiative that especially caught our attention was EcoPeace, an organization with offices in Jordan, Palestine, and Israel that works through both "bottom-up" and "top-town" interventions to advance projects around "sustainable regional development" and "the creation of necessary conditions for lasting peace."[12] It was hugely affirming for us to discover an NGO working on cross-border water and sanitation issues that frames its mandate and structures its interventions in ways so similar to ours. EcoPeace forwards the idea that "water has no boundaries" and can stimulate awareness of and cross-border commitments to regional interdependence. Instead of viewing water and sanitation as consumer products, a mindset that inevitably produces competition and conflict in the politics of water, EcoPeace's educational initiatives present water and sanitation as basic human rights, essential to life on both sides of the wall. As they describe their strategy: "By collaborating on environmental and water security problems, an understanding between conflicting parties and a willingness to establish interdependence is forged."[13]

A major initiative of EcoPeace is the Good Water Neighbor project, a coalition of twenty-eight communities in Jordan, Palestine, and Israel that reside along two main water systems: the Jordan River/Dead Sea Basin, and the Mountain and Coastal Aquifers. While these projects focus on social organization around local water and waste, the initiative has expanded in recent years to include major cities in

12. Our discussion of Eco-Peace is based on materials on their website. Another initiative that caught our attention is the Arava Institute, who in collaboration with USAID, Ben Gurion University, and two Palestinian NGOs facilitates cross-border stakeholder workshops focused on strategies for mitigating the impact of pollution throughout watersheds.

13. "About Us," EcoPeace, accessed February 13, 2019.

shared cross-border watersheds, including six shared watersheds between Israel and Palestine.

It was striking to note that EcoPeace has not worked in Gaza. The NGO does not state why, but voices support of international efforts to build and provide sufficient electricity to operate new wastewater treatment plants in Gaza. The urgency in their account of Gaza's challenges mirrors the scientific research we have begun to explore to get a grasp on the severity of the problem, and the implications of dramatic economic and political asymmetry in the regional politics of water.

In short, Gaza does not have the capacity to manage and treat the waste of its 1.8 million inhabitants. Current treatment plants manage only a quarter of the wastewater that is generated in Gaza annually, caused by the lack of capacity of existing plants, but also by a lack of electricity needed to operate them. The result is that 90,000 CM per day of raw or partially treated sewage is discharged into the Mediterranean Sea and the Coastal Aquifer, Gaza's main source of drinking water. The Aquifer is recharged mainly by the Wadi Gaza watershed flowing down from the mountains. However, these water flows are controlled upstream by Israel, impounded and redirected to agricultural and settler communities by thirty-two dams, barriers, and reservoirs, preventing the water from flowing into Gaza.[14] The trickle that does finally arrive is contaminated by agricultural runoff. Tragically, in addition to sewage and runoff contamination, the Coastal Aquifer has become increasingly salinated in recent years, by seawater to the west and brackish water to the east. This is exacerbated by the increasing digging of wells in Gaza in recent years, as it desperately seeks water.[15] The United Nations forecast that Gaza's coastal aquifer will be irreversibly damaged by 2020.[16]

This is a humanitarian crisis of gargantuan proportions, in one of the planet's most densely populated spaces. Gaza needs more water, more sanitation infrastructure, and more electrical capacity. But what has provoked us most, from the perspective of cross-border thinking employed in this chapter, is that the impacts of Gaza's condition are not confined to Gaza. It is an essential strategic fact that they imperil Israeli public health as well. Again, water has no boundaries. Watersheds, aquifers, and coastal currents do not respect the nation-state. Mirroring the northbound flows of toxic waste and sediments from Tijuana to San Diego in our region, Gaza's sewage flows northbound up the Mediterranean coast, compromising Israeli beaches, and threatening the Ashkelon desalination plant, which supplies 20 percent of Israel's drinking water. This appears to be a generalizable territorial phenomenon, true not only of waste from Gaza. According to a recent study, "over 90 percent of sewage from Palestinian towns flows untreated into 162 kilometers of rivers and streams, polluting groundwater aquifers shared by two nations in this fractious land."[17]

14. Akram Hassa Al Hallaq, "The Israeli Policies in Depleting Gaza Strip Fresh Groundwater," *Journal of Human Sciences*, no. 16/17 (2009): 261–79; see also Lior Asaf et al., "Transboundary Stream Restoration in Israel and the Palestinian Authority," in *Integrated Water Resources Management and Security in the Middle East*, eds. Clive Lipchin et al. (New York: Springer, 2007), 285–95.

15. Khalid Qahman and Abdelkader Larabi, "Evaluation and Numerical Modeling of Seawater Intrusion in the Gaza Aquifer (Palestine)," *Hydrogeology Journal* 14, no. 5 (2006): 713–28; A. Selmi, "Water Management and Modeling of a Coastal Aquifer Case Study (Gaza Strip)" (PhD diss., University of Milan Bicocca, 2013).

16. *Gaza Ten Years Later* (UNCT OPT, 2017).

17. Glenn Yago, "The Path to Peace Runs Through Sewage," *Haaretz*, July 28, 2013.

CONCLUSION:
UNWALLING CITIZENSHIP

In this essay, we have proposed degrees of openness to working across lines. Our gesture here should not be interpreted as appeasement or backpedaling from urgent ethical and political positions. There can be no compromise with radical injustice and the harms it inflicts on the most vulnerable in particular: children and the elderly. Motivated by a deep commitment to social justice for Palestinians in Gaza, and the urgency of remediating human suffering, we have proposed exploring productive fractures within both Palestinian and Israeli society that might become seeds for more imaginative transborder thinking and doing. Despite the entrenched and extreme ideological positions and violence that get the most airplay, these are not monolithic societies.

The ethical implications of pursuing mutual interest as a mechanism for transborder thinking and action focusing particularly on the meaning of engaging Israeli demographics that have proved resistant to Palestinian demands for equality and national self-determination are an urgent point of departure. When we engage publics and policy makers who are not motivated by democratic norms, social justice, or basic human compassion, and who through habit or agenda are committed to the status quo, can we find the right "lever" to turn them as they are, in very practical ways, toward more just ends, or at least to produce harms that are less unjust? When the harms we seek to remediate are severe and urgent, ideals can become a hindrance. Ideals entrench people and trigger passion and collective reaction.

Obviously, the kinds of interventions that these strategies might produce will not yield immediate political, social, and economic transformation. They will not end occupation. The radical transformation of social attitudes and behavior in Israel requires a dramatic realignment of internal dynamics and external pressures that do not seem forthcoming anytime soon.

But right now, interest-based strategies might help remediate the impacts of occupation on real lives. Though this is not satisfying from the perspective of social justice, and may seem like a weak diffusion of the crisis, the implications of remediation in Gaza should not be underestimated.

WORKS CITED

"About Us." EcoPeace, accessed February 13, 2019.

Asaf, Lior, Nta Negaoker, Alon Tal, and John Laronne. "Transboundary Stream Restoration in Israel and the Palestinian Authority." In *Integrated Water Resources Management and Security in the Middle East*, edited by Clive Lipchin, Eric Pallant, Danielle Saranga, and Allyson Amster. New York: Springer, 2007.

Carmona, Matthew, Tim Heath, Steve Tiesdell, and Taner Oc. *Public Places Urban Spaces: The Dimensions of Urban Design*. Oxford: Architectural Press, 2003.

Cruz, Teddy, and Fonna Forman. "The Cross-Border Public." In *Public Space? Lost and Found*, edited by Gediminas Urbonas, Ann Lui, and Lucas Freeman. Cambridge, MA: MIT Press, 2017.

Forman, Fonna. "Social Norms and the Cross-Border Citizen: From Adam Smith to Antanas Mockus." In *Cultural Agents Reloaded: The Legacy of Antanas Mockus*, edited by Carlo Tognato. Cambridge, MA: Harvard University Press, 2017.

Forman, Fonna, and Teddy Cruz. "Changing Practice: Engaging Informal Public Demands." In *Informal Market Worlds—Reader: The Architecture of Economic Pressure*, edited by Helge Mooshammer, Peter Mrtenbck, Fonna Forman, and Teddy Cruz. Rotterdam: nai010 Publishers, 2015.

———. "Citizenship Culture and the Transnational Environmental Commons." In *Nature's Nation: American Art and Environment*, edited by Karl Kusserow and Alan Braddock. Princeton, NJ: Princeton University Press, 2018.

———. "Global Justice at the Municipal Scale: The Case of Medellín, Colombia." In *Institutional Cosmopolitanism*, edited by Luis Cabrera. New York: Oxford University Press, 2018.

———. "Latin America and a New Political Leadership: Experimental Acts of Co-Existence." In *Public Servants: Art and the Crisis of the Common Good*, edited by Johanna Burton, Shannon Jackson, and Dominic Wilsdon. Cambridge, MA: MIT Press, 2017.

———. "The Wall: The San Diego–Tijuana Border." *Artforum* (Summer 2016): 370–75.

———. "Un-walling Citizenship." *Avery Review: Critical Essays on Architecture*, no. 21 (Winter 2017): 98–109.

Freire, Paulo. *Pedagogy of the Oppressed*. New York: Continuum, 2007.

———. *Teachers As Cultural Workers: Letters to Those Who Dare Teach With New Commentary by Peter McLaren, Joe L. Kincheloe, and Shirley Steinberg Expanded Edition*. London: Routledge, 2005.

Gaza Ten Years Later. UNCT oPT, 2017.

Hassa Al Hallaq, Akram. "The Israeli Policies in Depleting Gaza Strip Fresh Groundwater." *Journal of Human Sciences*, no. 16/17 (2009): 261–279.

Hirschman, Albert O. *The Passions and the Interests*. Princeton, NJ: Princeton University Press 1977.

Mockus, Antanas. "Building a Citizenship Culture in Bogotá." *Journal of International Affairs* 65, vol. 2 (Spring/Summer 2012): 129–32.

"New San Diego-Tijuana Survey Holds Mirror Up to Border Cities." *Next City*, February 25, 2015.

Qahman, Khalid, and Abdelkader Larabi. "Evaluation and Numerical Modeling of Seawater Intrusion in the Gaza Aquifer (Palestine)." *Hydrogeology Journal* 14, no. 5 (2006): 713–28.

Selmi, A. "Water Management and Modeling of a Coastal Aquifer Case Study (Gaza Strip)." PhD diss., University of Milan Bicocca, 2013.

"Survey Says San Diegans, Tijuanans Want More Cross-Border Collaboration." *San Diego Union Tribune*, June 19, 2015.

Tognato, Carlos, ed. *Cultural Agents Reloaded: The Legacy of Antanas Mockus*. Cambridge, MA: Harvard University Press, 2018.

Yago, Glenn. "The Path to Peace Runs Through Sewage." *Haaretz*, July 28, 2013.

HYPER–PRESENT ABSENCE: SUGGESTED METHODS

Hadeel Assali

Understand the realities of Gaza and one also understands the real challenge of Palestine as a cause and the Palestinians as a people. —Edward Said[1]

1. Edward Said, "Bitter Truths About Gaza," in *Peace and Its Discontents: Essays on Palestine in the Middle East Peace Process* (New York: Random House, 1993), 47.

Trying to write about Gaza seems a monumental task. Breaking through dominant mainstream Western discourses requires a complete reeducation along with the patience of a historian, the commitment of an anthropologist, and the willingness to set aside deeply entrenched notions about the place. These notions tend to fall into two categories, consisting of either a discourse around humanitarianism—divorcing the situation in Gaza from the root causes of the current crisis—or a discourse on war and terrorism, equating it with Hamas. Although these two discourses are distinct they reinforce each other.

In this essay, I explain how these discourses became so dominant and vociferous—what I call hyperpresent—and how they have obscured a deeper understanding of the Palestine question. I describe the near absence of Gaza in more in-depth studies on Palestine and speculate on additional factors that may have led to this void. I conclude with recommendations for how to break through this blockage based on my own nascent and ongoing experience.

HUMANITARIAN GAZA

Before there was the Gaza Strip, there was Palestine.
—Ilana Feldman[2]

In the wake of Operation Cast Lead (OCL), Ilana Feldman published an article titled "Gaza's Humanitarianism Problem"in which she presciently warned of the dangers of severing humanitarian crises from the political conditions that created them.[3]
She opens her article with a quote from Israeli historian Avi Shlaim, who stated clearly that Israel's goal for the 2009 war on Gaza was "to ensure that the Palestinians in Gaza are seen by the world simply as a humanitarian problem and thus to derail their struggle for independence and statehood."[4] However, Feldman reminds us that the humanitarian crisis, which is rooted in the *Nakba* and the very creation of the bounded territory that became known as "the Gaza Strip" in 1948, was greatly exacerbated prior to OCL. In 2006, the world saw an unexpected landslide victory for Hamas in the Palestinian parliamentary elections. Despite international observers' patronizing demands for Palestinians to participate in a democratic process, despite the fact that the voter turnout was 75 percent—higher than any United States election in recent history—and despite the fact that international observers reported that the elections were professional, free, and fair, the United States and Israel rejected the results. Palestinians, tired of Fatah's rampant corruption, chose Hamas; the United States and Israel chose to punish them for making the wrong choice. Thus, the inhumane closure of Gaza tightened when Western interests could not thwart Hamas's rise to power, as had been done in the West Bank. What followed was a politically motivated siege, which intensified the blockade of goods and services, and prevented Gaza's inhabitants from moving in and out of the tiny strip of land, effectively imprisoning two million people. Thus, a new chapter in the crippling of Gaza began. The discourse of humanitarian crisis, which Feldman points out had emerged decades prior, was amplified with the multiple devastating bombing campaigns after OCL.

2. Ilana Feldman, *Police Encounters: Security and Surveillance in Gaza Under Egyptian Rule* (Stanford: Stanford University Press, 2015), 8.

3. Ilana Feldman, "Gaza's Humanitarianism Problem," *Journal of Palestine Studies* 38, no. 3 (April 2009): 22–37.

4. Ibid., 22.

Drawing from a vast literature on "the international humanitarian order" and from her own fieldwork in Gaza, Feldman demonstrates how "humanitarianism *always* has political effects."[5] Well-meaning humanitarian organizations, after all, *always* uncritically take "the Gaza Strip" as a naturally given bounded entity. Since their mandate is to alleviate immediate suffering in times of crisis, there is simply no time to historicize and frame Gaza as an integral part of Palestine—and, in fact historically, of the wider region. The territory was forcibly segregated and bounded to a landmass that came to be known as "the Gaza Strip" only after the *Nakba* of 1948, which, as Feldman explains, led to a huge influx of refugees. The United Nations subsequently classified the local population into "refugees" and "natives" to help determine aid distribution, creating deep social and political divisions among the population. Perhaps these were unintended outcomes of the humanitarian response, but their consequences continue to plague Palestinian communities to this day. Feldman points out that both the *Nakba* of 1948 and OCL of 2009 were man-made events, but that "humanitarianism is not an arena well-suited for pursuing accountability,"[6] nor for bringing Palestinians closer to the primary goal of returning to the lands from which they were displaced. This is in fact the humanitarian problem of Gaza of which Feldman speaks: the amplification of immediate crises at hand, while their root causes and possible political solutions fade into the background. It goes without saying that the ongoing humanitarian crisis in Gaza is real, and many

Gazans are in need of support, especially as their economy and freedom of movement continue to be strangled. However, as thinkers and practitioners committed to opening the Gaza Strip, it is our task to hold history and its players responsible so as not to allow an apolitical humanitarian discourse to maintain the status quo.

GAZA AS WAR

Since 2009, humanitarian discourse has played an even more prominent role in framing the Palestinian question, alongside another discourse transforming the issue from occupied-and-occupier or colonizer-and-colonized to one of warring parties, as Sara Roy describes.[7] Roy shows how these paradigm shifts increasingly pushed into the background the language framing the Palestinian condition as a direct result of the Israeli occupation. The war discourse accompanied deeply entrenched policies of territorial fragmentation and annexation, economic debilitation, and false claims of Palestinian sovereignty in the West Bank and Gaza, despite continued Israeli military control of the territories. Roy demonstrates how the silencing of framing the issue as one of occupier and occupied has enabled Israel and the complicit international community to transform the Palestinians into a seemingly humanitarian case of their own leaders' making. Palestinian leadership in the West Bank has largely fallen in line with these policies, especially since the Oslo agreement, while the Hamas leadership of Gaza has been portrayed as a hostile terrorist

5. Ibid., 24.

6. Ibid., 27.

7. Sara Roy, "Reconceptualizing the Israeli–Palestinian Conflict: Key Paradigm Shifts," *Journal of Palestine Studies* 41, no. 3 (June 2012): 71–91.

enemy in a conflict of warring parties. Of course, Hamas only emerged during the Intifada in 1987, nearly forty years after the *Nakba* created "the Gaza Strip" and its humanitarian crises. However, the policies and paradigm shifts that Roy discusses have enabled Israel to absolve itself of any responsibility for Gaza's suffering, pointing to Hamas as its source.

The first paradigm shift that Roy lays out is the denial of territorial contiguity, which has long been accepted by the international community in the so-called two-state solution. While this "solution" is becoming less and less of a possibility with the Israeli usurpation of more and more Palestinian territory in the West Bank, the fragmentation of the Palestinian population continues to remain a largely accepted reality, even though it is a direct result of ongoing Israeli policies. This is the first framework that must be dismantled in a project that imagines opening Gaza and all Palestinian enclaves where people have been denied their freedom of movement. The second paradigm shift Roy describes is the entrenchment and irreversibility of the occupation, which has taken a sinister turn in Gaza. Israel's "disengagement" in 2005 (its removal of settlements and direct military forces on the ground) has enabled it to falsely claim that Palestinians have sovereignty over the Gaza Strip. Since the "disengagement," the word "occupation" has essentially disappeared in reference to Israel's policies in Gaza. Instead, the rhetoric has transformed to one of "security," which forms the third paradigm shift.

The fourth paradigm shift has seen a move from "occupation" to control of "borders," which are in fact an ever-increasing buffer zone destroying everything in their path. This fourth shift has enabled the occupation to be transformed from a political and legal issue underpinned by international law to a border dispute where the laws of war—and not occupation—apply. This is how the humanitarian responsibility for the residents of Gaza moved from being Israel's concern to being a burden of the international community (the fifth paradigm shift). Hence, whenever Israel "allows" borders to be opened, and goods and people to be transferred, they frame it as a gesture of generosity and goodwill—not one of direct responsibility—while they continue to annex land and devastate any possibility of economic development in the Palestinian territories.

The US State Department's designation of Hamas as a terrorist organization has largely gone unchallenged by the international community. This has transformed Palestinians from political actors with a possibility to determine their own future to an impoverished population that is the victim of its own leadership, only receiving relief from organizations that Israel allows to operate in the Palestinian territories. The risks of engaging with a "terrorist organization" are high, due to the illegality of providing any "material support or resources" to such organizations.[8] These risks likely resulted in what Roy describes as "a profound paradigmatic shift" for donors, as they changed from "their role from practitioners of development to providers of relief."[9] Thus, we can see how the two discourses—of war/

8. See the US Department of State website description: "The term 'material support or resources' is defined in 18 U.S.C. § 2339A(b)(1) as 'any property, tangible or intangible, or service, including currency or monetary instruments or financial securities, financial services, lodging, training, expert advice or assistance, safehouses, false documentation or identification, communications equipment, facilities, weapons, lethal substances, explosives, personnel (1 or more individuals who maybe or include oneself), and transportation, except medicine or religious materials.' "Terrorist Designations and State Sponsors of Terrorism," US Department of State, accessed May 1, 2018.

9. Roy, "Reconceptualizing the Israeli–Palestinian Conflicts," 83.

terrorism and of humanitarianism—have merged, trapping Palestinians into a downward spiral of being blamed for their own conditions and a decreasing visibility of their political aspirations for liberation. It is imperative for Palestine scholars and others concerned with the situation in Gaza and other Palestinian territories to challenge the US State Department's list of terrorist organizations, which includes every single Palestinian group except the nonmilitary wing of Fatah.

The conversations around Gaza's humanitarian crisis have grown considerably, as if the UN report that predicted Gaza would be uninhabitable by 2020—published in the same year as Roy's article—was a self-fulfilling prophecy, with absolutely no indication that the leadership of the international community holds Israel directly accountable for its condition.[10] The consolidation of humanitarian Gaza, with the blaming of Hamas, is evident in a recent *New York Times* article.[11] Exemplary of the current mainstream framing of Gaza, the article claims that the "heart of the crisis is a crushing financial squeeze, the result of a tense standoff between Hamas, the militant Islamist group that rules Gaza, and Fatah, the secular party entrenched on the West Bank." The article barely mentions the Israeli siege, says nothing about the multiple bombardments that have devastated Gaza, and of course makes no mention of the 1948 *Nakba* that created the Strip in the first place. Instead, it focuses on Palestinian leadership, especially Hamas, and is thus complicit in washing Israel's hands of the situation.

This is the hyperpresence of Gaza—framed as a humanitarian crisis essentially blamed on Hamas, while Israeli responsibility disappears from the frame.

ABSENT GAZA

Moving from the mainstream and humanitarian framing to more in-depth studies of Palestine reveals troubling realities as well. A survey demonstrates that while numerous historical studies include Gaza within the larger framework of Palestinian history, there is a dearth of ethnographic engagement with its actual population, despite a proliferation of ethnographies of other parts of the Palestinian population since the 1970s.[12] The only exceptions are the works by Feldman and Rema Hammami. Other scholars who have worked on Gaza offer different reasons for the absence of ethnographies there.

For example, Sara Roy, a key Gaza scholar who is not an anthropologist but employs ethnographic methods, writes in 1986: "There are many methodological difficulties in conducting research on the Gaza Strip, difficulties which are consistently encountered and which often interfere with effective and accurate data collection and analysis."[13] She explains that these difficulties arise from restrictions on the release of information from Israeli sources, the unreliability of much of the data, and the shortage of information among Palestinian sources due to restrictions by the military occupation and the lack of academic institutional and financial support. She warns: "The many realities of Gaza ... have, over time, been ignored and untreated.

10. United Nations Country Team in the Occupied Palestinian Territory. "Gaza in 2020: A liveable place?" Jerusalem: Office of the United Nations Special Coordinator for the Middle East Peace Process [UNSCO], 2012.

11. David M. Halbfinger, "With Gaza in Financial Crisis, Fears That 'an Explosion's Coming,'" *New York Times*, February 11, 2018.

12. Khaled Furani and Dan Rabinowitz, "The Ethnographic Arriving of Palestine," *The Annual Review of Anthropology* 40 (2011): 475–91. Their fairly thorough survey demonstrates a proliferation of ethnographic works on Palestine since the 1970s.

13. Sara Roy, *The Gaza Strip: A Demographic, Economic, Social and Legal Survey* (Jerusalem: Distributed by the Jerusalem Post, 1986), i.

This fact makes Gaza a potentially explosive area perhaps more so than any of the occupied territories."[14] She concludes by reflecting on the unsustainable realities in Gaza and the need to change attitudes so the right questions can be asked, in order to stop what she foresaw as dangerous trends. "If attitudes are to be changed, then reality as it exists inside Gaza today must, as a first step, be acknowledged."[15]

Unfortunately, when Roy published another book twenty-one years later, little had changed.[16] Once more, she warns of the absence of Gaza from scholarship in the region: "The focus of my work has been on the Gaza Strip, an area consistently neglected by both Western and Arab scholars, ... and an area that remains painfully mischaracterized and misunderstood despite its political centrality."[17]

Similarly, Hammami's dissertation tells us in the introduction that it "is not a comprehensive social history of the Gaza Strip—a work that still needs to be written."[18] Later, she reiterates, "the general historical literature on Gaza suffers from a similar dominance of political focus, but is also quantitatively more limited. Two major Arabic works exist on the twentieth century history of Gaza; their focus is primarily on political history with some emphasis on economic life."[19] She continues, "Thus, this study attempts to redress two lacunae in writings on Palestine: the absence of work on Gaza as a whole, and the absence of work on the social and cultural history of Palestinian women."[20] Disappointingly, Hammami's own work remains unpublished, which limits its circulation.

Finally, Feldman acknowledges that she was "extremely lucky in the timing" of her fieldwork, which occurred during the later part of the Oslo period. Her American passport granted her access to the Gaza Strip. Despite this, however, she discovered in the course of her research that "the materials available for this investigation were both considerable and incomplete."[21] She attributes these gaps in Gaza's archive in part to the Israeli seizure of archival documents in Beirut, and Gazans' destroying these documents to prevent their seizure. As a result, many of the materials about Gaza are elsewhere. British Mandate–era documents, and perhaps Egyptian records, are held in the Israeli State Archives in their entirety, without being catalogued or classified. In fact, Gaza was even marginalized within the British Mandate's own filing system. This absence clearly had long-lasting ramifications, as can be seen not only in the archives, but also in the overall scholarship in and on Gaza.

The Journal of Palestine Studies (JPS) is published by the Institute for Palestine Studies, which is "the oldest institute in the world devoted exclusively to documentation, research, analysis, and publication on Palestinian affairs and the Arab-Israeli conflict."[22] The journal has been in publication since 1971, and an analysis of its subject index of 156 issues (through 2010) shows only twenty-four titles under the subject "The Gaza Strip," eight of which are specifically related to war (Operation Cast Lead in particular). In a 1985 article in the journal, Ann Lesch states, "The Gaza Strip tends to be forgotten when scholars and

14. Ibid., 4.

15. Ibid., 151.

16. Sara Roy, *Failing Peace: Gaza and the Palestinian Israeli Conflict*. (Ann Arbor, MI: Pluto, 2007).

17. Ibid., 1.

18. Rema Eva Hammami, "Between Heaven and Earth: Transformations in Religiosity and Labor among Southern Palestinian Peasant and Refugee Women, 1920–1993" (PhD diss., Temple University, 1994), 2.

19. Ibid., 10.

20. Ibid., 11.

21. Ilana Feldman, *Governing Gaza: Bureaucracy, Authority, and the Work of Rule, 1917–1967* (Durham, NC: Duke University Press, 2008).

22. "History," Institute for Palestine Studies, accessed May 1, 2018.

diplomats discuss the Palestine problem. Mention of a 'Palestinian state on the West Bank' or of a 'confederation between the West Bank and Jordan' often omits reference to the Gaza Strip or only adds it as an afterthought—'and, of course, the Gaza Strip.'"[23] Lesch concludes her article by warning of the ramifications if Israel continues "to turn a blind eye to the realities of Gaza and to the stark choices that it poses for Israel's own future.

The choice made will have a profound effect on the prospects for peace and the risks of war throughout the Middle East."[24] It seems to me that JPS has largely limited its analysis of Gaza to a heavy association with war as well—including a special issue on the 2014 military campaign, Operation Protective Edge (OPE). In an article titled "The Twelve Wars on Gaza," historian Jean-Pierre Filiu offers very important insights, and shares Edward Said's sentiments that Gaza is the core issue of the Palestine question:

> *Gaza is not only an integral part of Palestine, it is the only one that survived the 1948 Nakba without either being absorbed into Israel or annexed by Jordan. There was no place for an entity like Gaza in the Zionist plan, which is a major reason for the extreme brutality that Israel has visited on the territory's population throughout the twelve wars. But Gaza is there to stay as a collective embodiment of Palestinian nationalism: It is in Gaza that Palestinian independence was proclaimed, in Gaza that the fedayeen[25] first arose, in Gaza that the founders of Fatah gained their know-how, in Gaza that the first intifada started, and in Gaza that Hamas was established. More importantly perhaps, it is in Gaza that the Palestinian resistance movement was able to cause an Israeli withdrawal after its first occupation of the territory in 1956–57. The 2005 "unilateral withdrawal" was supposed to transform the occupation and render it less costly for Israel both financially and in terms of security. But as the four wars since then have shown, the "reformed" occupation has proved frustrating for the Israelis and devastating for the Palestinians. With no more Israeli settlers in the Gaza Strip, no religious sites that are disputed between Jews, Muslims, and Christians, and the 1949 cease-fire lines long accepted as a permanent border, agreeing on the parameters of peaceful coexistence should have proven easier in Gaza than in the West Bank. Yet, the twelve-war cycle has demonstrated quite the contrary. This might be because the core issue in Gaza holds the key to the Israeli-Palestinian conflict: Is Israel able to deal with Palestinians who are neither occupied nor dependent? It is a simple question, but one which has far-reaching implications. If the answer is resoundingly positive, Gaza, as the cradle of Palestinian nationalism, could become the cornerstone of an authentic peace between Israel and Palestine. Conversely, it is*

23. Ann M. Lesch, "Gaza: Forgotten Corner of Palestine," *Journal of Palestine Studies* 15, no. 1 (October 1985): 43.

24. Ibid., 59.

25. *Fedayeen* means freedom fighters in Arabic.

clear that there will never be hope for Palestine as a whole as long as Gaza remains under attack.[26]

Filiu's suggestion that Gaza is the key to the Israeli–Palestinian conflict echoes Edward Said's claim (in the first epithet) that Gaza's realities must be understood in order to grasp the challenge of the Palestine question. Similarly, Lesch's warning on the risks of war echoes Roy's own warnings on the explosive potential of a misunderstood Gaza.

Why have these warnings gone unheeded by Palestine scholars for the past thirty-plus years? Can we truly say that the lack of engagement with Gaza can be blamed on the difficulty of access to the region? It has not always been as inaccessible as it is today, so how to explain its absence? With the concentration of political power in the West Bank and the Palestinian Authority, it seems to me that Palestine scholars might take pause and reflect on the possibility of other causes for the lack of engagement. Fear of political Islam, the internalization of Israeli discourses on Gaza, and social class differences between Palestine scholars and Gaza's residents, who are perceived to be traditional/conservative, could be possible reasons worthy of reflection if there still remain serious aspirations for a unified Palestinian polity seeking liberation.

OPENING GAZA

In more recent years, particularly after OPE, there has been an increase in Palestine scholars attempting to "get at" Gaza in order to make sense of its seemingly exceptional condition. Most of these scholarly inquiries into Gaza tend to use metaphors characterizing Israeli practices of domination—and the metaphors are legion. The most common metaphor used by Gazans themselves is that of a prison, while scholars in the West have described it as a Bantustan, a laboratory, and showcase for new Israeli military technology, part of a larger settler-colonial project, a site of humanitarian violence, and even a metaphor full stop. Others have described it in terms of Foucault's biopower, which Achille Mbembe extends into his concept of *necropolitics*, the most accomplished form of which he finds in "the contemporary colonial occupation of Palestine."[27] Recently, several scholars were featured in a collection of short essays titled *Gaza as Metaphor*, which opens with an introduction that meditates on metaphors as stand-ins due to increasingly restricted access. They, too, mention the "plethora of metaphors: Open-air Prison, Terror, Resistance, Poverty, Occupation, Siege, Trauma, Bare Humanity. Conversely, a plethora of terms also invoke Gaza: Crisis, Grief, Exception, Refugees, Nationalism, Destitution, Tunnels, Ruin, Persistence."[28] Other suggested metaphors hint at Gaza's man-made conditions: zoo, cyst, isolated, concentration-place, but, they counter, "if Gaza seems awash in apocalyptic metaphors, it is also, resolutely, a site of life and resistance."[29] The contributors ask and attempt to answer what these metaphors reveal and what they render obscure. For now, metaphors are serving as stand-ins for ethnographic work *in* Gaza (which has become nearly impossible in recent years). However, to conclude, I would like to suggest a two-step process

26. Jean-Pierre Filiu, "The Twelve Wars on Gaza," *Journal of Palestine Studies* 44, no. 1 (November 2014): 59. Emphasis mine.

27. Achille Mbembe, "Necropolitics," *Public Culture* 15, no. 1 (2003): 27.

28. Dina Matar and Helga Tawil-Souri, eds., *Gaza as Metaphor* (London: Hurst, 2016), 1.

29. Ibid., 6.

for moving beyond these metaphors, to break through the blockade and increase the exchange of ideas with the population trapped in the Gaza Strip, in order to bring them into the wider conversations about Palestine's future.

STEP 1: HISTORICIZE

There is no shortage of historical studies of Palestine, and while its recent history is fiercely contested by Zionist historians, a deeper historical study demonstrates quite clearly the contiguity between Gaza, the rest of Palestine, and the wider region. Reaching a historical understanding of the region takes time and patience, and it is a deeply empathetic act that will be instructive for anyone seeking to imagine a different kind of future. Below, I provide a partial bibliography as a suggested starting point. Understanding the history of the region—and the debates about that history—is imperative for anyone seeking to contribute to its future.

STEP 2: ETHNOGRAPHY— ESTABLISH RELATIONSHIPS

One fundamental problem with most humanitarian missions and war analysts is their lack of meaningful engagement with the local population. Establishing long-lasting relationships is the hallmark of anthropology. One must learn to listen to the actual experiences, feelings, and aspirations of those most directly affected in order not to impose ineffective "solutions" or lazy analyses. Another important practice is to learn from local knowledge production. Gaza has an enormous number of research centers, universities, libraries, and independent scholars. At the end of this chapter, I provide a partial list of these resources. Using these, one might begin to break through the closure—and this can all happen using electronic communications— in order to move Palestine studies in a direction that remedies the continuing absence of Gaza by taking direction from the local population in reframing these debates to include their perspectives and aspirations.

RESOURCES IN GAZA

RESEARCH CENTERS

Massarat Center

مركز مسارات

Al Hourani Center

مركز الحوراني

Palestinian Planning Center

مركز التخطيط الفلسطيني

Center for Study of Planning and Development

مركز CPDS الدراسات السياسيه والتنمويه

Qattan Studies Center

مركز القطان للدراسات

Al Zaytouna Center

مركز الزيتونه

LIBRARIES AND UNIVERSITIES

The Red Crescent Library

الهلال الأحمر

Islamic University

الجامعه الاسلاميه

Al Aqsa University

جامعه الأقصى

Open Jerusalem University

جامعه القدس المفتوحه

Al Azhar University

جامعه الأزهر

Mansour Library

مكتبه منصور

The Municipal Office Library

مكتبه البلديه

SCHOLARS IN GAZA

Abdal Hafez Hamid	عبد الحافظ حميد
Salah Abd al Aati	صلاح عبد العاطي
Assem Adwan	عصام عدوان
Tahassein Abu Aasi	تحسين أبو عاصي
Salaah al Naamy	صالح النعامي
Adnan Abu Amar	عدنان أبو عامر
Abd al Rahman Abu Aabed	عبد الرحمن أبو عابد
Akram Abu Aanzu	أكرم أبو عزه
Salim al Mbeed	سليم المبيض
Sameer Abumdallah	سمير ابومدللة
Nahd Zqout	ناهض زقوت
Mahmoud Thabit	محمود ثابت
Tawqif Shoumr	توفيق أبو شومر
Saoud Abu Ramadan	سعود أبو رمضان
Ghazi al Sourni	غازي الصوراني

SOURCES ON GAZA'S HISTORY

Abu al-Naml, Ḥusayn. *The Gaza Strip 1948–1967: Economic, Political, Social and Military Developments.* (Arabic) Beirut: Research Center of the PLO, 1979.

Abu Seif, Atef, ed. *The Book of Gaza.* Manchester: Comma Press, 2014.

Al-Aref, Aref. *The History of Gaza.* Damascus: Arrab Publishing House, 2015.

Al-Farrā, Mohammad Ali 'Umar. *Khān Yūnus : Mādīhā Wa-Hādiruhā.* 'Ammān: Dār al-Karmil, 1998.

Al-Mubayyid, Salim. *Gaza and its Strip: Studies on the Eternal Place and the Civilizations of its People.* Cairo: Egyptian Books, 1987.

Al-Tabbā', 'Uthmān Mustafá. *Ithāf Al-A'izzah Fī Tārīkh Ghazzah.* Ghazzah: Maktabat al-Yāzijī, 1999.

Baroud, Ramzy. *My Father Was a Freedom Fighter: Gaza's Untold Story*. New York: Palgrave Macmillan, 2010.

Bitton-Ashkelony, Brouria, and Aryeh Kofsky. *Christian Gaza in Late Antiquity*. Boston: Brill, 2004.

Butt, Gerald. *Life at the Crossroads: A History of Gaza*. Nicosia: Rimal Publications, 1995.

Doughty, Dick. "Gaza—Contested Crossroads." *Saudi Aramco World* 45, no. 5 (October 1994): 2-5.

Dowling, Theodore E. *Gaza, a City of Many Battles: From the Family of Noah to the Present Day*. New York: E.S. Gorham, 1913.

Downey, Glanville. *Gaza in the Early Sixth Century*. Norman: University of Oklahoma Press, 1963.

Faysal, Numān 'Abd al-Hādī. *A'lām Min Jīl Al-Ruwwād Min Ghazzah Hāshim : Mundhu Awākhir Al-'ahd Al-'Uthmānī Wa-Hattá Al-Qarn Al-'ishrīn, 1800-2000*. Ghazzah: Maktabat al-Yāzjī, 2010.

Feldman, Ilana. "Interesting Times, Insecure States: The Work of Government and the Making of Gaza in the British Mandate and the Egyptian Administration, 1917–1967." PhD diss., University of Michigan, 2002.

———. "Everyday Government in Extraordinary Times: Persistence and Authority in Gaza's Civil Service, 1917-1967." *Comparative Studies in Society and History* 47, no. 4 (October 1, 2005): 863–91.

———. "Government Without Expertise? Competence, Capacity, and Civil-Service Practice in Gaza, 1917-67." *International Journal of Middle East Studies* 37, no. 4 (November 2005): 485–507.

———. "Home as a Refrain: Remembering and Living Displacement in Gaza." *History and Memory* 18, no. 2 (October 1, 2006): 10–47.

———. "Difficult Distinctions: Refugee Law, Humanitarian Practice, and Political Identification in Gaza." *Cultural Anthropology* 22, no. 1 (February 1, 2007): 129–69.

———. *Governing Gaza: Bureaucracy, Authority, and the Work of Rule, 1917-1967*. Durham, NC: Duke University Press, 2008.

———. "Waiting for Palestine: Refracted Citizenship and Latent Sovereignty in Gaza." *Citizenship Studies* 12, no. 5 (October 1, 2008): 447–63.

———. "Refusing Invisibility: Documentation and Memorialization in Palestinian Refugee Claims." *Journal of Refugee Studies* 21, no. 4 (December 1, 2008): 498–516.

———. "Gaza's Humanitarianism Problem." *Journal of Palestine Studies* 38, no. 3 (April 1, 2009): 22–37.

———. "Ad Hoc Humanity: UN Peacekeeping and the Limits of International Community in Gaza." *American Anthropologist* 112, no. 3 (September 1, 2010): 416–29.

———. *Police Encounters: Security and Surveillance in Gaza under Egyptian Rule*. Stanford, CA: Stanford University Press, 2015.

Filiu, Jean-Pierre. *Gaza: A History*. New York: Oxford University Press, 2014.

———. "The Twelve Wars on Gaza." *Journal of Palestine Studies* 44, no. 1 (November 1, 2014): 52–60.

Glucker, Carol A. M. *The City of Gaza in the Roman and Byzantine Periods*. Oxford: B.A.R., 1987.

Hammami, Rema Eva. "Between Heaven and Earth: Transformations in Religiosity and Labor among Southern Palestinian Peasant and Refugee Women, 1920–1993." PhD diss., Temple University, 1994.

Hevelone-Harper, Jennifer Lee. *Disciples of the Desert: Monks, Laity, and Spiritual Authority in Sixth-Century Gaza*. Baltimore: Johns Hopkins University Press, 2005.

Lambert, Leopold. "Rafah: A Short History of Bulldozing in the Palestinian Border Town." *The Towner* (blog), September 6, 2016. http://www.thetowner.com/rafah-palestine-bulldozing/.

Lesch, Ann M. "Gaza: Forgotten Corner of Palestine." *Journal of Palestine Studies* 15, no. 1 (October 1, 1985): 43–61.

———. *Israel, Egypt, and the Palestinians: From Camp David to Intifada*. Bloomington: Indiana University Press, 1989.

Mughni, Nihad Mahmud. *Architectural Heritage in Gaza City*. Ramallah: Riwaq, 2007.

Radunzel, Joel. "Operation Mapping: Cartography, Intelligence, and the 3rd Battle of Gaza, 1917." Master's thesis, Syracuse University, 2015.

Rashid, Harun Hashim. *Stories of Gaza City*. S.l.: Cultural Circle of the PLO, 1987.

Reilly, James. "Rafeq's Ghazza: An Early Exploration of a Secondary Town." In *Syria and Bilad Al-Sham Under Ottoman Rule: Essays in Honour of Abdul Karim Rafeq*, 91–97. Leiden: Brill, 2010.

Sacco, Joe. *Footnotes in Gaza*. London: Jonathan Cape, 2009.

Shachar, Nathan. *The Gaza Strip: Its History and Politics: From the Pharaohs to the Israeli Invasion of 2009*. Portland, OR: Sussex Academic Press, 2010.

Shriteh, Fakher. *Gaza—The Bleeding Wound*. Bloomington: Xlibris Corporation, 2014.

Sourani, Ghazi. *The Gaza Strip 1948–1993: Historical, Political and Social Studies*. Gaza: s.n., 2013.

WORKS CITED

Feldman, Ilana. "Gaza's Humanitarianism Problem." *Journal of Palestine Studies* 38, no. 3 (April 2009): 22–37.

———. *Governing Gaza: Bureaucracy, Authority, and the Work of Rule, 1917– 1967*. Durham, NC: Duke University Press, 2008.

———. *Police Encounters: Security and Surveillance in Gaza Under Egyptian Rule*. Stanford: Stanford University Press, 2015.

Filiu, Jean-Pierre. "The Twelve Wars on Gaza," *Journal of Palestine Studies* 44, no. 1 (November 2014): 52–60.

Furani, Khaled, and Dan Rabinowitz. "The Ethnographic Arriving of Palestine." *The Annual Review of Anthropology* 40 (2011): 475–91.

Halbfinger, David M. "With Gaza in Financial Crisis, Fears That 'an Explosion's Coming.'" *New York Times*. February 11, 2018.

Hammami, Rema Eva. "Between Heaven and Earth: Transformations in Religiosity and Labor among Southern Palestinian Peasant and Refugee Women, 1920–1993." PhD disseration, Temple University, 1994.

"History." Institute for Palestine Studies. Accessed May 1, 2018.

Lesch, Ann M. "Gaza: Forgotten Corner of Palestine." *Journal of Palestine Studies* 15, no. 1 (October 1985): 43–61.

Matar, Dina, and Helga Tawil-Souri, eds. *Gaza as Metaphor*. London: Hurst, 2016.

Mbembe, Achille. "Necropolitics." *Public Culture* 15, no. 1 (2003): 11–40.

Roy, Sara. *Failing Peace: Gaza and the Palestinian Israeli Conflict*. Ann Arbor, MI: Pluto, 2007.

———. "Reconceptualizing the Israeli-Palestinian Conflict: Key Paradigm Shifts." *Journal of Palestine Studies* 41, no. 3 (June 1, 2012): 71–91.

———. *The Gaza Strip: A Demographic, Economic, Social and Legal Survey*. Jerusalem: Distributed by the Jerusalem Post, 1986.

Said, Edward. "Bitter Truths About Gaza." In *Peace and Its Discontents: Essays on Palestine in the Middle East Peace Process*. New York: Random House, 1993.

"Terrorist Designations and State Sponsors of Terrorism." US Department of State. Accessed May 1, 2018.

TIMELINE

63 BC
Palestine falls under Roman control.

1291
Gaza joins the Mamluk Kingdom as an autonomous principality.

1516
Gaza becomes part of the Ottoman Empire conquered Palestine.

1906
Administrative line established between Sinai and the provinces of Jerusalem and Hejaz agreed by British-occupied Egypt and Ottoman Empire.

1917
The Ottoman Empire loses control over Gaza to the British.

The Balfour Declaration establishes support for Zionist plans for a Jewish homeland in Palestine.

1948
Israel proclaims itself an independent State on May 14th.

The Arab–Israeli war and Al Nakba ("the catastrophe") results in 700,000 Palestinians being expelled. Egyptian forces enter Gaza.

1949
Armistice agreement between Israel and Arab nations.

Through the loss of surrounding towns around Gaza, the Israeli-Egyptian armistice agreement distinguishes the boundaries of the Gaza Strip.

General Assembly resolution creates UNRWA to provide relief to Palestinian refugees.

1950
UNRWA opens eight refugee camps in Gaza.

1967
June 5th, Six-Day War results in Israeli forces capturing Gaza Strip, Old City of Jerusalem, West Bank of river Jordan, including East Jerusalem, and Golan Heights.

June 6th, Israel invades Gaza and builds settlements.

1973
October or Yom Kippur War.

1978–1979
Camp David Accords signed in 1978 that led to the 1979 Israeli-Egyptian peace treaty.

1981
Khalid Al-Islambouli assassinates Anwar Sadat.

1982
Israel withdraws from the Sinai Peninsula but maintains control of the Gaza Strip and splits the town of Rafah in two with the new militarized border.

1987
The First Intifada, Palestinians rise up over the occupation of the West Bank and Gaza Strip. Founding of Hamas.

1993
In secret meetings the Oslo agreement is reached that resulted in the mutual recognition of Israel and the PLO.

1994
Cairo Accord signed. The agreement transferred the Gaza Strip and the area encompassing Jericho to the newly established Palestinian Authority.

1995
Oslo II was signed. Under the agreement, Israel retains the majority of the West Bank and 35 percent of the Gaza Strip.

Yigal Amir assassinates Yitzhak Rabin.

2000
Camp David Summit ends without an agreement.

The Second (Al Aqsa) Intifada begins.

2002
Establishment of the Palestinian Land Authority; Israeli Operation Defensive Shield.

2004
Yasser Arafat dies. Israel assassinates Ahmed Yassin, along with his two bodyguards and nine civilians.

2005
Israel "disengages" from the Gaza Strip. Jewish settlements are removed and all settlers are evacuated. Israel continues to control Gazan airspace, sea access, and land crossings.

2006
Palestinians in West Bank and Gaza elect Hamas. Gazan underground cross-border raid captures Israeli solider. Israel launches Operation Summer Rains, first major ground operation by Israel since withdrawal in Gaza, followed by Operation Autumn Clouds.

2007
Battle of Gaza between Fatah and Hamas; results in Hamas governing Gaza and Fatah the West Bank. Israel intensifies its blockade of Gaza's air, sea, and land.

2008–2009
Twenty-two day Israeli ground invasion Operation Cast Lead (OCL).

2010
Gaza Flotilla Raid, or Operation Sea Breeze, or Operation Sky Winds, Israeli forces blocked Free Gaza Movement attempt to deliver aid.

2011
Egypt's interim government permits Rafah border crossings but with constant and sudden closures.

2012
Eight-day Israeli invasion, Operation Pillar of Defence, also known as Operation Pillar of Cloud; UN report published on whether Gaza would still be a "livable place" by 2020.

2014
Israeli launches Operation Protective Edge (OPE) on Gaza; Gaza Reconstruction Mechanism (GRM) established.

2014–2015
Palestinian Authority and Hamas form Palestinian Unity Government.

2018–2019
The Great March of Return.

CONTRIBUTORS

Salem Al Qudwa was born and raised in the eastern coastal city of Benghazi, Libya (1976). Al Qudwa is an architectural engineer who holds BArch (2003) and MArch (2013) from the Islamic University of Gaza (IUG), Palestine. His professional experience is a mix of design, academic teaching, and humanitarian architecture. He began his professional practice in 2005 by working with Egyptian architect Rami El Dahan on the design and rendering for the Palace of Justice in Gaza. In 2006, he joined Islamic Relief Worldwide as an Emergency Architect with a strong commitment to affordable design for people in need. He has managed re-construction projects ranging from primary healthcare clinics and schools to the rehabilitation of shelters for families living in marginalized and rural areas in Gaza. In 2012, he worked on the renovation of Rafah Cross Border Terminal between Egypt and the Gaza Strip. In 2018, he received the World Habitat Award for the Rehabilitation of Damaged Houses, Gaza Strip, Palestine. In 2019, shortly after defending his PhD in Design at the School of Architecture, Oxford Brookes University, England, he secured a position at Secours Islamique France as Shelter Manager for the Gaza Strip. In addition, he is a part-time research assistant in the anthropology department at McGill University, Canada.

Hadeel Assali is a filmmaker, a chemical engineer, and a PhD candidate in anthropology at Columbia University.

Tareq Baconi is the author of *Hamas Contained: The Rise and Pacification of Palestinian Resistance* (Stanford University Press, 2018). He is the Israel/Palestine and Economics of Conflict Analyst for the International Crisis Group. He was previously a fellow at Columbia University's Middle East Institute in New York and at the European Council on Foreign Relations in London. He holds a doctorate in International Relations from Kings College London, an MPhil in International Relations from the University of Cambridge and an MEng in Chemical Engineering from Imperial College London. His writings have appeared in Arabic in *Al-Ghad* and *Al-Quds al-Arabi*, and in English in *The New York Review Daily*, *The Washington Post*, *Foreign Affairs*, *Foreign Policy*, *The Guardian*, *The Nation*, *The Daily Star* (Lebanon), and *Al-Jazeera*. He has provided analysis for print and broadcast media, including *The New York Times*, *The New Yorker*, the BBC World Service, National Public Radio, and Democracy Now!

Teddy Cruz (MDes Harvard) is a professor of Public Culture and Urbanism in the University of California, San Diego Department of Visual Arts, and Principal of Estudio Teddy Cruz + Fonna Forman, a research-based political and architectural practice in San Diego. He is known internationally for his urban research on the Tijuana/ San Diego border, advancing border neighborhoods as sites of cultural production from which to rethink urban policy, affordable housing, and public space. Cruz + Forman lead a variety of urban research agendas and civic/public interventions in the San Diego-Tijuana border region and beyond. From 2012–13 they served as special advisors on civic and urban initiatives for the City of San Diego and led the development of its Civic Innovation Lab. Together they lead the UCSD Community Stations, a platform for engaged research and teaching on poverty and social equity in the border region. Recipient of the Rome Prize in Architecture in 1991, his honors include the Ford Foundation Visionaries Award in 2011, the 2013 Architecture Award from the US Academy of Arts and Letters, and the 2018 Vilcek Prize in Architecture.

Fonna Forman (PhD Chicago) is Professor of Political Theory and Founding Director of the Center on Global Justice at the University of California, San Diego and Principal of Estudio Teddy Cruz + Fonna Forman, a research-based political and architectural practice in San Diego. A theorist of ethics and public culture, her work focuses on climate justice, border ethics, and equitable urbanization. She is known internationally for her revisionist research on Adam Smith, recuperating the ethical, social, and public dimensions of his thought. Forman + Cruz direct a variety of urban research agendas and civic/public interventions in the San Diego-Tijuana border region and beyond. Forman is Vice-Chair of the University of California 2015 *Bending the Curve Report* on climate change solutions and serves on the Global Citizenship Commission.

M. Christine Boyer is the William R. Kenan, Jr. Professor of Architecture and Urbanism at Princeton University. Professor Boyer is an urban historian whose interests include the history of the city, city planning, preservation planning, and computer science. Before joining Princeton, she was Professor and Chair of the City and Regional Planning Program at Pratt Institute and had taught at Cooper Union, Columbia University, and Harvard University. Boyer received an award from the Department of Art and Archaeology Publication Fund, for publication of *Le Corbusier: homme de letters (1910–1947)* (Princeton Architectural Press, 2010). Her publications include *Dreaming the Rational City: The Myth of American City Planning 1890–1945* (MIT Press, 1983), *Manhattan Manners: Architecture and Style 1850–1900* (Rizzoli, 1985), *The City of Collective Memory* (MIT Press, 1994), *CyberCities* (Princeton Architectural Press, 1996), and *Not Quite Architecture: Writing around Alison and Peter Smithson* (MIT Press, 2017).

Alberto Foyo received his architectural education at the Polytechnic School of Architecture in Madrid, Spain, and at the School of Architecture and Allied Arts at the University of Oregon. During his formative years, he worked for various architectural firms in New York and in Vienna. In 1993, he established his independent practice in Manhattan. He is also a founding partner and director of Postopia, a think-tank based in the United States with satellite studios in Ukraine, Russia, and The Netherlands.

Postopia's work is focused on clean-up policies and cultural sustainability in the highly deteriorated urban environment of the ex-Soviet republics.

Nasser Golzari is an award-winning architect and academic. He has been practicing and teaching in the UK since 1990 and is the founder of Golzari—NG Architects in London. His practice has developed a reputation of working on sustainable community projects nationally and internationally with specific interest in issues of cultural identity and responsive environmental design. Over the past years he has been working extensively in Iran and Palestine with different organizations including Municipalities, UN-Habitat, British Council, as well as local NGOs. Golzari has co-founded the Palestinian Regeneration Team (PART) along with Yara Sharif and Murray Fraser. Nasser was the Founding Editor of *A3 Times* and *A3 Forum* and has been guest editor for a number of architectural magazines.

Yara Sharif is a practicing architect and academic with an interest in design as a means to facilitate and empower "forgotten" communities, while also interrogating the relationship between politics and architecture. Combining research with design, her work runs in parallel with the architecture practice NG Architects, London, and the design studio at the University of Westminster. Sharif co-founded the Palestine Regeneration Team (PART). She was also the recipient of 2013 RIBA's President Award for Research. Her ongoing research by design is entitled *Architecture of Resistance:*

Searching for Spaces of Possibilities under the Palestinian/Israeli Conflict (Routledge, 2017).

PART is a design-led research group that aims to search for creative and responsive possibilities that can heal the fragmented map of Palestine. In addition to working on different regeneration and self-help schemes both in Gaza and the West Bank, PART combines speculative ideas along with live projects as a means to stretch the physical as well as the imaginative Palestinian space. PART has been working over the past 18 years, on projects both in the West Bank and the Gaza Strip along with local communities to explore notions of stitching the fragmented landscape through responsive design. PART's work on Palestine was awarded the RIBA President's Medal for research in 2013 and 2016 and the Holcim Award for Sustainable Construction 2014.

Denise Hoffman Brandt, RLA is Director of the Graduate Landscape Architecture Program at the City College of New York and Principal of Hoffman Brandt Projects, LLC. Her work focuses on landscape as ecological infrastructure—the social, cultural, and environmental systems that generate urban form and sustain urban life. Selected speculative design research projects have focused on: refugee camps ("Relief Organism" in *The Right to Landscape*, Ashgate Press, 2011), carbon storage infrastructure (*City Sink*, Oscar Riera Ojeda, 2013), community flood recovery and adaptation ("Landlocked" in *New Orleans Under Reconstruction*, Verso, 2014), and climate-adaptive infrastructure ("City Sink—Sinking Cities" in *Now*

Urbanism, Routledge, 2015, and *Waterproofing New York*, co-edited with Catherine Seavitt Nordenson, Urban Research 02, 2016). Her recent critical writing includes "The Body in the Library, Or a Blood Meridian" (*Journal of Landscape Architecture*, March 2018), which discusses the role speculative practices can play in adapting the discipline of landscape architecture to dynamic socio-environmental forces.

Romi Khosla is an architect and consultant on urban and rural revitalization projects and has worked on international, regional, and national scales. With a double graduation from Cambridge University in economics and London's Architectural Association in architecture, he has worked as a Principal Consultant in conflict areas for resolution and regional revitalization programs for UNDP, UNESCO, and WTO, on employment generation, as well as urban regeneration for UNOPS. Khosla has been engaged on various UN missions in the Middle East, the Balkans, Tibet, China, Central Asia, and Cyprus. In 1972, he established Romi Khosla Design Studios and has designed and built over a hundred buildings, some of which have been awarded with national and international honours. Among them is the LEED Platinum-rated Volvo-Eicher Headquarters in Gurgaon, India, which was recently given the World Architecture Award — Steel Building of the Decade. In addition to his architectural and conflict resolution work, he has been an earth walker, traveling on foot among remote rural communities. His travels and research in the deeper Himalayas resulted in the publication of

Buddhist Monasteries in the Western Himalayas (Ratna Pustak Bhandar, 1979). His other books include *The Loneliness of the Long Distance Future* (Columbia University Press, 2002), and *The Idea of Delhi* (Marg Publications, 2006).

Craig Konyk is Chair and Assistant Professor of Architecture at the newly formed School of Public Architecture in the Michael Graves College at Kean University and is the founder of KONYK, an innovative architecture design studio. The firm creates designs that are rooted in the contextual underpinnings of the site, supported by that sustainability, to constitute a redefinition of the public realm. He has taught both at Pratt Institute's GAUD and Columbia University's GSAPP, where at the invitation of Riwaq, he led three GSAPP Studios to Ramallah. He has been awarded two NYFA fellowships, two ACSA Design Awards, six AIA New York Chapter Design Awards, and has exhibited work at Parsons School of Design, the Architectural League of New York, and the Storefront for Art and Architecture. Konyk has been named an Emerging Voice by the Architectural League of New York and a finalist for the Rome Prize in Urban Design by the American Academy in Rome. He has served on the Boards of the Architectural League of New York and *The Architect's Newspaper*. He designed the exhibition *Rise and Fall of Apartheid: Photography and the Bureaucracy of Everyday Life*, curated by Okwui Enwezor, which originated at ICP in New York, in September 2012, and traveled to the Museum of Africa in Johannesburg, South Africa, in February of 2014. Konyk was one of ten inaugural

Fellows at ARCHITECTURE OMI's Architecture Residency Program in the spring of 2017, where he participated in the EXIT Architecture Exhibition in 2019.

Rafi Segal is an architect and Associate Professor of Architecture and Urbanism at the Massachusetts Institute of Technology (MIT), where he directs the SMArchS Urbanism program. His work involves design and research on the architectural, urban, and regional scale, currently focusing on how emerging notions of sharing and collectivity can impact the design of buildings and the shaping of cities.

Chris Mackey is a building scientist and designer at Payette Architects as well as a graduate of Massachusetts Institute of Technology's (MIT) Masters of Architecture and Masters of Science in Building Technology programs.

Vyjayanthi V. Rao, (PhD Chicago) Co-director, is an anthropologist by training. Prior to joining Terreform, she held research and teaching positions at The New School for Social Research and at the University of Chicago, where she also received her doctorate. From 2002 to 2004 she served as the Research Director of the Initiative on Cities and Globalization, Yale University, and as the Co-Director of Partners for Urban Knowledge, Action and Research (PUKAR), an innovative urban laboratory in Mumbai, India. Her current work focuses on cities after globalization, specifically on intersections of urban planning, design, art, violence, and speculation. She has authored many articles on these topics in noted journals, is the

co-editor of *Speculation, Now: Essays and Artwork* (Duke University Press, 2015) and is completing a manuscript on the spatial transformation of Mumbai.

Sara Roy is a Senior Research Scholar at the Center for Middle Eastern Studies, Harvard University. She has published extensively on the Israeli-Palestinian conflict, with a focus on Gaza. She formulated the concept of "de-development" to explain the impact of Israeli policy on Gaza's economy. Her major work, *The Gaza Strip: the Political Economy of De-development*, is now in its third edition, published by the Institute of Palestine Studies (2016). Previously, she authored *Hamas and Civil Society in Gaza: Engaging the Islamist Social Sector* (Princeton University Press, 2011, 2014).

Royal College of Art, ADS7 is an educational and research design studio based in the MA Architecture program of the School of Architecture at the Royal College of Art, London. ADS7 proposes an alternative way of thinking and designing architecture as a collective political practice. The studio encourages students to work simultaneously in multiple scales, proposing architectural models and strategies for a wide array of collectives. ADS7's main research question is what kind of architecture could emerge when we think about and define ecology, subjectivity, and living, as indispensable political and architectural categories. Within this framework, and in collaboration with the Centre for Research Architecture at Goldsmith's University and Forensic Architecture with assistance from B'Tselem, GISHA, and OCHA OPT,

ADS7 participated in the border/ground workshop. "Collective Equipment for Gaza" emerged from this workshop and was developed during the fall semester of 2016–17. It forms part of a larger body of work that will be presented in a forthcoming publication by ADS7.

Mahdi Sabbagh is a practicing architect and urbanist in New York. He co-curated Palfest, the Palestine Festival of Literature in 2019, around the theme of *Urban Futures: Colonial Space Today*. He has since joined the Palfest organizing team. Mahdi was co-editor of *Perspecta 50: Urban Divides* (MIT Press, 2017), and his work has been published in the *Journal of Public Culture*, the *Jerusalem Quarterly*, and *Jadaliyya*. He holds a Masters in Architecture from Yale.

Meghan McAllister is an architect and urbanist based in the San Francisco Bay Area. Her professional work focuses on affordable housing, as well as projects for combating homelessness. Meghan was the co-editor of the 50th issue of the Yale architectural journal, *Perspecta 50: Urban Divides* (MIT Press, 2017). She also collaborated on the publication *Mexican Social Housing: Promises Revisited* (Actar, 2018). Meghan holds a BA in Growth & Structure of Cities from Haverford College and a Masters in Architecture from Yale.

Francesco Sebregondi is an architect and researcher whose work explores the intersections of violence, technology, and the urban condition. Since 2011 he has been a Research Fellow and Project Coordinator at Forensic Architecture and co-editor of its first collective publication *Forensis: The Architecture of Public Truth* (Sternberg Press, 2014). He is currently completing a doctoral research on the architecture of the Gaza blockade, at Goldsmiths University of London. Francesco's writings have been published in journals such as the *Architectural Review*, *Footprint*, *Volume*, the *Avery Review*, and *City*. He has taught a design studio at the School of Architecture, Royal College of Art (2013–15) and has been invited to deliver talks and workshops in many international venues. He lives and works between Paris and London.

Deen Sharp (PhD CUNY) is a geographer and the co-editor of *Open Gaza*. Sharp is the co-director of Terreform, Center for Advanced Urban Research, and a Post-Doctoral Fellow at the Aga Khan Program for Islamic Architecture at the Massachusetts Institute of Technology (MIT). He is the co-editor of *Beyond the Square: Urbanism and the Arab Uprisings* (Urban Research, 2016). Sharp has published in *Progress in Human Geography, the Arab Studies Journal, Jadaliyya, Public Books, Arcplan*, and contributed book chapters to several edited volumes.

Malkit Shoshan is the founding director of the Foundation for Achieving Seamless Territory (FAST), an Amsterdam and NY based architectural think-tank. FAST uses research, advocacy, and design to promote social, spatial, and environmental justice, equality, and solidarity. Shoshan is the Area Head of Art, Design, and the Public Domain (ADPD) Master in Design Studies at Harvard GSD. She is the author and mapmaker of the award-winning book *Atlas of the Conflict: Israel–Palestine* (Uitgeverij 010, 2010), and the book *Village: One Land Two Systems and Platform Paradise* (Damiani Editore, 2014). Her additional publications include *Zoo, or the letter Z, just after Zionism* (NAiM, 2012), *Drone: UNMANNED. Architecture and Security Series* (DPR–Barcelona, 2016), and the issue *Spaces of Conflict* for Footprint, TU Delft Architecture Theory Journal (JAP SAM Books, 2017), as well as *Greening Peacekeeping: The Environmental Impact of UN Peace Operations* (International Peace Institute, 2018) and *UN Peacekeeping Missions in Urban Environments: The Legacy of UNMIL* (FAST, CIC–NYU, 2018). In 2016, she curated the Dutch entry to the Venice Architecture Biennale, *BLUE: Architecture of UN Peacekeeping Missions*. Her work has been published internationally in newspapers, magazines, and journals, and exhibited in venues including the Museum Boijmans Van (2018), Harvard GSD (2017), UN Headquarters, New York (2016), Venice Architecture Biennale (2002, 2008, 2016), Experimenta (2011), Het Nieuwe Instituut (2014), The Istanbul Design Biennale (2014), Israeli Center for Digital Art (2012), and The Netherlands Architecture Institute (2007).

Pietro Stefanini is a PhD candidate in Politics and International Relations at the School of Social and Political Science at the University of Edinburgh. He was previously the Researcher and Advocacy Coordinator at the Palestinian Return Centre (PRC), an NGO with Consultative Status in the Economic and Social Council of the United Nations. He has authored a number of PRC reports, including *Voices of Return: Documenting Israel's Repression of the Great March of Return*, which was based on testimonies to the *UN* Commission of Inquiry into the 2018 protests in the Gaza Strip; and *Syria's Palestinian Refugees: An Account of Violence, Precarious Existence and Uncertain Futures*. His research on Israel's siege of the Gaza Strip has appeared in *Politics of Post-Conflict Reconstruction* by the Project on Middle East Political Science (POMEPS). Stefanini has been featured in a 2018 Al-Jazeera TV documentary *Seven Days in Beirut: Life Inside Burj al-Barajneh Refugee Camp*. He holds an MSc in Politics of Conflicts, Rights and Justice from the School of Oriental and African Studies, University of London.

Michael Sorkin, President of Terreform, is the co-editor of *Open Gaza*. Sorkin is an architect and urbanist whose practice spans design, criticism, and pedagogy. Since 2000, Sorkin has been Distinguished Professor of Architecture and Director of the Graduate Program in Urban Design at City College of New

York. He is the architecture critic for *The Nation*, contributing editor at *Architectural Record*, and author or editor of twenty books. Sorkin is a Fellow of the American Academy of Arts & Sciences, the recipient of the 2013 Cooper-Hewitt National Design Mind Award, and is a 2015 Guggenheim Fellow. He is also Principal of Michael Sorkin Studio, an international design practice that works in close collaboration with Terreform.

Helga Tawil-Souri is an Associate Professor in the Department of Media, Culture, and Communication and the Department of Middle Eastern and Islamic Studies at New York University. Helga's scholarship focuses on issues spatiality, technology, and politics in the Middle East, with a particular focus on Palestine/ Israel, how media technologies and infrastructures function as bordering mechanisms, and how territorial/physical boundaries function as cultural spaces. Her publications have addressed different aspects of contemporary cultural politics, including the internet, telecommunications, television, cinema, and video games, as well as physical markers such as ID cards and checkpoints. Her work analyzes how each of these technologies is shaped, used, negotiated, and sometimes resisted in their historical-political specificities. Tawil-Souri is the co-editor of *Gaza As Metaphor* (Hurst, 2016).

Omar Yousef is an architect and urban planner. He is Assistant Professor at Al-Quds (Jerusalem) University and academic coordinator of the MA program in Jerusalem Studies.

Visualizing Palestine (VP) creates data-driven tools to advance a factual, rights-based narrative of the Palestinian-Israeli issue. Our researchers, designers, technologists, and communications specialists work in partnership with civil society actors to amplify their impact and promote justice and equality. Launched in 2012, VP is the first portfolio of Visualizing Impact (VI), an independent, non-profit laboratory for innovation at the intersection of data science, technology, and design.

Fadi Shayya researches cities, design, technology, and militarization. He practiced as an urbanist and architect in Lebanon, Iraq, Kingdom of Saudi Arabia, and United Arab Emirates; taught at the American University of Beirut, the New School, and Manchester School of Architecture, and served as operations manager with VI. He is currently a PhD candidate in Architecture at The University of Manchester.

TERREFORM

Terreform is a nonprofit 501(c)3, urban research and advocacy group founded in 2005 by Michael Sorkin. Its mission is to investigate the forms, policies, technologies, and practices that will yield equitable, sustainable and beautiful cities for our urbanizing planet.

Board of Directors

Michael Sorkin (1948–2020)
Joan Copjec, PhD
Jonathan House, MD
M. Christine Boyer, PhD
Richard Finkelstein, ESQ
Makoto Okazaki

Staff

Michael Sorkin
President

Vyjayanthi Rao Venuturupalli, PhD
Deen Sharp, PhD
Co-Directors

Maria Cecilia Fagel
Executive Editor

Andrea Johnson
Research Director

Isaac Gertman
Design Director

Nic Cavell
Senior Editor

Hilary Huckins-Weidner
Development Director

Trudy Giordano
Studio Manager

Damiano Cerrone
DeNeile Cooper
Filippa Dahlin
Vineet Diwadkar
Aysegul Didem Ozdemir, PhD
Christina Serifi
Principal Researchers

Sarah Abdallah
Supriya Ambwani
Sofia Butnaru
Casey Breen
Corinee Butta
Netta Nekash
Vaishnavi Reddy
Oliver Wright
Editorial, Design and Research Associates

Terreform works in close affiliation with Michael Sorkin Studio, whose members donate their time and skills to its projects: Makoto Okazaki, Ying Liu, Jie Gu, Qiuyun Chen, Zhen Quan, Chen Shen.

Sponsors

Terreform depends on and thanks generous donors of the past and present, and looks forward to a league of future supporters, a network of like-minded people and organizations.

Elysium
Holcim Foundation for Sustainable Construction, George Sorkin, Michael Sorkin Studio, and an anonymous donor.

Megalopolis
Jean-Louis Bourgeois Elise Jaffe + Jeffrey Brown, Frank and Berta Gehry, Graham Foundation for Advanced Studies in the Fine Arts, Institute for Transportation and Development Policy, Southern California Institute of Architecture, Turenscape, The Venice Biennale—2010 American Pavilion.

Metropole
Carl Pruscha and Eva Schlegel, Furthermore—A Program of the J.M.Kaplan Fund, Safdie Architects, Rockwell Group, Snøhetta, Anette Brunsvig Sørensen + Svein Toensager, The City College of New York—Bernard and Anne Spitzer School of Architecture.

City
Elisabeth Block, Diller Scofidio + Renfro, Roberta Brandes Gratz, Ying Lui, Richard Menaker, David Grahame Shane, TEN Arquitectos.

Town
Richard Baron + Adi Shamir Baron, Michael Burns, Steve Diskin, Holly Kallman, Lisa Landrum, Daniel Monk, Yasmin Shariff, Holly Huckins + William Weidner.

Alumni

Manolo Ampudia
Brian Baldor
Glen Barfield
Julia Bartocci
Djuro Pavao Bartulica
Laura Belik
Leslie Billhymer
Sarah Blankenbaker
Sofie Blom
Irem Bugdayci
Mattea Cai
Robin Balles Cervantes
Patrick Collins
Nadia Constantos
Jack Curry
Deniz Celik
Marta D'Alessandro
Monica Datta
Kristina Demund Auptha Surli-Dev
Aleksandra Djurasovic

Laurel Donaldson
Nadia Doukhi
Christian Eusebio
Daniela Friedman
Alia El Gammal
Lior Galili
Sabine Gittel
Jonas Gonzalez
Madeline Griffith
Timea Hopps
Peter Jenkins
Sejin Rubella Jo
Shirish Joshi
Jaspuneet Kaur
Achilleas Kakkavas
Elena Kapompasopoulou
Gayatri Kawlra
Corina Kriener Michelle Kennedy
Riddhima Khedkar
Tarlan Khoylou
Patricia Lassance

Jair Laiter
Grace Lee
Louise Levi
Michela Barone Lumaga
Jonathan Marty
Brandon Martinez
Einatt Manoff
Max Mecklenburg
Keren Christina Mendjul
Asia Mernissi
Yao Mi
Karen M. Miller
Francis Milloy
Tolga Mizrakci
Chris Moyer
Madeline Muldoon
Andrew Moon
Dalia Munenzon
Jonathan Ngo
Michael Parkinson
Ana Penalba

Michelle Pereira
Tamar Roemer
Maria Bueno Rosas
Dina Said
Nikhil Sambamurthy
Laura Sanchez
Shiori Sasaki
Malica Schmidt
Benjamin Shepard
Fern Lan Siew
Liam Turkle
Hannes Van Damme
Amy Vogel
Elisabeth Weiman
Marcus Wilford
Bastiaan Woudenberg
You Wu
Christina Yoo
Zachary Zill